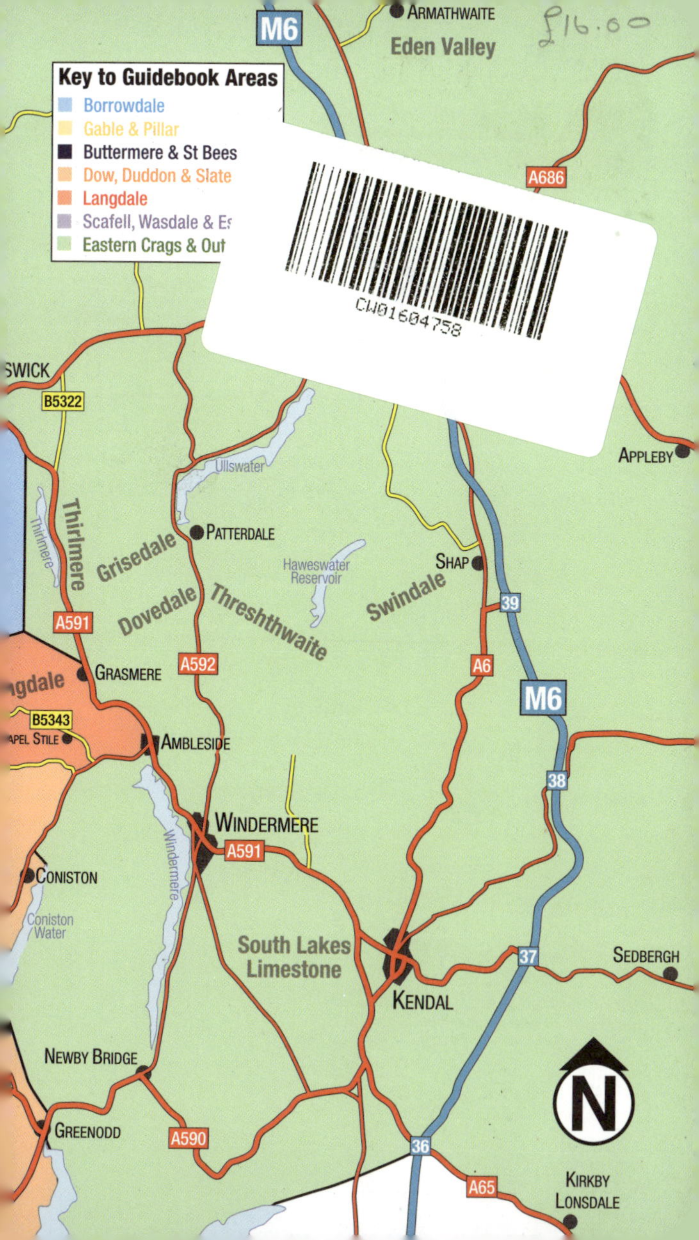
Key to Guidebook Areas
Borrowdale
Gable & Pillar
Buttermere & St Bees
Dow, Duddon & Slate
Langdale
Scafell, Wasdale & Es
Eastern Crags & Out
M6
Armathwaite
Eden Valley
A686
£16.00
CW01604758
Appleby
SWICK
B5322
Ullswater
Thirlmere
Thirlmere
Grisedale
Patterdale
Haweswater Reservoir
Shap
Swindale
Dovedale
Threshthwaite
39
A591
A592
A6
M6
Grasmere
gdale
B5343
APEL STILE
Ambleside
38
Windermere
A591
Windermere
Coniston
Coniston Water
South Lakes Limestone
Kendal
37
Sedbergh
Newby Bridge
Greenodd
A590
36
A65
Kirkby Lonsdale
N

Gable & Pillar

FRCC GUIDE

Published by
the Fell and Rock Climbing Club
of the English Lake District

Climbing Guides to the English Lake District

Gable & Pillar

by PC Rigby and SJH Reid
with assistance from
BJ Clarke, R Graham
and A Phizacklea

Photodiagrams by
PC Rigby
(Photographs Editor)

Maps by A Phizacklea
(Diagrams Editor)

Edited by SJH Reid

FRCC GUIDE

Published by
the Fell and Rock Climbing Club of the English Lake District

The Great Gable War Memorial. **Photo:** Eric Shaw

Dedication

After the First World War the FRCC purchased 3,000 acres of high fell land comprising "the rocks, buttresses, and recesses of Lingmell, Great End, Allen Crags, Green Gable, Great Gable, Kirkfell and other peaks east and west of Sty Head Pass" and presented it to the National Trust as a memorial to its members who had died in the conflict: this is the reason for the bronze plaque on the summit of Great Gable and the fact that the FRCC still holds a simple annual service of remembrance there to this day. Following the Second World War the club helped pay for the construction of a footbridge over the River Liza in Ennerdale as a memorial to its members who had died. As both these memorials are in the area covered by this guide it was felt fitting to dedicate this guide to those members of the FRCC who lost their lives in fighting to preserve those freedoms that we enjoy today.

World War I (1914–1918): JS Bainbridge, JG Bean, HSP Blair, AJ Clay, JN Fletcher, WHB Gross, E Hartley, SW Herford, SF Jeffcoat, EB Lees, SJ Linzell, LJ Oppenheimer, AJ Prichard, AM Rimer, RB Sanderson, HL Slingsby, GC Turner, BH Whitely*, JH Whitworth, CS Worthington.

World War II (1939–1945): D Adam, N Daley, FEW Dixon, JA Duncan, W Eden-Smith, WT Elmslie, RA Fanshawe, JWC Hawkins, R Hope, P Jackson, CB James, FF Thomas, T Willets

*BH Whitely was wrongly recorded as BH Witty on the original memorial. This mistake was only discovered recently, and was rectified by the club as part of the FRCC centenary celebrations in 2006; the original name was cut out and the correct one brazed into place.

1907–2007

The FRCC and Rock Climbing Guides to the English Lake District

The delicate moves on **Eagle's Nest Ridge Direct** (MVS), The Napes, were just as delicate around the time of the formation of the FRCC one hundred years ago. **Photo:** Abraham Brothers

The formation of the **Fell and Rock Climbing Club** was proposed at Coniston in 1906 at the instigation of Edward Scantlebury and Alan Craig, two of a "coterie of keen young mountaineers living on the southern confines of the English Lake District". Before the end of the year the club had over 40 members enrolled and was officially founded in 1907 when Ashley Abraham accepted the office of President. The first Club Journal was produced that same year and many new climbs were reported therein and in further annual volumes.

The Club published its first rock climbing guidebook in 1922 (*Doe Crag* by George Bower) and since that date has produced a continuous series of definitive guidebooks to Lake District rock climbing. These guidebooks are written and published by volunteers who update the text and check new climbs, many of which have been, and continue to be, pioneered by Club members.

The Club now has over 1000 members and owns several club huts both in the Lake District and elsewhere. Membership has always been open to applicants of either sex who can demonstrate an ongoing interest and enthusiasm for climbing in the Lake District. Enquiries regarding the FRCC and its guidebooks should be addressed to the current Club Secretary or Guidebooks Editor, whose addresses are available from the Club's website at www.frcc.co.uk or from the BMC.

Previous Editions

Gable:
1925 HS Gross
1937 CJ Astley Cooper
1948 CJ Astley Cooper, W Peascod, AP Rossiter
1969 PL Fearnhough
1977 PL Fearnhough

Pillar:
1923 HM Kelly
1935 HM Kelly
1952 HM Kelly, W Peascod
1968 AG Cram
1977 AG Cram

Gable and Pillar:
1991 D Kirby, J Loxham

Present edition: 2007

British Library Cataloguing in Publication Data
Rigby, P.
Gable & Pillar – [9th Series.] –
(Climbing guides to the English Lake District) –
(FRCC guide)

ISBN 978-0-85028-047-0

Front Cover: Craig Matheson cuts loose on The Wasdale Roof (E3), Napes Needle. Photo: Al Phizacklea

Frontispiece: The first ascent of North West Climb (MVS), Pillar Rock, 8th June 1906. The climbers in descending order are: F Botterill, LJ Oppenheimer, A Botterill and Dr JH Taylor. Both Oppenheimer and Taylor had cameras and took photographs during the ascent. Taylor probably took this image. **Photo:** FRCC Archive

Designed and typeset by **Vertebrate Publishing**, Sheffield, a division of **Vertebrate Graphics**. www.**v-publishing**.co.uk.

Produced by The Ernest Press, Glasgow, G44 5QD. www.ernest-press.co.uk.
Distributed by Cordee, 3a De Montfort Street, Leicester, LE1 7HD. www.cordee.co.uk.
Printed in China through Colorcraft Ltd., Hong Kong

Contents

Diagrams are shown in italics

A team on the top moves of **Tophet Wall** (HS), The Napes. **Photo:** Stephen Reid

Introduction

This guidebook is the first rock climbing volume in a new series of definitive climbing guides to the Lake District, one of the most popular climbing areas in the British Isles. This guide deals with part of the north-west corner of that area; Gable and Pillar. It is published by the Fell and Rock Climbing Club of the English Lake District, which has been responsible for producing definitive guides to the area since 1922. It is intended that the full Ninth Series will eventually comprise:

1. *Lake District Winter Climbs*
   (published in conjunction with Cicerone Press)
2. *Gable & Pillar*
3. *Buttermere & St Bees*
4. *Eastern Crags & Outcrops*
   (including Eden Valley and South Lakes Limestone)
5. *Dow, Duddon & Slate*
6. *Scafell, Wasdale & Eskdale*
7. *Langdale*
8. *Borrowdale*
9. *Lake District Rock* (Selected Climbs)

Gable & Pillar describes the wonderful climbing on and around Great Gable at the head of the Wasdale and the remote climbs of Ennerdale, including the mighty Pillar Rock, one of the finest crags in the Lake District.

For the first time in an FRCC rock climbing guide colour photos have been used for crag diagrams, and virtually every crag has been covered in this way, no easy task on complex multi-pitch crags such as Pillar Rock and the Napes. The writers, photographers and the Photographs Editor are to be congratulated on the outstanding collection of photodiagrams that has resulted. It's worth mentioning though that photodiagrams are not a totally new idea for the FRCC; the first series of guides (those slim

Left: The Wasdale Crack (HS), Napes Needle, the original route of ascent in 1886 and still popular today. **Photo:** Phil Rigby

volumes with the magenta covers) made extensive use of monochrome photodiagrams, and prior to that they featured in the club's earliest journals: photo-topos are at least 100 years old!

This guide describes some of the most isolated and remote crags in the Lake District, places to get away from the crowds and where even the noise of traffic is unlikely to be heard, a rare thing in our crowded country. The price to be paid for such solitude is inevitably a long approach walk, but the rewards are great, even greater if you are prepared to carry an extra load and camp high by some still tarn or sparkling gill. It also contains some of the most historically significant crags and climbs in Britain, places where the very sport of rock climbing was born, and some of the most beautiful views in the British Isles – indeed the view from Westmorland's Cairn near the summit of Great Gable is reckoned to be the finest in the Lake District. All this makes for a heady mixture and, given good weather and a modicum of effort, this small book will be your guide to some of the most enjoyable days on rock that you are likely to experience anywhere in the world.

Stephen Reid (Editor) March 2007

The celebrated view from Westmorland's Cairn, Great Gable: from left to right, Ill Crag, Broad Crag, Scafell Pike and Scafell, with Piers Gill and Lingmell in the foreground. **Photo:** Stephen Reid

General Notes

Terminology

A ***wall*** is almost vertical, or slightly overhanging. A ***slab*** is less than vertical. A ***glacis*** is a very easy-angled slab. An ***arête*** is a sharply-angled rib or ridge. Climbs and pitches are measured in metres (m). The terms ***gill*** and ***ghyll*** (meaning stream or gully) are interchangeable. ***Fell*** is the Lakeland word for hill.

Grades

The standard British double-grade system is used. On first acquaintance this may be puzzling to visitors from overseas used to climbs having a single grade, but in fact it is relatively simple and once understood provides a great deal of information about the climbs. All the climbs in this guide require the use of leader-placed natural protection and on any route given an adjectival grade a full rack suitable to the climb being attempted should be carried. Grades are very personal, being influenced by an individual's stature and physique, their willingness to climb above protection, and their preference for a particular style of climbing.

Adjectival Grades

These give the overall grade of the climb in good weather conditions, taking into account such factors as technical difficulty, rock quality and protection. The grades are: Moderate, Difficult, Very Difficult, Mild Severe, Severe, Hard Severe, Mild Very Severe, Very Severe, Hard Very Severe, Extremely Severe, with the standard abbreviations being used in the text. The Extremely Severe grade is open ended and is currently divided into E1, E2, through to E11, though the hardest climb described in this book is E9.

Plus and Minus Grades

In this volume, adjectival grades have been further subdivided by use of a minus sign (-) to indicate routes that are considered easy for the grade, and a plus sign (+) for those thought to be hard. This system replaces the traditional graded list and needless to say, just like a graded list, it is completely subjective.

Technical Grades

These are included for each pitch of 4a and above on routes of VS and above. This grade is an attempt to assess the pure technical difficulty encountered on each pitch and once again is open-ended. The grades to date are: 4a, 4b, 4c, 5a, 5b, 5c, 6a, 6b, 6c, 7a.

Aid, Bolts and In situ Protection

The placing of bolts is a subject which has aroused much emotive discussion during recent years. In the interest of care and concern for crags and the mountain environment and a belief that British climbing in general should continue with the principle of leader-placed removable protection, the FRCC are generally in accord with the guidelines on the use of bolts for the protection of routes as set out by the BMC. It is agreed that in the Lake District bolts are only acceptable on certain quarried crags and some agreed limestone and sandstone outcrops. Climbers are asked to adhere to this policy and refrain from the temptation to place bolts on any natural crags.

Retro-bolting has taken place on a number of routes in the Lake District but only after consultation with the first ascentionist of that route. In order to avoid any conflict, please ensure that this policy is maintained.

A number of route descriptions in this guide contain references to in situ protection including pegs, slings and wires. The history of these frequently dates back to the first ascent. There can be no guarantee that the fixed gear mentioned will still be in place when you climb the route or, more importantly, if it is there, that it will be of any use. It is well known that in situ gear will deteriorate to a fraction of its original holding power due to the elements. This can occur in a matter of months rather than years, particularly where wires or hard steel blade pegs are concerned. Therefore it is for the individual climber to assess the reliability of any in situ protection encountered.

Fixed abseil points have been found around some of the crags over the years. They should be thoroughly inspected before use and, if found to be doubtful, backed up with new equipment.

Stars and Quality

The star system of indicating the quality of a climb has been established for many years in Britain and climbers have long come to expect a three star route to be something extra special, not just in terms of the particular area being described, but vis-à-vis other climbs in the Kingdom as a whole. Whilst the original aim of this practice was laudable, giving only a handful of climbs three star status has brought its problems, particularly on remote mountain crags such as many of those covered in this guidebook. Three star routes attract queues and queues create polish whilst nearby almost as good 2½ star climbs that could do with a bit of traffic often languish in obscurity and become lichenous. This problem is compounded further down the starring scale and research has shown that many routes that were unstarred in previous guides to this area actually provide very good climbing. To remedy these problems many more stars

UK Adjectival Grade	UK Technical Grade (approx)	UIAA (alpine) Grade	European Equivalent	USA Equivalent	Australian Equivalent
Moderate		I, II	1	5.1, 5.2	4, 5
Difficult		II, III	1, 2, 2+	5.2, 5.3	5, 6, 7
Very Difficult		III, III+	2, 2+, 3–	5.2, 5.3, 5.4	6, 7, 8
Hard Very Difficult		III+, IV, IV+	2+, 3–, 3, 3+	5.4, 5.5, 5.6	8, 9, 10
Mild Severe		IV, IV+	3–, 3, 3+	5.5, 5.6	10, 11
Severe		IV, IV+, V–	3, 3+, 4	5.5, 5.6, 5.7	10, 11, 12
Hard Severe		IV+, V–, V	3, 3+, 4, 4+	5.6, 5.7	12, 13
Mild Very Severe	**4a, 4b, 4c**	IV+, V–, V	3+, 4, 4+	5.6, 5.7	12, 13, 14
Very Severe	**4a, 4b, 4c**	V–, V, V+	4, 4+, 5	5.7, 5.8	13, 14, 15
Hard Very Severe	**4c, 5a, 5b**	V+, VI-, VI	4+, 5, 5+, 6a	5.8, 5.9	15, 16, 17, 18
E1	**5a, 5b, 5c**	VI, VI+	5+, 6a, 6a+	5.9, 5.10a	18, 19, 20
E2	**5b, 5c, 6a**	VI+, VII–, VII	6a+, 6b, 6b+	5.10b, 5.10c	19, 20, 21
E3	**5c, 6a**	VII, VII+	6b, 6b+, 6c	5.10d, 5.11a, 5.11b	20, 21, 22
E4	**6a, 6b**	VII+, VIII–, VIII	6c, 6c+, 7a	5.11b, 5.11c, 5.11d	22, 23
E5	**6a, 6b 6c**	VIII, VIII+, IX–	7a, 7a+, 7b	5.11d, 5.12a, 5.12b	23, 24, 25
E6	**6b, 6c**	IX–, IX, IX+	7b, 7b+, 7c, 7c+	5.12b, 5.12c, 5.12d, 5.13a	25, 26, 27, 28
E7	**6c, 7a**	IX+, X–, X	7c+, 8a, 8a+	5.13a, 5.13b, 5.13c	28, 29, 30
E8	**6c, 7a**	X, X+	8a+, 8b, 8b+	5.13c, 5.13d, 5.14a	30, 31, 32

have been used in this guide than in previous editions and they are now intended to indicate quality on a much broader scale, viz:

★★★	Good climbing, on good, mainly clean rock, with purpose to the line.
★★	Mostly the above.
★	Some good climbing and a permutation of the other two factors.
	Of interest to only a minority of climbers, but should not be written-off completely.

It will be seen that a three star route no longer needs to be one of the best in the country, though it will provide an entertaining (and possibly adventurous) outing. This represents a substantial change in the starring policy adopted in earlier FRCC guides.

When selecting a route from the huge range available, it is also worth remembering that stars are only a means of narrowing down the choice, particularly for the infrequent or first-time visitor. No matter how many stars a route may have, if it sounds attractive in the guide, be prepared to go to its start and see what it looks like. It is then up to that route to "sell" itself. Many good climbs are missed for the lack of making this effort.

All stars have been allocated in good faith but the condition of a climb can deteriorate quite quickly and make a mockery of its stars. If this has happened to your route, sorry. No system is perfect and it is only meant to be a "guide".

It is particularly difficult to rate new or unrepeated routes. Therefore, these have been given "hollow" stars as a provisional assessment. Feed-back would be welcome – thank you.

In addition to quality of line and rock, the influence of the climate on the quality of a route should not be underestimated. Cleaner air and higher ambient temperatures have encouraged growth of mosses and lichens and those attempting starred routes on high crags in damp greasy conditions whilst being assailed by midges are unlikely to enjoy the experience as much as those doing the same climbs on a still dry sunny day after a long period of drought. The stars in this guide are assigned for the latter conditions not the former, and on high crags a certain amount of (hopefully dry) moss and lichen should be considered part of the experience. Gable Crag and Pillar Rock, despite their rough volcanic character, are only in condition during dry weather (even in mid summer Gable Crag does not see the sun until 7pm).

Sadly, existing routes on a few of the crags unearthed in the 1960s and '70s continue to decline, seemingly now in an accelerating downward spiral. Once popular routes, in particular on Bowness Knott and Anglers'

Crag, have become even more overgrown and consequently are shunned by today's climbers. Perhaps, particularly when one considers the section **Caring for the Natural Environment while you Climb** on page 14, we should we let nature take its course on such crags and acknowledge that maybe they should never have been gardened so enthusiastically in the first place.

Finally, some crags will be found more pleasurable due to the improved descents or ways off, especially where abseil points have been located. But as always be responsible for your own safety, don't rely on in situ slings, carry spares for that purpose and avoid using the abseil rope directly around trees as this damages the trunk. Abseiling can be a good alternative way off and may sometimes ease erosion on descents.

Unrepeated Routes

Climbs that are not known to have been repeated, have their grades suffixed by a (**?**).

New Routes and Corrections

To aid writers of future guidebooks, please post comments, corrections, and details of all new climbs on the FRCC website www.frcc.co.uk. Several "New Routes books" exist in the area, including the Log Books in FRCC huts. However, these may not be checked regularly and first ascensionists are urged to also record their route on the website above or it may be missed. Please provide all relevant details in the usual format including grades, dates, first ascensionists and style of ascent.

Location of Crags

The location of each crag is indicated by its national grid reference. Beware those crags where the name on the map may be some way from the grid reference shown, and those where the climbers' name for a crag or other feature is different from that on the map – such instances are detailed in the text. The aspect of the main faces has been included to aid the choice of crags. The altitude given is based on a mean sea level of zero. The terms 'true left' and 'true right' are used to describe the position of a crag in a valley or gill relative to the direction of flow of the stream. The terms 'left' and 'right', unless otherwise stated, mean as the climber faces the climb.

Maps

The Ordnance Survey Explorer Series 1:25 000 *sheet 4 (The English Lakes – North-West Area)* covers the bulk of the area. Harveys also produce an excellent set of maps at this scale (their Super Walker series), but the climber is perhaps better served by their collaborative map with the

British Mountaineering Council, *Lake District* at 1:40 000. At 1:50 000, the Ordnance Survey's Landranger maps numbers 89 and 90 cover the area in this guide.

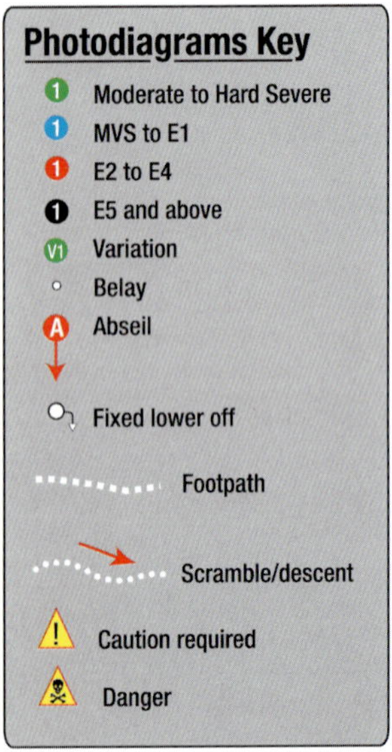

Photodiagrams

For the first time in an FRCC guide full colour photodiagrams of almost every crag and buttress covered have been included. The amount of work required to produce these, particularly on high remote crags, has been immense, requiring many visits and the climbing of almost every route. However it is possible that some small errors remain and if in doubt it is probably better to rely on the written description rather than the photodiagram. The symbols used should be fairly self explanatory.

Photographs

The Editor has little sympathy for those who criticise photographs in climbing guides yet don't carry a camera themselves. Tracking down good climbing photographs for guidebooks is always a difficult task and the FRCC Guidebook Committee would like to express their gratitude to all those who submitted photographs for consideration. To those whose photographs were not selected this time, please do not be discouraged, and please keep up the flow of new material. Anyone interested in supporting this aspect of guidebook work should contact the Guidebook Photographs Editor whose address, together with details of current guidebook work being undertaken, is available from the Club's website at www.frcc.co.uk.

Safety Advice

Climbing is a dangerous pastime that can seriously damage your health! Details of climbs recorded in this guidebook, together with their grades, reference to in situ or natural protection, and locations, are made in good faith having been compiled from first ascent or past descriptions, checked and substantiated where possible with consensus comments.

Unfortunately climbs can change; holds fall off, rock becomes dirty, in situ gear deteriorates or disappears. Even a minor alteration can have a dramatic effect on the grade or seriousness of a route. It is therefore essential that climbers judge the condition of any route before committing themselves.

The contents of this guidebook are believed to be correct. However, neither the FRCC nor its members and their friends involved with its production can be held responsible for any omissions or mistakes, nor liable for any personal or third party injuries or damage, howsoever caused, arising from its use. In this claims-conscious age, climbers are recommended to obtain suitable insurance cover. The BMC now provides third party liability cover for members and members of affiliated clubs.

Campsites, Bunkhouses, Camping Barns & Club Huts

Within the Lake District there are numerous camping barns, bunkhouses and campsites. To find out more about these contact details are given on page 345. There are also many climbing club huts, most of which are available to non-club members - contact the BMC for a list.

Wild Camping

Wild camping (ie camping outside of a proper campsite) is generally allowed on the fells above the 300 metre contour as long as one is above the final (intake) wall and not within 100 metres of habitation. Any campsite used should be left as it was found and all litter cleared.

Access & Conservation

Access to the crags described in this guide will be taken for granted by the majority of users but in fact in some cases it may have been achieved only through years of patient negotiation. Fortunately, the National Trust, Forestry Commission, United Utilities, or other private owners who are broadly sympathetic to climbers, own most of the crags described. In a few cases however, the situation remains delicate and increasing numbers of climbers are only likely to make it more so. Here is an area in which we can all help, not only by cherishing this region in the manner it deserves, parking thoughtfully, co-operating with farmers and landowners, following the country code, observing bird restrictions, picking up litter at crags and so on, but by ensuring that others do the same. Outsiders look on climbers as a group and inconsiderate behaviour by a few will be seen, rightly or wrongly, as a reflection upon us all. The onus is on all of us to make certain that it doesn't happen in the first place.

Several of the crags described in this guide carry **Bird Restrictions** in the spring (typically from 1st March to 30th June), and crags that have been restricted regularly in the past are indicated in the text. However, the situation changes from year to year and climbers visiting any crag in the Lake District should make efforts beforehand to find out if there are Schedule 1 birds or ravens in residence on the crag they intend to visit. Usually restricted crags will be signed, but this may not always be the case and all climbers should acquaint themselves with the latest known details which can be found on the BMC website at www.thebmc.co.uk or on the FRCC website at www.frcc.co.uk. Where birds have not nested in any particular year, the ban may be lifted earlier. If there are birds nesting, and there is an agreed restriction, then please be prepared to change your plans according to the agreement. It may be that only some parts of the crag are restricted, so other routes can be climbed. If this is the case it will be indicated on the signs. For more information on **Bird Restrictions** please see the notes on page 20.

"Gardening" of new routes (removing earth and vegetation wholesale from a crag, in other words) was once a fairly commonplace occurrence, and some classic climbs have resulted. However far more climbs that were extensively cleaned in such a manner have since become overgrown again and there is no doubt that many plants (possibly some quite rare) were needlessly uprooted for a fleeting moment of glory. With increasing pressure on our remaining wild places such behaviour is no long acceptable and, whilst cleaning out the occasional nut placement may be essential for safety, the climber should be aware that even that may be technically illegal. **Caring for the Natural Environment while you Climb** on page 14 discusses the duty of care that the climber owes to the environment.

Right: Styhead Pass signpost (long since disappeared), from left, P Unna, WE Webb, EE Stock, terrier and CW Barton. **Photo:** Barton Climbing Book, FRCC Archive

WASDALE
SCAWFELL 3

Geological Notes

by Dave Bodecott

Lake District climbing is synonymous with the Borrowdale Volcanic Group and these form the main crags of interest in this area. There are rare Skiddaw Slate crags however, but these are of minor climbing interest.

There is a core of granite underlying the Lake District that is thought to be as shallow as 2000 metres below surface. Metamorphism caused by this granite has affected the Skiddaw Slates in places, e.g. at Bowness Knott, Ennerdale.

The Skiddaw Slate Group represents a huge pile of blue-grey mudstones, with some sandstones, several thousand metres in thickness, that were deposited in a deep ocean during the early to mid Ordovician between 490 and 460 million years ago.

As the deep ocean became a major plate boundary in the form of an active collision zone (positioned then south of the Equator) between the American and Eurasian plates, large volumes of volcanic outpouring that became the Borrowdale Volcanic Group were generated. A thickness in excess of 7000 metres of material was ejected between 460 and 450 million years ago. It is this series of rocks that form the high crags of Gable and Pillar.

The volcanic crags are mostly formed by the Lower Borrowdale Birker Fell Formation. The dominant rock types are andesite and rhyolite lavas.

The lavas are interspersed with explosive volcanic products. These rocks were formed by violent volcanic activity, ash fall and high temperature gas-rich outbursts, then material was often eroded and locally reworked in lakes to give a laminated sedimentary character particularly to the finer grained rocks. This explains the variations on some crags from rough coarse high-friction volcanics, to the smooth fine-grained layered sequences. The volcanic crags are infinitely variable in rock texture with gas escape pockets, crystals, quartz veins and tension cracks often seen, but ultimately it is the influence of the sun and long spells of dry weather that are most crucial in defining "climbability".

The distinctive dome of **Great Gable**; glaciated volcanic scenery. **Photo:** Eric Ostell

Some time after the Borrowdale Volcanic period, the area was uplifted by the Caledonian mountain-building phase (395 million years ago). Erosion of these mountains enabled shallow tropical seas and limestone sedimentation to extend across the area during the Carboniferous (350-300 million years ago). The remnant of this limestone veneer is preserved (along with extensive haematite mineralisation and the later Carboniferous Coal Measures) to the west of our area, although there are no limestone climbing crags as on other flanks of the Lake District.

Further uplift during the Hercynian mountain building phase (300 million years ago) as continental drift brought the landmass into the northern hemisphere trade winds, led to the onset of desert conditions during the succeeding Permian and Triassic periods.

Finally, in this brief summary, the effects of glacial and inter-glacial periods are ubiquitous. As the leader brings up his or her second from a perched belay, the eye casts across the amazing scenery of the over-deepened valleys, truncated spurs, hanging valleys, roche moutonnées and moraines. The last ice left only yesterday (ca. 10,000 years ago) in geological terms!

Acknowledgements

British Geological Survey.
http://www.bgs.ac.uk
Cumberland Geological Society.
http://www.cumberland-geol-soc.org.uk
Dr. Andrew Bell, Open University.

Caring for the Natural Environment while you Climb

by Simon Webb & Peter Davies

Great Gable rises high over the central Lake District fells and the valley of Ennerdale that runs out towards the west coast. In this spectacular valley and its neighbouring fells you can find the complete range of upland vegetation in full splendour. Clear freshwater lakes and sparkling rivers, steep and mossy woodlands, swathes of purple heathland on the fellsides and, on the highest ridges, a low-growing montane heath of lichens and club mosses. By the time you reach the coast most natural vegetation is lost to agriculture. In the area covered by this guide, you climb amongst heathers, rare arctic-alpines, colourful flowering herbs and dwarf trees, you share cracks with ferns, and cliffs and fells with breeding birds.

What sort of vegetation is found on the upland crags and in the gullies?

The most impressive examples of upland vegetation are found amongst the cliffs and gullies of the Lake District high fells which have the specialised soils and climatic conditions that are favoured by upland plants. The steep ground and cliffs often provide refuge from the impact of grazing sheep – in fact increasing sheep numbers over the past 50 years have led to a huge reduction in heathland vegetation. Thus the heathery vegetation we see on crags and steeper slopes only survives there because it is away from the hungry mouths of grazing sheep. These areas are important as they provide reservoirs of heathers and flowers that can re-colonise the uplands now that conservation organisations are negotiating lower sheep numbers. The best examples of heathland have many different types of heather; ling, bell heather, bilberry, crowberry, cowberry and bearberry can all be found in a mixture of colours and textures.

There are more trees too on the crags than on the open fellside, as regenerating trees are also nibbled away by sheep and only on the steeper slopes (or where grazing pressure is very low) can they get beyond the

Bilberry is one of the plants that dominate the Lake District heathlands

Juniper clings to the crags and steep slopes
Photos: Simon Webb

seedling stage. Some of the Lake District upland trees are rare and specialised. Juniper, a low-growing native evergreen prickly conifer with berries that smell strongly of gin when they are purple and ripe, is probably the best known. A special dwarf juniper inhabits crags above 500 metres.

The Lake District is also the English stronghold for arctic-alpine plants which thrive in the cold harsh conditions of high latitudes and high altitudes. At the end of the last ice-age (some 10,000 years ago) they would have dominated Lake District vegetation, but now they are restricted to the highest ground, and areas where soils are richer in lime and basic minerals; damper crags, seepages, especially north and east-facing coves and gullies are their favoured habitat. Arctic-alpines found within this guidebook area include alpine saw-wort, yellow saxifrage, shrubby cinquefoil, mossy saxifrage and alpine cinquefoil.

Roseroot is an indicator of more lime-rich vegetation and often marks out the most important areas of mountain vegetation
Photo: Simon Webb

Gully side-walls, and ledges with richer and deeper soil, are also home to a type of plant assemblage called tall-herb ledge vegetation. This looks for all the world like part of an alpine hay meadow growing high in the mountains. Tall colourful herbs such as wood cranesbill, globeflower, water avens, wild angelica, and roseroot, cover ledges and gully bottoms in a luxuriant and spectacular show of mountain colour.

All such upland vegetation is rare and is vulnerable to the impacts of climbing because it is so restricted in where it can grow. Plant numbers are very low in some cases (and therefore even a small amount of damage can be significant): such plants are easily damaged by route preparation or "gardening".

Breeding birds are also of key importance

The fells and cliffs described in this guidebook are of outstanding importance for their breeding birds.

Of particular importance on Gable and in Ennerdale are the peregrine falcon and raven: many climbers will be familiar with these two birds which are covered in more detail in the chapter **Bird Restrictions** on page 20.

Another bird which there is increasing concern about is the **ring ouzel** which also has a stronghold in this guidebook area. More than half the UK population of ring ouzels have been lost between 1988 and 1999. This led to its recent (2002) red listing as a bird of conservation concern.

There is increasing conservation concern about the ring ouzel
Photo: RSPB

The ring ouzel (*Turdus torquatus*) is a member of the thrush family and is closely related to the blackbird. Adult males are all black except for a white crescent on the breast and a yellow bill. The wings have a silvery appearance due to white feather edgings. The male sings its loud and mournful song from trees or rocks, although if disturbed near the nest they make a harsh 'chack chack' call. The female is similar but duller, and young birds often lack the breast crescent. Juveniles have brown plumage.

This mountain blackbird is migratory, spending winter in Spain and Africa. They return to breed in the Lake District in gullies, rocky areas, or scree slopes of the high fells above the 250-metre contour line. They usually nest in mature heather, or occasionally under bracken, but very often on rock ledges or steep slopes, laying several eggs in a neat cup-shaped nest. Two broods are often reared. They are omnivorous during the breeding season; they eat earthworms, leatherjackets, insects and spiders. Moorland berries such as bilberry, crowberry and rowan are important in the late summer as they stock up on food before migrating. The ring ouzel is one of our least studied birds and scientists are not clear on the causes behind the huge population decline. There are many possible factors: changes in grazing levels, agricultural improvement, afforestation, disturbance, pollution, habitat loss in wintering areas, problems on migration routes and climate change. The Great Gable and Ennerdale area holds an estimated 25 to 35 pairs of ring ouzels. Please respect these 'mountain blackbirds' and the crags and environment that they rely on. Ring ouzels are clearly declining and we need to make sure we do not destroy their nesting habitat or reduce their Cumbrian breeding success. It is therefore extremely important when climbing on crags that have heather or bilberry covered ledges, that this vegetation is not removed, or the crag 'gardened'.

Where are the most vulnerable and important areas in this Guidebook?

The vegetation described above (heathers, trees, arctic-alpines and tall herb ledge) is widespread in the uplands of the Lake District and needs protection across its whole range. It really is so rare and vulnerable that any example of it that is left is important to conserve. The following section describes the most extensive and richest areas we know about within the area covered by this guide. However, if a place is not mentioned below it does not mean that it is not important and does not matter.

The areas around Pillar and Steeple are very variable. Some are ecologically poor others extremely rich. Pillar Rock itself is made of quite acidic rock and, as many plants like a base-rich environment, the main climbs are of lower ecological value. Much of Pillar Rock is covered with junipers though, and great care and respect needs to be shown here. The area around West Waterfall is probably the richest area on the Rock itself and is best avoided. Without doubt the botanically finest area in the Ennerdale valley is Hind Cove. Here is the healthiest Cumbrian population of shrubby cinquefoil. This plant's only UK locations are in the Lake District and Teesdale. This would be really vulnerable to gardening or winter climbing in poor conditions.

A code of conduct:

How climbers can help protect upland vegetation, rare plants and breeding birds.

Climbers (or other people involved in outdoor recreation activities) are not generally responsible for the decline in the extent and quality of wildlife habitats in the UK. However the nature of the sport is that it takes you to the most sensitive parts of the landscape, to the refuges unaffected by grazing pressure, and to the places best suited to the rare plants. Climbers need to be aware that they are going to these special places and must take extra care not to damage or disturb them.

The following best practice gives some pointers:

- Adhere to the negotiated restrictions to protect nesting birds. These are annually updated and available on the FRCC or BMC websites. If you experience obvious 'alarm calling birds' retreat from the area even if there is no bird restriction in place.
- Take care not to damage the crag flora. Route preparation (or gardening) is a significant threat to rare upland vegetation. If new route preparation will result in the destruction of upland vegetation or bird habitat then it should not go ahead. Gone are the days when it is acceptable to dig routes out of the hillside; the environmental price is far too high. More detail on this subject can be found in the *Lake District Green Climbing Guide* published by the BMC in 2006.
- Any trees growing above the 600 metre contour are likely to be really important ecologically or a rare species or both. These are not good places for runners, belays or lower-offs. Please respect mountain trees, they have a tough enough life as it is!

The law – what does it say?

Natural vegetation and birds are an important part of our heritage and the Government has enacted strong laws to protect them. These laws apply to both landowners and those enjoying outdoor recreation. This legal framework is part of the UK's national and international obligations towards conservation.

Much of the upland landscape is within Sites of Special Scientific Interest (SSSIs). Although there is much of interest to conserve outside these sites, SSSIs do form the central core of the statutory conservation system in the UK. This wildlife law doesn't just give powers to designate and protect special sites, it also provides for many positive initiatives to conserve our wildlife, including mechanisms for grants, management agreements, action plans, as well as open access provision.

In general terms all wild birds and their nests and eggs are protected by law with heavy penalties for disturbance.

Natural vegetation is also protected by legislation both within SSSIs and beyond. Reckless damage to an SSSI carries severe penalties with a £20,000 maximum fine. In addition to general protection there is a considerable number of the rarer plants and animals that receive additional protection.

These laws are strong but, if you take time to find out about the birds and natural vegetation in the mountain environment, it is unlikely that there will be conflicts. Following the codes of conduct and best practice is always a better alternative to court cases or permanent bans on climbing.

A "hanging garden" of colourful tall herb ledge vegetation **Photo:** Simon Webb

Summary

If future generations are to continue enjoying the Lake District, it is essential that we all contribute towards its long term conservation. Crags, cliffs and gullies are the most important locations of upland vegetation, home to rare plants and ferns and to threatened birds. These places are sensitive and vulnerable and climbers must take extra care to minimise their impact. Climbers (in both summer and winter) can play an important role in protecting the mountain environment. The best places for climbing are often the most important locations of upland vegetation and home to rare plants and ferns. They also provide nesting locations for a range of upland and sea birds. These places are sensitive and vulnerable, but if climbers take extra care to minimise their impact, and follow the best practice described above, then climbing and nature conservation can happily co-exist.

Simon Webb (Natural England, www.naturalengland.org.uk) *&*
Peter Davies (Cumbria Bird Club, www.cumbriabirdclub.org.uk)

Bird Restrictions

by Kevin Howett & Peter Davies

As mentioned on page 16, several crags described in this guide carry **Bird Restrictions** in the Spring. The notes below have been drawn up jointly by the Lake District National Park Authority, the National Trust, the Cumbria Raptor Study Group, Natural England, the BMC Area Committee and the FRCC. They are only intended to cover the Lake District and outlying areas of Cumbria though they may be found useful elsewhere.

All birds, their eggs and nests, are protected by the Wildlife and Countryside Act 1981. Certain rare or more endangered species are further protected by increased penalties under the 1981 Act and must not be intentionally or recklessly disturbed when nesting. These birds are listed in the act and are referred to as Schedule 1 species. Many are ground nesting or tree nesting birds, some are found on sea cliffs, but the Schedule 1 bird species that climbers may most commonly encounter on crags in the Lake District is the peregrine falcon. Some agreed restrictions also apply to ravens (though these are not Schedule 1).

Photo: RSPB

Peregrines

Peregrines are the largest falcons in the British Isles. They can be recognized by their distinctive profile, often sighted from the crag, as they plummet groundwards to seize some unsuspecting prey. Seen from below, they are pale coloured birds with dark tips to the tail and wings. Their call is a piercing shriek, once heard never forgotten, particularly if you are leading at the time! When disturbed this is uttered repeatedly for long periods. Peregrines hunt over a variety of habitats catching medium sized birds, mainly feral pigeons, by swooping at speeds of up to 200km an hour to seize them. The optimum and preferred nesting sites of peregrines in the United Kingdom are rocky coastal areas, cliffs and inland crags, but the actual nest site is not at all obvious, being just a shallow scrape in the soil. Some indication may be given by streaks of white guano (bird droppings) down an area of the crag, though this may merely be a roost site for the male rather than a nest. Peregrines are fairly common in the Lake District which is one of their most important European habitats, but they are rare elsewhere. In fact the United Kingdom supports approximately 14% of the European population. Of these, in Cumbria, there are usually about 85 nesting sites which hold one or more birds each year and approximately 65 pairs attempt to breed each season. This is 6% of the UK's total population and is considered to be the densest breeding population in the world. The Cumbrian birds are especially important because of the population numbers and productivity which is enabling the birds to spread and re-colonise other areas in the UK. They are particularly vulnerable to the weather, disturbance, poor food supply, and illegal activities such as shooting, poisoning, and egg and chick theft. In 2000 there were 83 occupied territories of which 46 pairs reared 111 young. However, in 2002 only 32 young were reared and this was the worst recorded breeding season for 30 years, predominantly due to appalling weather, but also to increased robberies. Climbers can assist here by reporting any suspicious characters they see near peregrine nest sites.

Ravens

Photo: RSPB

Ravens are very large black birds, similar to a rook but a third bigger. They have distinctive deep "pruk-pruk" and "grok" calls and are great aerial acrobats that delight in soaring and tumbling. Ravens, while not protected in the same way as peregrines and eagles, are still under potential threat from increased disturbance, and there are some voluntary restrictions in the Lake District on their account. Their nests are very large piles of twigs.

Bird Restrictions

Bird Restrictions are agreed annually between the Lake District National Park Authority, the National Trust, the Cumbria Raptor Study Group, Natural England, the BMC Area Committee and the FRCC. The area of crag agreed to be avoided can vary depending upon various factors including the layout of the crag. Some pairs also vary their choice of nesting site each year either within a crag or between different crags and so agreements may change from year to year. In general, they only apply to the most popular crags but this does not mean that it is necessarily alright to climb on all other crags during this period; even where a crag is not subject to a restriction, if you suspect a bird (particularly a peregrine) is nesting on it, you should heed the advice below. Areas where birds are known to nest should be avoided for a period running from the 1st March to 30th June in the case of the peregrine, and from 15th February to 31st May for the raven.

How the law affects you

The law states that it is an offence to 'intentionally' or 'recklessly' disturb a Schedule 1 bird 'at, on or near' the nest. It is also an offence to recklessly or intentionally disturb 'dependent' fledged young. These 'fledglings' are young birds that have just moved away from the nest but are still dependent to some extent on their parents for food and protection.

It is clear and unambiguous what 'at' and 'on' mean in this legislation, but the law does not stipulate a definition for 'near'. Nor does the law stipulate what constitutes 'disturbance'. It would be difficult to do this, as each bird species is different, and indeed individual birds are different. As a result, the prosecution would call upon expert witnesses to testify that disturbance occurred. It would also have to be shown that it was intentional or reckless.

Many peregrine falcon sites are monitored under licence by Raptor Study Groups, and it is important that climbers follow some basic guidance in order to minimise disturbance (and allow both birds and climbers to continue to coexist) as well as to make sure they are not breaking the law. Apart from possible prosecution, when arrested, police can confiscate your climbing equipment as evidence to present at the trial which may take a long time to come to court.

The following information will give a basic knowledge of Schedule 1 bird behaviour for climbers to judge for themselves what action to take. It is not intended to be definitive, but to be a general guide.

Climbers visiting any crag in the Lake District should make efforts beforehand to find out if there are Schedule 1 birds or ravens in residence on the crag they intend to visit. Usually restricted crags will be signed, but this may not always be the case and all climbers should acquaint themselves with the latest known details which can be found on the BMC website at www.thebmc.co.uk or on the FRCC website at www.frcc.co.uk. Where birds have not nested in any particular year, the ban may be lifted earlier. If there are birds nesting, and there is an agreed restriction, then please be prepared to change your plans according to the agreement. It may be that only some parts of the crag are restricted, so other routes can be climbed. If this is the case it will be indicated on the signs.

At the crag

If you visit a crag not listed as having an agreement, but then notice activity from a peregrine or other Schedule 1 bird in the vicinity, the guidance below will help you decide what to do. It can equally be used for some other nesting birds you may come across, such as ravens. Obviously, your choice of what can be done will depend on the extent of the crag and its topography as well as other factors outlined below.

As you walk into the crag keep a look out for peregrines and other birds. Peregrines in particular may be calling as they fly about the area. When you arrive they may be disturbed but this is quite normal intuitive disturbance. Try and move out of their line of sight as quickly as you can and then wait and see if they settle down and try to spot where they originate from. This will enable you to decide whether there is a nesting site that is being used near the climb that you are hoping to do, and to assess from the criteria below about disturbance, whether you feel your presence will be detrimental.

If the nest site is not directly beside where you are going to climb, the configuration of the crag means you can be separated from line of sight from the nest site to some extent, or the crucial period of egg incubation (see below) in cold weather is past, then you will probably find that the birds will have calmed down after the initial disturbance and climbing does not disturb them off the nest for long periods.

If the birds continue to appear aggressive and agitated and are staying away from the nest, then you should find another climb further away from the site, on another part of the crag, or indeed another crag, as to continue climbing could cause damaging disturbance by keeping the parents off the nest for too long.

How do you judge disturbance?

Most birds will act instinctively to protect their nest site when they perceive a threat. They will frequently make an initial reaction to human presence, calling, often repeatedly or aggressively. They will then either realise there is no threat and will settle down, or, if they continue and you then move away from them, they will then stop their instinctive behaviour.

It can be difficult for non-ornithologists to judge when a peregrine's call changes from normal activity to that of a protection call, but listen for a more aggressive tone. If the female then flies from the nest and stays away, or continuously circles the crag area calling, then they have been disturbed and it becomes detrimental to breeding success.

How close is too close?

There are no hard and fast rules to determine when you might be too close as so much depends upon the tolerance of the individual bird. If the crag is very popular with climbers, then any nesting birds may be habituated to climbers' presence. Such peregrines may be able to accept climbing in quite close proximity, as long as it is around the other side of an arête or on a separate buttress. Of one thing you can be sure is that climbing very close or directly onto the nest will cause damaging disturbance. At crags in remote areas where there is little climbing activity, birds may be disturbed even at some distance. Of particular importance is the line of sight. If the bird can see you it is far more likely to be disturbed. The best policy is to err upon the side of caution and if in any doubt retreat.

The most important period of nesting

For most birds the most sensitive periods are up to egg-laying, and when they have just laid eggs; for peregrines this period can be from February to late April when the ambient air temperature is still low. A later sensitive period is when the chicks have just hatched (for peregrines, mid to end of May). If adults are repeatedly or continually kept off the nest by climbers, then the eggs or chicks will quickly cool and die, or become available to predation. Obviously there is an even greater risk in cold conditions, and the position of the nest (on a north or south-facing crag) and the time of day will also be important factors to take into account. For ravens, the period in mid-April to mid-May, when they are feeding their chicks, is critical as this process needs to be constant throughout the day or the chicks will starve.

What to do if challenged or arrested

Even with the best of intentions, it is possible that, having obeyed the above guidelines, you may be accused of disturbing a bird, or of climbing on a crag where you should not have done. If asked to leave, then please do so without fuss, but please ask and note the name of the person requesting you to leave, the organisation they represent, and the reason you have been asked to leave. If the worst happens and you are arrested, then as soon as possible make full notes of the circumstances leading up to your arrest with especial detail on the position of any nests vis-à-vis your climb and the behaviour of any birds. These notes will form vital evidence if the case goes to court, which may be months or even years after the event. In all circumstances please report the details to the BMC.

Kevin Howett (Mountaineering Council of Scotland,
www.mountaineering-scotland.org.uk) *&*
Peter Davies (Cumbria Bird Club, www.cumbriabirdclub.org.uk)

Acknowledgements

Gable, Photodiagrams & Action Photographs

Work on this edition of *Gable* has been hugely helped by the following climbers who all gave up their time in the quest for knowledge, and made the research of this guide such a memorable experience. It hasn't all been done in glorious weather (and I'm sure a few would have preferred the drive to Yorkshire!). In alphabetical order the following all shared a rope on more than one occasion and gave copious amounts of encouragement and a few moans as the venue of Gable was mentioned while making plans on Thursday evenings at Armathwaite: Dave Armstrong, Kevin Avery, Pete Botterill, Al Davis, Dave Bodecott, Rob Fone, Tom Foster, Alan Greig, the late Mike Hetherington, Mark Hetherington, Mark Magas, John Moore, Alan Murray, John Pattison, Dan Varian and John Williams. My heartfelt thanks go to each and every one of them for their companionship on the hill.

A special note of gratitude to Al Phizacklea for his excellent action photographs and to the Barrow team of Joe Holden, John Holden, Craig Matheson, Rob Matheson, Steve Merry and Keith Phizacklea for giving their time and energy on the other side of the lens. Two other "climbing models" who deserve an extra word of praise are Pete Sterling and Ian Grimshaw who braved bitter weather and swirling clag when the sun was shining in Borrowdale but a photograph of Green Gable Crags was needed at the last minute. The agony of their freezing hands was prolonged even further due to the photographer being blown off his feet at regular intervals by the gale.

Thanks to Barry Clarke who acted as a runner checking out many esoteric gems (and adding a few of his own!), when I was laid up with injury.

Special mention to Lakeland raconteur and writer Tony Greenbank for his many amusing phone calls of encouragement.

On the technical front thanks go to Tom Prentice, Ben Hodgson, Captain Quark (Oliver Jackson) and Peter Hodgkiss for their patient technical advice and to FRCC Editor Stephen Reid for his enthusiasm

Photo: Jane Rigby

throughout. I am also indebted to Al Phizacklea and Alan Greig for help with taking crag photos, text ideas and checking photodiagrams.

Lastly a big thank you to my wife Judy, and daughters Kate and Jane, who have put up with my endlessly losing bits of manuscript and the annoying 'double-click' of the mouse in the living room corner!

Phil Rigby, 2007

Pillar & Editorial

First and foremost in acknowledging assistance with the ***Ennerdale*** section of this guide, thanks should go to Gareth Browning (Forestry Commission Forester for Ennerdale) who kindly allowed a rarely granted permit to motor up the valley's forest tracks; without this it is unlikely that the author would have found any second willing to accompany him more than once. As a result of the permit though many friends have assisted in checking routes for this guide. Chris King ranks foremost amongst these with visits too numerous to count. His constant enthusiasm and good humour, even on Scoat Fell Crag, made the somewhat daunting task considerably easier. Amongst the others forbearing enough to offer several times, Sally Baxendale and latterly Martin Armitage were gluttons for punishment, with Jonathan Preston, Graham Watson and Colin Wornham all putting in more than one appearance. Martin was even inveigled into repeating The Greater Traverse, admittedly over two days rather than in the original five hours. Ed Cross, Geoff Cram, Chris Eilbeck, Jim Loxham, Doug Elliot, Tony King, Tony Stephenson and Bill Young have all assisted with historical information. Finally, in addition to endless hard days on the hill, Sally has also put up gracefully with my regular absences as yet another evening is spent in my office wrestling (not always successfully) with apostrophes and semi-colons, and all the other tasks that make up the lot of both author and editor.

In addition, from the editorial point of view, this guide would not have been complete without the exceptional work of the authors in selflessly going climbing as often as possibly in order to check routes; their work though is based on that of all the previous guidebook writers whose contributions are acknowledged in the previous editions listed on page 4. More than anything though, this guidebook has been 'made' by the painstaking work of Phil Rigby who has produced all the photodiagrams single handed, and then spent a massive amount of time fine tuning them, on the often conflicting advice of the rest of the team. Al Phizacklea who has just seen twenty-five years of diagram drawing replaced, has none-the-less embraced the new style of guide with enthusiasm and has produced as fine a set of maps for this guide as you are likely to find in any similar publication. Historical photos were provided by Iain Whitmey, Sir Chris Bonington (researched by Frances Daltrey, Chris Bonington Picture Library), Bill Birkett, Eric Ivison, Chris Eilbeck, Bill Young and Mike Cocker, and the latter also uncovered, during his researches into the Wasdale Climbing Book, several earlier ascents of routes than those previously known. Eric Shaw has, as ever, been ready with his camera, and numerous other climbers have contributed photographs. Some of these are professionals who would normally charge for their work, but have been happy to forgo their usual fee to support a good cause – the continuance of club-published definitive guidebooks; their names are recorded in the text. In addition we once again express our gratitude to the Abraham family for allowing us free use of the wonderful photographic record of George and Ashley Abraham. We are grateful also to Simon Webb and Peter Davies for the timely chapter on the climber and the environment, whilst Peter's section on bird restrictions (written in conjunction with Kevin Howett) is again included. The geological section was written by Dave Bodecott, and Ron Kenyon has compiled all the information sections at the rear of the book with the exception of the advice on mountain accidents which was written by John Ellerton, and the crag guide which was the work of Max Biden. The onerous burden of proof reading was kindly undertaken by Al Davis (who has personally eliminated no less than a thousand redundant commas), Max Biden, Al Phizacklea, Phil Rigby, Alan Greig and Sally Baxendale so any msitkaes are their fault. Vertebrate Graphics have once again done a sterling job with the layout, and Peter Hodgkiss, at an age when most people would long ago have retired, has had to force himself to make yet another climbing trip abroad to oversee the printing.

Photo: Chris Bonington

Stephen Reid, 2007

Historical

Great Gable, Green Gable & Kirk Fell

1884–1936

Seen from a distance, Great Gable has no great rock face to attract the eye, and it is therefore not surprising that some fifty years elapsed after the first ascents of Pillar Rock and Scafell Crag before the first climb on Gable was recorded. This was in 1884, when the Needle Ridge was climbed by WP Haskett Smith.

It is true that in 1828 the Needle had been both observed and sketched by the father of JW Robinson, but no further attention seems to have been paid to this remarkable feature of the Napes Ridges until its first ascent by WP Haskett Smith in 1886. This ascent, apart from it being a notable solo effort in itself, had a considerable influence on the future of British rock-climbing. It was the subject of an article in the Pall Mall Gazette in 1890, and there can be little doubt that its spectacular appearance in photographs drew wider attention to Cumbrian rocks as a climbing ground.

OG Jones, whose book did so much to stimulate British rock-climbing, was stirred to pay his first visit to the Lake District by the sight of a photograph of the Needle in a shop in the Strand.

The Needle soon commenced to be, as now, the most popular climb in the district, and the first ascent by a lady was made by Miss Koecher in 1890. During the next decade the pioneers completed the ascents of the main ridges; both the Arrowhead and the Eagle's Nest Ridges being climbed in 1892. GA Solly's lead of the Eagle's Nest Ridge Direct, on a cold April day, must rank as one of the outstanding feats of Lake District climbing history. In the same year Gable Crag attracted attention, the Oblique Chimney being climbed by Dr Collier. Tradition has it that the crag was

Right: A busy day on The Napes circa 1900 with teams on **Needle Ridge** (D) and **Napes Needle** (HS). **Photo:** Abraham brothers

OG Jones and HC Bowen on the first ascent of **Kern Knotts Crack** (VS) in 1897.
Photo: Abraham brothers

used for business purposes by 'Moses,' the illicit whisky distiller, but no record remains of his routes. Other climbs on the crag soon followed the ascent of Oblique Chimney, the fall of the Engineer's Chimney in 1899 marking the end of the first epoch.

Kern Knotts was the discovery of OG Jones, who ascended the Chimney in 1893 and the Crack in 1897 – having climbed the Crack on a rope the previous year. It may be of interest to record that in the early days a chockstone was lodged at the top of the niche, and was removed by SW Herford when found unsafe.

From 1900 to 1918, exploration on Great Gable remained almost at a standstill. A few new routes were made, but the only notable achievement was the conquest of the West Buttress of Kern Knotts in 1912, by Sansom and Herford; the climb being at that time the most difficult ascent in the district. 1919 was a notable year in climbing history, and Great Gable did not escape the wave of exploration which swept over Pillar and Scafell. Kern Knotts was converted into a boulder problem by HM Kelly, the possible moves being still further increased in more recent years. On the Napes, the energy of Fergus Graham, Frankland, Kelly, and others has left little for future explorers; although a few unconsidered trifles were picked up in 1934. Gable Crag remained in comparative obscurity, the last problem of interest, that of the Engineer's Slabs, not being solved until 1934.

Since the last guide was written two new climbing grounds have been developed.

Green Gable Crags were apparently visited as long ago as 1910 when Epsilon Chimney was discovered by a Fell and Rock Climbing Club party. No further interest seems to have been taken in the crags until the visit of Fergus Graham in 1925, but a fuller exploration was made by GG Macphee in 1927. There is little likelihood of these rocks providing any more new routes.

Boat Howe, on Kirk Fell, first attracted the attention of T Graham Brown in 1912, but it was not until 1925 that he, together with George Basterfield, actually visited the crags. In conclusion, it is not inappropriate to mention that the summit of Great Gable was chosen as the site of the Fell and Rock Climbing Club War Memorial, indicating as it does, the place which Great Gable holds in the history of British Climbing.

CJ Astley Cooper, 1936

Stanley Watson leading **Sepulchre** (VS), Kern Knotts. This classic layback pitch fell down in 1981 and the route is now E3. **Photo:** Abraham brothers

1936–1948

It seems strange that the 1948 Gable guide did not contain an updated historical section. Truth to tell though, during what were largely the war years, little of note occurred, the most significant events perhaps being the ascent of Tophet Grooves by Jim Birkett and Vic Veevers, and the girdling of Tophet Wall by Arthur Dolphin and Bernard Black. Considerable exploration of Green Gable Crags and Boat Howe also took place.

1948–1968

Ever since the sport of rock climbing began, Great Gable has been the practice ground of Lakeland cragsmen. The imposing nature of its walls and pinnacles attracted many of the early pioneers of the sport, and it is hardly surprising that most of the plums had been picked. Largely owing to the preparation of the new Guide, however, interest in the area was renewed and many more lines were discovered under the moss and heather. Kern Knotts, which had been dismissed as worked out years ago, yielded many variations on old routes plus an additional Very Severe, The Cenotaph; the direct finish to Sepulchre still remains an unsolved problem at the present time, however. Exploration on the Napes has been sparse, although the climbing of Crocodile Crack, Alligator Crawl, The Pod, and the Merry Monk, all in the Eagle's Nest area, have made that section of the crag a veritable maze of routes. The big overhanging crack of Tophet Wall still waits a first ascent, however. The often wet and forbidding Gable Crag has provided a variety of routes, including two new Extremes, The Tomb and The Slant, which must rank as hard as anything in the area. On Engineer's Slab, that magnificent wall of rock which was climbed well ahead of its time by Balcombe in 1934, two new Very Severes, The Troll and Interceptor, have filled in the gaps.

PL Fearnehough, 1968

1968–1976

Since the last edition exploration has been rather sporadic, probably due to the scarcity of really good lines, However, some worthwhile routes have been found, particularly on Gable Crag. The mystery of the Unfinished Arête of Engineers Slabs has been solved; Paul Ross finished his Unfinished Arête way back in 1958. This is now incorporated into The Jabberwock. John Wilkinson, led by Rod Valentine and Dave Miller, found some more routes on Gable Crag, giving him a total of 9 routes on the crag, and Geoff Cram and Bill Young girdled the main buttress of Engineer's Slab.

Roper and Rogers found some good routes on Boat Howe and, although pitons were used for direct aid on the first ascent, Fangorn and Numenor are a couple of worthy additions.

Possibly the biggest breakthrough was The Vikings on Tophet Wall, with an amazing free lead by Richard McHardy. I said in the last edition that this route was still waiting for an ascent and, sure enough, Richard rose to the bait, and across on Kern Knotts, Jeff Lamb knocked off the direct finish to Sepulchre. So maybe if I mention that the roof above Tophet Wall has up to now defeated would-be ascensionists, the new hard men may provide us with yet another plum.

PL Fearnehough, 1976

1977–1990

With the last recorded new route in the 1977 edition of this guide being in 1974 the Historical section of the present edition starts from that date. The Gable area was for many years, and still is, only to a much lesser degree, the habitat of the lower grade climber and mountaineer with its strong traditional links, restricted choice of routes and crags plus its remoteness from the 'scene' all contributing to suppressing its rate of development.

During 1974 Kern Knotts was rudely, but only temporarily disturbed from its 12 years of hibernation by the addition of El Vino (E2) and The Kraken (E1) by Tony Stephenson and Stuart Miller, both in the same day. Gable Crag also receiving a rare new route during a visit by Pete Long and John Adams who climbed the very steep line of Vindolanda (E2) using a peg for aid.

It was late in 1976 that a raiding party from Carlisle gave a hint of renewed interest in the established crags of the area when Jeff Lamb and Steve Clegg added The Crysalid (E2) to Kern Knotts, a steep and fingery problem of excellent quality.

In most other guides the addition of only 3 new routes in any one year would be a non-event, but in 1977 Pete Whillance and Dave Armstrong did exactly this and showed the real potential yet to be exploited on the traditional crags, that is if you had both the eye and the talent. Supernatural, which climbed a very steep and intricate line left of Tophet Wall, gave Gable its first E5. The bold Sarcophagus (E3) on Gable Crag and the Cayman (E2) on the Napes completed the trio. All these routes were of excellent quality. The locals who were shaken but not visibly stirred had no defence against such a talented and selective approach to poaching.

The Gable area came under scrutiny once again from Carlisle raiders during April and May 1978 when Jeff Lamb and Pete Botterill firstly added Triffid (E2) to Kern Knotts, then with the help of John Taylor, moved on to quickly and successfully take up the gauntlet thrown down by Pat Fearnehough in 1977 and climbed the very steep cracked headwall on Tophet Wall to give Sacrificial Crack (E4). Four days later Jeff Lamb and Pete Botterill returned to add another E4 to the left-hand end of Tophet Wall, Golden Calf.

The area was at last slowly starting to take on a much needed character change with the addition of high quality routes in the extreme grades.

Any momentum gained over the previous few years quickly ebbed with 1979 and 1980 producing only four new routes, the best being The Angel of Mercy (E1) on Gable Crag by Jeff Lamb and Pete Botterill. During 1981 Kern Knotts finally and irretrievably had the cobwebs brushed away with the addition of five extremes, four in one day by a strong Carlisle team who also provided a solution to the problem created by the loss of Pitch 1 of Sepulchre in a rockfall. Kern Knotts had now become a balanced crag with climbing available at most grades.

August of 1984 saw Pete Whillance and Dave Armstrong in action again on Tophet Wall where they forced the superb line of Incantations, the first E6 for Gable. Many aspirant E6 mechanics have had the unusual opportunity, thanks to television, of rehearsing the route from the comfort of their armchairs, from where all things are possible. Don't be fooled it still requires talent and a lot of neck. At least we have all witnessed the fact that Dave Armstrong is not always cool and calm and does resort to the occasional expletive.

The next surge of activity was triggered off by the publication of the F&RCC New West Supplement in 1985, for climbers now had the route information which also showed up the gaps.

The prize of 1986 went to Colin Downer and Andy Hall who brought the Borrowdale scorched earth policy to Gable Crag and created Snicker Snack (E3), a superb classic crack climb left of Engineer's Slab. This beautifully cleaned strip of rock was to be a constant reminder to all of us of yet another lost opportunity.

In 1987, with guide book checking, The Napes came under scrutiny and this, as always, results in a cluster of new routes with the best being The Tormentor (E4), a very committing slab climb, by Al Phizacklea and Tony Greenbank (yes, the original) and Amos Moses (E1) by Pete Long and Terry Parker.

Whilst attention was being focussed on The Napes, Colin Downer and Andy Hall came in on the blind side and scored two direct hits on Gable

Crag with Dream Twister (E3) and Powder Finger (E3), once again producing routes of excellent quality and showing their ability to pick off the best lines and everyone else's inability to spot them before the event.

1988 saw a spread of activity throughout the area with parties touring the crags, mopping up and infilling during an excellent long Summer. Steve Hubball and Steve Brailey contributed eight new routes to Green Gable, the first new route activity for 55 years, at grades compatible with the existing, the best being Abacus (HVS).

The good weather also brought Ron Kenyon to the valley where we at last sorted out the various options to Buttonhook Route on Kern Knotts by climbing Close to the Wind (E1).

Both Gable Crag and The Napes were to benefit from the good weather when Al Phizacklea, temporarily unemployed as a result of industrial action, added 6 routes to Gable Crag and one to The Napes as part of his 63 route bumper season in the Lakes. The Tombstone (E3) on Gable Crag was his best effort which filled in the gap between The Tomb and The Jabberwock.

1989 was to prove disappointing with very little activity, the only exception being that of Al Phizacklea, Dai Lampard and Bob Wightman who tiptoed across Tophet Wall on a very bold and sustained traverse line to create The Satanic Traverses (E5) (a very topical name at the time).

The general apathy of 1989 spilled over into 1990 when only Moggy Traveller (E4) and Fat Freddie's Cat (E3) were recorded during the summer months, both routes being variations on the left-hand end of Kern Knotts and climbed by Al Phizacklea, Andy Rowell and Dave Kells.

When looking through the first ascents list and route descriptions it soon becomes obvious that not all development is good or desirable development with the lines that are justifiably popular and here to stay having been carefully and selectively chosen for their quality and appeal, but not just to the first ascensionists. 1977 and 1981 were perfect examples of this selective approach when Pete Whillance and Dave Armstrong added routes to Gable Crag and The Napes which all carry star ratings and receive repeat ascents. This approach was by no means exclusive to them as born out by routes such as: Sacrificial Crack, Golden Calf, Snicker Snack, Dream Twister, The Tormentor, all excellent routes that are guaranteed to get repeat ascents or at least attempts.

The other extreme to this will unfortunately always be found close at hand where many routes, although having been extensively gardened during their exploration, have still resulted in poor quality climbs with repeat ascent being rare. Nature has its own way of correcting this brief intrusion but over enthusiastic and often unnecessary gardening can and

Left: Jeff Lamb hangs from the 'mother of all jams' during the first ascent of **Sacrificial Crack** (E4), The Napes. **Photo:** Pete Botterill

does create long term problems. The scars can take many years to heal and the critics are constantly in the wings waiting for the opportunity to prove their point.

The present edition, unlike its predecessors, now contains routes across all the grades giving a more balanced climbing picture but differs from many other guides in not being top heavy on both grade and quality. In spite of the modernisation process since the last edition the area retains its strong traditional links with many lower grade classic rock climbs on its mountain crags that can still provide superb days out in a relatively quiet mountain atmosphere. The difference now is in the choice of available crags and hopefully some of the increasing number of climbers will be tempted onto the alternative crags thereby reducing the pressure on The Napes and Tophet Wall.

Unlike the previous writer, I shall not be giving hints as to the remaining last great problems or 'plums', do it the hard way, go out and find them if they exist. Alternatively, try repeating any of the many fine recorded routes, the rewards for most would be much greater and the quality guaranteed. There can be few climbers around that have totally exhausted the available routes at their grade and below. Alternatively, work at it, and go up a grade.

It only now requires the armchair critics to adopt their usual and predictable positions when assessing the guide's route descriptions, grades and star rating for the whole of the guide book production process to be completed.

Some things never change.

Dave Kirby, February 1991

1991–2006

Nearly 100 routes have been added to the Great Gable guide since 1991. Not exactly a flood of new routes over 16 years, but still respectable for a Lakeland mountain whose crags all lie above the 500 metre contour and for the most part only come into condition in the summer months. A number of these additions are of a high quality and should bring the area back into vogue again, especially the excellent development of Boat How.

Late in 1991 Al Phizacklea and John Holden, typically put that year's new guide out of date with a very active day on the fell and found three more gaps on Kern Knotts adding Toss Pot (E2), Young Shavers (E2) and West Buttress Eliminate (E1) before moving on to The Napes and squeezing in Aquiline Slab (E2).

After this initial surge of activity by the Barrow team new routes came in more of a steady trickle.

In 1993 Ian Turnbull and Colin Downer explored the overhanging rock right of Incantations on Tophet Wall and found a hard place in Golgotha (E6).

Paul Ross spotted the potential of Boat How while walking his Jack Russells around Ennerdale. The crag had had a less than flattering description in the previous guide. He returned later in June 1995 with Dave Birkett and Sue Wood. Their objective was the unclimbed central pillar which Ross described as 'An E3 leader's answer to Indian Face as a fall from the crux would result in a deck out!' Birkett led Flagship originally graded E4, protected by skyhooks and small RP's. The team then went on to remove the last aid point from Fanghorn (E3) and added a harder top pitch. Even though a stunning half-page photograph of Dave Birkett leading Fanghorn appeared in Climber (October 1995, printed back to front!) Ross still had the crag to himself for the next year and a half! The following summer he added the excellent Scenic Cruise (HVS) on the cleaner West Face of Boat How with Paul Greenwood, and in the spring 1997 teamed up with Pete Armstrong to add Final Voyage (E1), before departing for the USA. Later that year Al and Keith Phizacklea visited Boat How and climbed Trim and Incline (E3), an excellent addition to the West Face.

Over on The Napes in 1999 Martin Armitage and Tessa Kennedy added the Cannon Stone (E1), which gets the record for the longest pitch but unfortunately includes an alarming detached block. While on Kern Knotts Karl Telfer added the bold Grimalkin (E4), and Napes Needle saw its first new route in over 50 years when Stephen Reid and Ron Kenyon added Sick Heart River (E2) on the east side of the pinnacle. Rick Graham and Ted Rogers took over the development of Boat How first with the addition of a number of high quality pitches including Numenor with Direct Finish (E2), Voyager (E3) and Jolly Roger (E2). They later returned and climbed Keel Haul (E3) and together with Andy Jones added the blockbuster Poseidon Adventure (E4).

The new millennium saw the beginning of work on the guide and Phil Rigby and John Williams added Nine Lives (E3) on Kern Knotts. Lakeland guru Dave Armstrong made an appearance to continue the Carlisle link with Great Gable by adding The Cat's Whiskers (E4), on Kern Knotts. Rigby and Rob Fone then added the serious and deceptively short Mausoleum (E6), on the wall right of Innominate Crack and filled another gap on the Cat Wall with Cat Napping (E5).

Perhaps it was also fitting that the new millennium saw the UK's first reported E10, John Dunne's Breathless on the impending headwall left of Sacrificial Crack on Tophet Wall, a route which only succumbed after some 14 attempts. However, repeats by Dave Birkett and Dave McLeod have resulted in a consensus grade of E9.

The fells were out of bounds for most of the 2001 season as the Foot and Mouth disaster closed down the county and many hefted flocks were lost. As the county began the process of regeneration in 2002 only two new routes were climbed, both on Napes Needle. Phil Rigby and Kevin Avery added Thirty-nine Steps (E3), a super direct version of Sick Heart

River, and on the Wasdale side a direct line through the large overhang of the top block gave Phil Rigby and Tom Foster the Wasdale Roof (E3), a highly entertaining problem.

After an exploratory walk under Westmorland Crags Stephen Reid saw the potential for new routes on these neglected broken buttresses and ribs. That year (2003) he added 22 new routes, a record for development of one crag, and unlikely to be seen again in the Lake District. (Prove me wrong!), the best of these being the delightful rib of Not a Cairn in the World (HVS) climbed with Chris King and the short off-width jamming spectacular of Westmorland Crack (E2) led by Trevor Suddaby. Over on the Napes, Al Phizacklea and John Holden added five routes in the space of a week. The best being Turdus torquatus (E2) to the left of Abbey Buttress and Gharial (E1), which takes a slim pillar of rock left of its bigger brother Crocodile Crack. They returned the following year and added three more routes to this part of the crag.

In 2005 Barry Clarke, while helping out with descriptions of some of the lower graded routes found plenty of spare rock on Gable Crag and added 12 routes (11 climbed solo), and pointed to the potential of linking some of the many short, clean buttresses on this side of the fell.

Boat How once again came under the spotlight in 2006 of the Barrow team of Al Phizacklea and John Holden, who worked some of the remaining spare rock and came up with three routes the best being Groyne Strain (E1) on the East Buttress. On hearing of more developments at Boat How, the crag aficionado Ted Rogers drafted in Ken Forsythe for a piece of the action and they added two short but worthy E2s, Topsail and Spinnaker. This crag has certainly matured over the last 17 years with the addition of 20 new routes/pitches and is no longer a backwater in Ennerdale.

What next? Well take a look at the new photodiagrams in the comfort of your home/bar/campsite and make plans, start walking and fill in those gaps! There is still one left on Napes Needle and what about the direct start to Voyager?

Phil Rigby, March 2007

Pillar Rock & Ennerdale

1826–1934

That Pillar Rock should have attracted mankind over one hundred years ago is not surprising in view of its situation and unique appearance – an isolated crag on the breast of a mountain flanking one of the most desolate dales in the Lake District. The very remoteness of its surroundings, as well as the apparent inaccessibility of its summit, doubtless fascinated as well as awed the shepherds and others whose work or inclination took them within its neighbourhood, and its solitariness naturally became a challenge. Farm fireside talk and inn gossip probably clothed it with a certain amount of romance, and early writers included it in their Guides as one of the notable features of the district. It also gained notoriety from Wordsworth, who indicated it, erroneously, as the scene of the fatal accident which inspired his poem, 'The Brothers,' published in 1800. So that, when the first ascent was actually achieved, it only increased the allurement of Pillar Stone, as the Rock was known in those days.

It is not very difficult to assign to this first ascent its due place in relation to our sport, for in it can be recognized the first seed of English rock-climbing. The climbing of rocks as an art in itself parted ways with mountaineering as then known, i.e. the attainment of a summit of a mountain by the least arduous route, for here was a definite attempt to get to a summit – not of a mountain – by way of difficult rocks.

John Atkinson, of Croftfoot, Ennerdale (variously described as cooper and shepherd), was the man who became associated with this landmark of British rock-climbing, and his feat was given due prominence in the two county newspapers of the day, the date of the ascent being given in both cases as July 9th, 1826. One of them stated that, "tho' the undertaking had been attempted by thousands, it was always relinquished as hopeless." Seemingly journalistic licence was known in those days. Still it is evident that the Pillar had a great reputation, and that many efforts had been made to reach its top.

Atkinson is believed to have used the way now known as The Old West, and it is understood that Messrs J Colebank, W Tyson, and J Braithwaite, all shepherds, followed his route the same year, though it is stated by a writer in the West Cumberland Times, of August 8th, 1891, that they reached the top by the East Side. There may be some ground for this statement, for shepherds must certainly have played the most prominent part in those early attempts. It seems very likely that they were on intimate terms with the crag, especially the east side of High Man, for the grassy ledges lying between the top of Walker's Gully and Low Man must have proved a great temptation to sheep straying from the fellside above, and consequently many of them would have to be rescued. Unfortunately, there is no record as to when the 'Old Wall' was built to prevent such straying; a knowledge of this might have thrown some light on the earliest ascents. Because of this early acquaintance with the east side, it has been hinted by RST Chorley, in his historical investigations (***Fell and Rock Journal***, 1926), that even the first ascent may have been made from this and not from the west side.

For some unaccountable reason a period of twenty-two years elapsed before the next recorded ascent, when what might be described as the first tourist ascent, was made by Lieut Wilson (RN) He was followed by CAO Baumgartner, JG Whitehead, and CW Hartley, all in 1850. These may not have been the only persons who had ascended Pillar by this time, as Mr Baumgartner says he found on the top "a bottle … containing a paper recording the names of preceding visitors," and it is to be regretted that he does not give their names.

The feat was now, by the frequency of its accomplishment, becoming less fearsome, and Mr George Seatree estimates that an approximate summary of ascents from 1826 to 1875 is as follows:

1826 to **1850**	6 ascents
1850 to **1866**	22 ascents
1866 to **1873**	31 ascents
1874	10 ascents
1875	50 ascents
Total	119 ascents

Early pioneer John Robinson. Probably taken in the Abraham's studio. **Photo:** Abraham brothers

In spite of conflicting reports, it is traditionally held that the first few ascents were made by The Old West Route, with the possible exception of Baumgartner's, this, according to a letter of his, being by the east and north sides (which sounds rather like the Old Wall Route). Mr Whitehead also claims, according to Mr J W Robinson, to have done the Corner above the slab, i.e., the one into which the Pendlebury Traverse leads.

In the early sixties a little more certainty creeps in, and new courses were discovered. We learn from Mr Seatree's 'List of First Ascents' that "the first known ascent of the east side" was made in 1861 by the Keeper of the Lighthouse, St Bees, and four friends. Messrs Conybeare, Butler and others also climbed the East Face, although there is some doubt whether they did the Notch on this occasion or went by 'Easy Way' variation. A still newer route was made in the early seventies by Gardiner and the Pendleburys, though one can only look upon this as substantial variation of the Slab and Notch Climb. An earlier guide stated that Messrs Barnes and Grave worked out the Old Wall Route in the early sixties. Further investigation proved this to be unlikely as, firstly, William Grave was only born in 1848, and, secondly, an extract from his diary (*Climbers' Club Journal*) gives his ascent with Matthew Barnes as being made on August 7th, 1870, 'by a slab on the east side.' Nevertheless, Seatree says (*FRCC Journal*, vol 2, p 16), referring to 1866: "In that year also there occurred successful attacks on the 'Old Wall' and 'Great Chimney' route, now seldom climbed, by Messrs Matthew Barnes, A Barnes, W Grave, G Scoular, Hermann Woolly, R Whitwell, W G Holland, James Moore and Tom Leigh. The Rock now began to attract our womenfolk, and Miss A Barker had the honour of the first ascent for her sex in 1870. Miss Mary Westmorland accompanied her brothers (Thomas and Edward) up it in 1873 or 1874, and Mrs Ann Creer was the third in 1875. The latter year also saw the introduction to the Rock of that most interesting character, the Revd James Jackson, self and well styled the Patriarch of the Pillarites, a title which might now well be claimed by Mr Lawrence Pilkington, who as a boy of fourteen climbed the rock, with his elder brother, in 1869. It was also in 1875 that Mr Seatree himself became a devotee, and during the next ten years he guided many parties to the shrine on the summit. He claims to have made the first ascent of The Curtain (*FRCC Journal*, vol 2, pp 15 and 17), with Stanley Martin, on September 14th, 1874, though it is hard to reconcile his description with the climb as we know it today. His devotion was wholehearted, and much of our knowledge of the early history of the Rock is due to the care with which he collected every scrap of information relating to his beloved crag."

An interesting point to note at this juncture is the fact, to which Mr Seatree called attention, that hitherto the climbing had been done ropeless, and this is probably the reason why there was not a great deal of variation in the quality of the routes taken in the first fifty years. One can, therefore, understand his surprise on seeing JW Robinson carry a rope when they first met in the eighties.

With the advent of that prince of pioneers, Mr WP Haskett Smith, a change came over the scene, and, following the general new developments in rock-climbing, more difficult routes were worked out (*vide* **List of First Ascents**). Messrs JW Robinson (a name particularly associated with Pillar), WC Slingsby, and G Hastings, all assisted in the impetus which he gave to exploration. It was this decade which became memorable in the annals of climbing on Pillar Rock because of the long siege laid to the North Climb, for Haskett Smith, along with his brother Edmund, reached the Stomach Traverse at least as early as 1884. Less than a year after the first ascent of the climb in 1891, GA Solly led a party up it, and proved that the descent into Savage Gully could be avoided by the Hand Traverse, a fact further emphasised by J Collier's successful attack on the Nose about twelve months later.

Exploration of the Rock kept pace with that on other crags in the Lake District, and 1899 and 1901 saw the fall of Walker's Gully and Savage Gully respectively, a fitting culmination to the gully epoch of the sport. The successful attack on the New West Climb by the brothers Abraham, in 1901, recalled the further possibilities of this almost forgotten face;

but a more significant sign of the times (the development of modern rock-climbing) was the magnificent victory over the north-west angle of the Rock in 1906. It was ten years, however, before the west face was thought of again, when the South-West Climb paved the way in 1911 for the grand assault on it in 1919, with its afterthoughts in 1920 and 1923, though curiously enough the men who had shown the possibilities of this side in 1901 went to the north-east for their next conquest in 1912.

The High Man with its multiplicity of routes was becoming well-nigh exhausted, but Low Man had still secrets to reveal, and some homeric efforts at gardening on the West Wall of Walker's Gully, a labour which took the best part of two days, yielded in 1928 the magnificent Grooved Wall Climb. This was matched later by the two superlative routes on the north face, evolved in 1932 and 1933. These were, incidentally, the outcome of the Girdle Traverse, so ingeniously and fearlessly worked out a year earlier by its authors, a grand climax to the girdling aspect of cragsmanship in the Lake District.

Before closing this brief history, the name of LJ Oppenheimer should be mentioned. That Pillar Rock should have made an appeal to him was an inevitable reaction between such a striking natural object and a man of his artistic temperament. It was the lodestone of his wanderings in the Lake District, and though he did not achieve any of the glamour associated with being the leader of a first ascent, it was mainly due to his optimism that Savage Gully and the North-West Climb were done.

Finally one must recall the extraordinary demonstration of interest in Pillar Rock shown by both climbers and the general public on Easter Sunday, April 4th, 1926, a century after the first ascent. It is hardly an exaggeration to say that there were scores of climbers and non-climbers who reached its top by devious routes, whilst on the fellside ledges, above and on both sides of the Rock, were large numbers of lookers-on perched like so many sea-birds on their cliffs. The culminating moment of that day occurred, for me, as I reached the scree on the west side after descending the New West. It carried me back to days of veneration and awe, for before me stood a very elderly farmer and his wife gazing up at the great sweep of cliff before them. "Ay, it's a Grand Stone," he said simply. A sentiment, surely, that has echoed time and again in many a cragsman's heart.

HM Kelly, 1934

1934–1968

During the late thirties most of the exploration on Pillar Rock was done by parties led by AT Hargreaves and SH Cross, culminating in the ascent of Shamrock Tower. In this period A Birtwistle visited the Rock and

Left: The Nose of **North Climb** (MS), Pillar Rock. **Photo:** Abraham Brothers

Early climbers on **New West Climb** (VD), Pillar Rock. **Photo:** Abraham Brothers

climbed the difficult slabs on the left of the South-West Climb, naming the route South-West-by-West.

Then came an extraordinarily long period of inactivity on the Rock. For 18 years no new climbs were reported on Pillar although some routes were found on Black Crag and Haskett Buttress. The first route on Anglers' Crag was done in 1938 while the remainder were reported in the late fifties by climbers from West Cumberland. W Peascod led the most obvious routes on Bowness Knott in 1950 and the rest were discovered nearly 10 years later.

In the drought of 1959, G Oliver climbed the obvious line on the west face of High Man and named the route Vandal. This was, in fact, one grade harder than any previous climb on Pillar. On the same day M de St Jorre climbed Goth, the big corner on the west face of Low Man. Again came a period of inactivity until climbers who lived close at hand began taking an interest in the Rock. Beginning with Scylla, many of the most obvious lines on the north and west faces were climbed. The era of routes named from particle physics then began and a considerable number of climbs were found on Shamrock and the north face of Low Man, often only after extensive gardening. People were seen carrying ice-axes on hot summer days for this purpose. Some new ideas covered rock previously climbed, notably Boot Strap, and the final result has been a great deal of very pleasant climbing in superb and comparatively remote surroundings, always one of the unique values of climbing on Pillar Rock. Most of the best lines appear to have been climbed but there is still a great deal of unclimbed rock in and around Ennerdale, although the prospective explorer may well require 'green fingers'.

AG Cram, 1968

1968–1976

The intensive development of the Rock reached a peak in 1968 with some ten major new routes being found. This development has continued with the discovery of a further nine routes, as usual mainly by local climbers. A notable addition is the Greater Traverse – a girdle of the main faces including Shamrock and totalling nearly 1,800 feet.

The dynamic Bill Lounds set a ferocious new standard with a free ascent of Black Widow, and also created the precedent of ten hard routes in one day! Other free ascents, including that of Scylla Direct by Jeff Lamb, have meant that the only aid on the Rock is now one sling on Gondor.

Bill Lounds on the first ascent of the classic **Thanatos** (HVS), Pillar Rock, 18th May 1968. **Photo:** Chris Eilbeck

Two other less pleasant events should be reported. For some ten years it has been possible for the relatively small number of visiting rock climbers to drive up the Ennerdale Valley to a point below the Rock – particularly useful on a short visit. However, access is now banned (see approaches) beyond the car park at Bowness Knott. A second particularly sad event had been the annual destruction of Robinson's Cairn by mindless persons unknown.

On a more cheerful note, the 150th anniversary of the first ascent of the Rock was celebrated with great zest on the 9th–10th July, 1976. Large numbers of people reached the summit, some by the original Old West Route and many by harder routes.

The recent changes have, of course, not affected the Rock at all. Pillar Rock is still a very pleasant and peaceful place to climb. Long may it remain so.

AG Cram, October 1976

1976–1990

Pillar Rock or 'The Rock' as it is affectionately known by local climbers has always been the 'Cinderella Crag' among the mountain crags of Lakeland. In the early days, its remoteness from centres of climbing popularity, bad communications and lack of transport held its development in check, and 'The Rock' has always lagged behind other mountain crags as standards have risen over the years. Even in 1990 it only boasts three routes harder than E2.

Development of the crag has been largely undertaken by locally based climbers and activity reached a peak in the 1960s when climbers could drive up the Ennerdale valley to below the crag. The loss of vehicular access spelled the death knell for 'The Rock' as ascents of new routes dwindled and, with the exception of the popular classics, the existing routes started to revert back to nature.

In HM Kelly's 1934 Historical Notes he makes reference to the Revd James Jackson, "self and well styled the Patriarch of the Pillarites." A century later that title may well go to Bill Young who has been actively involved in the development of the crag for some 20 years, being on the first ascents of Scylla in 1963 and Tapestry in 1980, with many in between.

The late 1970s saw the freeing of Gondor by the late Gordon Tinnings and until the exact line of his ascent became widely known, many epics ensued as climbers attempted to free climb the original way.

The 1980s opened with a quantum leap in difficulty. Tapestry, a bold E4 on the North Face of Low Man by local climbers Tony Stephenson and Chris Sice, re-kindled interest in new routes on Pillar and other routes soon followed. Cunning Stunts is notable and aptly named. This was followed in 1984 by The Straits of Messina (E4), the hardest route to date, climbed by Pete Whillance and Dave Armstrong.

Development then slackened somewhat, no doubt partly due to the wet summers in the second half of the decade. However, Jim Loxham was active during this period when weather permitted and notable additions were Over the Hill in 1987, a companion route to Soliton on the wall of Walker's Gully, climbed with Pete Botterill, and in 1988 Patriarch of the Pillarites with Stuart Miller. A notable event (for Pillar) in 1988 was the on sight lead of Pauli Exclusion Principle and The Terrorist, both E2 by Bob Wightman and Al Phizacklea, giving two new hard routes in one day.

There are still many new lines in the modern idiom (i.e. bold, short and hard) to be climbed on Pillar but until access improves, or climbers are prepared to make the long approach, new additions will continue at a trickle.

Two other crags worthy of mention are Black Crag in Wind Gap Cove and Haskett Buttress in Mirklin Cove. The former has seen attention from Jim Loxham and several worthwhile routes have been pioneered, making the crag well worth a visit. Haskett Buttress was visited by Al Phizacklea and Bob Wightman in 1988 and four new routes were climbed in one day, all named after the theme started by Don Greenop in the early 1970s. Thus, all the routes on this buttress have the initials DS, and rather peculiar names e.g., The Detrital Slide in 1969 and in 1988 The Dipso Somnambulist.

All the crags in the Pillar area are quiet and, unusual these days, one can often have them to oneself. It is expected that the new guidebook will stimulate renewed interest in the area, I hope that it will still be possible to find peace and solitude on its crags.

Jim Loxham, December 1990

1991–2006

The first new routes added to Pillar Rock came not long after the publication of the previous guide when Stephen Reid who had undertaken to write the Pillar section for the FRCC's selected climbs guide ***Lake District Rock*** began tackling some of the obvious gaps noticed during his researches. The results, Gorre (E1) and Caucus Race (E3), spurred Colin Read to dig out his little black book and hot foot it up to West Cove where over two days in 1995 he and Graham Swainbank put up Hawkeye (HVS) and Sundance (MVS) on the immaculate rock of the West Face of High Man. Apart from the odd minor addition, nearly all the remaining new routes on Pillar were climbed by Reid and various friends in the course of guidebook research; particular mention should be made of Chris King who led many of the harder pitches. Goodbye to All That (E1) from Reid and Steve Stout, and Mirror, Mirror… (E2), the latter a bold lead by King, were the best of this crop. Delving back into the past, Mike Cocker's historical researches enabled Reid and King to make a probable second ascent of North-West-by-West (or Mallory's Route) on the West Face of Low Man first climbed by George Mallory and Alan Goodfellow in 1913, a line previously untraced. The only other new route worthy of mention was Photogenic (E2) on the Shamrock from Al Phizacklea and John Holden, though to their chagrin they found that they had been beaten to the main pitch by two days by the inevitable King/Reid team.

Elsewhere in Ennerdale things were quiet for a long while; the only exception being the further exploration of Anglers' Crag by Des Johnson between 1995 and 1997. In 2005 though, Phizacklea and Holden, realising that the guidebook research team was moving rapidly westwards, stepped in and developed the small but immaculate Spire Crag: of their new climbs the best is undoubtedly Inspired Slab (E2), though it was subsequently discovered that they were pipped to the post for the central corner by Cocker and party. All the remaining new routes are in Mirk and Mirklin Coves and were discovered during guidebook operations by Reid, King, Sally Baxendale and Sarah Bailey.

There is still unclimbed rock aplenty in Ennerdale, including a few noteworthy blank areas on Pillar Rock that could provide some very hard pitches, and, though the excursions of the last few years have meant that there is now a little less for anyone else to go at, it is to be hoped that they gain as much enjoyment from exploring it all as we have.

Stephen Reid, March 2007

Great Gable from Wasdale

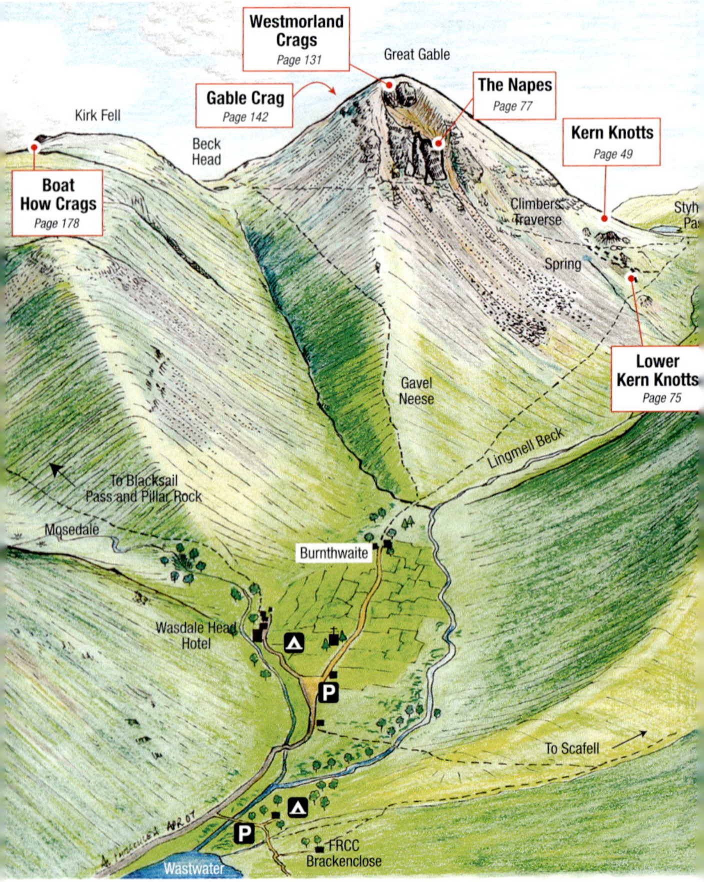

Great Gable

by Phil Rigby

Great Gable's distinctive pyramid shape at the head of Wasdale makes it the archetypal Lakeland mountain. The same can also be said of its four climbing centres which range from the relaxed outcrop style crag of *Kern Knotts* to the dark brooding north-facing *Gable Crag*. Nicely filling in the gaps between these two are the airy mountaineering ridges and faces of *The Napes* and the imposing buttress of *Tophet Wall* which looms over the red screes of *Great Hell Gate*.

All of these crags can be easily reached in a leisurely one and a half to one and three-quarter hours from Seathwaite or Wasdale, or ***Gable Crag*** can be reached in just over an hour if approached from the top of Honister Pass.

No other Lakeland mountain offers this variety of climbing, meaning that you can explore Great Gable over many visits and still find something new and exciting.

Kern Knotts

Grid reference:	**NY 215 096**	Altitude:	**520m**
Faces:	**South-West**	Approach:	**1hr 15 mins**

Kern Knotts is a superb crag in a fine situation with stunning views of Wasdale Head and the Scafell range. It is very steep and compact and provides climbing of high quality and character on sound rough rock which dries quickly and its sunny aspect means that it is one of the first mountain crags to come into condition early in the season.

The main feature (seen well when approaching from Sty Head) is a steep wall at its right-hand end set at right angles to the rest of the crag. This wall boasts two famous crack climbs from the early days of Lake District exploration; ***Kern Knotts Crack*** and ***Innominate Crack***. Around the corner left of this is the deep gash of ***Kern Knotts Chimney*** and further left again is the shorter ***Kern Knotts West Chimney***. At the extreme left end of the crag is the very clean ***Cat Wall*** which has distinctive rock bands running across its face and provides many excellent single pitch routes.

Wasdale Head in early summer. **Photo:** Phil Rigby

Around the base of the crag is scattered a fine selection of boulders with excellent bouldering used by the early pioneers for a "wet day's sport".

Approaches:

From **Wasdale Head** follow the track to Burnthwaite then take the Sty Head path situated on the north side of Lingmell Beck. Break off the track at ***Lower Kern Knotts*** and scramble over scree and boulders to join the **Climbers' Traverse** below ***Kern Knotts*** (1hr 15mins).

From **Seathwaite**, Borrowdale (1hr 20mins), take the path to Sty Head Pass and, from its highest point at the Mountain Rescue box, follow the **Climbers' Traverse**, a gently rising track which crosses the south flank of Great Gable. The path is rather vague at first but soon becomes better defined and ***Kern Knotts*** is reached in a few minutes.

Descent:

An easy descent makes this an ideal crag for a multi-route day: easiest on the left.

The climbs are described from **left** to **right**.

Pyfo	55m	VD		1962

A poor route. Start at a small buttress at the extreme left end of the crag. Climb the buttress and make a traverse rightwards avoiding the top of the crag for as long as possible.

Kern Knotts & Tophet Wall

Cat Wall

Caterwaul	25m	E1		1992

Start 2 metres right of the large sloping heather ledge below a short crack in a blank wall.

(5b). Climb easy rock to reach the short crack. Ascend the crack to a small bulge and make an awkward move to gain the sloping ledge above. Traverse leftwards to a shallow impending groove just right of the chimney on ***Flake Climb***. Ascend the groove to a ledge and finish up a thin crack in the wall above.

The Cat's Whiskers	40m	E4		2000

An eliminate up the wall between ***Caterwaul*** and ***Feline Crack***. Start directly below a crack 3 metres right of ***Caterwaul***.

(6a). Climb easy rock to a thin crack in the steep wall. Climb the crack and move rightwards to a ledge. Gain the gangway above (***The Catwalk***) and traverse left for 2 metres. Climb up to a good nut runner and pull up right to an obvious flat hold; blind moves up and left gain a standing position on the flat hold. Climb leftwards on small holds to better ledges above and follow easier rocks direct to the top.

Feline Crack	35m	VS	★	1979

Interesting climbing up the obvious vertical crack at the left end of the crag.

1 25m (4c). Ascend easy slabs to the steep crack which is climbed with interest to a sloping ledge; step left to a good rest. Step back right and

Kern Knotts

Cat Wall

1	Caterwaul	E1	
2	The Cat's Whiskers	E4	
3	Feline Crack	VS	*
4	Flake Climb	VS	
5	Grimalkin	E4	***
6	Cat Napping	E5	
7	Pussy	E4	***
8	Moggy Traveller	E4	**
9	Sylvester	E3	***
10	Fat Freddie's Cat	E2	**
11	Kern Knotts West Chimney	VD	*
12	Nine Lives	E3	

Photo: Phil Rigby

continue up the thin finger crack above, followed by easier climbing to a large open book corner on the right.

2 10m. Climb the corner to the top.

Flake Climb	30m	VS		1919

Start at the obvious broken crack just right of ***Feline Crack***. Good value.

(4c). Climb easy slabs to the steep crack and ascend the crack to a sloping ledge *(**The Catwalk**)*. Traverse the ledge leftwards for 15 metres to the foot of a short steep chimney; climb this to the top.

Grimalkin	44m	E4	★★★	1998

Bold climbing up the banded wall. Start directly below a prominent short hanging corner at a thin ragged crack.

1 24m (6a). Climb the crack using small holds on the left and make committing moves rightwards to reach the corner and good runners. Climb up and rightwards across the fingery bulging wall to reach a slim groove. Climb the groove more easily to a good ledge.

2 20m (5a). Climb a short wall to a large glacis, then another wall right of a corner to easier ground and the top.

Cat Napping	20m	E5+		2000

A taxing fingery climb up the short hairline crack and groove 3 metres right of ***Grimalkin***. Start below the crack.

(6b). Climb a short wall to a ledge. Boldly climb the wall past a small bulge to reach the hairline crack. Launch up the crack with difficulty to a good hold at the base of a small corner (junction with ***Pussy***). Climb the corner direct and step right onto a sloping ledge below a thin crack. Climb the crack and groove to the top.

The next three routes all share the same start and the first 10 metres of climbing. Start just left of a blunt arête which is bounded by a shallow groove on the left.

Pussy	40m	E4	★★★	1989

No soft touch! An intriguing route on perfect rock, that makes a right-to-left rising traverse of the banded wall. Run out towards the top.

1 30m (6a). As for ***Sylvester***, climb the groove to a large spike. Step right onto the steep cracked wall and climb up to an obvious square-cut overhang. Pull leftwards around the overhang into a shallow scoop. Make difficult moves leftwards to reach a short hanging corner (junction with ***Grimalkin***). Climb the corner to a small flake and continue leftwards, following the narrow ramp, until forced to make delicate moves to gain a good ledge above.

2 10m (4b). Climb the rounded rib on the left of the corner above, to the top.

Moggy Traveller	20m	E4-	★★	1990

Steep climbing on perfect rock. Well worth the ride.

(6a). As for *Sylvester*, climb the groove to a large spike. Step right onto the steep cracked wall and climb up to an obvious square-cut overhang; pull around the overhang leftwards into a shallow scoop. Climb up steeply into a short groove and climb it to the top.

Sylvester	25m	E3	★★★	1981

The first of a new breed of wall climbs on *Cat Wall*. A problematic pitch which sees a number of failures; it requires a level headed approach up the smooth crux groove.

(5c). Climb the groove to a large spike. Step right onto the steep cracked wall and climb up to a small sloping ledge. Step back left and climb the awkward groove to reach good holds at the top.

Fat Freddie's Cat	20m	E2+	★★	1990

Another good climb which has the merit of being independent from its neighbours. Start just left of *Kern Knotts West Chimney*.

(5c). Climb easy rocks to reach an awkward crack right of the blunt arête. Climb the crack to a small ledge on the left, step back right and climb the steep right-hand shallow groove to the top.

Kern Knotts West Chimney	32m	VD	★	1897

The obvious chimney bounding the right-hand side of *Cat Wall* gives a traditional route which will be found to be very awkward by those unfamiliar with the time-honoured techniques required. Start below the chimney.

1 **16m.** Easy rocks lead to the chimney; this is climbed to a platform using a variety of classic contortions.

2 **16m.** Climb the crack above to a ledge at 8 metres followed by easier rocks to the top.

Nine Lives	33m	E3		2000

A deceptively steep eliminate up a short hanging gangway on the wall 3 metres right of *Kern Knotts West Chimney*. Start at the toe of the buttress.

(6a). Climb easy cracks for 5 metres to the start of the short gangway. Ascend the gangway leftwards to a good flat hold. Climb steeply up a short hanging crack above and pull onto the wall above. More steep moves are needed to reach a good ledge. Climb a short hanging crack in a rib and ascend the rib to a large ledge; the wall above leads to the top.

Right: Lee Proctor prepares to leave the resting ledge on **Sylvester** (E3), on the superb 'banded' Cat Wall, Kern Knotts. **Overleaf:** A team out in the midday sun on **The Buttonhook Route** (HVS), Kern Knotts. **Photos:** Mark Glaister

Kern Knotts

Central Area

1	Fat Freddies Cat	E2	**
2	Kern Knotts West Chimney	VD	*
3	Nine Lives	E3	
4	West Buttress	MVS	**
5	West Buttress Eliminate Superdirect	E1	*
6	The Kraken	E1	**
7	The Loch Ness Monster	E1	
8	The Crysalid	E2	***
9	Central Climb South Face	MVS	*
10	Triffid	E2	***
11	Triffid Right Hand Finish	E3	*
12	Kern Knotts Chimney	HS	**
13	The Young Shavers	E2	
14	Kern Knotts Buttress	HVS	
15	Misfit	E2	*

Photo: Phil Rigby

Central Area

Kern Knotts West Buttress	33m	MVS	★★	1912

The steep buttress 4 metres right of ***Kern Knotts West Chimney***. Start at the toe of the buttress.

1 16m (4b). Climb the steep broken crack to a large spike below a V-groove. Pull up the groove and make an awkward step left on to a good foothold then follow a good crack leftwards to a flat ledge. Move up left until a step back right can be made on good jugs to a large broken ledge.

2 17m. Easier rocks on the left are followed to the top.

West Buttress Eliminate Superdirect	30m	E1	★	1991

A worthwhile eliminate. Start at a thin crack in the centre of the wall, just left of the prominent lower corner in the middle of the buttress.

(5b). Climb the centre of the wall to a large spike (junction with ***Kern Knotts West Buttress***). Pull up directly, to the right of the V-groove, to a shallow scoop. Climb the scoop, step left to a short crack and ascend it. Step right, and climb more easily to a short hanging groove; climb the groove to the top.

Variation

The original route started up the corner on the right using hollow flakes to gain the large spike.

The Kraken	35m	E1	★★	1974

Better than it looks: a puzzling start leads to a fine finish. Start in the centre of the the prominent lower corner in the middle of the buttress.

(5b). Climb the short corner and make a long reach right to good holds. Pull up steeply on flat holds and move leftwards to a small ledge below the mossy corner. Ascend the corner until good holds lead out to the left arête in a fine position. Climb up more easily to a small corner and the top.

Variation

(5b). The upper corner can be climbed direct, once the holds are found under the moss!

The Loch Ness Monster	E1	33m		2000

Best left undisturbed. Start below the obvious diagonal crack just right of ***The Kraken***.

(5b). Climb the difficult crack to reach good flat holds, pull steeply up right onto a blunt rib and climb the rib past a good spike runner to a short mossy groove. Ascend the groove and short wall above to a small overhang. Pull through the overhang and trend rightwards to finish up a slab.

The Crysalid	30m	E2	★★	1976

An excellent exercise in steep fingery climbing with the crux at the top. Start at a blunt rib 4 metres right of the corner of the *The Kraken*.

1 15m (5a). Climb the rib to reach a long diagonal crack in the steep slab, and follow it rightwards then climb a short mossy wall to the base of the steep upper groove: small stance on the left.

2 15m (5c). Step right and climb the steep groove with commitment to a good hold on a doubtful flake. Step left onto a slab and follow this to the top.

Central Climb South Face	37m	MVS	★	1919

Follows the right-to-left weakness across the wall. Start 4 metres left of *Kern Knotts Chimney* and just right of a grassy crack.

1 25m (4b). Climb the wall and crack to a ramp which leads more easily rightwards to a large detached pinnacle. Climb steeply up for 12 metres then traverse left to a small stance below and left of the steep groove.

2 12m (4b). Continue left to the base of a steep scoop which is climbed to a good finishing hold.

Variation Start VS 1933

A better although more difficult start.

1 (5a). A few metres right of the original start is an obvious steep thin crack; climb it, followed by easier rocks, to the pinnacle on Pitch 1 and continue to the belay as for the original route.

Central Climb Variation 33m E1 1956

The original ascent of the first corner of *The Kraken*.

(5b). Climb the starting corner of *The Kraken*, then move right and up to a small spike. Climb mossy slabs to a reach the gangway, move left and pull into the steep finishing scoop (good flake finishing hold).

The next two routes climb the steep hanging cracks which meet to form an obvious 'V' near the top of the buttress.

Triffid	30m	E2+	★★★	1978

Difficult technical climbing up the left-hand of the V-cracks. Start at the obvious finger crack 2 metres left of the large gash of *Kern Knotts Chimney*.

(5c). Climb the steep finger crack to a large perched pinnacle (as for the *Variation Start to Central Climb South Face*). Climb past the pinnacle and climb a short wall to reach the bulging crack on the left. Climb the bulging crack via a rib on the left, and continue with interest up

Left: Adam Wilde and Mandy Davenport finish the day off with **Kern Knotts West Buttress** (MVS), Kern Knotts. **Photo:** Stephen Reid

the narrow V-groove to a small overhang. Pull over the overhang and climb more easily to a good ledge.

Triffid Right-Hand Finish	30m	E3+	★★	1981

An intimidating route with a mystifying crux. Start as for *Triffid*.

(6a). Climb the steep crack to a large detached pinnacle (as for the *Variation Start to Central Climb South Face*). Climb directly up the bulging wall below the overhang, take the right-hand crack through this, then climb the wall above and another small roof to the top.

Kern Knotts Chimney	50m	HS	★★	1893

The prominent chimney on the Wasdale side of the buttress. An old classic with a fine finish – a mirror-like one that is, due to the polish applied by many generations of tweed, nails and elbow grease. Start directly below the chimney.

1 30m. Climb easily to a large platform. Ascend the chimney passing a chockstone en route. Pass under a leaning block to a belay on the other side of the buttress.

2 20m. Step off the block onto the slab and make delicate moves up to reach better holds. Easier climbing leads to the top. The slab may be avoided by going left but that would spoil the fun!

Above: Barry Clarke back and foots his way up **Kern Knotts Chimney** (HS). **Photo:** Phil Rigby

The Young Shavers	30m	E2		1991

Takes the left wall of *Kern Knotts Chimney* via a hanging groove and corner. Start just right of *Kern Knotts Chimney*, below a slim pillar of rock.

(5c). Climb the narrow pillar to a junction with *Kern Knotts Chimney*. From the top of the pillar step left across onto the wall and boldly climb up and leftwards, then back right, to the hanging groove (and runners!). Make an awkward move to reach a good ledge below the steep corner; climb this, moving right to finish.

Left: Rob Knight gets some protection in for the steep crux groove of **The Crysalid** (E2), Kern Knotts. **Photo:** Mark Glaister

The next seven routes all finish at the top of the buttress at a large leaning block. From here they all finish up the top pitch of *Kern Knotts Chimney*.

Kern Knotts Buttress	49m	HVS		1919

A steep route up the left edge of the buttress. Start at a wide crack below a prominent narrow pillar of rock, 4 metres to the right of *Kern Knotts Chimney*.

1 12m (4b). The steep crack leads to a large platform.

2 17m (5b). Step back down right to reach a small spike hold on the buttress front. Pull across steeply rightwards to a small niche, and climb on good holds to a broken ledge. Follow the left edge of the buttress (avoiding easier ground further left) to finish on sloping holds.

3 20m. Pitch 2 of *Kern Knotts Chimney*.

Misfit	50m	E2	★	1981

Strenuous climbing up the front of the buttress. Start below the overhangs in the centre of the buttress at a small rock pillar.

1 30m (5c). Climb a short cracked slab to the lower overhang. Step left and climb the thin hanging crack through the roof to a good hold on the right. Pull up onto a good foot ledge (junction with ***Buttonhook***). Move up rightwards into a slim groove that leads to a broken ledge. Step left and climb the hanging crack and blunt rib to the top.

2 20m. Pitch 2 of *Kern Knotts Chimney*.

The Buttonhook Route	50m	HVS+	★★★	1934

A very steep exposed climb that threads its way up the front of the buttress. Start at the foot of the buttress at a small rock pillar. It is worth combining the pitches for a classic lead.

1 10m (5a). Climb the short slab to the first overhang. Pull steeply rightwards around the roof to a jug. Climb the crack above to a small ledge.

2 20m (5a). Step off the ledge and follow good holds leftwards to a short groove. Climb the groove then trend rightwards to a prominent pinnacle on the right edge of

Above: John Pattison reaches the jug on **The Buttonhook Route** (HVS), Kern Knotts. **Photo:** Phil Rigby

Right: Phil Rigby leading **Misfit** (E2), Kern Knotts. **Photo:** Mike Hetherington.

the buttress. Climb the shallow stepped groove in an airy position to an awkward finish.

3 20m. Pitch 2 of *Kern Knotts Chimney*.

Cracks Area

The next routes start below the fine wall of rock set at right-angles to the rest of the crag. This is split by the twin lines of *Kerns Knotts Crack* and *Innominate Crack*.

Close to the Wind	45m	E1	★	1988

Interesting climbing up the left edge of the face. Start below a short groove at the toe of the face. The start is rather bold.

1 25m (5b). Climb the right-hand side of the groove to a horizontal break and runners. Step up and right to a short hanging groove that is capped by a small overhang. Pull steeply up the groove and climb a right-facing flake to a shallow groove. Climb the groove on good holds more easily to the top

2 20m. Pitch 2 of *Kern Knotts Chimney*.

Pharos	45m	E2		1991

Takes the slim cracked wall just left of ***Kern Knotts Crack***. Worth doing even though blinkers are needed to avoid adjacent routes.

1 25m (5c). Climb ***Kern Knotts Crack*** for 2 metres, then step left and climb over an overlap to a short crack. Follow the slender wall above, using a series of shallow cracks, to a narrow foothold. Step right and finish up the short ragged crack to the top.

2 20m. Pitch 2 of *Kern Knotts Chimney*.

Kern Knotts Crack	42m	VS	★★★	1897

The wide left-hand crack gives a climb of great character. Start directly below the crack.

1 22m (4c). Climb the crack to a sentry box at 8 metres. Either jam the walls of the sentry box to a narrower crack above (only good technique or sheer determination will pay off this way), or climb the

"I found today that the first chockstone in Kern Knotts Crack, *which is usually used for swinging out of the 'Niche', was on the point of coming out. I therefore removed it. It can be had on application at the Wastwater Hotel. This rendered the climb considerably harder, but quite safe."*
Seigfried Herford, ***FRCC Journal 1911***

Overleaf: Kevin Avery and Rob Fone get **Close to the Wind** (E1), Kern Knotts.
Photo: Phil Rigby

Kern Knotts
Cracks Area

1	The Buttonhook Route	HVS ***
2	Close to the Wind	E1 *
3	Pharos	E2
4	Kern Knotts Crack	VS ***
5	Innominate Crack	VS ***
V1	Innominate/Sepulchre combination	E1 ***
6	Mausoleum	E6
7	Sepulchre Direct	E3 *
8	Cenotaph Left-hand	E3 *
9	The Cenotaph	HVS
10	El Vino	E2 *
11	Tosspot	E2

right wall on small holds until a long step back left can be made to reach the narrower crack. Follow the fine crack to finish on top of the pinnacle.

"Brute force and ignorance go a long way here."
FRCC Journal 1907

2 20m. Pitch 2 of *Kern Knotts Chimney*.

Innominate Crack	40m	VS-	★★★	1921

The right-hand crack, and one of the classic crack climbs of the Lake District. Start directly below the crack.

1 20m (4b). Follow the twin cracks until forced into the right-hand one. Climb the crack above until awkward moves can be made to gain a wide crack just below the top of the pinnacle. Climb the crack to the top.

2 20m. Pitch 2 of *Kern Knotts Chimney*.

Innominate/Sepulchre Combination	35m	E1+	★★★	1975

A fine pitch which makes good use of the bottomless groove at the right-hand side of the wall. Start as for *Innominate Crack*.

(5b). Climb *Innominate Crack* for 7 metres to a line of good holds, follow these diagonally right to the base of the large bottomless groove and climb the groove, with interest, to the top.

Mausoleum	35m	E6		2000

A short but serious start up the wall right of *Innominate Crack*. Start at a pointed block 2 metres right of *Innominate Crack*.

(6b). Pull onto the wall to reach a short diagonal crack on the left. Climb the crack and surmount a small overlap to gain a standing position on good footholds (poor skyhook). Make committing moves up the wall to reach good jugs. Step left to the bottom of the groove of *Sepulchre Direct* and climb this relatively easily to the top.

The large niche to the right was once the home of the huge block now resting on the scree below it, its fall being caused by an earthquake in 1981 – beware there is still some loose rock around. With it went **Sepulchre** (VS, 1930) and the sad demise of one of the classic laybacks of the Lakes.

Sepulchre Direct	37m	E3+	★	1981

Thin smeary climbing under the large roofs right of *Innominate Crack*: the high point of a Carlisle Mountaineering Club beginners' meet! Start at the foot of the obvious easy-angled groove below a large roof.

Right: Mike Hetherington, laybacking on **Innominate Crack** (VS), Kern Knotts.
Photos: Phil Rigby

(6a). Climb the groove to the roof and make difficult moves around the roof to a resting foothold. Traverse left below the roof to reach better holds at the bottom of the large groove. Climb the groove to the top. Take care to avoid rope drag under the end of the roof.

Cenotaph Left-Hand	34m	E3+	★	1981

A monumental pitch with a very strenuous finish. Start, as for ***Cenotaph***, below the obvious easy-angled groove below the overhangs.

(6a). Climb the right wall of the groove to reach a short hanging groove in the large roof. Pull into the steep groove above and climb with caution (unstable blocks) to the large groove above. Climb this to a good crack and ascend the crack leftwards to good footholds under the roof. Pull leftwards around the roof and climb the steep crack with determination to better holds on the left. You'll be glad to know that the top is reached more easily.

The Cenotaph	35m	HVS		1955

The original ***Cenotaph*** route, breaking out right into the obvious large hanging groove. Start below the obvious easy-angled groove below the overhangs.

(5a). Climb the wall to reach a short hanging groove in the large roof. Bridge over roof with caution (unstable blocks) to a large groove above. Climb the groove to below the upper overhang. Make an awkward move right into the obvious bottomless groove and ascend it more easily to the top.

El Vino	34m	E2	★	1974

Interesting climbing up the narrow groove right of The ***Cenotaph***. Start directly below the upper groove at an easy wall.

(5c). Climb the wall to a grassy ledge. Climb the large open groove to the large overhang, pull through the overhang on the right, and make strenuous moves to stand in the narrow groove above; climb this to the top.

Tosspot	32m	E2		1991

Climbs the short narrow groove below the large overhang. Start as for ***El Vino*** at an easy wall.

(5c). Climb the wall to a grassy ledge. Pull into the steep narrow groove and climb up the large roof. Move right under the roof and climb the blunt rib and wall to the top.

Kern Knotts Chain	135m	HVS	★	1928

A left-to-right girdle of the crag with some fine positions although the second pitch does get very close to the ground! Start at the top of ***Flake Climb***.

1 25m (4c). Reverse ***Flake Climb*** to the bottom of the steep crack.
2 23m. Traverse slightly down and rightwards over easy rocks to reach *West Chimney*. Climb the chimney to a good ledge just below the final wall.
3 25m (4b). Follow the ledge rightwards to join the gangway on ***Central Climb***. Reverse the gangway to the large pinnacle (Pitch 1 belay). Look after your second!
4 18m (5b). Traverse rightwards onto a large platform right of *Kern Knotts Chimney*. Step down right to reach a small spike hold on the buttress front. Pull across rightwards to a small niche and climb on good holds to a broken ledge. Traverse right to an obvious pinnacle on the edge of the *Kern Knotts Crack* face.
5 14m (5a). Traverse the steep wall on the right into *Kern Knotts Crack* at the height of the pinnacle, then traverse right into, and finish up, *Innominate Crack*.
6 30m (4a). Pitch 2 of *Kern Knotts Chimney*.

Original Finish

Originally the climb traversed into ***Sepulchre*** and finished up Pitch 2 of ***Cenotaph*** but this has become far harder since the fall of the block out of *Sepulchre*.

Kern Knotts East Buttress

About 30 metres further right of *Kern Knotts Crack* is the *East Buttress*. *Kern Knotts Corner* climbs the obvious leaning corner.

Eastern Bloc	47m	VS		1989

Start just left of ***Kern Knotts Corner***. The block has been toppled.

1 27m. Climb up and left to a dirty groove, then pull up and right onto the arête to reach a large ledge. Climb up onto another large ledge above.
2 20m. Walk left below the upper rib to a cave and climb the wall on the left to a rounded finish.

Kern Knotts Corner	35m	VS		1932

A good route. Start below the obvious leaning corner.

1 27m. Pleasant climbing up the corner and slabs leads to a large jammed block. Climb over the block and up to a ledge on the left. Easy climbing leads to a good ledge.
2 8m (4c). Climb the puzzling and strenuous undercut crack on the left.

Kern Knotts
East Buttress

1	Eastern Bloc	VS
2	Kern Knotts Corner	VS
3	Leap Year	MVS
4	The East Buttress	VS

Photo: Phil Rigby

Leap Year	36m	MVS		2004

Start 4 metres right of *Kern Knotts Corner*.

1 26m (4c). Climb past a small sentry box to a ledge, move up a rib above to a small spike, then pull right to gain a smaller ledge. Step left and climb the steep crack and short groove to a large rock ledge.

2 10m. Move right and finish up the chimney.

The East Buttress	40m	VS+		1924

Start below a rough clean wall, 10 metres right of *Kern Knotts Corner*.

1 30m (4c). A bold and balancy first pitch: either make strenuous moves on small holds up the wall or climb the shallow groove on the left. Continue up and slightly rightwards on easier rock to reach slabby mossy ledges below the top section of the wall. Starting at the right-hand end of the wall, traverse left along a sloping ledge, then straight up a small crack to a ledge; all very precarious and with poor protection.

2 10m. Climb the wide chimney above and finish up the right arête.

Lower Kern Knotts GR NY 215 095 Alt 460m F South-West

This micro crag (possibly the smallest in the Lakes – but no prizes for finding a smaller one!) is situated directly below *Kern Knotts*, and just above the Wasdale/Styhead path.

Lower Kern Knotts

1	The West Route	D	3	The Crack	VD
2	Rob and Angie's Wedding	VD	4	The Slab Climb	VS

Photos: Phil Rigby

The West Route	12m	D		1924

The wall 3 metres left of ***The Crack*** starting at the toe of the buttress.

Rob and Angie's Wedding	12m	VD		2004

Climbs a tiny groove, arête and slab just to the left of ***The Crack***.

The Crack	8m	VD		1893

The obvious crack in the middle of the rock.

The Slab Climb	8m	VS		1920

The wall right of ***The Crack*** passing an overhang on the right and taking the slab above on small holds.

Lower Kern Knotts West

GR **NY 214 096** Alt **470m** F **South-West**

Situated slightly higher than, and approximately 70 metres left of *Lower Kern Knotts* is the larger *Lower Kern Knotts West*. The crag has a distinctive lower slab topped by a bilberry terrace and steep upper wall.

Lower Kern Knotts West

1	The Buttress	HS	3	Slab and Chimney Variation	VS
2	Slab and Chimney Route	VD			

The Buttress	27m	HS		1921

Start 3 metres right of the open vegetated groove. The route finishes at a prominent jutting block.

1 15m. Climb slightly rightwards for 5 metres, step left and continue straight up on small holds to a vegetated ledge.

2 12m. Go straight up from the belay to a small ledge. Continue up a shallow groove on good holds to finish left of the jutting block.

Slab and Chimney Route	30m	VD		

Climbs the right-hand slab and obvious narrow chimney on the upper wall: start below the cleanest part of the slab.

1 21m. Climb the slab to an obvious detached block on a vegetated ledge: move past the block and scramble rightwards over vegetated ledges to belay below the chimney.

2 9m. Climb the chimney.

Variation VS

2 9m (4c). Climb the striking forked off-width crack direct.

The Napes

Grid reference: **NY 210 101** Altitude: **650m**
Faces: **South-West** Approach: **1hr 45 mins**

Rightly considered to be the birthplace of English rock climbing, *The Napes* provide a varied range of mountaineering routes and modern hard classics. The unique *Napes Needle* is one of its main attractions but the crag has lots more to offer at all grades, including some very airy climbs and all climbers, whatever their ability, will find something to enjoy here.

"What's makk'n ye chaps fash ye'r ses' seah mich aboo't crags noo-a-days, isn't t' fells gud enough for ye?"
Will Ritson (Landlord of the Wasdale Head Inn in the 1870s) speaking about the Gable Crags, and quoted by George Seatree, Wasdale Head in "Auld Will" Ritson's Time, *FRCC Journal 1911*

At the right-hand end, overlooking the screes of ***Great Hell Gate*** is the stunning ***Tophet Wall***, which has an intimidating atmosphere, and possesses some awe inspiring Lakeland classics, including ***Tophet Wall***, ***Incantations***, ***The Vikings***, ***Golden Calf***, ***Sacrificial Crack***, ***Supernatural*** and the futuristic ***Breathless***. To the left is the main ***Napes*** area and its historic ridges, ***Needle***, ***Eagle's Nest***, and ***Arrowhead***, many harder more modern routes, such as ***The Cayman*** and ***Amos Moses***, plus of course, the ***Needle*** itself. Although most of the climbs are on sound rock, care should be taken when on the ridges, as any stonefall will rake the gullies and their walls, eventually crossing the busy path at the bottom. Most of the crag is quick drying and it holds the sun late into the day.

Approaches:

From **Wasdale Head**, follow the bridleway to Burnthwaite, then take the Sty Head path situated on the north side of Lingmell Beck which, after crossing Gable Beck, gradually steepens, traversing the scree slopes well below the *Napes*. Break off the track at ***Lower Kern Knotts*** and scramble over scree and boulders to join the **Climbers' Traverse** below ***Kern Knotts***. Follow the track west to reach ***The Napes*** (1hr 45mins). It is worth noting that 200 metres or so west of ***Kern Knotts*** a small cave will be seen in the rock wall just above the path. If you descend 50 metres directly below the path at this point an excellent spring will be found.

The Napes & Westmorland Crags

1 Sphinx Ridge
2 Rainbow Ridge
3 Arrowhead Ridge
4 Abbey Buttress
5 Eagle's Nest Ridge Direct
6 Eagle's Nest Ridge Ordinary
7 Needle Ridge
8 Chantry Buttress
9 Scrimshanker Area
10 Belfry Buttress
11 Lucifer Ridge
12 Brimstone Buttress
13 Tophet Ridge

Westmorland Crags
Connecting Ridge
Great Hell Gate Descent
Back Staircase Descent
Great Hell Gate
10
pes East
9
13
Hell Gate Pillar
Tophet Wall
11
12
Photo: Al Phizacklea

It is also possible but unpleasant to leave the Sty Head path just after the bridge over Gable Beck and follow the steep **Moses Trod** path up Gavel Neese (the south-west shoulder of Great Gable), continuing directly up the scree past a large block (***Moses's Finger***) to join the Climbers' Traverse. This takes just as long as the approach via ***Kern Knotts*** and is not recommended due to its unrelenting steepness and looseness.

From **Seathwaite**, **Borrowdale**, follow the path to Styhead Pass and from its highest point, follow the **Climbers' Traverse**, a gently rising track which crosses the south flank of Great Gable. The path is rather vague at first, but soon becomes better defined and passes under ***Kern Knotts*** before continuing on to ***The Napes*** (1hr 45mins).

Approaching from the east, the first crag reached is ***Tophet Wall***, which towers above the wide scree chute of ***Great Hell Gate***. The track continues west below ***Napes Needle*** which stands at the bottom of ***Needle Ridge***. Just further on, the path enters ***Needle Gully***, which is followed steeply upwards, past a large chockstone, until a scramble out left leads to the Dress Circle, a platform which gives the best viewpoint of ***Napes Needle***. Alternatively the ***Dress Circle*** can be gained by the classic scramble of **Threading the Needle** (M). This popular way is reached by following the highly polished route which goes through the ***Gap***, the cleft between ***Napes Needle*** and ***Needle Ridge***. The path continues west from the ***Dress Circle***, underneath the impressive arête of ***Eagle's Nest Ridge Direct***, where it drops down to a crevasse formed by a large detached flake of rock (***Fat Man's Agony***) at the foot of ***Abbey Buttress***. A tricky descent leftwards gives access to ***Eagle's Nest Gully***. The path continues more easily across the bottom of ***Arrowhead Ridge***, into ***Arrowhead Gully***, and on towards the distinctive ***Sphinx Rock***.

Descents

Descents from ***Tophet Wall***, ***Needle Ridge*** and ***Eagle's Nest Ridge*** are by scrambling up to the junction with the main ridge of the crag, following this to its top and then going down the screes of ***Great Hell Gate***. A shorter alternative from the ***Tophet Wall*** area is to use ***The Back Staircase***, a diagonal scramble from the ridge above ***Tophet Wall*** into ***Great Hell Gate***. Both these descents are worn and require caution. Descent from ***Arrowhead Ridge*** is by scrambling up, then going west to meet the top of the steep rocky path that leads down towards the ***Sphinx Rock***, or continue into ***Little Hell Gate*** and descend the scree. The general descents described are lengthy, **but on no account try to ascend or descend the gullies which are loose and dangerous**. It is also possible to abseil off the area above ***Crocodile Crack*** from a variety of ledges. There are slings in place but teams should check these carefully before abseiling. This saves a long walk back to the base of the crag. Another alternative for the routes in this area is to down climb ***Eagle's Nest Ordinary Route***.

Napes West Area

This is the area to the west (left) of *Napes Needle*. The routes are described from **left** to **right**.

High up *Little Hell Gate* (the scree area to the left of the crag), a square buttress separates the main scree chute from a slabby grassy branch on the left. The grassy central section of the buttress is flanked by two rock ribs. **Chestnut Edge** (25m, VS 4b, 2006) follows the left-hand rib and is disappointingly cracked and unsound. **Lost Ridge** (23m, S, 2006), the green-flecked right-hand rib, is more solid apart from a few loose flakes at 3 metres and may prove a more attractive proposition than scree-shuffling.

Approximately 30 metres left of, and at a slightly lower level than, the *Sphinx*, a prow-like buttress guards the upper reaches of *Little Hell Gate*.

Isis Crack	10m	S		2006

Climbs the striking wide crack on the right-hand side of the buttress.

Gain the crack awkwardly and follow it to the top.

Sphinx Ridge	15m	VD		

The ridge immediately behind the *Sphinx* gives a short section of climbing.

Climb easy rocks to a groove. Step right onto polished footholds adorning the thin rib on the right and continue up easy scrambling to the top.

The Sphinx or **Cat Rock**	5m			1889

Was this Lakeland's first boulder problem? Now harder after the *Cat's Tail* has disappeared down the scree.

(5a). Tricky moves up the back of the *Sphinx* from the gap. Very airy. Remember the moves down!

Sphinx Crack	10m	VD		

The short parallel-sided crack behind and right of the *Sphinx*.

Burning Sphinxter	22m	VS		2004

Interesting climbing, with a hard start and delicate finish: well-protected throughout. Start about 12 metres right of the notch behind the *Sphinx*, below a steep right-facing corner.

(5a). Climb the corner, over the roof, to a good flake. Traverse right delicately to reach a crack-line just left of the edge of the buttress and climb this to the top.

Gremlin's Crack	15m	HVS		1946

An exercise in jamming up the obvious steep crack in the right wall of *Sphinx Ridge*. Start about 12 metres up the gully.

(5a). Climb the crack with interest.

Right of *Sphinx Rock*, the crag is very broken and grassy for 40 metres, until the deep *Arrowhead Gully* is reached. This was described in the first FRCC guide to Great Gable (1925) as "an uninteresting gully abounding in loose rock and vegetation. Most distinctly a place to be avoided at all costs." The writer of this guide has seen no need to reassess this description.

Rainbow Ridge	32m	S	★	1922

A delightful climb on good rock. Scramble up *Arrowhead Gully* then up steep grass leftwards for about 40 metres, to reach a clean slab of light coloured rock to the left of a large overhanging nose and square chimney.

Climb the steep slab to a small ledge at 6 metres. Climb up left on good holds to a detached block. Traverse right to the arête and follow it to the top. Alternatively, from the small ledge, traverse directly right to the arête and climb up this to the top.

Crowley's Chimney Route	30m	VD?		1894

Only recently rediscovered and probably unrepeated. The route description is based on the first ascent account. Start at the obvious chimney between *Rainbow Ridge* and the large overhanging nose of rock to its right.

Climb the chimney and at the top move round a corner and make a 5 metre traverse to a moss filled crack. From the crack hand-traverse to the ridge, approximately one metre above the lower traverse. Climb directly up the ridge until it is possible to traverse right into *Square-Cut Gully* below the final chock stone, which is passed on the left.

Square-Cut Gully	30m	S?		1895

The gully between *Rainbow Ridge* and *Scimitar Ridge*. Only recently rediscovered and probably unrepeated. The route description is based on the first ascent account. Start at two rock ribs at the back of the gully.

Climb up 2 metres to a narrow ledge on the right. Traverse left and continue up the ribs, which merge into one. Traverse across the rib to a block on the right. An oblique crack leads to grassy slabs and a cave. Exit on the left and finish up the easy chimney above.

Left: Al Davis contemplates the moves onto the back of **The Sphinx** (5a), The Napes.
Photo: Phil Rigby

The Napes West & Arrowhead Ridge
1 Lost Arrow Spire VS*
2 Arrowhead Ridge Direct VD**
3 Abbot E3*
4 Costello E3
5 The Pod VS
6 Turdus torquatus E2**
7 The Merry Monk MVS
8 Abbey Buttress S***
9 Eagle's Nest Ord. Route (part) VD**
Arrowhead
A
Photo: Phil Rigby
Napes Needle
Arrowhead Gully
Eagle's Nest Gully

Scimitar Ridge	45m	VD		1919

A narrow curving ridge which divides *Arrowhead Gully* into two grassy runnels. The approach involves an insecure scramble up grass.

1 **20m.** From the base of the ridge, scramble up the left branch of the gully until it is possible to gain the ridge on the right via a 3 metre high corner. Continue up the ridge via a mantelshelf onto a prominent ledge slightly to the left.

2 **25m.** Climb the slab and move up and leftwards to a block on the left edge of the slab; finish up the crest.

Lost Arrow Spire	27m	VS	★	2006

Start a short way up *Arrowhead Gully* at the foot of the wall below and right of the arrow tip. Enjoyable climbing with good protection.

(4c). Climb up to gain the prominent crack from the left and follow it to a diagonal break. Climb leftwards along the break to a shallow corner and follow this delicately to reach the notch behind the tip of the *Arrow*.

Arrowhead Ridge Direct	80m	VD	★★★	1896

An excellent airy climb, characterised by the distinctive *Arrowhead* at the top of the steep section. Start at the lowest point of the ridge on the left.

1 **15m.** Easy scrambling leads to steeper rock. Climb up to a good ledge.

2 **25m.** The steep ridge above is climbed, either direct, or round the corner from the right, to reach a pinnacle. Step off the pinnacle onto a slab then climb up steeply on good holds to the top of the *Arrowhead*. It is also possible to traverse left around the base of the *Arrowhead* to the gap behind but this misses the point!

3 **10m.** Stride across the gap and traverse a horizontal section of the ridge.

4 **30m.** Scramble up the ridge passing the *Strid* en route.

Arrowhead Ridge South-East Variation 40m VD 1925.

An alternative to Pitch 2 of *Arrowhead Ridge Direct*. It can be reached from below, but the best way is to climb *Arrowhead Ridge Direct* to the pinnacle on Pitch 2, then descend a groove on the right for 8 metres, where a short ascending traverse is made to a good stance on the *Easy Way*.

Climb the slab and a short way up the corner above, move out left onto the true arête, then go straight up to the top of the *Arrowhead*.

Red Arrow	32m	VS		2004

A direct line up the right-hand arête of the *Arrow* with delightful slabby climbing. Start directly below the arête from a blocky rake overlooking *Eagle's Nest Gully*.

(4c). Make an awkward pull over the initial nose, then climb the slab above for about 10 metres until the lower part of the sharp upper arête can be gained. Follow this direct to the top of the *Arrowhead*.

To the right of ***Arrowhead Ridge*** is the wide basin of ***Eagle's Nest Gully*** – another gully that is best avoided.

Arrowhead Ridge Easy Way	60m	D		1892

The easiest way up the ridge unfortunately avoids the *Arrowhead*. Start 20 metres up *Eagle's Nest Gully* above the large chockstone, just left of a large smooth slab.

1 22m. Climb easy grassy ledges up left, then right, until a short traverse left can be made to reach the gap behind the *Arrowhead*.
2 8m. From the gap, traverse right and go up a short crack to reach the ridge proper.
3 30m. Scramble along the ridge, passing the ***Strid*** en route.

The next seven routes all start up on the left side of ***Eagle's Nest Gully***, below a conspicuous clean slab with an overlap at half height. This is about 40 metres higher than the point where the path crosses the ***Gully***. The easiest approach is by a grassy rake on the flank of the ***Arrowhead***, which runs parallel to, but 10 metres higher than the ***Gully***.

Time and Place	35m	E2	★	1982

A fine sustained pitch requiring a bold approach. Start below the central short crack at the bottom of the slab.

(5b). Move left along the grass ledge to the foot of a shallow corner (which can be used for runners but not for hands or feet!) to reach a diagonal break. This is followed to the right edge of the slab, where a good jamming crack is climbed for 8 metres or so, until it is possible to step left into the centre of the slab to a delicate finish (as for *The Tormentor*).

Left: A perfect day on **Arrowhead Ridge Direct** (VD), The Napes. **Photo:** Stephen Reid

The Tormentor	35m	E4+	★★	1987

Technical and intimidating climbing up the centre of the slab. Start as for *Time and Place*.

(6a). Gain the lower left edge of the slab by climbing the short crack and stepping left along a grassy ledge. Pull onto the slab and, after 2 metres, follow a faint weakness up and right to a runner, then pull back to good holds at the foot of a diagonal crack (junction with *Time and Place*). Follow the crack until in the centre of the slab, then make some very scary moves straight up to the overlap (undercut hold and runner). Pull over and right on improving holds to another diagonal break and finish up the thin crack above.

Murin Buchstansangur	25m	E2		1988

A mischievous little climb up the slender area of rock right of the obvious large upright rectangular block on the east wall of *Arrowhead Ridge*.

(5b). Pull into a little corner below an overlap just right of a wide crack. Climb thin parallel cracks up to a diagonal break then the pillar above following its left-hand edge to the top.

Cutlass Ridge	30m	VD		1922

High up the gully is a large upright rectangular block just left of a grassy groove. Start just right of the groove.

Climb the steep buttress to a crack at 8 metres which is followed for a further 8 metres to a steep slab. Ascend the slab and climb easily to join *Arrowhead Ridge* at the *Strid*.

Sabre Ridge	30m	VD		1920

The steep ridge that divides *Eagle's Nest Gully* about 50 metres above the chockstone.

Climb the arête for 7 metres, then go up the sharp left edge to a ledge. A short section of arête above is followed by scrambling to the top.

The following climbs are situated on the left wall of *Abbey Buttress*. The next two lines share the clean prow on the opposite side of the gully to *The Tormentor*.

Abbot	24m	E3-	★	2007

A well positioned steep line with good protection.

(5c). Climb a cracked rake running up the foot of the wall until a good flake on the left, low on the steep wall, can be reached. Reach

Right: Rob Matheson searching for invisible holds on **The Tormentor** (E4), The Napes.
Photo: Ed Luke

a smaller flake above (thin sling) then step left and pull up to the arête with difficulty. The crack on the left side of this leads to the top.

Costello	23m	E3		2007

A companion to ***Abbot***.

(5c). Follow ***Abbot*** to the thin sling flake, then stretch right to a small wire in a thin crack. Follow a series of holds in a shallow crease above to another small wire, then pull out right to finish.

The Pod	30m	VS		1968

The steep pod-shaped crack on the left-bounding wall of ***Abbey Buttress***. Not as hard as it looks but often wet. Start about 25 metres above the path that crosses ***Eagle's Nest Gully***.

(4c). Scramble up easy rocks below the pod-shaped crack. Climb the crack, exiting left at the top. Broken rocks lead to the ridge.

Turdus torquatus	75m	E2	★★	2003

An excellent, well-protected route to the left of ***Abbey Buttress***, finishing up a memorable crack. Start in the bed of ***Eagle's Nest Gully***, 12 metres above the point where the path emerges from behind the large detached flake below ***Abbey Buttress***.

1 38m (5b). Ascend a short groove containing a suspect wedged block. Traverse left to the arête, and reach a small spike above, then use a curious pocket to stand on a foot-ledge on the right (the start can be made bolder by climbing direct to the curious pocket without any runners). Move up, then back left, to the arête, to reach the thin crack which leads to a grass ledge. Scramble up to a large ledge below a prominent square-cut roof.

2 10m (5a). From the crack behind the belay, step right and climb the wall to below a square-cut roof. Jam the crack through the roof and follow the ridge above to a large block belay.

3 7m. Scramble leftwards to belay below the overhanging corner.

4 15m (5b). Climb the corner, continuing with excellent jams to a strenuous and awkward finish. A superb pitch.

The Merry Monk	30m	MVS		1968

A pleasant route up the thin crack-line about 5 metres right of the ***The Pod***. Start as for ***Turdus torquatus***.

(4b). Climb the thin crack, which is awkward to start. Continue up a shallow scoop, moving out left near the top.

Left: Rob Matheson jamming the top pitch of **Turdus torquatus** (E2), The Napes.
Photo: Al Phizacklea

Napes Central Area

The next routes start at the foot of *Abbey Buttress*, marked by the large detached flake of rock, which forms *Fat Man's Agony*, a tight squeeze on the path.

Abbey Buttress	58m	S	★★★	1909

A classic climb with a devious and intimidating second pitch. Start at the foot of the buttress behind the large detached flake.

1 20m. Climb straight up to a ledge, step right and follow a steep crack to a ledge.

2 20m. Climb steep rock above to a wide ledge at 4 metres. Traverse left for 5 metres and then go straight up for 8 metres whereupon a traverse back right below an overhang can be made onto an arête that leads on good holds to a large ledge.

3 18m. Climb the cracked blocks immediately right of the grassy gully to a ledge. Ascend the corner on the left to a junction with ***West Chimney/Eagle's Nest Ordinary***.

Variation VD 1913

The lower part of this route has disappeared down the scree after a large rock fall, leaving just the second pitch.

2 17m. Go straight up the wall on good holds to the overhang on the ordinary route, which is followed to the top.

Eagle's Chain	110m	VS	★	1945

An airy left to right girdle starting at the foot of ***Abbey Buttress***, crossing ***Eagle's Nest Buttress*** high up and finishing up ***Tricouni Rib***.

1 20m. Pitch 1 of ***Abbey Buttress***.

2 10m. Move right and climb the wall to a ledge, then continue the traverse right, crossing ***Little John***, into the ***West Chimney*** of ***Eagle's Nest Ordinary***.

3 10m. Cross the wall on the right onto ***Long John*** and follow this, trending left, to a platform above ***West Chimney***.

4 14m (4a). Traverse horizontally right onto ***Eagle's Nest Ridge Direct*** where a delicate and exposed step down is made into the ***Crow's Nest*** using sloping and polished holds (small wires to protect the second). Step down again then traverse right to the grassy crack of ***Eagle's Crack***. Climb the crack for 2 metres then traverse right to another grassy crack.

5 28m (4b). Step down and traverse delicately right across the steep wall to gain ***Crocodile Crack*** above the crux. Climb the crack for about 4 metres then make a slightly descending traverse right, crossing ***The Cayman***, to a belay on ***Alligator Crawl***.

The Napes
West & Central Areas

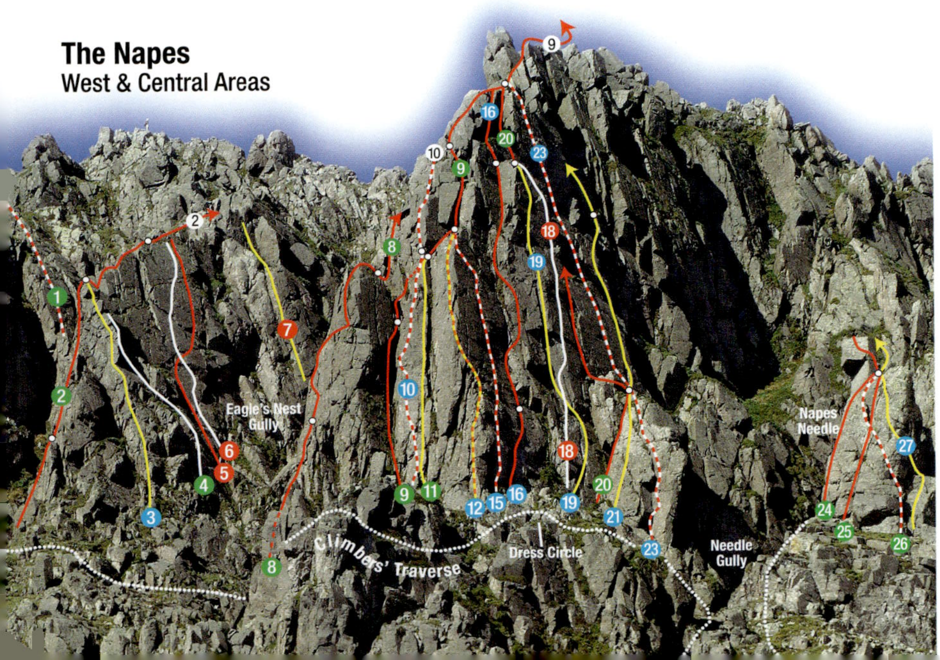

1	Scimitar Ridge	VD	
2	Arrowhead Ridge Direct	VD	***
3	Red Arrow	VS	
4	Arrowhead Ridge Easy Way	D	
5	Time and Place	E2	*
6	The Tormentor	E4	**
7	Murun Buchstansangur	E2	
8	Abbey Buttress	S	***
9	Eagle's Nest Ord. Route	VD	**
10	Long John	HVS	*
11	Ling Chimney	VD	
12	Eagle's Nest Ridge Dir.	MVS	***
15	Centennial Climb	VS	*
16	Eagle's Crack	VS	
18	The Cayman	E2	***
19	Crocodile Crack	HVS	***
20	Alligator Crawl	HS	*
21	Tricouni Rib	MVS	
23	Amos Moses	E1	**
24	The Arête	HS	***
25	The Crowley Route	HS	
26	The Lingmell Crack	HS	*
27	The Obverse Route	MVS	***

See close up diagram for missing numbers.

Photo: Phil Rigby

6 18m (4a). Make an upward diagonal traverse right to a junction with Pitch 3 of *Tricouni Rib* at the step across the gully, then continue up *Tricouni Rib*.

7 10m (4a). Pitch 4 of *Tricouni Rib*.

The right side of *Abbey Buttress* is marked by the deep grassy cleft of *West Chimney*. The following two climbs start at the bottom of this chimney.

Little John	26m	S		1947

A steep route up the wall left of *West Chimney*. Start from the top of a pedestal 10 metres up the chimney on the left wall.

Climb the slab on its left side to where it steepens. Ascend the grassy right-slanting crack to below an overhang. Make an awkward move over the overhang and climb the grassy crack to the top.

Eagle's Nest Ordinary Route (West Chimney)	107m	VD	★★	1892

A fine old traditional route. Start below the grassy chimney.

1 30m. Easy rocks lead to the bottom of *West Chimney* which is climbed, either by bridging, or by the right wall *(Pope's Variation)*.

2 12m. Climb up and right through a crevasse to the top of *Ling Chimney* then go up a smooth slabby groove to a belay in the corner.

3 12m. The awkward chimney above is followed by the ridge on the left.

4 18m. A chimney on the left is followed by easy scrambling up broken rocks to the foot of a tower.

5 35m. Pull up the short steep crack to an exposed rock ledge and move right into the boulder-choked chimney. Follow the scratches and scramble along the ridge.

Variation 12m VS

3 (4c). The hanging groove just left of the stance can be climbed instead of the chimney.

Long John	42m	HVS+	★	1928

Delicate climbing up the strip of rock dividing *West* and *Ling Chimneys*. Pitch 1 on its own gives a superb climb at VS. Start below a pinnacle just left of *Ling Chimney*.

1 33m (4c). Climb straight up to the bottom of the left-hand crack of Ling Chimney, then step left and climb the centre of the slab, until forced out left onto the edge. Climb up to a ledge which leads back right into the centre of the slab. Ascend the slab trending left to a platform above *West Chimney*.

2 9m (5a). From the top of the pinnacle, a poorly protected and difficult move is made onto the wall above. Climb the wall more easily to a ledge.

The Napes
Central Area

9	Eagle's Nest Ordinary Route (top part)	VD	**
11	Ling Chimney	VD	
12	Eagle's Nest Direct	MVS	***
13	Conversation Killer	HVS	
14	Aquiline Slab	E2	
15	Centennial Climb	VS	*
16	Eagle's Crack	VS	
17	Gharial	E1	*
18	The Cayman	E2	***
19	Crocodile Crack	HVS	***
20	Aligator Crawl	HS	*
21	Tricouni Rib	MVS	
22	Cannon Stone	E1	
23	Amos Moses	E1	**

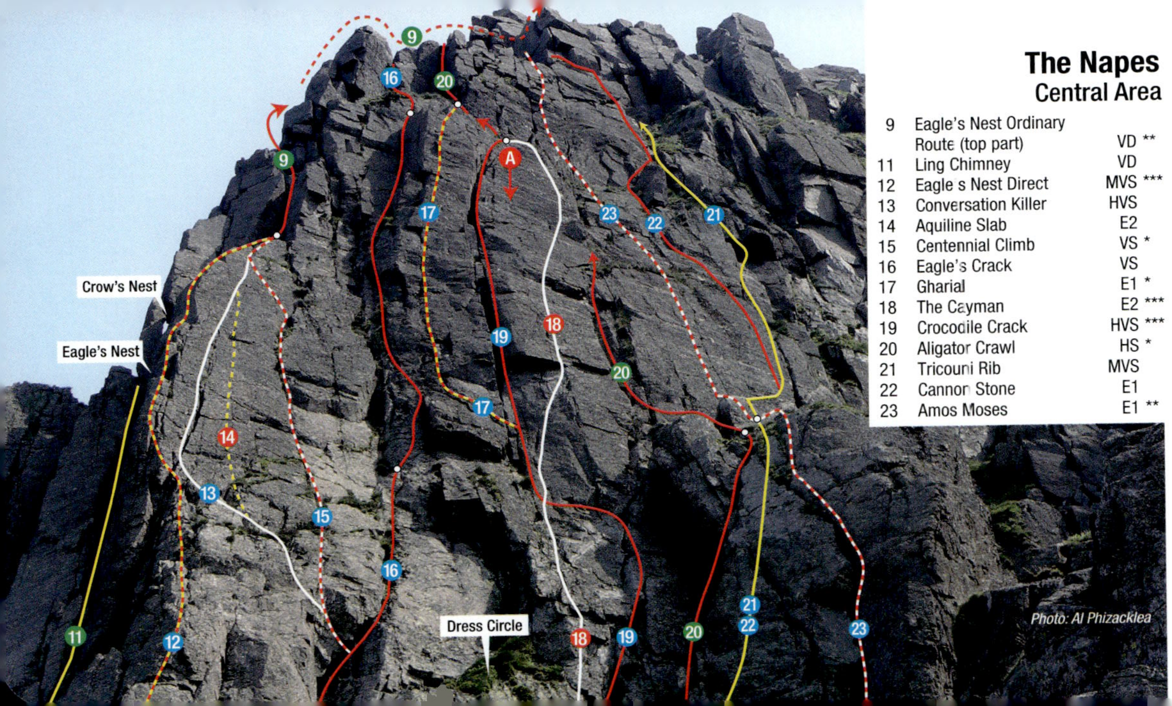

Photo: Al Phizacklea

Ling Chimney	40m	VD		1899

The narrow grassy chimney on the left of ***Eagle's Nest Ridge Direct***. Start directly below the chimney.

Climb easy rocks to the bottom of the left-hand of two cracks and then climb this crack to a chimney which is followed to a junction with the ***Eagle's Nest Ordinary***. Finish as for Pitches 3, 4, and 5 of that route.

Eagle's Nest Ridge Direct	45m	MVS	★★★	1892

A bold Lakeland classic giving delightful open and delicate climbing up the blunt arête overlooking the ***Dress Circle***. Start directly below the arête on a sloping ledge.

(4a). Climb up steeply on good holds bearing right to a ledge overlooking the ***Dress Circle***. Climb up and left to the arête using two parallel cracks, then step up to the ***Eagle's Nest*** (a small platform); continue up for 5 metres to the ***Crow's Nest*** (another small platform). Climb the slab above boldly on sloping holds to a good ledge. Belay in the corner above below the chimney of Pitch 3 of ***Eagle's Nest Ordinary***. Either **descend** or continue via that route, if doing the latter, its Pitch 3 variation is worthwhile.

The next four routes all share a common start with ***Eagle's Crack*** – the obvious slab and crack capped by an overhang above the middle of the ***Dress Circle***.

Conversation Killer	38m	HVS		1992

Takes the prominent diminishing right-hand crack on the right side of ***Eagle's Nest Ridge***. Start as for ***Eagle's Crack***.

(5a). Climb the slab and crack for 4 metres, swing left onto a rib using a good hold and pull up and climb a short crack to a small ledge. Climb leftwards to a prominent detached spike, step left and climb the right-hand diminishing crack and short wall above, to a good ledge. The grade assumes holds on ***Eagle's Nest Ridge Direct*** are not used!

Aquiline Slab	40m	E2		1991

Hard moves squeezed up the slab between ***Conversation Killer*** and ***Centennial Climb***. Start as for ***Eagle's Crack***.

(6a). Climb the slab and crack for a couple of metres then step down and left to enter a sloping niche in the left wall. Ascend the niche and continue up leftwards, past a grassy break, until below the centre of

Left: John Holden making the delicate and bold moves on the crux of **Eagle's Nest Ridge Direct** (MVS), The Napes. **Photo:** Al Phizacklea

a clean slab between two vertical crack systems. Climb the slab directly, keeping out of the cracks, past a difficult blank section, until easier ground leads straight to the belay on *Eagle's Nest Ridge Direct*.

Centennial Climb	40m	VS	★	1992

Climbs the thin broken crack running through overlaps just left of ***Eagle's Crack***. Start as for that route.

(4c). Climb the slab and crack for a couple of metres then step down and left to enter a sloping niche in the left wall. Climb the niche then move rightwards to gain a thin vertical crack running through overlaps. Climb the crack to a niche. Step left, and ascend a wall of excellent rock to belays in the corner of ***Eagle's Nest Ridge Direct***.

Eagle's Crack	62m	VS		1940

Entertaining climbing, but the loose flake on Pitch 2 requires care. Start below the slab capped by a prominent overhang.

1 20m (4c). Climb the slab to the overhang, step right to the rib and continue up the crack above for 7 metres to belays on the left wall.

2 30m (4c). Follow the crack over doubtful blocks until a bold mantelshelf move is made onto an obvious ledge on the right undercut rib. Climb up and left to regain the crack above the overhang and ascend the crack to thread belays.

3 12m. Climb the crack and mossy slab above to a grass ledge. The short crack just left of ***Eagle's Corner*** leads to the ridge.

Gharial	47m	E1	★	2003

A good pitch up the slim pillar left of ***Crocodile Crack***. Start up ***The Cayman***.

(5b). Pull through the first overhang of the ***The Cayman***, and continue straight up to join ***Crocodile Crack*** at the base of the good crack. Climb the crack to just above the large overlap on the left, then make a long reach leftwards to reach the mantelshelf on ***Eagle's Crack***. Climb straight up the slab then follow the thin crack up the steeper rock to a ledge, avoiding the poised block out left. The upper arête is climbed on good holds up the front face, to a good ledge.

The Cayman	60m	E2	★★★	1977

A high quality climb up the slender face right of ***Crocodile Crack***. Start just left of ***Crocodile Crack*** below an overhang.

1 45m (5b). Climb the overhang and crack above to where ***Crocodile Crack*** crosses the face. Step right and climb the thin diagonal crack to an overlap. Surmount this and continue up the wall above to the

Right: John Hudson tackling the first overlap on **The Cayman** (E2), The Napes.
Photo: Al Phizacklea

next overhang. Pull over and move up and right to a ledge on the arête. Ascend the steep arête in a fine position to a good ledge.

2 15m. Pitch 4 of *Eagle's Corner*; grassy chimneys to the ridge.

Crocodile Crack	58m	HVS	★★★	1960

An excellent climb up the obvious wide crack above the *Dress Circle*. Start at the bottom of a flake crack to the right of the main crack line above.

1 43m (5a). Climb the flake crack for 8 metres then make a long step left into the main crack. Ascend the crack to an overhang at 15 metres. Continue up the widening crack, past a small ledge on left, and then move up the crack again to a good ledge.

2 15m. Climb a grassy chimney on the right to join the ridge above.

Alligator Crawl	57m	HS	★	1960

A good climb that finds the easiest way up this part of the buttress. Start below the wide chimney which is bounded by an oblique overhang.

1 15m. Climb the chimney to a ledge.

2 27m. Step off the top of the block onto the wall to reach a good crack. Climb the fine crack to a good belay ledge.

3 15m. Climb a grassy chimney on the right to join the ridge above.

Tricouni Rib	65m	MVS		1925

Very overgrown: start at easy grass and rock just right of the chimney of *Alligator Crawl*.

1 20m. Climb easy rocks to a large grass ledge then up to the top of a large prominent pinnacle.

2 15m (4b). Step off the pinnacle and traverse right on small holds to the edge of the buttress. Climb the edge, then the face above, to a stance.

3 20m (4a). Climb the right edge of a gully, move up, then step across the gully to an undercut rock on the right; awkward moves up its left edge are followed to a frightening finish on steep grass. Belay in a corner higher up.

4 10m (4a). Climb easy rocks right of the belay then traverse left into a broken chimney which leads to *Eagle's Nest Ridge*.

Cannon Stone	75m	E1		1999

The slim pillar right of *Amos Moses* gives one of the longest pitches on *The Napes*. Great care is required with a large block on Pitch 2 which if dislodged, in addition to its potential to maim the climbers on the route, would also be likely to cause carnage amongst those in *Needle Gully* waiting to

Left: Rob Matheson approaching the jaws of **Crocodile Crack** (HVS), The Napes.
Photo: Al Phizacklea

climb the *Needle* – for this reason **it is suggested this route is avoided at busy times**, or indeed avoided all together. Start just right of the chimney of *Alligator Crawl*.

1 25m. Climb the blunt rib and wall above to a large grassy ledge.

2 50m (5b). From the large pinnacle, step down and right into a wide crack. Ascend the crack and slab above trending left to a groove left of a frighteningly large detached block. Climb the groove, and gain a standing position on the block. Boldly pull off the block on good holds to a small overhang and jammed ***Cannon Stone*** (runner recommended before loading the cannon, preferably to one side so that it does not shoot through your rope!). Pull up onto the thin slab above and climb it to a bulge. Step left and ascend a ragged crack and easier rock above to a good ledge.

Amos Moses	60m	E1	★★	1987

A direct line up the buttress right of ***Alligator Crawl*** giving excellent climbing. Start at the bottom of the large subsidiary buttress below the right-hand end of the ***Dress Circle***. The buttress is split by a wide right-slanting crack.

1 25m (5a). Gain the crack from the left using a small rib and climb it past two bulges to a slab. Climb up to a large grass ledge and pinnacle.

2 35m (5b). Climb the pinnacle and step onto the wall below a prominent finger crack. Ascend the crack with difficulty to a small ledge and move up and left to the foot of an obvious groove above a bulge. Pull rightwards into the groove with difficulty and climb more easily to a stony ledge.

Crinkler's Crack (HVS, 1973) took a meandering line in this area but has been badly affected by rock fall.

Eagle's Corner	70m	MVS		1924

Start below a grassy chimney level with and opposite the base of *Napes Needle*.

1 25m. Scramble up grass and climb the chimney to grass ledges above.

2 15m. Scramble up left, cross an incipient chimney, and climb the edge of the buttress to a stance and junction with ***Tricouni Rib***.

3 15m (4a). Traverse left along a ledge for 5 metres to a corner. Step round the corner and continue traversing left on small holds, crossing ***The Cayman***, to a wide crack. Climb the crack to a large grass ledge.

4 15m. Climb the grassy chimneys to the ridge.

The unpleasant *Needle Gully* to the right was accurately summed up in the 1925 guidebook as "unsuitable for any number of climbers" .

Napes Needle

Lakeland's celebrated pinnacle is a great attraction for many climbers and provides a unique experience and memorable day for teams as they sit, stand, do headstands and pose on its tiny flat top! The *Needle* has been brought into the 21st Century with the addition of some modern harder climbs. Many of the routes share the same belay below the top block on the *Shoulder* and use a common final pitch for both ascent and descent. The top moves have acquired a particular glass-like sheen and require care.

If the crack is treated like a horizontal bar, a leg can be thrown over either end or corner, by a short man. On my first ascent, I used the right hand, but several years after, probably for want of bar practice, I couldn't work the gymnastic on that end, and tried the left corner with success. As to the figure in the print, all I wish to say is, "These be my struggles but not my pants."
G. Bennett Gibbs, *Fell and Rock Journal 1909*

Descent:

It is strongly recommended that the leader lowers the second to a belay on the *Shoulder* and then down-climbs to that point. Then, having lowered the second back to the ground, the leader should down-climb via *The Arête* whilst safeguarded by the runners either placed on the ascent and left in place for this purpose (**NB:** the second will need to clip the rope into these whilst descending!), or placed by the second while descending.

"Would a Swiss guide attempt a thing like that?"
An awestruck John Wilson Robinson to Walter Parry Hasket Smith on his first sighting of Napes Needle (1885).

Napes Needle
Wasdale Face

1	Direct Obverse from the Gap	E1	
2	The Wasdale Roof	E3	*
3	The Wasdale Crack	HS	***
4	The Arête	HS	***
V	Slingsby's Variation	HS	
5	The Obverse Route (part of top pitch)	MVS	***
6	Needle Ridge	VD	***

Photo: Al Phizacklea

WARNING: There have been a number of accidents to parties caused by attempting to abseil from the summit.

The routes are described from **left** to **right** starting on the west side of the *Gap*, that is the narrow cleft between the *Needle* and the rest of the crag.

The Wasdale Roof	17m	E3	★	2002

A short and exciting roof problem which climbs the large overhang formed by the top block that overlooks Wasdale Head. Possibly the shortest and most photogenic E3 in the Lakes!

(5c). Climb the *Wasdale Crack* to the slab. Move left and climb a short rib to the left end of the overhang. Step right onto the thin wall and pull boldly directly over the roof to reach good holds which lead to the top.

The Wasdale Crack	17m	HS	★★★	1886

The original way and a very popular route with two entertaining and contrasting pitches. Start below the obvious wide crack down and right of the *Gap*.

1 13m. Climb the awkward crack, facing left, then right to its finish; then ascend an easy slab to the *Shoulder*.

2 4m. Mantelshelf onto a narrow ledge (easier from the right) Traverse left onto the face and climb delicately to the top.

The Arête	20m	HS	★★★	1894

The west arête gives a delightful pitch; start at the bottom of *The Wasdale Crack*.

1 16m. Traverse delicately horizontally right until a pull round onto the arête can be made. Climb the arête to the *Shoulder*.

2 4m. As for *The Wasdale Crack*.

Slingsby's Variation 1904

Climb the slanting crack just right of *The Wasdale Crack* to join *The Arête*.

The Crowley Route	22m	HS		1893

The rather artificial slab between *The Arête* and *The Lingmell Crack*.

1 18m. Climb the slab crossing *Lingmell Crack* en route to the *Shoulder*.

2 4m. As for *The Wasdale Crack*.

The Lingmell Crack	22m	HS	★	1891

The obvious crack on the side facing Lingmell.

1 18m. Climb the crack over a small overhang to a ledge then up to the *Shoulder*.

2 4m. As for *The Wasdale Crack*.

The Obverse Route | 24m | MVS | ★★★ | 1912

A fine route with a brilliant top pitch which is well worth seeking out. Start just right of *Lingmell Crack*.

1 18m (4b). Climb the steep slab right of the crack on small holds to the *Platform*, then a large flake, followed by a slab, to the *Shoulder*.

2 6m (4b). Hand-traverse right, along the horizontal crack under the top block (and over the *Gap*) to gain its northwest arête (opposite *Needle Ridge*). Soak up the exposure, then make steep moves on good holds up the arête to gain the top.

Sick Heart River | 22m | E2+ | ★★ | 1999

A sensationally exposed climb up the east arête – a real find after *Napes Needle* had remained dormant for over half a century. Protection is marginal in the upper section. Start on the eastern side of the *Needle* at the foot of the polished groove of the *Gap*.

1 18m (5c). Climb towards the *Gap* for a few metres and then follow the obvious traverse line leftwards to the *Platform*. Climb the arête initially on the left, then on the right (crux) before climbing leftwards to the *Shoulder*. Alternatively, from the *Platform*, it is slightly easier but not as aesthetic to bridge against the huge flake for 3 metres before moving right to the arête; this also allows better protection to be placed.

2 4m (4b). Mantelshelf onto the ledge on the top block that overlooks the *Gap* and move up directly to the top.

Variation: Thirty-Nine Steps 18m E3+ ★★ 2002

An excellent direct line through *Sick Heart River*. Start at a short hanging groove just right of the arête leading to the *Platform*, at the foot of the *Gap*.

1 (6a). Climb the steep groove to gain the *Platform*. Climb the arête direct initially on the left then on the right to reach jugs below the final steep section. Continue directly up the right side of the arête to the *Shoulder*.

Direct Obverse from the Gap | 13m | E1+ | | 1928

A serious little route with a nasty landing. Start from the *Gap* directly below the arête. Worth doing for the positions.

(5b). Climb the arête boldly and with difficulty to reach better holds, then continue straight up the edge to join the exposed upper arête of *The Obverse Route* and pull up steeply to the top. It is also possible to take a diagonal line leftwards to the *Shoulder* and then follow Pitch 2 of *The Obverse Route* at the same grade (E1+).

The *Needle* can be girdled at two different heights. Both require an exercise in diplomacy and rope management of nightmare proportions!

Napes Needle East Face & South Face inset

1	The Arête	HS***	5	Sick Heart River	E2**
2	The Crowley Route	HS	V	Thirty-nine Steps	E3**
3	The Lingmell Crack	HS *	6	Direct Obverse Route	E1
4	The Obverse Route	MVS***			

Photos: Al Phizacklea and Phil Rigby

The Higher Needle Girdle	18m	MVS		1921 (or before)

A clockwise girdle of the top block, starting and finishing at the *Shoulder*. It can also be reversed.

(4b). From the *Shoulder*, make a descending traverse leftwards under *The Wasdale Roof* . Make an awkward move up the edge on the left to reach the crack under the top block. Move steeply around the arête on the left to reach the horizontal crack of *Obverse Route*. Traverse this leftwards to regain the *Shoulder*.

The Needle Perimeter	30m	MVS		1941

An anti-clockwise lower girdle which starts and finishes at the *Gap*. It too can be reversed.

1 20m. Descend down ledges to the *Wasdale Crack* and continue right to the arête, then cross a slab past the large flake on *The Obverse Route* to the *Platform*: belay.

2 10m (4b). Move down right and traverse horizontally right for 3 metres along a strenuous crack that leads back to the *Gap*.

Napes East Area

This broken area of interrupted buttresses runs eastwards (ie rightwards) from *Needle Ridge* (directly behind *Napes Needle*) towards *Lucifer Ridge* (on the left-hand edge of *Tophet Wall*). Some of the upper routes can be reached by scrambling up steep grass but a better way is to combine them with one of the lower climbs.

Descent:

From the top of *Needle Ridge* scramble up to a junction with a broad grassy ridge which forms a link to the mountain, then descend down into *Great Hell Gate*. This scree descent is worn and requires caution.

Needle Ridge	114m	VD	★★★	1884

A classic and justifiably popular route that is frequently used, both as a beginners' introductory climb, and as part of a mountaineering route to the summit of Great Gable. Start from the *Gap* behind the *Needle*.

1 12m. Climb the very polished slab above the *Gap* to a short shallow chimney that trends left to a block belay on the edge of the ridge below a steep wall. Alternatively, start from *Needle Gully* (to the left of *Needle Ridge*), at the lowest point of the ridge, and follow the arête on good holds to the same stance.

2 18m. The crack in the steep wall above, followed by easier rocks, leads to a blocky ledge. Scramble along the crest of the ridge for 7 metres to a stance.

The Napes East Area

1	Tricouni Rib	MVS
2	Cannon Stone	E1
3	Amos Moses	E1 **
4	Eagle's Corner	MVS
5	The Arete	HS ***
6	The Crowley Route	HS
7	The Lingmell Crack	HS *
8	The Obverse Route	MVS ***
9	Needle Ridge	VD ***
10	Salome	VD
V1	Salome Variation	VS
11	A Laudable Ox	VS
12	Chantry Buttress Dir.	HVS *
13	Chantry Buttress	S *
14	Zeta Climb	VD
15	Buzzard Wall	VD
16	Crumbs from a Rich Man's Table	MVS *
17	Scrimshanker	VS *
18	Hamshanker	MVS
19	Skorkian Crack	VS
20	Belfry Crack	MVS *
21	Belfry Buttress	HS

Above: Matt Groves on the upper part of **Needle Ridge**, VD, The Napes. **Photo:** Dave Willis

3 **15m.** Climb the chimney above for 4 metres, then step left onto the edge and follow this to a ledge. Either climb the short corner on the right, or pull delicately direct to a large ledge.

4 **34m.** Climb the groove above which leads to the crest of the ridge, step around this (possible belay) and follow a straight crack in the wall overlooking the gully which leads back onto the crest. Alternatively, climb the groove for 3 metres and then traverse right under the overhang and finish direct.

5 **35m.** Easy scrambling along the gendarmed crest to the main ridge of *The Napes*. The **descent** down to *Great Hell Gate* lies 20 metres along the main ridge, down a red scree chute.

Salome	80m	VD		1954

Start at the foot of a grassy crack in the slabs, near the bottom of the east side of the *Gap*.

1 **18m.** Climb the crack then traverse left along the rising grassy ledge to a platform. Continue until a swing right round a nose is made onto a slab that leads on small holds to a large block and ledge.

2 **28m.** Make an awkward step right to gain a crack which is climbed to a large ledge. Easy rocks lead up to a belay behind a large block.

3 **24m.** The wall behind the block is climbed with difficulty, then bear right to the foot of an obvious chimney that leads to a rock ledge. Climb the crack on the right to a large ledge.

4 10m. From the left-hand end of the ledge, move up to the break in the *Needle Ridge*.

Variation VS 1954

Start 7 metres right of *Salome*.

1 32m (4c). Climb 5 metres into a grassy gully then swing left onto the slabs. Move up a metre, then climb the groove on the right, underneath the overhang, step left and then go straight up the steep delicate slab. Move left to the belay at the end of Pitch 1.

A Laudable Ox	20m	VS		2007

Start at the right-hand side of *Napes Needle*, 7 metres right of the foot of the gully leading to the *Gap*, in the same place as the *Variation Start to Salome*.

(4b). Climb a rough slab to a short left-facing corner with a perched block at its top. Step right onto the fine hanging slab and climb this to the top.

Chantry Buttress Direct	27m	HVS	★	2003

The obvious crack. Start at the lowest point of the buttress.

(5b). Climb the widening crack up the front of the buttress to a ledge and finish directly over the bulging wall above.

Chantry Buttress	30m	S	★	1921

An independent clean little buttress about 30 metres right of *The Needle*. Start at the lowest point of the buttress.

Easy scrambling for 8 metres to a grass ledge. Climb the slab on the right followed by a steep crack to a ledge. Pull leftwards across a steep wall to a groove. Ascend the groove then make an awkward exposed step right to reach good holds which lead to the top; block belay.

The next four routes climb the buttress above the large steep grassy bay above *Chantry Buttress*, at the right end of which is the obvious leaning groove of *Scrimshanker*. These routes are best reached by climbing a route on *Chantry Buttress*. It is also possible to extend them by finishing up *Belfry Buttress*, *Belfry Crack* or *Skorkian Crack*.

Zeta Climb	43m	VD		1924

Start midway across the slab left of *Scrimshanker* and just right of a grassy groove.

1 18m. Ascend the rocks just right of the groove to a grass niche, then make an ascending traverse left to a grass ledge.

2 25m. Climb up the slabs on the left to a ledge which is partly occupied by a large block. Ascend the short wall on the left to a large ledge, followed by easy slabs and steep grass.

Buzzard Wall	23m	VD		1922

The slab right of *Zeta Climb*. Start right of a conspicuous recess.

Climb the wall, trending right to a grassy corner at 7 metres, then follow the clean slab on the right up to a large ledge. The short wall above leads to a grass finish.

Crumbs from a Rich Man's Table	23m	MVS	★	2007

The hanging arête left of ***Scrimshanker***; start directly at its foot.

(4b). Climb a steep groove just left of the arête to meet ***Buzzard Wall*** at a good spike. From this, traverse right and follow the arête to a good ledge, then a crack just left to another ledge; the top lies just above. To keep within the grade finish up ***Belfry Buttress***, or take the following variation:

Variation Finish VS+ 2007

2 **17m.** Climb easy rocks to a stance below the upper rocks.

3 **20m.** (5a) Climb the crack on the left side of the buttress to a ledge, then pull left to a vertical crack which leads with difficulty to a ledge. Move up and right to cross above the gully on the right by precariously monkeying across the wedged flake!

Scrimshanker	30m	VS	★	1965

An interesting route up the obvious leaning corner. Not for slackers! Start below the corner, at a V-groove.

(4c). Climb the steep groove for 6 metres to a good ledge on the left. Pull back right into the wide crack and follow it, exiting left at the top to belay.

Hamshanker	25m	MVS		2003

A reasonable route on clean rock. Start at the right side of the bay below a wide crack leading up rightwards.

(4c). Climb the wide crack to stand on a protruding flake. Follow the steeper crack up leftwards to finish.

The next three routes are situated on the clean buttress of rock below the top part of ***Needle Ridge***. It is best to reach them by using a combination of routes on the lower buttresses.

Skorkian Crack	15m	VS		1954

An entertaining ascent of the off-width crack 8 metres left of ***Belfry Crack***: it can easily be reached from below the top pitch of ***Needle Ridge***.

(5a). Climb the crack to the chockstone and continue to a ledge. An easy chimney leads to the top.

Belfry Crack	20m	MVS	★	1925

A good climb up the obvious crack in the centre of the buttress.

(4b). Either ascend easy rocks on the right of the crack, then step left onto a ledge below the crack, or climb direct to the same point. Climb the crack until a ledge on the left is gained. Make a difficult step back right into the crack and follow it to a platform from where easy rocks lead to *Needle Ridge*.

Belfry Buttress	18m	HS		1968

Start 2 metres right of the *Belfry Crack*.

Climb the awkward groove to the top of a pedestal then go straight up the wall to a large ledge. Climb the short slab to *Needle Ridge*.

Tophet Wall

Tophet Wall is the large and impressively steep buttress which rises abruptly out of the sweeping screes of *Great Hell Gate*. A magnificent mountain crag with an unforgettable atmosphere. In mid-summer this south-east facing crag gets the sun until mid-afternoon but can suffer from a chill wind later in the day – early start recommended.

Descents:

From the top of the climbs follow the ridge north until it joins the broad saddle which connects *The Napes* and *Westmorland Crags*, then descend into west into Great Hell Gate which is followed down to the base of the crag. A shorter alternative is to descend **The Back Staircase** (M, 1913), which follows a narrow diagonal scramble from near the top of *Tophet Wall* into *Great Hell Gate*.

The routes are described from **left** to **right**.

Set back at the left-hand side of the crag is a distinctive clean wall split by a wide crack; the left edge of this wall is taken by *Lucifer Ridge*. The following four routes are reached by easy scrambling.

Jaga	123m	VD		1951

Climbs the grassy area of rock on the left side of *Lucifer Ridge*. Start below an obvious sentry box.

1 18m. Climb the wall until level with the sentry box then traverse left into it.

2 18m. Leave the sentry box on the right and climb the wall above, trending right to a large grass ledge.

The Napes Tophet Wall

1	Lucifer Ridge	VD *
2	Lucifer Crack	S *
3	Hell Raiser	E2 *
4	Tophet Bastion	VD *
5	Tormentil	MVS
6	Brimstone Buttress	MVS
7	Golden Calf	E5 **
8	Tophet Grooves Direct	E1 *
9	The Vikings	E3 ***
10	Tophet Grooves	HVS *
11	Incantations	E6 ***
12	Golgotha	E6
13	Supernatural	E5 ***
V1	Supernatural Direct Finish	E5 *
14	The Satanic Traverses	E5 ***
15	Breathless	E9 **
16	Tophet Wall	HS ***
17	Demon Wall	VS *
V2	Demon Wall Upper Trav.	HVS
18	Sacrificial Crack	E4 ***
19	The Tartarus Trip	E2
20	Tophet Ridge	VS *
21	Hell Gate Pillar	MVS
22	Hell Bent	E4

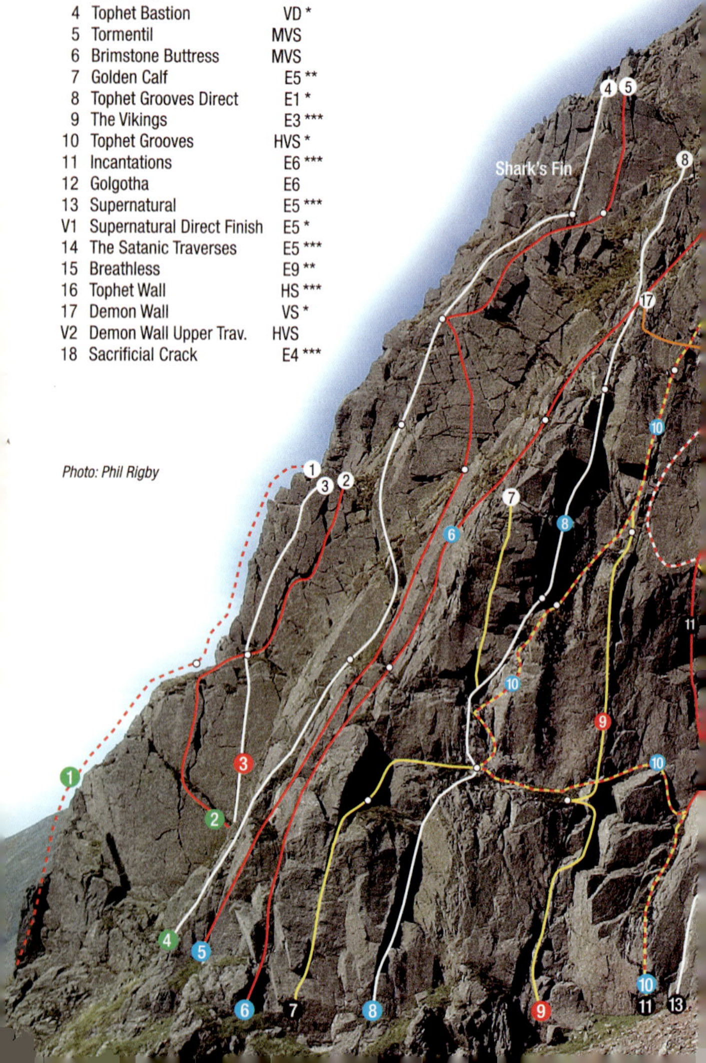

Photo: Phil Rigby

Westmorland Crags
Hell Gate Pillar
Great Hell Gate
6
19
16
V1
11
18
13
15
V2
13
16
11
V1
15
A
V2
16
17
18
21
20
22
13
14
12
13
19
17
18
16

3 30m. Traverse left for 7 metres, climb the ridge ahead until it finishes under a nose of rock, then hand-traverse left on good holds, finishing up a nose of rock at its end.
4 20m. Climb easy slabs and then a prominent rock tower.
5 12m. Climb the slabs immediately behind the tower, trending right to a stance.
6 25m. Continue up slabs and a small rock wall to a small ledge. Climb the rocks under the overhang, working first right, then left to the top.

Lucifer Ridge	43m	VD	★	1934

Start at the foot of the distinctive rocky ridge.
1 12m. Easy climbing leads to a stance at the side of the steep arête.
2 16m. Descend a little, then climb the face on the left of the arête to the top of a pinnacle, or alternatively, climb up the corner above the belay. Step across the gap and climb the arête on good holds to the ledge above Pitch 1 of *Lucifer Crack*.
3 15m. Follow the arête direct on good holds to the top.

Lucifer Crack	30m	S	★	1925

A pleasant route. Start from a grass ledge below and right of the crack.
1 13m. Traverse the grass ledge leftwards to a crack about 6 metres above its start. Climb into a niche and follow the crack to a large ledge.
2 17m. Climb the cracked wall above the ledge in a fine position.

Hell Raiser	26m	E2	★	1987

A short technical route up the thin crack in the wall right of *Lucifer Crack*.
1 12m (5c). Climb the crack with interest to a large ledge.
2 14m (5b). Climb a bold little wall just right of the left arête to sloping pockets. Pull up to good holds, step right and finish directly up a thin crack just left of the big flake.

The next three routes start at the foot of the obvious large diagonal ramp which runs above the main wall.

Tophet Bastion	82m	VD	★	1919

A good mountaineering route up the left side of the crag. Start at the bottom of a broken arête on the left-hand side of the ramp.
1 20m. Easily up the arête to a grass ledge then climb the steep corner on the right to a rock platform. It is possible to bypass the corner by the steep wall on the right.
2 17m. Climb the slab above for 8 metres to a ledge then step left around the corner and up a steep arête to a stance.
3 12m. Step right and climb straight up to the bottom of a groove at 7 metres. Climb the groove direct (crux, and awkward as it is easy to

face the wrong way!) to the top (the groove can also be avoided on the left but you know you shouldn't).

4 **16m.** From the belay, scramble up steep grass to the obvious feature of the ***Shark's Fin*** high on the left.

5 **17m.** Starting from the right, climb the edge of the rib to the foot a crack in a V-groove. Climb the crack by its left wall, exiting left at the top.

Tormentil	81m	MVS		2003

Pleasant variations up the right flank of ***Tophet Bastion***. Start 3 metres right of ***Tophet Bastion*** at a slim pillar.

1 **35m (4a).** Climb the slim pillar which leads to a slab (this is also taken by the short variation to ***Tophet Bastion*** which avoids the steep corner); climb this finishing delicately up the right rib above, to gain a loose grass ramp. Belay below the middle of the slab on the left.

2 **31m (4a).** Climb the slab directly, passing to the right of a small rectangular overlap, to finish on the arête of ***Tophet Bastion***. Scramble up the ridge for a further 16 metres to belay below the ***Shark's Fin***.

3 **15m (4a).** Follow twin cracks to the right of the rib of ***Tophet Bastion*** and continue up the awkward wide crack to finish.

Brimstone Buttress	69m	MVS		1938

Climbs the obvious short steep right-angled corner on the left edge of the main crag. Very overgrown and loose.

1 **20m (4b).** Climb the crack into the corner then step onto the right wall where small holds lead up until the crack can be rejoined. Scramble up to a belay below a sweep of slabs.

2 **17m.** The slabs above are climbed trending right to the edge then directly up, finishing via a shallow scoop.

3 **32m.** Climb the ridge direct to a large ledge, then move up the arête, first on the left, then on the right, to the top.

The crag now becomes very impressive with a huge overhanging wall on the left-hand side.

Golden Calf	42m	E5	★★	1978

A classic product of the '70s, giving powerful climbing up the left side of the overhanging wall. Only for idol worshippers. Start 3 metres from the left edge of the crag below a thin diagonal hanging crack.

1 **17m (6a).** Climb the crack direct to a large ledge.

2 **8m (4a).** Traverse easily right to a belay below a hanging groove.

3 **17m (6b).** Climb the groove until it is possible to bridge up to reach a thin hanging crack on the left. Ascend the crack passing two distinct steepenings with difficulty, to the top.

Tophet Grooves Direct	78m	E1	★	1991

This combination of direct variations on ***Tophet Grooves***, needs a good spell of weather to dry. Start below the obvious diagonal groove at the left side of the crag.

1 18m (5b). Climb the groove with interest to a good ledge on the right.
2 18m (5b). Climb the scoop above passing a doubtful block to the overhang; step right a metre and climb directly over the bulge to a stance.
3 24m (5b). Step right and climb the mossy wall direct to a good ledge. Move left and climb leftwards back into the main groove then tackle the puzzling overhanging cleft through the roof. An easier groove above leads to a large grass ledge.
4 18m (4a). Scramble over easy ground to the foot a prominent rib and climb it to the top.

The Vikings	57m	E3+	★★★	1969

The archetypal Lakeland crack climb: it requires a determined approach. Start directly below the crack at an upstanding block. It is better to combine the first and second pitches.

1 15m (5b). Climb leftwards to reach a steep crack. Ascend the crack then step right into another crack and make an awkward pull into the corner above. Climb the corner and pull out left at the top to a good ledge.
2 27m (5c). Move back right and climb the overhanging crack with increasing difficulty to gain the obvious flared niche. Pull steeply out of the niche and climb directly to a grassy crack. Climb the crack to a large pedestal belay on ***Tophet Grooves***.
3 15m (4b). Continue up the crack and groove above to the top.

Tophet Grooves	79m	HVS	★	1940

The original route, which was the first to breach the left side of the main buttress. Start below a nose about 3 metres right of the obvious upstanding block.

1 17m (5b). Climb the nose direct stepping left into a grassy groove that leads easily rightwards to a large sloping ledge.
2 12m (4a). Descend the groove slightly then climb the crack to a large pedestal. Traverse the narrow grass ledge leftwards to belay below a mossy groove.
3 15m (5a). Climb the groove, passing doubtful blocks, to the overhang, then traverse right across a mossy scoop onto a rib. Move up the rib and then step left back into the groove (small belays).

Right: Tom Foster at the top of the overhanging crack on **The Vikings** (E3), The Napes.
Photo: Phil Rigby

4 20m (4c). Step right and climb the mossy wall to a ledge, then ascend the grassy crack on the right to a large pedestal belay.
5 15m (4b). Continue up the crack and groove above to the top.

Incantations	87m	E6+	★★★	1984

A superlative test piece with two powerful pitches. Since the first ascent, the poor peg and a number of holds and placements on the second pitch have gone making this pitch an even more difficult lead. Start below the nose as for *Tophet Grooves*.

Above: Pete Whillance, with his trademark waist belt and bandolier, leading **Incantations** (E6), The Napes. **Photo:** Chris Bonington

1 22m (5b). Climb the nose and up an easy groove rightwards to a large sloping ledge.
2 35m (6b). A serious and sustained pitch with no real rests. Difficult and bold moves lead up the overhanging wall (wires out left but difficult to place). Continue up the wall (wires behind expanding flakes) to reach a thin right-slanting crack in the steep slab above. Climb the crack to ledges, then move rightwards over a bulge and step up right onto the *Great Slab*. Climb up to the *Demon Wall* lower traverse then move left to a good pinnacle belay.
3 30m (6b). Climb the rib above the belay, then step right to below a thin right-slanting crack in the overhanging wall. Climb the wall (Friends) to a jug beside the peg, move right, and pull into the groove above (junction with *Supernatural Direct Finish*). The groove and its right-hand branch lead to the top. Originally the peg was gained by difficult moves up a thin crack culminating with a desperate clip.

Golgotha	48m	E6		1993

Steep and fingery climbing between *Incantations* and *Supernatural*.
(6c). Climb the first pitch of *Supernatural* to the large ledge. From the middle of the ledge climb directly up the steep wall to good holds on

Right: Steve Merry pulling through the steep overlap on **Supernatural** (E5), The Napes. **Photo:** Al Phizacklea

the top of an overlap. Make a long reach up and left (peg runner), then pull onto the steep little slab above (junction with the groove on *Supernatural*). Swing out left on tiny holds and enter the short hanging groove above; up this, then move leftwards to good holds. Pull onto the slab above via the rightward-slanting crack of ***Incantations*** and climb the crack to small ledges, continuing straight up to a good ledge and pinnacle belay.

Supernatural	82m	E5	★★★	1977

A magical route with a committing and serious middle pitch which follows an intricate line up the steep wall right of ***Incantations***. Start at steep shallow groove just right of a large grassy groove.

1 25m (5c). Climb the groove, moving right at the top onto the wall. Move up and make a difficult pull left onto the rib and ascend it to a good ledge and pinnacle.

2 32m (6a). Climb the steep wall above the pinnacle to a bulge (the peg out left on ***Golgotha*** being out of bounds if you want the full out of body experience). Pull onto the steep hanging slab above and traverse it leftwards with difficulty to reach the base of a steep groove; climb the groove to a welcome spike and rest. Step right and climb a rib and groove that lead to good holds on the ***Great Slab***. Step left and climb the slab until an easy traverse can be made leftwards to a ledge and large pinnacle belay.

3 25m (5b). Climb directly up the rib above the belay to a ledge on the right, then up a mossy slab on the left to a sloping ledge. Traverse right along the ledge, then move up and right round the rib on good holds. Climb the wall and V-groove to the top.

Supernatural Direct Finish E5 ★★ 1984

An alternative, but much harder, final pitch to ***Supernatural***, taking in the overhanging headwall. Start from the pinnacle belay at the top of Pitch 2.

3 30m (6b). Climb down rightwards for 5 metres then ascend directly to below the overhanging wall. Worrying moves are made past a peg runner to below a small overhang. Climb the thin crack and pull into the base of a large groove then follow the right wall of the groove and the continuation groove above to the top.

The Satanic Traverses	30m	E5	★★★	1989

A devilish space walk across the lip of the central overhanging wall climbed by ***Incantations***, ***Golgotha*** and ***Supernatural***. Start at the left end of the belay ledge of Pitch 1 of ***Tophet Wall***.

Left: Dave Birkett begins the crux section of **Breathless** (E9), Tophet Wall.
Photo: Steve Crowe

(6a). Step left and climb up 3 metres to a small pocket which is used to place a Rock 4 or 5 in a vertical slot, then reverse back down to the belay ledge. Traverse leftwards just above the overhang to a small spike, then move down to the spike on Pitch 2 of ***Supernatural***, and continue leftwards, using tiny footholds on the very lip of the overhanging wall, to a junction with the crack of ***Incantations***. Move left and climb a line of good holds to a rib (junction with ***Tophet Grooves***). Climb the rib and trend back right up a grassy groove to the pinnacle belay of ***Supernatural***. Only fiendish rope work will save the second from a swing into the gates of Hell!

Breathless	26m	E9	★★	2000

A death-defying and audacious route up the smooth impending top wall of the crag. The climbing is merely E8 to the good hold but then increases steadily in difficulty, with the final move being the hardest. Relax and breath deeply on this route if you can! Start at the belay at the top of Pitch 2 of *Tophet Wall*.

(7a). Climb the thin crack (2 blade peg runners) to a good hold (2 good peg runners). Climb directly to an obvious loose block (very poor thin blade runner), then climb the unrelenting hard and dynamic upper wall leftwards to gain the crux.

Tophet Wall	75m	HS	★★★	1923

A magnificent mountain outing winding its way through very impressive rock architecture. Probably the best route of its grade in the Lakes. Take several slings and start to the right of a rightward-leaning crack/corner in the centre of the wall.

1 20m. Climb the thin wall just right of the steep crack (thin tape runner on flat spike just right of the start of the hard bit if you look), until a step left can be made into the crack, which is followed awkwardly to a ledge. An ascending traverse right leads to a good ledge at the foot of a short dark wall (the ***Original Start*** traversed easy ledges from the right to this point).

2 17m. The short wall above is climbed boldly to a broken ledge. Traverse left to a groove and climb it to a slab and spike belay on the right.

3 38m. A fantastic pitch! Semi hand-traverse 10 metres rightwards in a sensational position to a crack and climb up to a small ledge, then follow the crack up rightwards. Alternatively continue the traverse a

Right: Joe Holden shows his father John how to run out the magnificent top pitch of **Tophet Wall** (HS), The Napes. **Photo:** Al Phizacklea

Overleaf: Wil Hurford and Jill Reid on the dramatically situated lower pitches of **Tophet Wall** (HS), The Napes. **Photo:** Stephen Reid

bit further and climb directly up to the same point. Climb the small pinnacle on the right, then step left into the crack which is followed to an airy pull out right onto a flake pinnacle. Easier climbing up the wall leads to a belay on a narrow footpath. **Descend** by following the footpath rightwards to a scramble down to *Hell's Gate Screes*.

Demon Wall	76m	VS+	★	1945

An interesting route that requires a delicate touch in some exposed positions. Start below the obvious rightward-slanting narrow ramp immediately right of *Tophet Wall*.

1 18m (5a). Climb the ramp to a good spike, then make a difficult and committing pull out left onto the steep wall which is followed up to a good ledge.

2 18m (4b). Step right round a bulging corner into a grassy recess. Climb its left wall on small holds to a ledge which is followed back left to a junction with Tophet Wall below a large corner.

3 20m (4c). *The Great Slab*. Ascend *Tophet Wall* until a line of good flake holds encourage a break out left onto the open slab from the relative security of the corner. A rising traverse is made across the slab in a superb position to a spike belay on the edge.

4 20m. Traverse left, crossing *Tophet Grooves*, then step left round a corner onto easy ground. Follow the pockmarked slab to the finish.

Variation: The Upper Traverse HVS 1974

A recommended alternative taking a higher traverse line under the overhanging wall.

3 27m (5a). Climb the corner on Pitch 2 of *Tophet Wall* to gain the obvious leftward-rising hand-traverse line, directly below the overhanging wall. Follow this and, at its end, climb a mossy groove into a slabby recess (junction with *Tophet Grooves*). Pull over to easy ground.

Sacrificial Crack	66m	E4	★★★	1978

A very intimidating crack climb of great character. The route takes the frighteningly overhanging crack at the top right-hand side of the crag. Off-width virgins beware! Start as for *Demon Wall*.

1 18m (5a). As for Pitch 1 of *Demon Wall*.

2 25m (5b). A poorly protected pitch. Climb the rib just left of *Demon Wall* Pitch 2 to a broken ledge, move right then pull over a bulge into the right-hand of two short grooves (directly in line with the crack on Pitch 3). Climb the groove to a belay just right of the crack at a shattered pinnacle.

3 23m (6a). Climb the crack with a dynamic move left at half height, followed by a long reach to a sinking jam below the recess. A strenuous pull gives access to the recess and a possible rest. Follow the crack with interest to the top.

The Tartarus Trip	52m	E2		1987

Takes in the short bulging wall below *Tophet Wall*, before finishing up the obvious square pillar on the right arête of the crag. Start on a grass ledge below a left-hand hanging V-groove, above the original start to *Tophet Wall*.

1 15m (4b). Climb the V-groove to block belays below the bulging wall.
2 25m (5c). Make bold and tricky moves over the bulge onto easier ground. Traverse right to the arête (*Tophet Ridge*) and climb the front of the square pillar above, in an exposed position, to a good ledge.
3 12m. Easy climbing to the top.

Tophet Ridge	52m	VS	★	1932

A good climb up the steep right arête of the crag. Start below an obvious groove on the right side of the ridge, opposite *Hell Gate Pillar*.

1 30m (4c). Climb the left wall and a groove to gain the ridge and follow it to a good rock spike and grass ledge on the right. Make an awkward move onto the spike and climb the steep wall (crux) to reach better holds. Climb more easily to a grassy corner.
2 22m (4b). Climb up, past a large block, to a horizontal crack. Hand-traverse the crack into a short corner (junction with *Tophet Wall*), pull up onto the top of a pinnacle on the right and climb more easily to the top. The original pitch climbed up rightwards from the belay but is now very overgrown.

Back of the Napes	37m	MS		1942

This climb lies on the right side of *Tophet Ridge*, on a wall facing *Hell Gate Pillar*. It is steep, damp, loose and thoroughly unpleasant. Start 8 metres up the scree from the foot of *Tophet Ridge* where the wall is grooved.

1 10m. The broken wall leads to a ledge. Belay at the foot of a steep groove.
2 15m. Traverse right and climb the steep wall by an awkward traverse right, followed by a traverse back left, into a short crack that leads to a corner.
3 12m. Traverse right to broken rocks and climb these or alternatively traverse left onto *Tophet Wall* at the foot of Pitch 4 and finish up this.

Tophet Girdle	117m	VS	★	1945

A left to right traverse of the *Tophet Wall* face incorporating *Tophet Bastion*, a traverse of the *Great Slab* and the upper pitches of *Tophet Wall*. A splendid outing with some superb positions. Start as for *Tophet Bastion*.

1 20m. As for Pitch 1 of *Tophet Bastion*.

2 18m (4a). Traverse right to the top of Pitch 1 of ***Brimstone Buttress*** then work up and right to the edge which leads via a shallow scoop to a belay (rock requires care).

3 16m. Climb easy slabs above to the top of the overhanging groove of ***Tophet Grooves Direct*** then follow the grass ledges rightwards to the pedestal belay at the top of Pitch 4 of ***Tophet Grooves***.

4 23m (4c). Traverse the ***Great Slab*** by reversing Pitch 3 of ***Demon Wall*** into a corner and a junction with Pitch 2 of ***Tophet Wall***, which is then followed to its belay (remember to protect the second).

5 15m (4a). As for Pitch 3 of ***Tophet Wall***.

6 25m (4a). As for Pitch 4 of ***Tophet Wall*** until a break leads off right, crossing ***The Tartarus Trip***, and round a rib into a corner. The shattered ridge on the right is climbed, followed by easy scrambling to the top.

Hell Gate Pillar

Above and right of *Tophet Wall* is a pinnacle-like ridge that divides *Great Hell Gate*. The lower end of this ridge forms a steep little buttress containing the following two routes; both have sections of loose rock.

Hell Gate Pillar	30m	MVS		1934

Start about 7 metres above the foot of the ridge on the ***Tophet Wall*** side.

(4a). Climb the slab to the overhang then cross the slab on the right using small holds to a corner. Step down and round the corner on the right to a scoop; climb this, followed by a short wall on the right, to a ledge. The corner on the left leads to an easy arête (rope drag can be a problem).

Hell Bent	25m	E4		1987

Climbs the steep arête on the ***Tophet Wall*** side of the pillar. A short but serious climb.

(5c). Climb the steep arête direct (skyhook runner in hole), passing a small overhang at 15 metres, to a hollow block. Step right then pull back left and go up the steep wall above on good holds to easier ground. Block belays.

Westmorland Crags

Grid reference: **NY 211 102** Altitude: **800m**
Faces: **South** Approach: **2hrs**

Once a neglected venue with only one climb recorded, until it was rediscovered in 2003 and given a new life with the frenzied addition of over 20 new routes! The climbs all have a mountaineering feel and enjoy magnificent panoramas, which makes up for the broken nature of the crag. Haskett Smith noted in 1894 that a number of 'neat problems' had been climbed here on the way to the summit of Great Gable: it is thought that he may have made the first ascents of *Westmorland's Gully*, *Pinnacle Ridge* and *Chockstone Chimney*.

The rock is generally clean and quick drying, though there are a fair amount of loose holds around (feeding source for ***Hell Gate Screes***!), so great care should be taken not to send blocks down towards the ***Napes*** below.

It is best to use the flat area near ***Westmorland's Cairn*** at the top of the crag to gear up, then descend various easy gullies to get to the foot of the routes, most of which start above the very broken lower section of the crag.

Approach:

From **Honister Pass**, via Green Gable and Great Gable summit, (2 hrs).
From **Wasdale Head**, via Burnthwaite, Gavel Neese and ***Little Hell Gate*** (2 hrs).

All directions are given as though looking up, unless stated otherwise.

Near the left-hand end of the crag is **Westmorland's Gully** (reasonable **descent** at M) and about halfway down where it eases, on its right (looking up), is a fine prow.

Rusty's Rib	20m	MVS	★	2003

Exposure, spaced gear and tuneful holds, make for an exciting little climb.
(4a). Climb the left edge of the lower prow wall to a large ledge and poised boulder. Move up into a shallow niche on the right wall, and traverse horizontally right around onto the front face, and onto a small ledge on the right. Climb up steeply just right of the overhanging prow and step left onto it. Finish up the rib above.

Westmorland Crags

1	Rusty's Rib	MVS	*
2	Tubular Balls	HVS	*
3	Sparrowfart Rib	S	
4	Blazonry	VS	
5	Pinnacle Ridge	M	**
6	Chequered Cracks	MVS	
7	Hotel du Lac	E1	
8	Westmorland Ridge	VD	
9	Pinncairnle Rib	VS	*
10	Westmorland Crack	E2	**

Photo: Al Phizacklea

Tubular Balls	20m	HVS	★	2003

A fine pitch requiring a cool head and....

(4c). Climb the lower wall by its right arête (no gear) to the small ledge. Traverse left a metre and climb the prow direct (good wire round on the left wall).

When looking from above, directly below *Westmorland's Cairn* will be seen a diagonal open scree gully (*Central Gully*) which is divided in two by a rock rib. The ridge forming the outer edge of this gully is *Pinnacle Ridge* which is a popular scramble.

The next two routes finish on *Pinnacle Ridge* and start from the bottom of the crag, some 30 metres down the *Hell Gate Scree*'s side of the grassy ridge which connects *Westmorland Crags* to the top of *The Napes*.

Sparrowfart Rib	45m	S		2003

Start very early, 3 metres below a large block embedded in the scree, and 10 metres above a square block which marks the start of *Pinnacle Ridge*.

1 **20m.** Climb a short wall to a rake, cross this, and climb the pinnacle-shaped wall behind, pulling out right onto a small ledge and finishing up a wide crack.

2 **25m.** Cross the wide grassy rake, and climb the clean rib that has a wide crack on the right and a slim groove on the left near its top, finishing up the slim groove. A good but somewhat disconcerting pitch with lots of hollow holds. A short scramble brings you to *Pinnacle Ridge*.

Blazonry	30m	VS		2006

Fifteen metres down and right of *Sparrowfart Rib*, a grassy gully is found slanting up to the left; 17 metres up the gully on its right side is a rectangular pillar of rock between two grassy breaks, easily identified by its curious white striations: start at the foot of the pillar.

1 **14m (4c).** Climb the centre of the pillar until, at 10 metres, a steep move gains a ledge on its right arête. Continue up to a good ledge.

2 **16m.** Climb a slabby wall and wide crack on the left to reach a large ledge. Continue up walls and ribs until a short traverse right gains *Pinnacle Ridge*.

Pinnacle Ridge	150m	M	★★	<1894

Start 50 metres right of *Sparrowfart Rib*, just right of a 5 metre high square buttress, 25 metres down and left of the entrance to *Central Gully*.

Scramble up well-trodden low rocks and ledges behind the 5 metre high buttress, with a steeper section up a short corner, to reach the *Pinnacle* after 90 metres. Go left behind this then up a steep wall (well-marked) on the left to gain the crest. Up this then along a horizontal section with short rises for a further 60 metres to reach a lawn and path to the top.

The next routes are all best reached from the top of the crag by **descending** *Central Gully*. The first obvious feature, reached from a short way down *Central Gully*, is a smooth slab with a slim groove in it. The following three routes all start from a block belay at the foot of the right-hand side of the slab.

School's Out	18m	S	★	2003

A fine little pitch.

Climb the slab leftwards to a block on the arête, and thence to a large platform. Climb the wide crack on the left to the top.

Dad's Day Slab	18m	VS	★	2003

(4c). Follow the slim groove direct to the platform. Step right off this and climb flakes to the top.

Wha's the Crack?	18m	HS		2003

Climb the obvious wide crack at the back of the groove right of *Dad's Day Slab* to just below its top. Step left onto the slab and finish via a short groove.

To the right of *Dad's Day Slab* are four narrow ribs, the central two having an obvious V-groove between them.

Chocks Away	28m	MVS		2003

The poised blocks that gave this route its name were trundled after the first ascent but the rock still needs treating with care. Start below the V-groove at a clean bulgy buttress.

(4a). Climb the buttress to a slab and move up leftwards to grassy rock so as to step into the groove from the left. Climb the groove exiting leftwards and squeeze up a narrow chimney between two hanging ribs.

Just right of the V-groove is a vague mossy groove and 2 metres right again is another clean bulgy buttress leading to a more pronounced moss-filled chimney.

Cairnshung Face	30m	HS		2003

Climb the bulgy buttress to a slab and continue up the mossy chimney mainly via its left wall. Where the chimney eases, take to the face on the left and climb it to a ledge. Climb up behind a pinnacle and make an awkward exit via a short corner on the left.

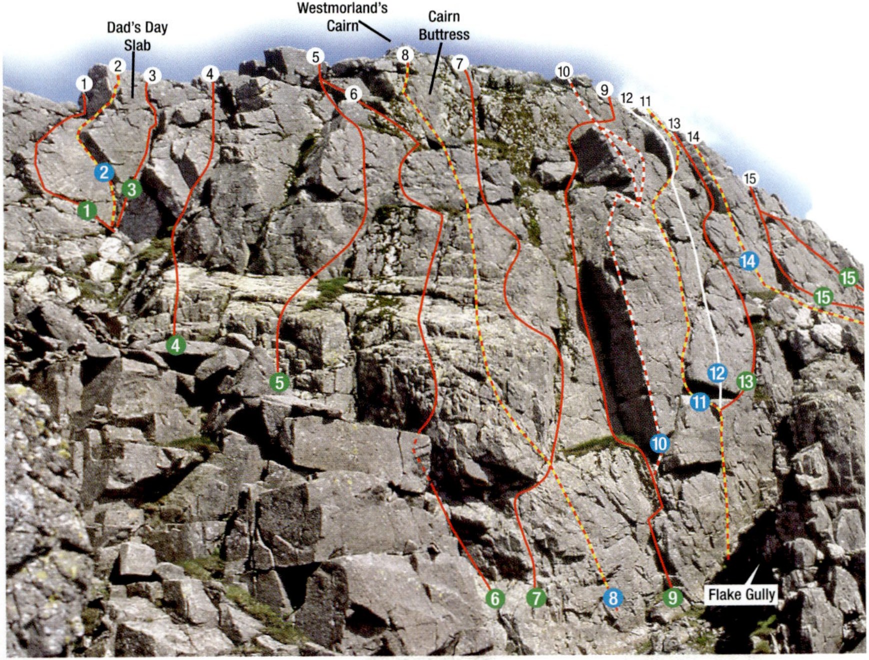

Westmorland Crags

Upper Crag

1	School's Out	S *
2	Dad's Day Slab	VS *
3	Wha's the Crack?	HS
4	Chocks Away	MVS
5	Cairnshung Face	HS
6	The Cairnbrian	HS
7	Cairn Climb	HVD *
8	Cairn Direct	VS *
9	Chockstone Chimney	HVD
10	Not a Cairn in the World	HVS **
11	Cairn Nuts Crack	VS
12	R & R Special	MVS **
13	Crackerjack	S *
14	Pinncairnle Rib (part)	VS *
15	Westmorland Ridge (part)	VD

Upper Crag as seen looking across Central Gully from Pinnacle Ridge, which appears in the left-hand corner.

Photo: Stephen Reid

Towards the bottom of the right-hand branch of *Central Gully*, a subsidiary gully (*Flake Gully*) branches off rightwards behind the obvious feature of the *Great Flake*. *Cairn Buttress* is the long wide slabby buttress that rises directly to *Westmorland's Cairn* from this junction. It is guarded by an overlap at 4 metres.

The Cairnbrian	40m	HS		2003

Takes the left side of *Cairn Buttress*. Start directly under the centre of the overlap.

1 25m. Climb a wide easy left-slanting crack-line to just before its end in a grassy niche on the left flank of the buttress. Pull boldly up the steep wall on the right on jugs to gain the slab above. Climb directly up this to follow a thin crack, pulling out left at its top, and climbing the sharp arête on the left to a poised block belay on a big ledge.

2 15m. Go leftwards along a grass ledge for 3 metres and climb a wide crack behind a big spike. The awkward corner beyond leads to the top.

Cairn Climb	40m	HVD		2003

An enjoyable mountaineering route. Start as for the *Cairnbrian*, directly under the centre of the overlap.

1 25m. Climb up to the overlap, traverse rightwards underneath it and climb up into a large depression (*Chockstone Chimney* is on the right). Climb the groove on the left, exiting leftwards onto the buttress. Go straight up to a vague ramp and move right up this to its end, before stepping leftwards to a crack. Climb the crack to a poised block belay on a big ledge.

2 15m. Climb up to a narrow grass ledge and traverse right along it to a mossy left-facing corner (loose block). Climb the corner to a break and finish up the wide crack above.

Cairn Direct	40m	VS	★	2003

Crosses *Cairn Climb* and takes the centre of *Cairn Buttress*. Start at the bottom of *Flake Gully*, below the right-hand end of the overlap.

1 25m (4b). Climb the steep wall to a large depression just right of the long overlap (alternatively, start one metre up *Flake Gully* and climb a left-slanting crack to the same point). Step down left and pull over the overlap near its right-hand end, moving leftwards to easier ground. Climb directly up the front of the buttress on excellent holds to a poised block belay on a big ledge.

2 15m (4b). Climb the clean slab above moving leftwards into a slim mossy groove. Go up this and exit to the right of some large poised blocks to finish at the cairn.

The next buttress to the right is *Flake Gully Buttress*.

Chockstone Chimney	38m	S		1913

Climb a wide crack and blocky pinnacle under the hanging arête on the left side of *Flake Gully Buttress* and move up left to a grass ledge and the foot of the chimney. Follow the chimney avoiding the upper chockstones by a short groove on the left. Traverse right to a possible belay behind the huge flake. Climb leftwards up a groove formed by two huge slanting blocks to a large ledge. Climb straight up the mossy wall above.

Not a Cairn in the World	38m	HVS	★★	2003

The arête gives a superb climb. Start as for *Chockstone Chimney*.

1 18m (5a). Climb to the top of the blocky pinnacle and then up the ramp and arête to gain a ledge at the foot of the arête proper. Follow this boldly (Micro-Friends) to a huge pinnacle flake belay.

2 20m (4c). Step off the flake onto the wall behind, and climb the wall direct, via a small V-groove, to a ledge. Follow the left-hand crack in the wall above to the top.

Variation 1

1 Follow *Cairn Nuts Crack* to gain the arête – this was the original way.

Variation 2 2003

2 (4c). Equally good: follow Pitch 2 for 3 metres then step onto the rib on the left and follow this to the ledge.

The following routes lie on the right-hand side of *Flake Gully Buttress* and start about a third of the way up *Flake Gully* at a right-slanting crack-line (*Crackerjack*).

Cairn Nuts Crack	38m	VS		2003

1 18m (4c). Climb the diagonal crack for a few metres to gain a ledge on the left. Move left and climb the striking off-width crack to a huge pinnacle flake belay.

2 20m (4c). Step off the flake onto the wall behind and move up a metre to a right-slanting traverse line. Follow this rightwards under a cracked prow and traverse rightwards onto a hanging arête – all rather exciting. Climb up to a ledge and take the right-hand crack in the wall above to the top.

R & R Special	38m	VS	★★	2003

A delightful little eliminate up the buttress between *Cairn Nuts Crack* and *Crackerjack*. Exposed climbing on perfect rock with excellent protection.

1 18m (4c). Follow the right-slanting crack for 3 metres then step left and pull directly over the roof on excellent holds. Go straight up the wall above, crossing a right-slanting crack/groove-line, direct to a huge pinnacle belay.

2 20m (4b). Start just right of a large block and climb the right arête of the wall behind to below a cracked prow. Climb the prow direct then take any line up the wall behind.

Crackerjack	38m	S	★	2003

1 18m. Follow the diagonal crack-line in its entirety moving left near the top to avoid loose blocks: ledge belay.
2 20m. Move right into the open serpentine groove and follow it to a large ledge. Move up then step right onto the arête which leads to the top.

Sixteen metres down *Central Gully* from *Flake Gully*, a grassy slope on the right (looking-in) leads up to a flake crack springing from the left side of an overhang in *Central Gully*.

Chequered Cracks	17m	MVS		2006

Start at the flake crack.
1 10m (4c). Climb the flake crack to a block-strewn ledge.
2 7m (4b). The crack, via a triangular niche in the steep wall behind the ledge proves awkward and leads to the *Great Flake* ridge.

Hotel du Lac	25m	E1		2006

Five metres right of *Chequered Cracks*, a pillar of rock projects boldly towards the Wasdale Head Inn (hence the name). A fine first pitch, but serious, with little protection.
1 13m (5a). Climb the gully on the right of the pillar for 4 metres, then step left onto the pillar and climb it, trending slightly leftwards to a small ledge. Continue up a short wall to a block-strewn ledge atop the pillar.
2 12m (4b). Move up the steep wall above, keeping right of the crack, to a ledge. Avoiding the easy ground, step left onto a wall and climb it to reach the summit of the *Great Flake*.

To the right of the absolute bottom of *Central Gully*, and just as easily gained from below, is one of the earlier routes of the crag.

Westmorland Ridge	50m	VD		1932

Good climbing interspersed with scrambling. Start at the foot of a small buttress to the right of the entrance to *Central Gully*.
1 26m. Climb the steepest bit of the wall on excellent holds, followed by grassy scrambling slightly rightwards to a left-slanting groove at the foot of the left flank of the *Pinnacle*.

Left: Leave your worries behind: Stephen Reid on **Not A Cairn in the World** (HVS), Westmorland Crags. **Photo:** Trevor Suddaby

2 11m. Cracks up the wall are climbed to the top of the *Pinnacle*. Drop down to a large ledge beyond on the left atop a cubic buttress.
3 13m. Either climb a left-slanting ramp ahead, or traverse left to a short chimney and climb this (much easier) to the same point. Easier rock leads to the top.

The remaining routes are best reached by descending *Central Gully* to the bottom of the dividing rib (but above the broken ground below) and traversing rightwards until a scree slope at the base of the *Pinnacle* is gained. The *Pinnacle* is very obvious from above, lying about 20 metres left of the *Great Flake* looking out. On the east face of the *Pinnacle* is a steep crack-line and to the left of this a fine arête.

Pinncairnle Rib	45m	VS	★★	2003

Two fine pitches separated by a scramble. Start from a flat chockstone on the left side of the arête.
1 25m (4b). Climb the arête on its left-hand side to a belay on the *Pinnacle*. Scramble 20 metres leftwards to belay below a narrow chimney in the upper wall (this is just right of the open groove of Pitch 2 of *Crackerjack*).
2 20m (4b). Climb directly up the fine slab to the left of the chimney.

Westmorland Crack	25m	E2	★★	2003

A mini classic up the hanging crack-line in the overhanging east face of the *Pinnacle*. A good selection of Friends is useful. The second should take a belay at the bottom of the crag to avoid a slow slide down *Great Hell Gate*!
(5c). Climb up to the impending off-width. Thrutch up this with difficulty to gain the overhanging jamming crack above (it is also possible to climb the outside of the off-width on small holds, but this makes the placing of runners very difficult). Follow the crack on perfect jams to a good ledge and finish up the wide crack in the corner.

To the right of the *Pinnacle* is *Pinnacle Gully*.

Hell Gate Chimney	40m	MVS		2003

An interesting route, though marred by the possibility of an easy escape leftwards onto *Westmorland Ridge* on the second pitch. Start at the base of the upper section *Pinnacle Gully*, a few metres right of the chockstones.
1 15m (4a). Climb a slab and rib on the right and step right into a deep chimney which leads to the *Pulpit*.
2 25m (4b). From the left side of the *Pulpit*, follow a crack diagonally leftwards up the wall to ledges. Traverse right towards the arête and climb the wall direct, passing a hanging block on the right. Finish up the easy rib.

Hellfire and Brimstone	40m	HVS		2003

Technically easy for the grade but rather bold. Start at a slab just up and right of ***Hell Gate Chimney*** and just left of a prominent rock rib.

(4c). Climb the slab to the overhang and avoid this by traversing left across the chimney to the ***Pulpit***. Immediately pull back rightwards into a hanging groove and climb this until it is possible to exit rightwards onto a slab. Climb the narrow slab directly above, overcoming an overlap with difficulty and keeping left to finish.

Ten metres up and right is ***Cave Gully***, the cave being formed by a huge chockstone. To the left of ***Cave Gully*** are two grooves.

Adam's Groove	35m	E2		2003

A better and longer route than it looks from below, up the more defined left-hand groove. Watch out for some loose holds.

(5c). Climb dirty rock to gain the top of a dubious block. Hard climbing up the groove above leads to an exit left onto a slab. Follow the broken crack above to the top.

Caitlin's Climb	35m	E1+		2003

The slim groove to the right is quite hard for the grade.

(5b). Climb up to the crack (and gear) with difficulty. More hard moves gain easier ground. Carry on in the same line, overcoming an overlap, to the finishing slab.

The next routes are 30 metres right of ***Cave Gully***, on the ***Red Walls***; identified by a slender pinnacle/flake on the left and a steep right-to-left diagonal grass rake in the centre.

Of Beauty	22m	VS		2006

Takes the arête of the slender pinnacle/flake at the left end.

1 12m (4c). Climb the arête (the one facing Great End) to the summit. Descend to the neck and belay on blocks.

2 10m (4b). Climb the clean strip of wall between two mossy breaks to the top.

Tango Magenta	13m	MVS		2006

Start below and right of the bottom of the grass rake, at a 6 metre high trapezium-shaped wall surmounted by a block.

(4b). Climb the right side of the wall and move up left to the block; stand on this and climb the thin crack and wider crack above to finish.

Borrowed Time	9m	VS		2006

Takes the flying arête at the right end of the main red wall.

(4b). Climb the wall just left for a couple of metres, then move right onto the arête. Tiptoe up this to the top.

Just above and right of ***Borrowed Time*** lies another, smaller, wall.

Thee Groove	9m	VD		2006

Climb the V-groove, roughly in the centre of the wall, and the short wall above.

Ringing Flakes	9m	S		2006

The left-trending line of flakes just left of ***Thee Groove***.

Gable Crag

Grid reference:	**NY 212 105**	Altitude:	**800m**
Faces:	**North**	Approach:	**1hr 30 mins – 2 hrs**

Gable Crag is the extensive crag on the Ennerdale side of the summit of Great Gable, a superb high-level mountain crag with excellent buttresses of rock. The steep fellside below the crag gives an airy atmosphere on many of the routes. High in the centre of the crag is the classic *Engineer's Slabs*, a magnificent clean buttress and, despite the terminology 'slab', a steep wall with high quality and sustained routes, most of which follow well-protected cracks. Between the crack-lines however are a number of superb and intricate wall routes which require a high level of nerve and concentration. The other buttresses also offer some excellent routes which take a little more effort to reach. The crag requires a good spell of dry weather to come into condition. *Aaron's Slab* area gets the sun until midday while the main section of crag only gets the sun very late in the day, which can result in cold conditions. However it is the perfect shady place to climb on a hot summer's day. Some of the harder routes may require a moderate amount of cleaning, especially the bolder routes on *Engineer's Slabs*: this can easily be done by abseil.

Approaches:

The easiest approach is from the summit of **Honister Pass**. Follow the old tramway incline west up the hillside behind the quarry car park for one kilometre, then turn south onto a well-marked track that runs along the side of Grey Knotts. Keep on the main track below Brandreth then break off right to a small stile. Follow a vague path beyond the stile to join the lower path of **Moses Trod** which leads to Stone Cove below ***Gable Crag***. Climb directly up the boulder slope to the crag or follow a good path to Windy Gap and an easy traverse below the crag. (1hr 30mins).

Great Gable – from Seathwaite & Honister Pass

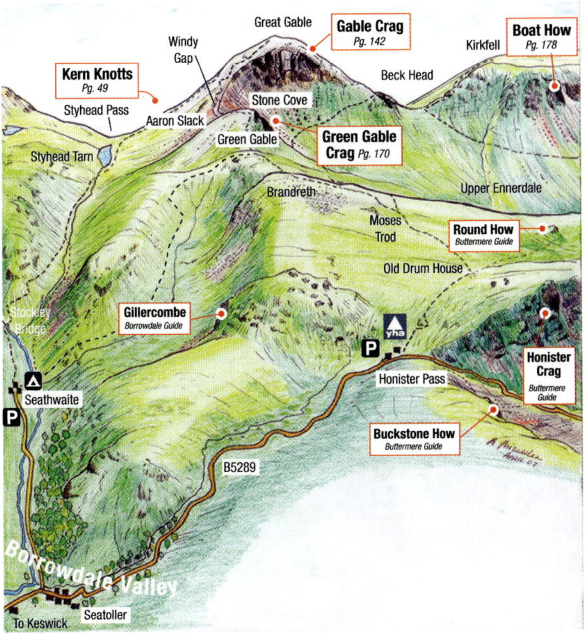

From **Wasdale Head**, follow the track to Burnthwaite, then take the Sty Head path. After the bridge over Gable Beck turn left and follow the Moses Trod path up the steep south-west shoulder of Great Gable (Gavel Neese). Just below the prominent Moses's Finger boulder, follow a rising traverse line leftwards across the scree to the col at Beck Head. Ascend the shoulder of Great Gable for 200 metres, where a narrow track (North Traverse) leads off left under ***Gable Crag***. (2hrs).

From **Seathwaite** take the path to Sty Head Tarn, then turn north up Aaron Slack to the col of Windy Gap. A short descent leads to the North Traverse path below ***Gable Crag***. (2hrs).

From **Black Sail Youth Hostel** an easy walk leads to Stone Cove and Windy Gap, then join the North Traverse below the crag. (1hr 30mins).

Descents:

Easy descents can be followed east or west down the walkers' paths around either end of the crag. This involves a long walk and the steep approach scramble for ***Engineer's Slabs*** has to be re-ascended. Another

Gable Crag

A Approaches to Slant Buttress (caution when wet)
B Bottle-Shaped Pinnacle
C Oblique Chimney
D Easy Sheep Walk (caution)
E Engineer's Slabs
F The Central Gully
G Sledgate Ridge area
H Smuggler's Chimney
K Barney Buttress
P Prayer Mat Buttress
S Slant Buttress
W Windy Ridge

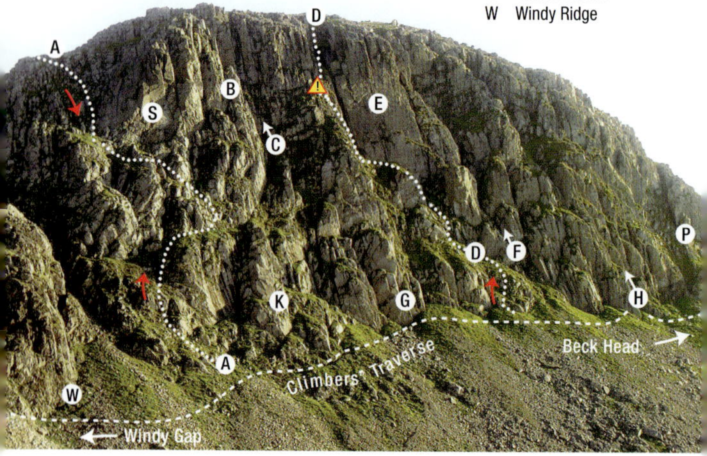

alternative is to descend the precarious *Easy Sheep Walk*. Various abseils can be used from some routes; a spare sling or length of old rope should be taken.

The routes are described from **left** to **right**.

Windy Ridge	37m	S		1944

This climb lies on the isolated buttress nearest to *Windy Gap*, with a wide scree gully on its left and a narrow scree gully on the right. 10 metres up and right of the toe of the buttress are two open grassy grooves 3 metres apart. This climb starts up the left-hand one.

1 23m (4a). Gain the groove from the right and follow it awkwardly, using the rib on the right, to a ledge. Climb up a steep wall to another ledge, then follow the steep groove above on indispensable but disposable holds to a grass ledge.

2 14m. Step left and follow the slabby ridge (some loose blocks), until scrambling leads to the top. Descend the rake leading rightwards into the narrow scree gully.

Marie Celeste	34m	MVS		2006

Good climbing up the groove and slab just right of *Windy Ridge*. Start as for that climb.

1 20m (4a). Climb the rib on the right of the right-hand open grassy groove to a sloping ledge on the left. Move right and follow the steep shelving groove, using holds on its right wall, to a good ledge.

2 14m (4b). Step right to below a recently created pink-hued slab. Go up a crack in the slab, past the overlap (crux), to a short rib leading to easier ground. Scrambling leads to the descent rake on the right.

Coronet	24m	MVS		2005

The fine diamond-shaped slab high on the right flank of *Windy Ridge*. Start at the left-hand end of a steep wall, 40 metres up the narrow scree gully.

1 12m (4a). Climb up using hollow holds and skirt a block on its right. Move up easier rock to a grass stance below a roof barring access to the slab.

2 12m (4a). Pull over the roof to gain the sinuous cracks in the slab. Follow the slab on excellent rock, keeping just left of the cracks to the top. **Descend** by moving up and crossing easy slabs rightwards into the narrow scree gully.

Slant Buttress

The next climbs are situated on the buttress high at the left end of the crag. The striking diagonal ramp-line of *The Slant* can be easily identified. This area is well worth the extra effort to reach as the routes have great atmosphere. The best approach is by descending the wide grassy gully left (right looking out) of the buttress. The approach from below requires care especially when wet. There is a good abseil thread at the top of the buttress.

Aaron's Slab	39m	MVS		1959

Start at the foot of a clean slab, 5 metres left of the start of *Mallory's Left-Hand Route*.

1 27m. Climb the slab, firstly in its centre, then by its right-hand edge, to a small grass ledge. Follow the slab above to a large ledge.

2 12m. Traverse left and climb either the steep crack, or the steep left edge of the wall.

Mallory's Left-Hand Route	30m	VD		1908

Start at the left-hand edge of the buttress, to the right of a large detached block, at the left end of an obvious diagonal flake crack.

Gable Crag
Slant Buttress

1 The Serpent E1
2 Vindolanda E4**
3 The Slant E2*
4 Mallory's Right-Hand Route MVS
5 The Bandersnatch HVS
6 Potheen MVS
7 Barney Buttress VD

Photo: Al Phizacklea

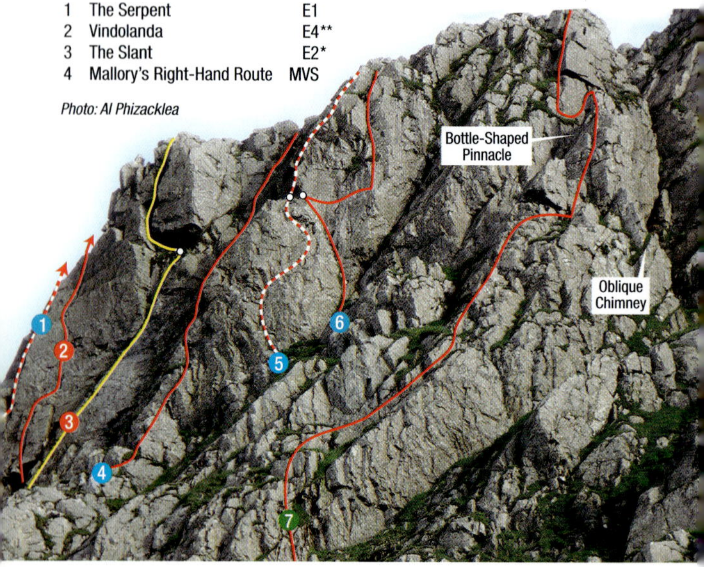

1 **12m.** Pull up onto the wall and climb the diagonal crack to a small ledge on the right.

2 **18m.** Step left and climb the slab for 12 metres to where a short difficult traverse right to a large block leads to easier rocks and a good ledge. Easy scrambling to the top.

The Serpent	32m	E1		1970

A slippery customer. Start at the obvious left to right curving crack.

1 **20m (5b).** The crack that is both awkward and strenuous is followed, trending right into the niche above. It is also possible to gain this niche by traversing in from *The Slant*.

2 **12m (5a).** Climb the crack above the slab, through the overhang, to the top.

Vindolanda	35m	E4	**	1974

The prominent steep crack-line at the left end of the crag gives a sustained and difficult exercise in jamming. The original start gained the crack leftwards from *The Slant*.

(6a). Climb the awkward slot through the roof below and left of the main hanging crack. Move right and ascend the crack with difficulty past a small pod to reach a slab. Climb the slab and corner to easy ground and a belay.

The Slant	45m	E2-	★	1968

A fine route in a tremendous position which takes the obvious gangway and groove. The route has suffered from neglect over the years but is worth seeking out in a dry spell. Start below the bulging wall, just left of the gangway.

1 30m (5b). Climb the bulging wall, pull onto the bottom of the sloping gangway and follow this to a flake crack below an obvious V-groove. Enter the groove, which is often wet and very mossy (crux), and climb it to a large stance on the right.

2 15m (5a). Traverse 3 metres left to the impressive chimney/groove and climb it to the top, passing an overhang at half height.

Mallory's Right-Hand Route	37m	MVS		1908

Start at the right-hand end of the buttress below a steep crack.

1 30m (4a). Easy rocks on the right lead to the bottom of a crack. Climb the strenuous crack to a ledge and loose rocks.

2 7m. The loose grassy chimney leads to the top.

Variation Start 30m MVS 1968

A better start to the route.

1 (4a). Climb a slab on the left by an upward diagonal traverse to a flake crack on the right. Follow this to the main crack.

The Bandersnatch	47m	HVS		1970

An interesting route on steep clean rock to the right of *Mallory's Right-Hand Route*. Start 10 metres right and up from *Mallory's Right-Hand Route* below a steep groove

1 22m (5a). Enter the groove from the right (long reach) and climb it exiting right, then go diagonally right up steep slabs to the edge of the buttress. Traverse left below the overhang then climb straight up to a grass ledge.

2 25m (4c). The arête above is climbed, first on the right, then on the left, via a huge block to the top.

Potheen	40m	MVS		1970

Start at an open grassy chimney, 10 metres above and right of *The Bandersnatch*.

1 10m. Climb the easy grassy chimney and crack to belay as for Pitch 1 of *The Bandersnatch*.

2 30m (4b). Descend 2 metres, traverse right across slabs to an arête, and climb straight up to below a steep crack. Climb it, and the short groove above to the top.

The next two routes start at the small buttress at the base of the crag, approximately 50 metres right of ***Windy Ridge*** and 12 metres above the path.

Barney Buttress	160m	VD		1939

The longest route hereabouts. Start below a narrow slabby buttress which is bounded by a broad grassy bay on the left (cairn).

1 10m. An easy buttress to a broad grass ledge.
2 13m. Climb the steep wall ahead by an obvious curving crack. At its top move back right and follow an arête to a rock crevasse.
3 25m. Step over the crevasse and scramble easily up grass to the upper ridge.
4 20m. Start down on the left of a sharp rock rib and continue straight up.
5 20m. Follow a comfortably inclined slab on the right with good holds bearing right at the top. Move up to belay below a grassy corner.
6 18m. Move 3 metres right and up to a wedge-shaped block. Continue up to belays below a huge impending block.
7 7m. Climb the steep gully on the right to a stance behind the block.
8 15m. A loose vertical crack followed by a steep slab leads to the top of the ***Bottle-Shaped Pinnacle***.
9 3m. Make an awkward descent into the gap.
10 18m. Follow the ridge ahead to reach a gully. Go up this for a metre or so before traversing rightwards out to the exposed rib which leads to a ledge.
11 11m. Continue up the ridge to the top.

Variations

There are easier alternatives on the right to Pitches 2, 4 and 7.

Mayan Slab	30m	S		2005

Start 3 metres to the right of ***Barney Buttress***.

1 10m (4a). Climb the slabs to a grassy stance: belay on the right.
2 20m (4a). Move up the groove above for 4 metres, then step left to follow slabby ramps up the wall on the left. At the crevasse just above, stride across to the right and move around into a hidden groove. Up this to the top. **Descend** by crossing the grassy gully on the left then follow the grass ramp down leftwards.

Oblique Chimney Area

The next three routes start from a grassy area high above the base of the crag. This is reached by a long difficult scramble up steep grass or by ascending the *Easy Sheep Walk* and traversing in.

Oblique Chimney	23m	VD		1892

The chimney situated high on the crag to the right of the ***Bottle-Shaped Pinnacle***.

Climb the right wall of the chimney, passing two caves, to exit right at the top onto scree. Belay well back.

On the lower right wall of ***Oblique Chimney*** is a large, but fading, rock-fall scar. The following route starts just right of this from approximately the same height as the base of the ***Bottle-Shaped Pinnacle*** and some 6 metres right of ***Oblique Chimney***.

Corkscrew Slabs	53m	VS		1958

1 **18m.** Easy rocks and grassy scrambling right of the rock scar lead to a grass ledge with a wide crack on the left. Climb the crack to another ledge.

2 **35m (4b).** Traverse left, climb the groove, then make a delicate ascending traverse across slabs on the right to a small ledge below the bulge, which is passed on the right to steep but easier ground.

Moonshiner	40m	HS		1958

The short steep wall 6 metres left of the ridge taken by the ***Easy Sheep Walk*** descent. Start at a rib, 5 metres left of a large flake.

1 **15m.** Climb the rib to a grass ledge.

2 **25m.** Step onto the rib above from the right and climb directly up to a small grass ledge below a crack. Step left onto a small ledge and then climb up, trending right to the top.

Sledgate Ridge Area

The next three climbs are on a small clean buttress right next to the path and 15 metres left of the distinctive jamming crack of *Sledgate Ridge*. **Descent** from these routes is down a steep grassy gully on the left.

Jongleur Wall	16m	E1		2006

The left wall; fine wall climbing with sketchy protection. Start just slightly left of, and 5 metres below, a cluster of loose flakes.

Gable Crag

Central Area

1	Jongleur Wall	E1
2	Troubadour	MVS
3	Inca Grooves	S
4	The Slay Ride	E3 *
5	Sledgate Ridge	HS **
6	Cerca Trova	VS
7	Moonshiner	HS
8	Engineer's Chimney	VS
9	Trundle Ridge	VS
A	Abseil	
S	Easy Sheep Walk approach/descent	

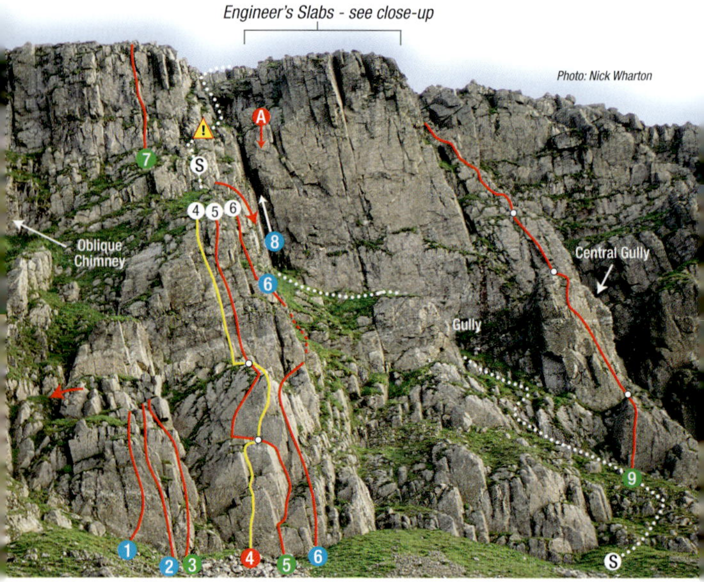

(5a). Climb diagonally rightwards up the wall to below the flakes. Move up and right to gain a ledge then continue up the wall to the top.

Troubadour	15m	MVS		2006

The blunt right arête of the buttress.

(4b). Climb directly up the arête finishing up the hand-sized crack.

Inca Grooves	22m	S		2005

A series of grooves up the right side of the buttress.

(4a). Follow the right side of the crack for 4 metres then move right up a slab to reach a grassy recess. Step right and climb a flake crack up rightwards into a corner, making a stiff pull out at its top. Follow rough rock to finish.

The following climbs start below the slim buttress of rock that runs from just above the path to below and left of the main central wall of *Engineer's Slabs*. Any of them makes an excellent approach to the routes on *Engineer's Slabs*.

The Slay Ride	75m	E3	★	1988

Interesting climbing with a very bold first pitch. Start 3 metres left of the obvious crack of ***Sledgate Ridge***.

1 **25m (5c).** Gain a small ledge, move right to a hollow flake, then climb the steep wall above to a ledge. Climb the diagonal crack above which leads to a large ledge and belay in a little bay on the right (junction with ***Sledgate Ridge***).
2 **20m (5c).** The thin crack leads via a very long reach to an easy arête which runs to a large grass ledge.
3 **30m (5b).** A small ramp leads to the left-hand crack which is followed to a horizontal break. Climb the arête above to where it ends and then cross a square groove on the right to a belay.

Sledgate Ridge	73m	HS	★★	1958

Three fine pitches. Start at the obvious crack (crux) in the steep little wall.

1 **20m (4b).** The difficult crack can be avoided by an easy chimney on the right – but you would only feel guilty! The water worn grooves on the right are followed for 10 metres, then the wall on the left to a large ledge.
2 **18m.** From the left end of the ledge climb the wall, then grassy slabs on the right to a large grass platform.
3 **35m.** Climb the wall above to a ledge below three vertical cracks. The central crack leads to the top. A scramble across rightwards and a descent of a short gully leads to the foot of ***Engineer's Slabs***.

Cerca Trova	62m	VS		2006

Good sustained climbing up a series of cracks in the right side wall of ***Sledgate Ridge***. Start one metre right of the easy chimney start to ***Sledgate Ridge***.

1 **20m (4b).** Climb the thin crack and rib to a ledge. Follow easier slabs and a wall to reach a small triangular grass ledge just below and right of a short crack with a pinnacle at its base.
2 **12m (4b).** Step left and climb the short crack and the fine scooped wall above to gain a large terrace. Scramble up right to a large flake on the right edge of the wall.
3 **14m (4b).** The proper way may be up the chimney on the left but this is very mossy. Instead, clamber over the flake and hand-traverse rightwards onto the side wall from where thin cracks and a wider crack above lead to a ledge with blocks.

Gable Crag

Engineer's Slabs Area

1	Engineer's Chimney	VS
2	Powder Finger	E3 **
3	Dream Twister	E3 **
4	The Troll	HVS *
5	The Angel of Mercy	E1 **
6	Interceptor	VS **
7	Snicker Snack	E3 ***
8	Engineer's Slabs	VS ***
V	Left-Hand Finish	VS
9	Mome Rath	E2 *
10	The Tombstone	E3 *
11	The Tomb	E2 ***
12	Sarcophagus	E3 ***
13	Unfinished Arête	HVS *
14	The Jabberwock	HVS **

A Abseil

Photo: Al Phizacklea

4 16m (4a). Climb the groove on the left, then follow easier grooves slightly to the right, to reach the top of ***Sledgate Ridge***. Scramble up for 30 metres to reach the ***Easy Sheep Walk*** descent route.

Engineer's Slabs Area

The following routes are all situated on the main central wall that starts about half way up the crag, with the dark cleft of *Engineer's Chimney* at its left-hand end and the sharp arête of *Unfinished Arête* on its right. The best approach is by scrambling up steep broken ground to the right of a small broken buttress directly below the wall, or use *Sledgate Ridge* or one of its neighbours as a warm up route.

Descents:

For teams wishing to climb a second route on the wall, it is possible to descend the precarious **Easy Sheep Walk** (M, 1890) which follows steep broken ground to the left of ***Engineer's Chimney*** (on the right if facing out). Many teams also abseil from gear (check first) from a ledge above the left side of the face (above and right of ***Engineer's Chimney***). Care should be taken at the top to avoid dislodging blocks. There is also an abseil from the very top of ***Sarcophagus***, but this is only practical if you have 60 metre ropes.

Engineer's Chimney	36m	VS		1899

The deep cleft which bounds the left side of ***Engineer's Slabs*** gives a traditional and difficult chimney climb.

1 16m. Easy climbing leads to where the chimney divides.

2 20m (4a). Climb the left-hand branch of the chimney, using the left wall as required, until a strenuous pull through the narrows gives access to the wider chimney above. Climb past a chockstone to a crack in the left wall which is followed to the top. The narrow section of the chimney can be avoided on the left wall by an ascending traverse to a large flake and back again above the crux.

Powder Finger	45m	E3+	★★	1987

A technical route up the slim hanging groove just right of ***Engineer's Chimney***. Start from a grass ledge 3 metres right of ***Engineer's Chimney***.

(6a). Easy rocks lead to a ledge and loose blocks. An awkward pull into the groove on the left is followed by sustained climbing up to the overhang, then step right onto the arête and gain a rest point (thin tape on spike). Move up to a poor flake (another thin tape here, but difficult to arrange), then make some committing and strenuous moves rightwards over the bulge to a good hold on ***Dream Twister***.

From a standing position on this hold, traverse back left and up to a crack (junction with ***Spirit Level***), then continue left into a shallow groove, which leads to the top (beware rope drag).

Dream Twister	45m	E3-	★★	1987

Fine open well-protected climbing with a sustained crux section. Start as for *Powder Finger*.

(5c). Easy rocks lead to a ledge and loose blocks. Pull into the groove on the left, exiting right at the top onto the wall and a good ledge. Climb the wall direct to the overhang. Pull over this using the crack above, moving left at its top into a wider crack curving rightwards to a good ledge. The short crack above leads to a large grass ledge and thread belay.

Spirit Level	92m	E1+	★★	1971

A traverse across the main wall of ***Engineer's Slabs***, providing a good route of contrasting pitches on excellent rock. Care is required to protect the second. If the first pitch is wet, it can be avoided by climbing ***Dream Twister*** to a junction with the ***Spirit Level*** traverse line.

1 22m (4a). Climb ***Engineer's Chimney*** moving out left to a ledge and belay.

2 13m (5b). Difficult moves lead across the overhang on the right to the edge. Climb the crack above for 6 metres, then traverse right, crossing ***Dream Twister***, to a stance on ***The Troll*** (above the block overhang).

3 10m (5a). Traverse horizontally right, crossing ***The Angel of Mercy***, then continue diagonally right to join ***Interceptor*** at the short traverse on Pitch 2. Reverse the traverse and groove of ***Interceptor*** down to the sentry box belay.

4 10m (5b). Traverse right, crossing ***Engineer's Slabs***, onto a blank section of the wall above the overlap. Delicate and worrying moves now lead to ***Sarcophagus***, followed by easier climbing to a stance on Pitch 2 of ***The Tomb***.

5 12m. Easy climbing right and up leads to the sloping ledge on ***The Jabberwock***.

6 25m (4c). Pitch 3 of ***The Jabberwock***.

The Troll	60m	HVS	★	1967

To the right of ***Dream Twister*** is an obvious jammed block overhang about 25 metres up the face. Start directly below the block.

Left: Nick Wharton delicately laybacking **Dream Twister** (E3), Gable Crag.
Photo: Al Phizacklea

1 28m (5b). Climb the wall on small but good holds (some suspect) to the block overhang. The crack on its right leads with difficulty to a ledge.

2 32m (5a). Step right and climb the steep slabs for 12 metres to a break, then traverse right, making awkward moves into the flake-line of ***Snicker Snack***. Follow this then step right into a groove just left of ***Interceptor*** that leads to the top.

The Angel of Mercy	60m	E1+	★★	1979

To the right, and above the roof of ***The Troll***, is a steep wall split by a crack which provides the crux pitch of this fine route. Start as for ***The Troll***.

1 25m (5a). Follow Pitch 1 of ***The Troll*** to a nut belay below the roof.

2 35m (5b). Move up and traverse rightwards across the sandwiched slab to gain the crack. Follow the crack, which gives excellent climbing, to where the angle eases, then climb the ramp up and right to below a wide overhanging crack splitting the headwall. Difficult moves lead up the crack to the top.

Variation Start 25m HVS- 2006

1 25m (5a). Start as for ***Interceptor***. Climb directly past two grass ledges and follow a thin crack to below the roof, then step left to the belay.

Interceptor	65m	VS+	★★	1967

An excellent companion climb to ***Engineer's Slabs*** and of a similar grade. It works its way through the overhangs between ***Snicker Snack*** and ***Engineer's Slabs***, starting about 3 metres left of the start of those two routes.

1 30m (4c). An awkward pitch with difficult route finding. Climb up to the left end of a grass ledge, then straight up to gain another grass ledge at its right end. An ascending traverse right on small holds leads to the twin cracks of ***Engineer's Slabs*** and the sentry box (care should be taken to protect the second).

2 15m (4c). Climb straight up the groove-line above to the overhangs, traverse left into two parallel cracks (***Snicker Snack***) and climb these to a stance by a huge flake.

3 20m (4c). Layback the flake, traverse right to a groove, and climb it until a prominent spike on the right can be reached. Climb the rib to the top.

Snicker Snack	57m	E3-	★★★	1986

Superb well-protected climbing taking the thin crack-line up the steep wall between ***The Angel of Mercy*** and ***Engineer's Slabs***. Start in the middle of the wall as for ***Engineer's Slabs***.

Right: Angela Soper and Val Hennelly soaking up the atmosphere on **The Angel of Mercy** (E1), Gable Crag. **Photo:** Mark Gear

1 45m (5c). Climb the wall of ***Engineer's Slabs*** for 12 metres, step left and follow the straight crack through the overlap, then continue up the thin crack-line above to belay at the huge flake of ***Interceptor***.

2 12m (5b). Climb the flake, traverse right and surmount a small overhang to gain a thin crack about 3 metres left of the finishing groove of ***Interceptor*** and follow this to an awkward finish.

Engineer's Slabs | 60m | VS | ★★★ | 1934

An outstanding Lakeland climb of great character, taking the obvious crack and groove-line up the centre of the wall. Start just left of a groove in the middle of the face.

Above: Mark Gear bridging up the V-groove at the top of **Engineer's Slabs** (VS), Gable Crag. **Photo:** Paul Hennelly

1 26m (4c). The wall leads past a small pinnacle to the foot of a crack. Climb the crack for 5 metres to twin cracks on the right which lead to a chimney and sentry box.

2 34m (4c). Traverse right for 2 metres into a crack and climb this for 8 metres to a ledge, followed by a layback crack to a good ledge. The chimney above gives access to the fine groove that leads to the top. Many teams avoid the classic delights of this final groove by following the ***Left-Hand Finish*** up the jagged crack on its left wall. This leads to the arête and a junction with ***Interceptor*** at the spike, then up the ridge above – but doesn't entitle you to tick the route!

Mome Rath | 58m | E2 | ★ | 1989

A direct route up the broken crack-line running down from the final groove of ***Engineer's Slabs***, with a wild finish up the impressive hanging rib. Start just right of ***Engineer's Slabs***.

1 33m (5b). Climb the poorly protected wall onto easier ground that leads over ledges to the base of the crack-line. Follow the crack above, over some doubtful blocks, to the overhang, pull over strenuously, and follow the crack above to a junction with ***Engineer's Slabs***, and a belay at the foot of the layback crack.

2 25m (5c). Step left and climb the overhanging groove in a superb position exiting left at the top. Follow the break-line above over flakes to a junction with ***Interceptor*** which is followed to the top.

The Tombstone	64m	E3	★	1988

Bold and serious climbing with the second and third pitches taking the steep wall just left of *The Jabberwock*. Start 4 metres right of *Engineer's Slabs*.

1 15m (5b). Climb diagonally right to gain a sloping ledge. From this, follow a line of good holds which lead up and right, crossing *The Tomb*, to the large flake belay on *Sarcophagus*. A poorly protected pitch.

2 22m (5c). Step off the top of the flake and climb directly to the overlap (runners). Pull over this on small holds and make a difficult move up (skyhook runner) to gain a flake just left of the crack and below the big ledge of *The Jabberwock*. Move up to the big ledge then traverse left to a shallow groove which leads to a good belay on *The Tomb*.

3 27m (5b). Climb the wide crack above for 10 metres, step right and climb the flake to a bottomless black sentry box. Pull out right onto *The Tombstone* to join the top pitch of *The Jabberwock*, then traverse left immediately, utilizing a doubtful block to finish up a crack.

The Tomb	68m	E2+	★★★	1966

Another high quality route that requires a confident approach, with good but widely spaced protection. Start 5 metres right of *Engineer's Slabs*.

1 18m (4c). Traverse right and up to gain the obvious sentry box. Climb this, and the wall above leftwards to a ledge, then step left to belay below a break.

2 20m (5c). The wall on the left is climbed on small holds for 6 metres to a rest point (protection slot above). Move right under the overlap to its end (where protection is possible but can be strenuous to place). Pull through the overlap onto a small ledge and traverse right into a steep crack which leads to a good stance. The overlap can be avoided by climbing the left wall until it is possible to traverse back right above it.

3 30m (5a). Climb the groove above to the overhang and step left into the open groove which leads to the top.

Sarcophagus	64m	E3	★★★	1977

A technically absorbing face climb which ascends the blank wall below the traverse of *The Tomb*, then the overhang and break above. The route requires steady nerves on its poorly protected second pitch. Start as for *The Tomb*.

1 18m (4c). As for Pitch 1 of *The Tomb* to the sentry box. Climb up stepping right from the wall above to a large flake.

2 18m (5c). Step up left to a small block at the right end of a grass ledge. Step off the block and make a series of increasingly committing

moves up the wall to join ***The Tomb*** at the end of the traverse. Move left to a thin crack, climb up to the overlap (good runners) and pull over strenuously, stepping right onto a narrow ledge (small nut belays). An exciting pitch.

3 28m (5b). Move up and left into a groove/crack-line. Follow this and jam the crack above, to finish up a groove left of the groove on ***The Tomb***.

Unfinished Arête	63m	HVS	★	1934

Interesting climbing up the obvious arête that marks the right edge of the face. Start just right of ***The Tomb***, where the grass ledge begins to fall away to the right.

1 15m (4b). Traverse right to below a sentry box. Climb up and right to a small groove that leads to a grass ledge below the arête.

2 23m (5a). Climb the arête to a small overlap. Traverse right, then up to a grass ledge. Continue up the arête to a sloping ledge with shattered blocks (junction with ***The Jabberwock***). A bold pitch.

3 25m (4c). As for Pitch 3 of ***The Jabberwock***.

The Jabberwock	75m	HVS	★★	1970

An excellent route with a wild finish: it takes the obvious steep crack and grooved headwall at the right end of the face. Start from the lowest point of the wall, just right of the final gully on the approach scramble.

1 22m (4c). Climb the cracked wall to ledges on the right of a large flake.

2 28m (5a). Climb the crack, passing a large ledge at 18 metres, to a sloping ledge and shattered blocks (junction with ***Unfinished Arête***).

3 25m (4c). The short slab on the left leads to a very exposed groove which is climbed to the top on good holds (**beware loose blocks**).

Above: Paul Hennelly leading the top pitch of **The Jabberwock** (HVS), Gable Crag. **Photo:** Mark Gear

Left: Dan Varian eyeballs the next hold on **The Tomb** (E2), Gable Crag. **Photo:** Mark Magas

The next climb takes a crack in the upper west face of a large pinnacle in the upper left-hand side of *Central Gully*. Access to the pinnacle is from the top of the *Engineer's Slabs* face by scrambling up and right for 50 metres until above and right of the pinnacle (which is easily identified by having several blocks perched on its top). Abseil down the gully on its right-hand side to a grass terrace situated just below and right of the crack.

The Short Crack	12m	HVS		1988

A good bit of contrived fun.

(5b). Traverse left on sloping holds to gain the crack, and go up it to the top on excellent jams.

Returning to the bottom of the crag:

Trundle Ridge	75m	VS		1970

A pleasant climb up the left-bounding rib of *Central Gully*. Start a few metres up and left of the lowest rocks of the ridge in a grassy corner below a steep wall split by a thin crack.

1 15m (4b). Climb the wall just right of the crack to a grass saddle.
2 25m (4b). Behind the saddle is a slab. Climb the slab, then continue up a steep crack to the top of the square-cut tower (rock requires care).
3 10m. Descend a few metres and cross a chimney by a jammed block, then scramble up to a grass ledge and block belay on the left.
4 25m (4b). From the right end of the stance step right and gain the arête. Climb the arête for 2 metres then move left onto the cracked slabs. These are followed until moves back right regain the arête, which leads to a large stance. The top of the crag is reached after 60 metres of scrambling.

The Central Gully – Direct Finish	70m	VD		1896

The large broken gully right of *Engineer's Slabs* provides an easy scramble to the top of the crags. There are a few pitches of Difficult standard and the top crack, if climbed direct, is Very Difficult, but all difficulties can be avoided on the left. In winter the route can be transformed to star quality status.

Heinz Route	170m	S		1947

The broken right-bounding buttress of *Central Gully* is full of variety, but not recommended. In its lower section the route takes in a large pinnacle before bearing off left, following a series of ledges and chimneys to the top.

Right: Climbers on **Engineer's Slabs** (VS), left and **The Jabberwock** (HVS).
Photo: Phil Rigby

Gable Crag

Smuggler's Chimney Area

1	Nothing To Declare	E2 *
2	Smuggler's Chimney	VS **
3	American Dream	S
4	Smaug	HVS *
5	Guest Appearance	HVS
6	Sundowner	S
7	Strike While It's Hot	E1

Photo: Al Phizacklea

Smuggler's Chimney Area

Nothing to Declare	50m	E2	★	1988

Although the climbing is a little disjointed, each pitch is on excellent rock and has something to offer. Start just left of ***Smuggler's Chimney*** at the base of a clean slab.

1 10m (5a). Climb the slab trending left to gain a crack on the left edge at mid-height (runners); step right and continue delicately to a large ledge.

2 25m (5b). From the right-hand side of the ledge, step right and climb a thin crack for 5 metres, then pull out right on the wall to gain a good ledge. From the right-hand side of the ledge, make a very long stretch up to a flake which leads back left to another ledge on the bulging wall. The short pillar on the left leads to a large terrace. Belay a long way back.

3 15m (5a). From the foot of a small gully (the true continuation to *Smuggler's Chimney*), climb up and right to stand on a cluster of

spikes. Step up and swing back left round the rib, then continue up a cracked wall passing a niche to a block belay.

Smuggler's Chimney	37m	VS	★★	1909

Otherwise known as Struggler's Chimney! An absolute must for the small die-hard masochistic traditionalist. Start below the deep narrow cleft.

A sketch in the ***Wasdale Climbing Book of Gable Crag*** in 1890 by Lakeland legend John Robinson shows a walled enclosure, formerly a small hut, used by whisky/graphite smugglers. The enclosure is shown in the area high above ***Smuggler's Chimney***. Find it if you can!

1 10m (4a). Climb to the foot of the chimney either by the flake on the right or a crack on the left. Both ways are rather vegetated.

2 27m (4c). The inside of the narrow chimney is climbed with difficulty to a large terrace.

American Dream	82m	S		1988

Start at the foot of the ridge, 10 metres right of *Smuggler's Chimney*.

1 30m. Climb the pleasant ridge to a large sloping grassy recess below a steep wall.

2 32m. Climb the wall by a crack on the left then, just below a grass ledge, swing left on good holds to regain the ridge. Continue up the ridge to belay below a small square-shaped buttress with a chimney on its right.

3 20m. From the right, climb a ramp to gain a flat pinnacle below the chimney. From the pinnacle, either climb the chimney direct or step right round a bulge to a good ledge and easy ground.

Smaug	63m	HVS+	★	1988

Start about 12 metres up and right of *American Dream*, just right of a steep dirty green corner. Very good and varied climbing; the last pitch taking the wide crack high up.

1 40m (5a). Scramble up to the base of a V-groove, then move left and climb the obvious crack in the slab on the left to its top. Belay below the rib.

2 15m (5b). Step right and climb the thin crack just right of the rib to below a steep crack.

3 8m (4c). Climb the excellent overhanging off-width jam crack to the top (big Friends useful - especially those willing to give a helping shove!).

The following route is on the final small buttress starting 10 metres left of the foot of the open grassy gully that comes down from behind *Prayer Mat Buttress*.

Guest Appearance	27m	HVS		2006

Good climbing once the rather dirty start has been overcome. Start below the scooped recessed slab.

(5a). Climb into the corner on the right then traverse delicately left across the scoop to the arête. Follow this to the top.

Sundowner	50m	S		1958

A very overgrown climb wandering up the buttress left of the scree gully that separates ***Prayer Mat Buttress*** from the rest of the crag. Start well to the right of and up from ***Smaug***, below a steep prominent slab with a chimney on its right.

1 30m. Climb the left end of the slab to a grassy groove that splits the slab diagonally. Follow the groove rightwards, step across the top of a chimney and go up to a grass ledge below a crack. Traverse up and left round a corner, then climb directly up to a grass ledge.

2 20m. The slab above leads to a rake trending left. Leave the rake on the right and climb grass to a corner below a chimney containing fangs of rock. Ignoring the fangs, climb the surprisingly pleasant corner to an exit rightwards at the top.

Strike While It's Hot	22m	E1		1988

Left of ***Doctor's Chimney*** is a very steep mossy corner capped by a large roof, access to the bottom being over steep grass and connecting ledges.

(5b). Climb the overhanging corner to the roof. Strenuous moves on good jams lead through the roof until a step left can be made onto easier ground and into the break-line above.

Doctor's Chimney	30m	VD	★	1896

Between ***Prayer Mat Buttress*** and the main crag there is a steep scree gully: this chimney lies approximately 50 metres up this on the left. A real classic of the genre; climbing walls will not prepare you for this one!

Climb the chimney to a horizontal spike. Face right, move up and pull out right onto a pinnacle. Continue by a combination of bridging and back and footing to the top, taking care not to dislodge loose stones.

Prayer Mat Buttress

The most westerly buttress on *Gable Crag*.

Solenelle	25m	VS	★	2005

The crack immediately left of the steep wall left of ***Prayer Mat Buttress*** and right of a huge pinnacle. Start 11 metres left of ***Prayer Mat Buttress*** and scramble up for 8 metres to a slab at the foot of the wall.

Gable Crag

Prayer Mat Buttress

6	Sundowner	S		
7	Strike While It's Hot	E1		
8	Doctor's Chimney	VD	*
9	Solenelle	VS	*
10	Prayer Mat Buttress	VS	*
11	The Gable End	VS	
12	Notre Dame	MVS	*
13	End Zone	HVS	

(4b). Climb the slab trending left to reach the crack proper. Move up to a ledge on the left thus avoiding the grassy lower section. Step back right into the crack and follow it to the top.

Prayer Mat Buttress	30m	MVS	★	1926

A bold route starting from the lowest point of the buttress below an arête and just left of an iron spike.

(4b). Climb the arête to a small ledge at 10 metres. Awkward moves left lead to a sloping ledge, followed by an arête to a small rectangular ledge at 10 metres (the *Prayer Mat*). The overhanging corner on the right leads to a pleasant slab and the top (it is possible to go left from the *Prayer Mat* but this is not recommended).

Cloud inversion over Ennerdale with Kirk Fell and a misty Beck Head in the foreground.

The Gable End	25m	VS		1988

Start at the iron spike just right of ***Prayer Mat Buttress***. Fine open climbing.
(4b). Climb directly up to enter a short square-cut groove. Climb the groove, step right to a ledge, then go up the slab above direct to the top.

Notre Dame	25m	MVS	★	2005

A pleasant and direct route up the rib right of ***The Gable End***.
(4b). Climb the slabby wall, then the rib via a shallow groove. Continue directly up the arête to the top.

Photo: Tony Morley

End Zone	15m	HVS		1995

(5a). The slab 10 metres right of ***The Gable End***.

Transpire	16m	HS		2005

Opposite the top of ***Prayer Mat Buttress*** and across the scree gully is an arête with a thin crack running up its right-hand side.

(4a). Climb the thin crack up the arête, past a sentry-box, to a ledge. Make a steep pull into the niche above and continue to the finishing terrace.

Green Gable

by Barry Clarke & Phil Rigby

The climbing on Green Gable is all on *Green Gable Crags* at the head of the Ennerdale Valley and facing across towards *Gable Crag* on Great Gable.

Green Gable Crags

Grid reference:	**NY 214 106**	Altitude:	**750m**
Faces:	**West**	Approach:	**1hr 15 mins – 2 hrs**

These seldom frequented crags are situated far away from the crowds on the Ennerdale side of Green Gable, just below the summit. Although rather broken they provide some excellent lower grade mini-mountaineering routes in a stunning setting. The crag is quick drying and gets the sun from midday.

Approaches:

From **Honister Pass**, take the path behind the Youth Hostel over the summits of Grey Knotts, Brandreth, Gillercombe Head and over the top of Green Gable (1hr 15mins). Moses Trod can also be used but this involves a slog up scree at the end.

From **Seathwaite**, via Stockley Bridge, Sty Head Tarn, Aaron Slack and Windy Gap (2hrs). Alternatively, from **Seathwaite**, via Sour Milk Gill, Gillercombe, and over the summit of Green Gable (1hr 45mins).

From **Wasdale** ascend the Great Gable track to Beck Head via Gavel Neese and Moses Trod, then follow the cairned track up the north-west shoulder of Great Gable until a narrow track leads off left, the Climbers' Traverse, under *Gable Crag* to Windy Gap. Traverse the scree to the crag (2hrs).

From **Black Sail Youth Hostel**, an easy walk to Stone Cove and Windy Gap, then traverse the scree below the crag (1hr 30mins).

Descents:

The descents are on the left side of the crag except from the *Alpha Buttress*.

The routes are described from **right** to **left** i.e. from Windy Gap.

Green Gable Crags Right Side

1	Alpha	VD
2	Calculus	S
3	Omega	VD
4	Abacus	HVS *
5	Beta	VD
V	Beta variation	S
6	Gamma	D *
7	Delta	VS
8	Timshel	S

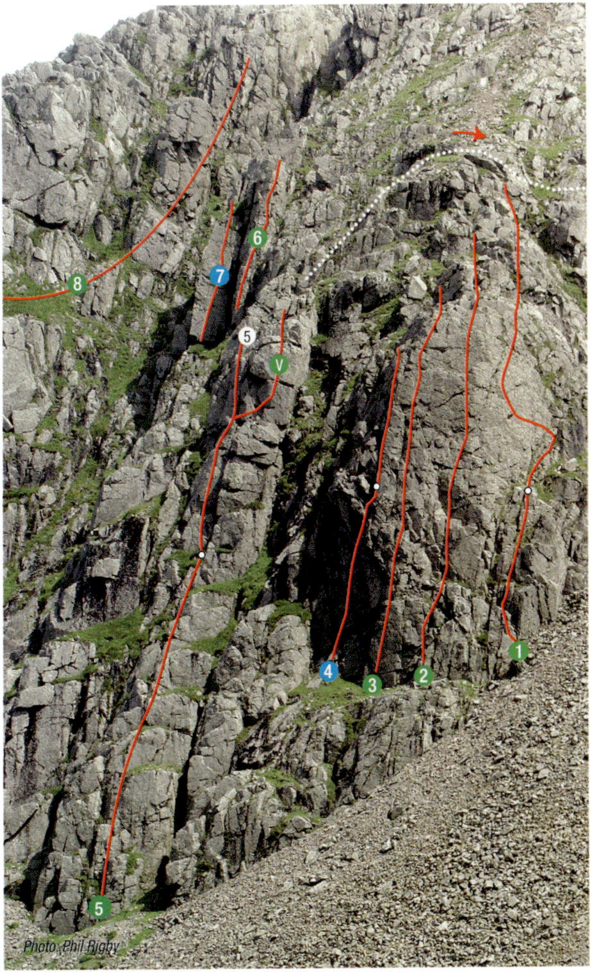

Alpha	30m	VD		1927

Start at the right-hand side of the first buttress.

1 20m. Climb the broken wall to a ledge and continue up to a platform: belay on the right.

2 10m. Retrace your steps for 2 metres and climb the steep wall on small but good holds, followed by easy climbing to the top.

Calculus	32m	S		1988

Five metres left of ***Alpha*** is a thin crack.

Climb the crack with difficulty to easier ground, which is followed direct to the top, finishing just left of ***Alpha***.

Omega	32m	VD		1988

Start at the left-hand edge of the buttress.

Follow the edge of the buttress, moving right below a broken overhang. The shallow groove above is climbed to a small overhang which is passed on the right to a ledge. Easy climbing to finish.

Abacus	35m	HVS	★	1988

A good route taking an impressive line on excellent rock. Start just left of ***Omega*** at a slab below a large overhang.

1 15m (5a). Climb the slab to the overhang, move right and pull round a rib to the bottom of a groove.

2 20m. Climb the arête.

Beta	40m	VD		1927

From ***Alpha***, walk downwards along the scree at the base of the crag: the start is on the left of a deeply cut chimney at the lowest point. The first pitch is broken, the second pitch rather better

1 25m. Climb the broken rib past an old peg. Scramble to the foot of a steep buttress.

2 15m. Gain a V-groove from the left and follow it to a good ledge. Climb the wall on the left of the small overhang to finish.

Variation S

2 15m. From the good ledge on Pitch 2, climb the wall on the right.

The next two routes start 35 metres up, on the right-hand side of the central wide grassy gully, below two small clean buttresses.

Gamma	20m	VD	★	1927

The narrow right-hand rib of steep rock: an excellent little route which makes a good upper continuation pitch to ***Beta***. It can be reached by scrambling leftwards from the top of ***Beta***.

Climb the rib to a ledge at 10 metres. Continue up the ridge to finish.

Green Gable Crags
Left Side

6	Gamma	VD*
7	Delta	VS
8	Timshel	S
9	Epsilon	MS*
10	Epsilon Chimney	D
11	Calaboose	S
12	Caleb	VD
13	Aaron	VS
14	Eta	MS
15	East of Eden	S
16	Fie	VS*
17	Green Peace	S
18	Theta	D
19	Arjuna	D
20	North Face	D

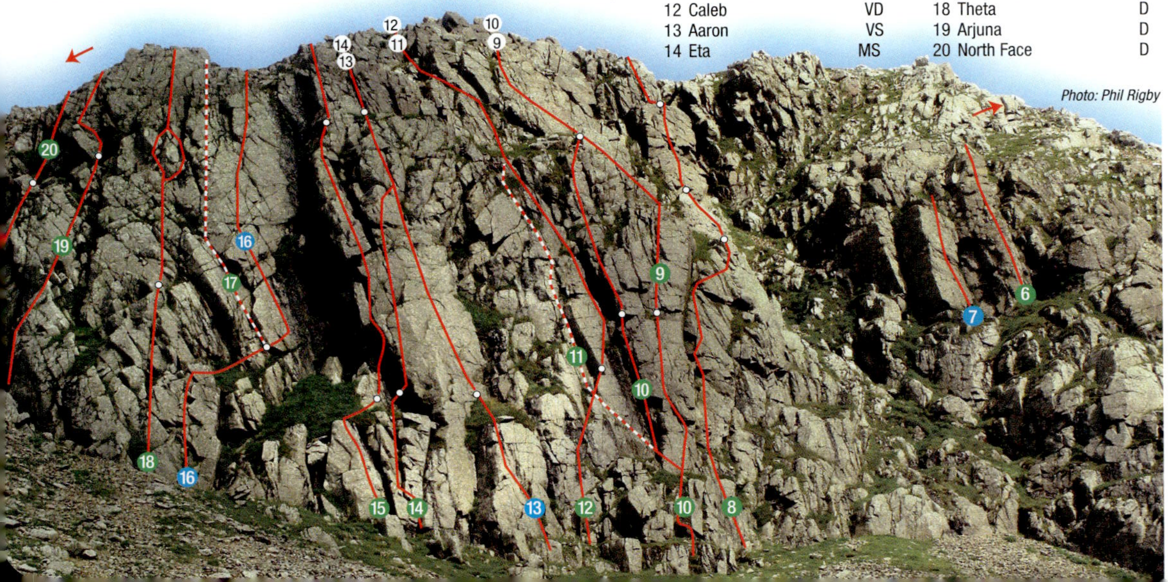

Photo: Phil Rigby

Delta	13m	VS		1928

(4b). The slab up the clean buttress left of *Gamma*. Steep, exposed and unprotected but a good pitch.

The next three routes are found by traversing left across the scree at the base of a wide grassy gully to a mass of slabs. The first route starts at a mossy slab 10 metres left of the gully and just right of a 4 metre high corner.

Timshel	80m	S		1988

An interesting expedition finishing on the summit of the mountain.

1 30m. Climb the mossy slab and corner-crack to gain the groove below the steep wall. Follow the groove, step right onto a slab, and then back left to a pinnacle. Traverse right for 3 metres to a flake and climb the wall to a grass ledge.
2 10m. Walk 10 metres up and right to belay near a smooth wall below a prominent buttress with an obvious central crack.
3 27m. Climb the smooth wall on its left to reach the buttress. Climb the centre of the buttress (beware hollow blocks) and the fine crack to finish. Belay well back on the left.
4 13m. A broken wall above is climbed at its centre.

Epsilon	60m	MS	★	1927

A good route with fine situations. Start at the foot of the first continuous slab.

1 20m. Climb the broken wall for 5 metres to a grass ledge. The slab above is climbed using a crack on the right, to a small grass ledge.
2 27m. After an awkward start, the slab above leads to a grass ledge. Continue up broken rocks to below a rough wall.
3 13m. From a small spike, climb the wall on good holds.

Epsilon Chimney	53m	D		1928

The cleft immediately left of *Epsilon* provides traditional chimney climbing. Better than it looks.

1 18m. Scramble up grassy rocks to the foot of the chimney. Climb the chimney past a chockstone to a good stance.
2 22m. Continue up the chimney past yet another chockstone to a ledge. The chimney, now having finished with you, allows the clean rib on the right to be climbed to the foot of a rough wall.
3 13m. As for Pitch 3 of *Epsilon*.

Calaboose	20m	S		2005

Pleasant wall and rib climbing, just left of ***Caleb***. Start by scrambling up to the foot of ***Epsilon Chimney***.

Step one metre left and climb the deceptive wall to the crevice below the corner-crack on ***Caleb***. Climb the left wall of the corner and the clean rib above to a ledge on the right. Use a diagonal crack to gain the arête on the left and, from the ledge just above, step left to finish nicely up the final rib and easier ground.

Eight metres left and below the foot of ***Epsilon Chimney*** is a small detached buttress taken by ***Aaron***. Three metres right of this is a broken wall where the following route starts.

Caleb	43m	VD		1988

1 18m. Climb the wall to a grassy ledge. Traverse 5 metres right to the obvious corner-crack.

2 25m. Step right and climb the steep wall immediately left of ***Epsilon Chimney***.

Aaron	47m	VS		1925

A good route with committing moves and little protection. Start at the middle of the small buttress.

1 12m (4b). Climb straight up, stepping left to finish up the edge to a grass ledge. Belay on the left wall.

2 35m (4b). Climb the wall above on good holds until an awkward move leads to a mantelshelf. Continue directly above to a ledge and by easier climbing to the ridge.

Eta	40m	MS		1927

Start 6 metres left of ***Aaron*** below a series of short broken ribs. Pitch 2 is a left-hand version of ***Aaron*** avoiding its tricky moves.

1 10m. Climb the rib in the centre to a large grassy recess; the lower one, not the one below the large mossy corner.

2 20m. Climb a rib on the right of the corner and up a rough slab. Step left onto a small rib and continue up until a traverse right is made onto a rock ledge.

3 10m. Climb the slab to finish.

East of Eden	48m	S		1988

Start at a wall just left of the broken ribs of ***Eta***.

1 10m. Climb the wall and break awkwardly out left at the top. Continue across to a large grassy recess on the right (on ***Eta***).

2 20m. Climb the small mossy slab above, followed by a short steep wall on the right, to a wide ledge on the front of the buttress. Go up to the overhang, step right into a chimney, then back left onto the ridge and up to a pinnacle.
3 18m. Climb easily up the broken arête.

Twelve metres left of the ribs containing ***Eta*** and ***East of Eden*** are broken slabs bounded by a steep grass bay on the right. The first slab marks the start of the next route.

Fie	45m	VS	★	1933

An excellent climb on good rock: start just right of the centre of the slab.
1 15m. Climb the slab to a grass ledge. Move 5 metres right to below a broken rib.
2 30m (4b). Climb the slab on the left of the moss to an overhang at 6 metres. Pass the overhang with the aid of a small crack just on the left and continue up the slab, trending to the right of a short arête. Finish up the right side of the arête.

Green Peace	45m	S		1988

Worthwhile for its second pitch. Start as for ***Fie***.
1 15m. As for Pitch 1 of ***Fie***.
2 30m. Move up right and climb the wide crack, passing left of the square overhang. Step right onto its top and climb the blunt arête on small holds to the top.

Theta	48m	D		1927

A pleasant route up the slab. Start at its centre, just left of ***Green Peace***.
1 18m. Climb the broken slab to a ledge. Continue up the slab on the left (crowned by a loose block) to a good stance.
2 30m. Follow the middle of the large broken slab to an overhang (which may be passed on either side) to a ledge. A short wall leads to the top.

Arjuna	38m	S		1988

Start at the left side of the crag at a broken wall, 3 metres below a small detached triangular spike.
1 25m. Climb the steep wall using a loose flake at 3 metres. Follow broken rocks to the foot of an obvious corner-groove on the right and continue up to the grassy corner below the overhanging chockstone.
2 13m. Pull up awkwardly and with caution on to the chockstone to gain good rock on the left wall. Finish up the arête.

Above: Pete Sterling and Ian Grimshaw battle the elements on **Alpha** (VD), Green Gable Crags. **Photo:** Stephen Reid

North Face	27m	D		1925

Seven metres above and left of *Arjuna* is a small buttress about level with the top of Pitch 1 of *Theta* and 3 metres right of a grassy gully.

1 **15m.** Climb the buttress to a niche. Move right and continue to a large grass ledge.

2 **12m.** Climb the mossy rib on the left wall of the large square overhang.

A **Girdle Traverse** of the crag (190m, VS or S, 1959) has been recorded going from right to left, but is not really worthwhile due to its disjointed nature: its description is on the FRCC website.

Kirk Fell

by Rick Graham, Al Phizacklea & Phil Rigby

All the climbing on Kirk Fell is situated on the north-east flank of mountain, overlooking the upper part of Ennerdale.

Boat How Crags

Grid reference: **NY 199 110** Altitude: **700m**
Faces: **North & West** Approach: **2 hrs–2hrs 15 mins**

An area of broken crags which overlook the upper part of Ennerdale; once neglected, they now boast a number of high quality routes. Standing out is an impressive central pillar of rock – the *Main Wall*, originally first breached by *The Prow of the Boat*. The rock is generally solid and very rough but some areas remain lichenous. It takes little drainage and in the summer gets the sun from late afternoon. The fine *West Face* receives the sun earlier. The crag has a unique feeling of remoteness and is well worth the extra effort needed to get there.

Approaches:

From **Wasdale** take the good path to Beck Head via Gavel Neese on Great Gable. At Beck Head, bear left up the east shoulder of Kirk Fell until just beyond the top of the steep section, then bear off rightwards to the top of the crag, which can be seen as a large protruding buttress. Either scramble down a short way to an idyllic gearing up and picnic spot in a grassy bowl and abseil to the routes, or follow an easy descent to the foot of the crags. Alternatively, from Beck Head, follow the Black Sail Pass track dropping across the Ennerdale side of Kirk Fell for 500 metres, to where the steep ground below the crag can be ascended (2hrs).

From **Honister Pass**, follow the old tramway incline westwards up the hillside behind the quarry car park for one kilometre then turn south off this at the point where the path is elevated onto the well marked track that runs along the side of Grey Knotts. Keep on the main track below Brandreth then break off right to a small stile. Follow a vague path beyond the stile to join the lower path of **Moses Trod** which leads to Stone Cove

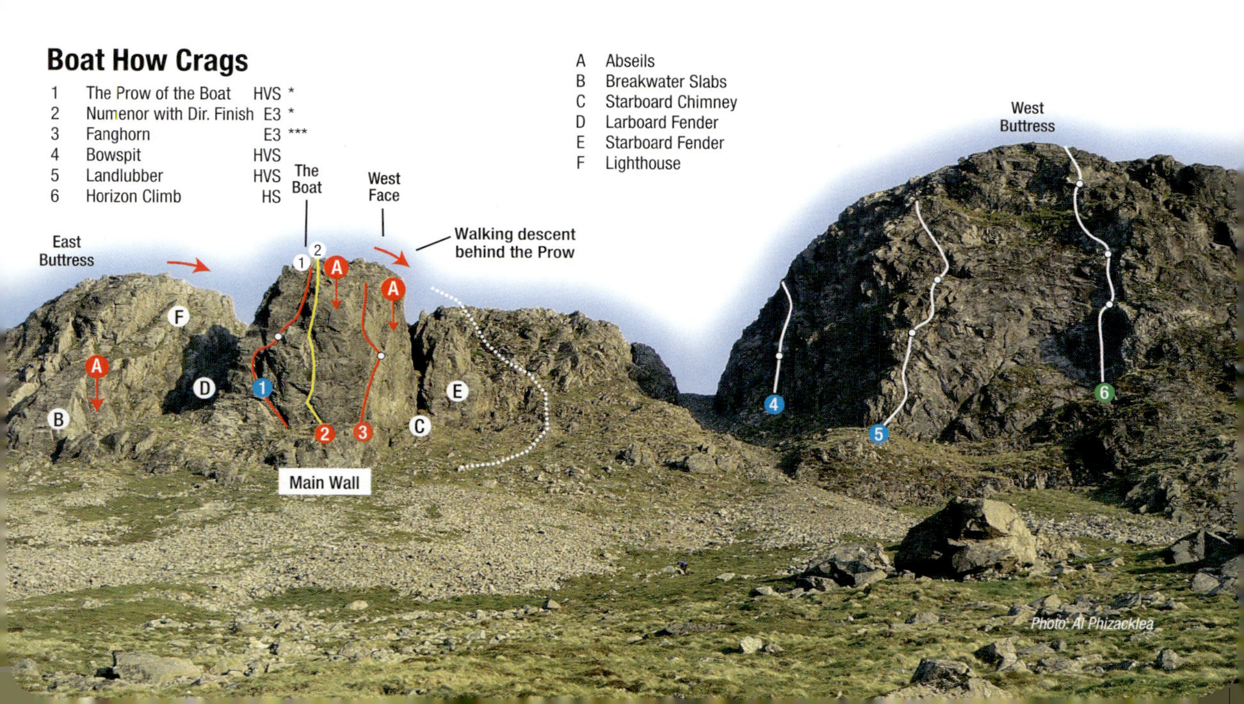
Boat How Crags
1 The Prow of the Boat HVS *
2 Numenor with Dir. Finish E3 *
3 Fanghorn E3 ***
4 Bowspit HVS
5 Landlubber HVS
6 Horizon Climb HS
A Abseils
B Breakwater Slabs
C Starboard Chimney
D Larboard Fender
E Starboard Fender
F Lighthouse
East Buttress
The Boat
West Face
Walking descent behind the Prow
West Buttress
Main Wall
Photo: Al Phizacklea

below *Gable Crag*. Continue the climb to Beck Head col, then follow directions as above (2hrs).

From **Ennerdale**, cycle to Black Sail Youth Hostel, then approach the crag via Black Sail Pass (2hrs 15mins in total).

Descent:

There is a good abseil from the top of ***Main Wall***; a large thread nearby allows a 50 metre abseil to the base - take a spare sling and short length of rope to link anchors. There is also an abseil down the ***West Face*** from near the top of ***Starboard Chimney***. Alternatively descend the wide gully on the right of the main crag, behind ***Starboard Fender***.

The climbs are described from **left** to **right**, in line with the normal approach.

Longshoreman's Arête	180m	M		1926

A worthwhile scramble gained by rocks and grass on the left flank.

Bonjour Matelot	28m	MVS		2006

A fine although slightly contrived first pitch on clean rough rock. Start 20 metres up and left of ***Coastguard Climb*** at a grass ledge below an easy-angled slab slanting up to the right.

1 20m (4b). Move left and up onto a block. Follow the arête rightwards for a couple of metres until the tiny hanging ramp on the right can be gained by a sensational move. Up this to a large spike and swing left onto a broad gangway which leads to a steep wall. Traverse right for 5 metres to a nook and block belays.

2 8m (4b). Optional: climb the steep mossy scoop above to easier rocks and the top.

Coastguard Climb	40m	VD		1926

Start about 70 metres up the scree gully at the extreme left end of the crag, at the bottom of a steep crack reached by awkward scrambling out of the gully.

1 8m. Climb the crack to a ledge.

2 20m. Follow ledges and grooves up left to a broken ledge.

3 12m. Climb the slab on the right to the ridge.

East Buttress

The *East Buttress* is a wide expanse of broken rocks, bounded on the left by *Custom House Arête* and on the right by *Sea Wall Arête*.

Esplanade Climb	170m	D		1925

A poor outing up the front of the *East Buttress* keeping approximately 10 metres left of the right edge. Start on a wide grass terrace above the lower rocks and about 70 metres below and slightly left of the obvious clean buttress of *Breakwater Slabs*.

Slabs and ribs lead up for 80 metres to a noticeable steepening. Climb up a series of grassy runnels on the right, past an obvious detached block near the top, until a ramp system leads left to easier slopes.

Sea Wall Arête, East Buttress	70m	D		1925

An interesting route which generally follows the right edge of the *East Buttress* just left of an open grassy gully.

1 15m. Scramble up to a ledge below a split block. Climb the strenuous crack to a rock stance.
2 13m. The right edge of the slabs above leads to a stance.
3 17m. Ascend a few metres, then go up the corner on the right, followed by slabs to below a large corner.
4 25m. Climb the left wall of the corner and the slabs above to the top.

Variation VD

3 23m. Climb the arête on the left to join Pitch 4 below the slabs.

Breakwater Slabs

The following routes, which can all share the same finish up the *Lighthouse*, are situated on *Breakwater Slabs* where the rock is good and dries quickly. The top pitches can be avoided by abseiling from a block on the right of the slabs.

Moss Slab	27m	HS	★	1939

A good climb taking the left edge of *Breakwater Slabs*.

Step right onto the arête and continue up the slab on the left until it steepens into a wall. Make an awkward traverse left, then go up and back right, finishing straight up the arête. Either finish up Pitches 2 and 3 of *Breakwater Slabs and Lighthouse* (35m) or abseil off.

Breakwater Slabs and Lighthouse	65m	S	★	1925

Start below the obvious crack in the centre of the slabs.

1 30m. Climb directly up the crack to a large grass ledge.
2 15m. Up the grass trending right to below some broken slabs.
3 20m. Climb the broken slabs, after which the climb steepens at the *Lighthouse*, the slabby rib overlooking the gully on the right. The holds remain good to the top.

Boat How Crags

Breakwater Slabs

1 Seawall Arête, East Buttress D
V Variation VD
2 Moss Slab HS *
3 Breakwater Slabs and Lighthouse S *
4 Groyne Strain E1 **
5 Breakwater Slabs, Grooved Arête VS *
6 Sea Shanty E1
7 Topsail E2 **
8 Spinnaker E2 *

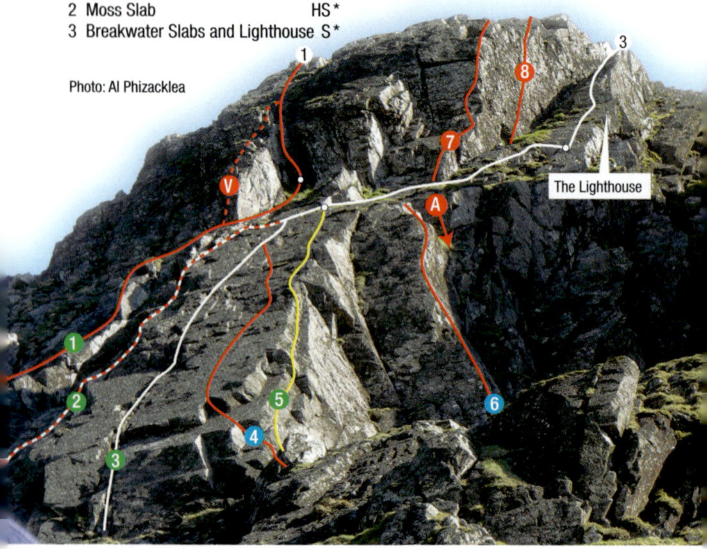

Photo: Al Phizacklea

Groyne Strain	26m	E1-	★★	2006

Excellent well-protected climbing; Ennerdale's answer to ***Aphasia***! Start as for ***Grooved Arête*** at the top of a large block.

(5b). Step delicately left to reach a small triangular niche, then smear leftwards to gain a higher recess in the slab. Follow the thin crack directly, moving left where it eases. Traverse right to finish up ***Topsail***, or abseil off from near the top of ***Sea Shanty***.

Breakwater Slabs, Grooved Arête	30m	VS-	★	1928

An excellent pitch up the right-hand arête of the slabs, starting above a jammed block.

(4c). Make an awkward step onto the arête from the right and follow a stepped groove on the right edge, pulling left over a bulge to a junction with ***Breakwater Slabs and Lighthouse*** below the broken slabs. Finish up Pitch 3 of ***Breakwater Slabs and Lighthouse*** (20m) or abseil.

Sea Shanty	10m	E1		2006

(5b). The short arête right of *Grooved Arête* is climbed on its right side to an awkward finish.

The next two routes start above the long traverse of ***Breakwater Slabs and Lighthouse***.

Topsail			
12m	E2	★★	2006

The arête overlooking the ***Lighthouse*** makes a good top pitch to *Groyne Strain*.

(5b). Climb slabs until they meet the arête. Pull across left for a good hold, then move back up right on hidden pockets. Climb straight up the wall with long reaches to ledges on the arête. Finish direct to a ledge and large block belays.

Above: Al Phizacklea tiptoes up the main brace on **Sea Shanty** (E1), Boat How. **Photo:** John Holden

Spinnaker	10m	E2	★	2006

The middle of the wall right of ***Topsail***. Start just right of an alcove.

(5c). Pull up steeply on small finger holds until it is possible to use a layaway to reach a good hold in a round hole. Continue more easily direct to the top.

In the wide gully up to the left of ***Main Wall*** is a small buttress called the ***Larboard Fender*** which has a short easy crack up the front. Between this and ***Main Wall*** is a small chimney called ***The Hatchway*** which marks the start of the following route.

Hatchway and Rigging	40m	VD		1925

A poor and disjointed route.

1 8m. Climb the ***Hatchway*** via its right wall to a large ledge.

2 7m. Scramble right to the bottom of a crack in a wall.

3 17m. **The Rigging**. Climb the wall to a spike on the left. Step across right into a groove and follow the crack to the top of a tower.

4 8m. Easy scrambling leads to the top.

Main Wall – The Boat

The steep face looking directly across the head of Ennerdale only receives the sun late in the afternoon. The rock is sound but areas remain lichenous and some routes may require cleaning before an ascent.

Larboard Arête	43m	S		1925

Start at the foot of the left arête of the main buttress of the *Boat*.

1 20m. Starting up a shallow groove, climb the arête to a ledge at 12 metres and continue up to another ledge.

2 15m. The groove to the left leads up to the top of the tower on *Hatchway and Rigging*.

3 8m. Easy scrambling to the top.

Final Voyage	45m	E1		1997

A line between *Larboard Arête* and *Prow of the Boat* starting just left of the latter. The first pitch can be climbed completely independently of *The Prow of the Boat* by some bold but steady climbing.

1 20m (5a). Climb up left of the *Prow* for 10 metres then traverse left to the edge (awkward to protect). After a couple of long reaches, move up and pull onto a cracked slab with nut belays and a poor stance (or continue).

2 25m (5a). Climb straight up over a steep little wall, then follow grooves on the right to the top.

The Prow of the Boat	55m	HVS	★	1940

A good climb giving two worthwhile pitches in spite of their dirty appearance. Start below an easy rib that leads up to an obvious V-groove running up just left of the front of the *Boat*.

1 25m (5a). Climb the easy rib and continue up the V-groove until a small resting ledge can be gained on the left. Traverse right across steep rock then up to good ledges. Good belay at the far right-hand end of the ledge.

2 30m (5a). Traverse delicately right for 4 metres to gain the bottom of a left-facing corner. Climb this corner passing a doubtful flake, go over a bulge, then diagonally left to a ledge below an overlap. Pull over the overlap and up the delicate slab above to the top. A poorer alternative is to traverse right from below the overlap to a rib which is followed to the top.

Boat How Crags Main Wall

1	Larboard Arete	S
2	Final Voyage	E1
3	Prow of the Boat	HVS*
4	Dehydroepianrosterone	E2*
5	Keel Haul	E3
6	Numenor with Direct Finish	E3*
7	Voyager	E3**
8	Flagship	E5***
9	Fanghorn	E3***
A	Abseil	

Prow Direct	50m	HVS	★★	

A good combination of pitches finding the best rock on this part of the crag.

1 25m (5a). Pitch 1 of *Prow of the Boat*.
2 25m (5a). Pitch 2 of *Dehydroepiandrosterone*.

Dehydroepiandrosterone	48m	E2	★	1996

A direct line on high friction rock. Start just right of the wide groove which forms *The Prow of the Boat*, at a narrow broken left-trending groove.

1 23m (5c). Enter the wide groove, then step right and follow the broken groove to where it narrows and steepens (crux). The dirty groove can be avoided by climbing the left rib (still the crux). After the narrow groove, a good belay ledge is found to the right below the prominent thin crack splitting the slab above.
2 25m (5a). Follow the thin cracks directly up the centre of the slab to finish up the friction slab. An excellent pitch.

Keel Haul	50m	E3		1999

Start just right of *Dehydroepiandrosterone*.

1 25m (5c). Climb the thin crack to join *Dehydroepiandrosterone* after 6 metres and follow it for a few moves before stepping right onto the steep wall. Climb through the bulges above by strenuous lay-backing and undercuts.
2 25m (5b). Climb the slab and rib on the left side of the upper slabs to the top.

Numenor with Direct Finish	50m	E3-	★	1999

Steep and strenuous climbing up the thin ragged crack-line and bulges 7 metres right of *The Prow of the Boat*. Well-protected throughout with good rests between the steep sections. An excellent line which greatly improves in proportion to the amount of cleaning done before the ascent. Start below a shallow leaning corner.

(6a). Climb the awkward leaning corner up to a bulge. Pull out right onto the steep wall, move up to the foot of the sharp crack and climb it over a bulge and up to the next bulge. Continue over two more bulges to the top.

Original Way E2+ 1969

(5c). Start as above, but traverse left at mid-height to gain a small stance, then join *The Prow of the Boat* at the bottom of the left-facing corner.

Voyager	40m	E3	★★	1999

Start from a hanging stance about 15 metres up *Numenor*.

(5c). Traverse sensationally rightwards at the level of the second peg on ***Flagship***; two hidden right-facing ramps provide holds and runners. From the peg, climb delicately upwards to gain the base of a groove (Pitch 2 of ***Fanghorn***) and finish up this.

Flagship	50m	E5	★★★	1995

The pride of Ennerdale, this route takes a bold line directly up the main wall of ***Boat How*** between ***Numenor*** and the arête of ***Fanghorn***. There are numerous RP placements between the pegs but only skyhooks will possibly prevent a deck out from the crux at 12 metres. It is however possible to step left into ***Numenor*** for a runner before the crux which reduces the seriousness of this pitch.

(5c). Climb a small slab to a peg at 4 metres. Sustained technical climbing continues straight up for about 15 metres past three short grooves to a peg on the right. Move back from the peg and make delicate moves left to reach small cracks and good placements. Continue straight up the small steep groove, pull out right, and follow slabs to the top. Superb!

Fanghorn	50m	E3-	★★★	1969

Tackles the proud arête between ***Main Wall*** and the ***West Face***, starting at the toe of the blunt arête on the right. A classic route with excellent rock and situations.

1 20m (5c). Climb up to a small corner to the right of the rib then make an awkward pull left onto the arête. Go straight up to an old peg which is passed with difficulty. Continue up a shallow groove to a good stance.

2 30m (5b). Traverse left across a flake and make a delicate move around a bulge into a hidden groove. Follow the groove directly to the top.

Original Way

2 30m (5a). Straight up the wide open groove above, then left to a shallow corner and up this to the top.

West Face

This steep wall of excellent clean rock looking down towards Ennerdale receives the sun shortly after mid-day.

Jolly Roger	50m	E2	★★	1999

An entertaining and varied climb which incorporates the original second pitch of ***Fanghorn***. Start below the open groove, 9 metres right of the arête.

1 20m (5c). Climb the groove past a spike and move up to an awkward slot in the overhang. Step left and climb a groove to a grass ledge.
2 30m (5a). Climb straight up the wide open groove above, then left to a shallow corner, and up this to the top. Alternatively finish up the Pitch 2 of *Fanghorn* for a better balanced route.

Trim and Incline	28m	E3+	★★	1997

A route up the centre of the wall, 15 metres right of *Fanghorn*.
(5c). Climb up to a hanging flake which has a poor nut and a loose block at its top. Make a series of long reaches up a set of 'steps' (skyhook), and then go right to a second good skyhook and a wire. Traverse left and up to reach a good hold and runners. Move up and make a long reach left above the diagonal roof, then climb directly up a shallow scoop to a belay on a ledge. Either abseil off, or finish up *Poseidon Adventure*.
(Under 6ft 2in? Then avoid the blind move over the roof by stepping left by the runner and climbing a shallow groove to the belay.)

Poseidon Adventure	50m	E4+	★★	1999

Start 5 metres right of *Trim and Incline*.
1 25m (6a). Climb the shallow groove/chimney and exit left at the overhang. Move left to the 'second skyhook placement' on *Trim and Incline* (which takes a poor wire). Climb directly up the wall above with difficulty to the apex of the roof and pull over this on dramatically improving holds to a good ledge.
2 25m (5a). Climb the rib defining the edge of the *North* and *West Faces*, gaining it from the right.

The Golden Rivet	38m	HVS-	★★	2006

Supersedes the earlier line of **Starboard Arête Direct** (MS, 1940) which was originally described as giving poor climbing on dirty loose rock.
1 14m (4c). Follow *Scenic Cruise* to where it traverses right at 6 metres, then climb the straight crack system to a grass ledge.
2 24m (5a). Climb the flake-line up a shallow rib above to where the rock bulges, then step down and traverse across the wall on the right to the edge overlooking the top of the gully. Pull steeply up a short groove then pull out right onto the edge of the rib and finish directly.

Bilge and Ballast HVS 2006
2 18m (4c). The direct finish to *The Golden Rivet* up the dirty grooveline; poor.

Right: Dave Birkett leading the first free ascent of **Fanghorn** (E3), Boat How, with Sue Wood belaying. **Photo:** Paul Ross

Boat How Crags West Face

9	Fanghorn	E3***
10	Jolly Roger	E2**
11	Trim and Incline	E3**
12	Poseidon Adventure	E4**
13	The Golden Rivet	HVS**
V1	Bilge and Ballast	HVS
14	Scenic Cruise	HVS***
15	Starboard Arete	S*
16	Starboard Fender	VD
V2	Starboard F. Direct Finish	HVS

A Abseil descent

Scenic Cruise	45m	HVS+	★★★	1996

A direct line up the steep *West Face* of the buttress. Sustained climbing on excellent quick drying rock. Start at the foot of *Starboard Chimney*.

(5a). Starting just to the left of *Starboard Chimney*, climb a left-leaning scoop/groove for about 6 metres then make a couple of interesting moves right to a crack-line. Step right and climb straight up, heading for the base of the steep groove at the highest point of the buttress. Pull out left and climb a delicate slab which leads to the top. The groove may be climbed directly but is harder.

The dangerously loose and grassy **Starboard Chimney** (30m, VD 1925) right of the *West Face*, which divides it from the *Starboard Fender* buttress, is not recommended.

Starboard Arête	63m	S	★	1926

Pleasant climbing on relatively clean rock which wanders across above the main wall. Start as for *Starboard Fender*.

1 10m. As for Pitch 1 of *Starboard Fender* to the grass ledge.
2 12m. Using the top of a large leaf of rock, go up and left into a corner. Make a descending traverse left into *Starboard Chimney* and a belay.
3 13m. Climb the wall on the left to a ledge and traverse it leftwards until it is possible to step down to a stance.
4 13m. Go up the wall on the left then make an ascending traverse leftwards over ledges to the *Capstan* (a large belay block).
5 15m. From the *Capstan*, climb the slabs above direct, or traverse right into a groove and follow this to the top.

Starboard Fender	35m	VD		1935

A poor route on the buttress right of *Starboard Chimney*.

1 20m. Climb to a grass ledge, either via the crack near the right corner of the buttress, or the short corner further right again. Continue up over broken rocks, step right onto a slab, and climb this to a large ledge.
2 15m. Traverse right and ascend easily to the top.

Direct Finish HVS

2 15m (4c). Climb the steep wall on the left to a recess, then finish up the left rib: bold.

Stern Girdle Traverse	101m	S		1926

A girdle of the *Boat* starting up *Larboard Arête* and descending *Starboard Arête*. It can be climbed in either direction, neither of which lead to the top of the crag!

1 20m. As for Pitch 1 of *Larboard Arête*.
2 15m. As for Pitch 2 of *Larboard Arête*.

3 15m. Descend slightly and traverse rightwards to a grass ledge. Continue traversing right and down to a large belay ledge and the *Capstan*.
4 13m. Reverse Pitch 4 of ***Starboard Arête***.
5 13m. Reverse Pitch 3 of ***Starboard Arête***.
6 12m. Reverse Pitch 2 of ***Starboard Arête***.
7 13m. Reverse Pitch 1 of ***Starboard Fender*** from the grass ledge.

West Buttress

Across a large open scree gully, right of the *Boat*, lies the large, broken and dirty *West Buttress*.

Bowspit	34m	HVS		2006

Start at a spike belay on a grass ledge, left of a short side gully cutting into the left wing of the ***West Buttress***, below the left-hand arête.
1 10m (4a). Climb the slabs delicately to a ledge and pull over a bulge to a higher grass ledge.
2 24m (5a). Use the rib on the left to reach the obvious undercut and pull out left to a flake. Traverse onto a ledge on the left and follow a steep mossy groove for 4 metres to where a footledge leads back right to the arête. Climb this on a series of superb jugs to the top.

Landlubber	68m	HVS		1969

A route that follows the shallow groove left of the large sweep of slabs in the centre of the buttress. Start 10 metres down and right of the point where the crag meets the large scree gully.
1 20m (4c). The short ramp leads up to the foot of a groove. Climb the groove, then the flake crack above, to a stance.
2 18m (4c). Climb up the break diagonally rightwards to a grass ledge, then go up a crack to a large stance.
3 30m (4b). Gain the prominent corner up and right, step left to a narrow mantleshelf, then continue left below a bulge to a large sloping ledge in a corner. Climb the left wall to the top.

The next route lies about 15 metres to the right of ***Landlubber***.

Horizon Climb	99m	HS		1926

A disjointed and poor route starting in a corner left of a small buttress, at the right-hand end of the large sweep of slabs.

Left: Keith Phizacklea taking in the view on **Scenic Cruise** (HVS), Boat How.
Photo: Al Phizacklea

Above: The upper reaches of Ennerdale with Kirk Fell and Boat How in the centre and the distinctive outline of Pillar Rock on the right. **Photo:** Phil Rigby

1 **20m.** Climb the corner to a grass ledge, make an ascending traverse right then go up steeply to ledges.
2 **16m.** The broken loose rocks above lead with care to a large sloping grass ledge; poor belays.
3 **18m.** Either traverse diagonally left and up over rocks and grass ledges to a broken corner, or step right from the sloping grass ledge and climb the arête.
4 **25m.** Scramble up and traverse right along a grass ledge.
5 **20m.** The easy ridge to the top.

Kirk Fell Gill

GR **NY 185 110** Alt **675m** F **North**

Kirk Fell Gill (1944) is the huge cleft passed on the right when approaching Boat How Crags from Black Sail Pass. It consists of about 150 metres of scrambling and has three waterfall pitches, the hardest being the top one (MS but rather depends on the amount of water flowing down it). All difficulties can be avoided.

Black Sail Buttress

Grid reference: **NY 194 111** Altitude: **620m**
Faces: **North** Approach: **2 hrs**

More properly called *Kirkfell Crags*. A remote dark and heavily vegetated crag high on the Ennerdale side of Kirk Fell with few rewards for such a long approach. The easiest way of identifying the climbing area from the surrounding broken fellside is by the large square overhang at half-height.

Approach:

From **Wasdale** take the path to Black Sail Pass then turn south onto the track up the northern spur of Kirk Fell for about 300 metres before contouring left, following a poor sheep track for 200 metres, to the base of the crag (2hrs).

Descent:

The best descent is by scrambling to the top of the buttress, then going north to meet the Kirk Fell northern spur track. Follow the track down to the sheep track used on the approach.

Three Blind Mice	75m	MVS		1969

A route up the relatively clean arête on the right-hand side of the crag. Start directly below the arête.

1 25m (4a). Straight up the arête to a stance.
2 25m (4b). Climb the wall just right of the arête to gain a leftward-sloping recess that leads up over a bulge to a large terrace.
3 25m (4b). Step off the block on the left, traverse delicately left across the slab to the arête, then climb the shallow groove to a ledge. Move left round a bulge and up the arête to the top.

The Cat Run	75m	MVS		1969

This route traverses right to left under the large overhang in the centre of the crag. Start below the shallow vegetated groove 6 metres left of the arête of *Three Blind Mice*.

1 45m (4a). Climb over ledges to the bottom of a break leading through overlaps. Follow the steep break on good holds for 15 metres, then go up diagonally left over easier ground to a large terrace: good belay below large block.
2 30m (4b). Climb the grassy groove just left of the large block, make an awkward step left onto the slab, and continue up to the large overhang. Traverse left on good holds to the extreme left arête, then climb up over easy grassy rocks to ledges.

Ennerdale

by Stephen Reid

This remote forested valley in the far west of the Lake District possesses several pleasant but remote crags likely to be of interest only to the seeker of solitude and one magnificent venue – *Pillar Rock*.

There are few facilities in this valley and vehicles are not permitted beyond Bowness Knott: whilst this makes for some long and arduous crag approaches, it also means that the crags are never busy, and in fact you are highly likely to have them to yourselves. The most convenient campsites are at Buttermere or Wasdale. There is a youth hostel at Gillerthwaite (handy for climbers as it entitles you to drive further up the track) and another at Black Sail near the head of the valley (vehicles are not allowed to this one).

The crags are described **clockwise** around the valley.

Bowness Knott

Grid reference:	**NY 109 155**	Altitude:	**160m**
Faces:	**South-West**	Approach:	**5 mins**

This is the collective name for a number of crags that lie on the south and south-western slopes of *Bowness Knott*, just above the car park at the end of the road.

Left of the car park are *Long Crag* and *Bowness Crag*: these comprise the main climbing area.

The climbing here is generally of poor quality and any good bits of rock or pitches are far and away outnumbered by poor rock (some holds need careful usage), heavily vegetated rock, or just the sheer poor quality of climbing. There are, however, one or two exceptions such as *Green Gash* which make an evening here worthwhile. The crags do catch any sunshine going and have a pleasant picture postcard outlook, but that is about all that can be said in their favour. The crags face south and west

Left: A team of three early climbers on **Slab and Notch** (M), Pillar Rock. The leader is rounding The Curtain on The Easy Way variation. **Photo:** Abraham Brothers

Ennerdale

Green Gable Crag
Pg. 170
Green Gable
Gable Crag
Pg. 142
Great Gable
Windy Gap
Brandreth
Stone Cove
Moses Trod
To Honister Pass
Beck Head
Boat How
Pg. 178
Haystacks
High Level Route
Robinson's Cairn
Scarth Gap
High Crag
Raven Crag
Pg. 203
Black Sail
High Stile
Memorial
Footbridge
Raven Crag
Buttermere Guide
Red Pike
The Knors
Buttermere Guide
Roadbridge
Bowness Knott 3km
River Lisa
Gillerthwaite
Sept 06.

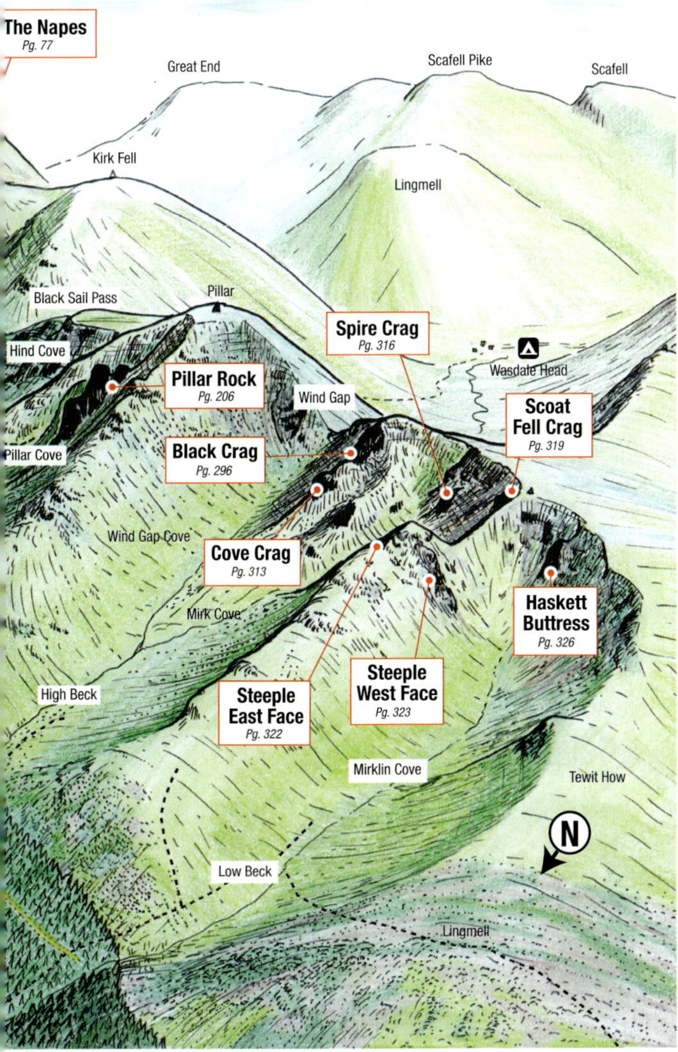
The Napes
Pg. 77
Great End
Scafell Pike
Scafell
Kirk Fell
Lingmell
Black Sail Pass
Pillar
Spire Crag
Pg. 316
Hind Cove
Wasdale Head
Pillar Rock
Pg. 206
Wind Gap
Scoat
Fell Crag
Pg. 319
Pillar Cove
Black Crag
Pg. 296
Wind Gap Cove
Cove Crag
Pg. 313
Haskett
Buttress
Pg. 326
Mirk Cove
Steeple
West Face
Pg. 323
High Beck
Steeple
East Face
Pg. 322
Mirklin Cove
Tewit How
N
Low Beck
Lingmell

across the lake and are easily reached via a gate opposite Bowness Cottage, 200 metres north of the car park.

There is likely to be an unsigned bird restriction on these crags between 1st May and 31st June. Please consult the FRCC website for details.

Directly above the gate is *Bowness Crag* and the green wall of *Labyrinth*. Further into the quarry (left) a derelict stone-wall leads up to *Green Gash*. The track ends below a large central scree slope which is unstable and best avoided (it is **not** suitable as a descent route), but it clearly defines the two crags. *Long Crag* is to its left and *Bowness Crag* to its right.

Long Crag

Descent:

Descent is to the immediate left (facing in) by scrambling down a bilberry ramp.

Black Crack Route	80m	HS		1950

Very vegetated, especially Pitches 1 and 3 – but a good route lurks in here somewhere! Start at the base of *Long Crag* below a large tree.

1 20m. Climb left of the tree and continue up the steep left edge to belay below the *Black Crack*.

2 15m. A thin slab leads to the crack which has excellent holds; belay on the left.

3 20m. Step right and climb the crack and steep wall on the right over blocks to easy ground, then traverse right to a tree belay beneath *Hyacinth Chimney*.

4 25m. Ascend the rib right of the chimney and continue up the fine crack, on hidden holds, to the top.

Two poor routes, **Snowstorm** (S, 1957), and **Tyrozet** (S, 1968), make their way up the extremely vegetated ground to the right.

Hailstorm	78m	HS		1950

Start 20 metres up the scree gully to the right of *Black Crack Route* at a large block set against a short red wall.

1 20m. Move upwards and left to a bracket, then climb direct to a ledge below a steep wall with a crack to its right.

2 20m. Climb the fine wall left of the crack to the top of the pinnacle and continue to the foot of *Hyacinth Chimney*.

3 8m. Climb the rib, right of the chimney, then move right to a stance below the final wall.

4 30m. Cross the rough slabs to the right and go up the corner crack, past a holly, to the top.

Wall Street	55m	E2		1981

Start as for *Hailstorm*.

1 25m (5a). Step off the block and climb the short, red wall. Continue to a terrace and birch tree below a black wall on *The Marriage*. Move 8 metres right to belay on an oak in a clump of trees.

2 15m (5b). Climb the green wall by a ramp leading leftwards; when it ends follow a steep groove direct to a tree belay below a bulging wall. All rather serious and unpleasant.

3 15m (5b). Climb up and right until it is possible to pull back left over a bulge and go up a good jamming crack to the top.

Variation 1981

2 15m (5a). Start 10 metres right of the clump of trees. Climb the strenuous crack past a wedged block, then leftwards to the tree belay.

The Marriage	48m	HVS+	★	1969

Start level with the top of a huge chockstone in the gully, 4 metres up the scree from the *Hailstorm* block.

1 12m (4a). Climb the impending groove into a dirty scoop and follow the left rib to heather and a birch belay.

2 12m (5a). Climb the corner on the right of the long black wall strenuously to the obvious break. An easier scoop leads to the foot of *Hyacinth Chimney*.

3 24m (5a). A fine pitch. The steep wall immediately behind the tree is climbed on small holds for 6 metres (using a tree), then slightly right using a thin finger crack. Make an awkward step left round a rib to a slab. Ascend diagonally left, then veer to the right up a corner. Continue via a stepped nose on the right, a short wall, and pleasant slabs to the top.

Don't attempt the **Bowness Girdle** (100m, S) without a shovel!

Bowness Crag

Scrambling by the old stone wall leads to the *Green Gash*, the obvious cleft tilted slightly to the right.

Descent:

Descend either by abseil from a convenient rowan tree about 5 metres back from the edge of *Green Gash* (double rope required), or, by scrambling up to an old wall which is crossed and then making an arduous and rather prickly descent down steep scree to the right of the crag.

Skyhook	50m	S		1964

Steep and interesting looking but spoiled by vegetation and a very large poised block at the start. Start 10 metres left of ***Green Gash*** at a small block below an overhang.

1 **25m.** Step up left and climb over a huge block of doubtful stability (if you dare). Continue over the bulge and up a mossy slab to a ledge. Go up the short gangway on the left, then move back right across the slab above the overhang and up to a tree belay.

2 **25m.** Climb straight up the slabs, keeping to the right edge overlooking ***Green Gash***.

Left Wall (E3? 5b) ascends an obvious series of overhanging grooves on the wall between ***Skyhook*** and ***Green Gash***, starting at an overhanging corner 3 metres left of ***Green Gash***; all seriously loose, friable and poorly protected.

Green Gash	40m	HVS-	★	1959

A tremendous adventure, this fine pitch cleaves ***Bowness Crag*** from top to bottom, and although mossy, this does not detract from the pleasure of the route; protection is good where it matters. At the time of writing the "obvious tree belay" mentioned in the previous guide has fallen from the top of the crag and is wedged across the first groove about 10 metres up the climb! The route is still possible with care and a bit of arboreal pot-holing though, and there are other trees to belay from and abseil off. Start by scrambling to the foot of the obvious cleft.

(4c). Ascend the corner/groove direct, moving left at the top and into a stepped groove to the left. A bulge near the top of the climb proves awkward. Either finish direct, or move right to the arête and finish up this to the obvious remaining tree belay. An **abseil descent** down the route is recommended: double ropes required.

Labyrinth	55m	VS		1959

A meandering artificial climb, with the odd nice move, but not really enough to make up for the approach or the descent. It takes the clean-looking green-grey walls directly above the gate opposite the cottage and about 150 metres right of ***Green Gash***. Start at a left-slanting gangway behind the right-hand of two large blocks embedded in the gorse, 10 metres right of a rowan.

1 **25m** (4a). Rather bold. Follow a clean pleasant gangway leftwards to the left end of a narrow horizontal ledge under a steep wall. Step left and up and then move out right at the top to a good ledge. Traverse

right then climb directly up for a couple of metres to belay beside a mossy glacis (shocking antique bolt belay!).

2 **15m.** Move up and right to climb a shallow slanting line with a detached block. After 10 metres, move horizontally right to jammed blocks, then further right to oak tree belays.

3 **15m (4b).** A good but bold pitch. The overhanging crack behind the tree is climbed strenuously towards the top with some difficulty (Friend 3.5 or 4). Move left to finish on steep vegetation etc and belay 15 metres up on the next rock outcrop. The **descent** is most unpleasant - scramble up to a wall, cross this, and then descend well right of the crag down the steep scree and gorse-ridden hillside.

Above and right of the car park (NY 109 154) are a number of outcrops including ***Oak Grove Crag***, ***High Crag*** and ***Hollow Ghyll Crag***. They have been explored in the past and are generally loose and/or vegetated, and are not recommended; even the peregrines avoid them.

Ennerdale Face of High Stile GR NY 166 146

The *Ennerdale Face of High Stile* is an intriguing collection of small buttresses (*The Knors* and *Raven Crag*) which can easily be seen from the valley high on the flank of High Stile. Although the approach from Ennerdale is just as feasible, they are traditionally gained from Buttermere, and are therefore described in the **Buttermere & St Bees** guide.

Proud Knott GR NY 182 120 Alt 500m F North

Proud Knott is heavily vegetated, and although a few routes in the easier grades have been climbed in the past, it is perhaps best left to the wilder inhabitants of the valley.

Raven Crag, Ennerdale GR NY 178 124 Alt 400m F North

Raven Crag lies on the south side of the River Liza and may be recognized as the lowest crag above the forestry fence on this side of the valley.

The crag is the third to the east from the beck and small waterfall, which comes down from the combe below *Pillar Rock*.

It is a fairly long crag sloping back at a deceptively easy angle, forming a broad backbone of rock. To the left (eastern side) of the crag is a short, very steep wall of good rock, about 25 metres high. The obvious **Central Corner** has been climbed (VS) but nothing else has been reported!

On the easier-angled front of the crag, the following two routes have been recorded, neither of which is very good. Above the crag are some slabs about 60 metres high which would give a continuation to the routes.

Centipede (100m, S, 1937) starts at the lowest point of the crag and aims to follow the crest of the buttress. Variations are possible almost at will, so no attempt has been made to describe the route.

Scarab (80m, VD, 1937) starts about 45 metres up and right of *Centipede*, and keeps more or less to the right of it.

It is possible to climb almost anywhere on the front face of this buttress, and with the combination of the upper slabs, and the routes in *Hind Cove*, *Great Doup* or *Pillar Rock*, a good mountaineering day can be had.

Hind Cove

GR **NY 178 122** Alt **600m** F **North-East**

Hind Cove is the spacious hollow crossed by the High Level Route, just before the ascent to Robinson's Cairn. It provides a few routes of an exploratory nature but is particularly important botanically, and further exploration involving "gardening" should be avoided: see the conservation notes on page 16.

Rib and Gully Climb (60m, VD, 1925) is situated on a prominent pillar-like outcrop of rock high up on the far left of the cove, and about the same level as *Hind Cove Gully*. A scree gully bounds it on the left. Starting from the foot of the crag, the rib is followed for about 25 metres, and leads to a grassy gully with a small cave pitch (10 metres). The gully is followed to the ridge of Pillar Fell.

The remaining climbs are situated high up the combe, on its right side, about 90 metres above the path. They are easily located by a conspicuous black cleft of *Hind Cove Gully*.

Hind Cove Buttress (80m, VD, 1923) forms the left wall of the gully. The route is fairly obvious.

Hind Cove Gully (1897) is the aforementioned black cleft, which provides an easy route. The main feature of the place is the depth that the fissure penetrates the hillside.

The *Slab Climbs* are situated on the right side of the gully, and are:

Route 1 (60m, VD, 1923) forms the right wall of the gully, the route being fairly obvious.

Route 2 (40m, VD, 1923) starts 9 metres to the right of *Route 1*, and keeps to its right, the finish being a couple of metres right of and below the finish of *Route 1*.

Great Doup (Pillar Cove) GR **NY 173 121** Alt **750m** F **North**

This is the the cove immediately east of *Pillar Rock*. It is of a similar nature to *Hind Cove*, and only an indication and brief description will be given, route finding being left to the skill of the mountaineers wishing to climb here.

"Two elephantine properties are mine,
For I can bend to pick up pin or plack,
And when this the Pillar Rock I climb,
Four-score and two's the howdah on my back.
P.P. Date of third ascent, May, 1878."

Note found on the body of the Rev. James Jackson, the self-styled "Patriarch of the Pillarites", who stumbled and fell to his death in Great Doup in 1878 at the age of 82 whilst on his way to make a solo ascent of Pillar Rock – the note was intended for the bottle on the summit.

Great Doup Pinnacle (40m, S, 1927) is situated on the immediate left of, and about 75 metres higher than, the start of *Great Doup Buttress*. A difficult rib is followed by a grassy scoop between two ribs and leads to a rock platform. A well defined crack leads to a steep wall which is followed to the top.

Great Doup Buttress (120m, D, 1889) is the most prominent central buttress situated at the head of *Great Doup*. Although the buttress presents such an imposing appearance, the climbing is only of a moderate nature. The climb starts at the lowest point of the buttress and trends right to follow the right-hand side of the buttress.

Western Buttress (30m, S, 1943) starts at the toe of a small buttress on the west side of *Great Doup*. Follow a corner into a groove, continue up the groove, and follow a crack in a slab on the left, then move left into a grassy groove which leads to the summit rocks.

Above: Early morning approach to Pillar via the High Level Route. **Photo:** Mark Gear

Pillar Rock

Grid reference: **NY 172 125** Altitude: **600m**
Faces: **North, South, East & West** Approach: **2hrs 30 mins**

Pillar Rock forms the central feature of the rugged north face of Pillar Fell and was the focal point for the earliest pioneers of rock climbing in the Lake District. As Harry Kelly rightly pointed out in the first guidebook to this area, "*Pillar Rock* is not at one's backdoor," but it is an imposing atmospheric venue offering superb climbs over a wide variety of grades on impeccable rock and worth every bit of the long approach.

Approach:

Pillar Rock is accessible from Ennerdale, Wasdale and Buttermere:

Ennerdale: This is the normal access route to the *Rock* for those having use of mountain bikes, as vehicles are not allowed past the Forestry car park at Bowness Knott (NY 109 153). Cycling reduces the two and a half hour walk-in by almost an hour – and it can be reduced even further by staying at either Gillerthwaite Youth Hostel (where there is a bunkhouse) or Gillerthwaite Field Centre. Follow the main valley dirt road for 7.5 kilometres, crossing the River Liza via a concrete bridge, until the Memorial Footbridge can be seen down to the left and a junction with the upper forest road. Turn right up this and continue another 450 metres or so to an unsigned path. Leave bicycles here and take the pleasant diagonal path to follow a stream into the combe. If walking, 50 metres past the concrete bridge, some wooden steps mark the start of a good (if wet) path which eventually joins the above route.

> *"...the most imposing view of the rock is to be gained by proceeding along the valley till opposite it, and then climbing up to its base. It is a fatiguing scramble, and it has been said that the cragsman taking this route, will find the way strewn with the graves of those who have preceded him."*
>
> CN Williamson, ***The Climbs of the English Lake District, All Year Round (1884)***

Wasdale: The traditional approach. From Wasdale Head (NY 186 088) take the path up Mosedale and branch up right towards Black Sail Pass. Just after crossing Gatherstone Beck, the path forks. Follow the upper, left-hand branch to Looking Stead. Carry on a short way on the main path up towards Pillar Fell where a small cairn and narrow path to the right marks the start of the **High Level Route**. This elegant and exposed well-marked track (first explored by that enthusiastic Lake District pioneer climber John Wilson Robinson ca 1881) contours the northern slopes of Pillar Fell. It soon splits and either branch can be followed (though the upper is the original one). The branches rejoin in Hind Cove only a short distance from **Robinson's Cairn** where the magnificent eastern profile of *Pillar Rock* can be seen (2hrs 30mins).

Buttermere: From Gatesgarth Farm (NY 194 150), follow the path to Scarth Gap. Do not descend to Black Sail Youth Hostel, but follow a path which starts a short distance down on the Ennerdale side and heads diagonally down in a westerly direction to reach the valley bottom at the **Memorial Footbridge** and a junction with the Ennerdale approach (2hrs 30mins to the crag).

All the above approaches are on the long side for a single day's climbing, but there are one or two good if small areas of flat ground on the ridge to the left of the stream as one approaches from Ennerdale (ie several hundred metres west of and a bit lower than Robinson's Cairn) which would make excellent campsites only 15 minutes from the crag.

Pillar Rock is practically conical in appearance; in fact there are two cones stuck together, forming the summits of *High Man* and *Low Man*. *High Man*, the highest point of the crag, is only accessible by climbing, which makes for difficult descents from some routes.

Looking from the north, on the left of the main crag is the *Shamrock*, a wide buttress of ribs and grooves which has a conspicuous heathery ledge (the *Great Heather Shelf*) running diagonally across its centre. Behind the *Shamrock*, to the east (left), and separating it from the bulk of Pillar Fell, is *Shamrock Gully*, and a short distance up the hillside above *Shamrock Gully* lies the **Shamrock Traverse**, a slabby rock rake which slants down leftwards to join the High Level Route, and which forms the **descent** for many climbs. Care should be taken not to mistake *Shamrock Gully* for the *Shamrock Traverse*, or indeed for any sort of descent which

Pillar Rock

1 Shamrock
2 Walker's Gully
3 North Face of Low Man
4 West Face of Low Man
5 West Face of High Man
6 Western Gully
7 Jordan Gap
8 Pisgah
9 Shamrock Traverse
(1) The Old West Route M**

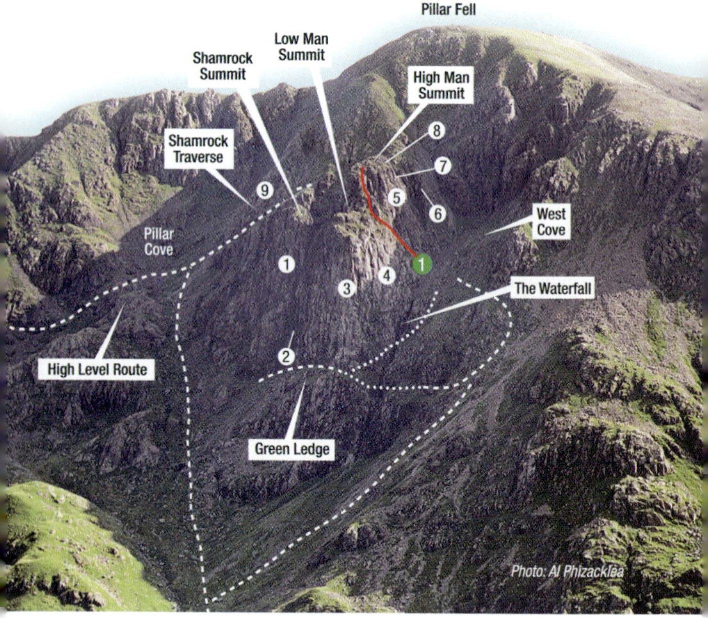

it most definitely is not! Separating the *Shamrock* from *Pillar Rock* to its right is the very obvious deep cleft of *Walker's Gully*. To the right of *Walker's Gully* is the *North Face of Low Man*, which rises vertically from the gully initially, then further right it becomes more broken in structure, the home for routes such as *North Climb*. The *North Face* increases in size moving rightwards, until it forms an arête (the *Bounding Buttress*) at the junction with the *West Face of Low Man*. A useful traverse, *Green Ledge*, runs under the full width of the *North Face of Low Man*, separating it from easier rocks below. Right again, and round the corner is the *West Face of Low Man*. At the base of the *West Face* is a deeply-cut gully known as the *Waterfall* (or *West Waterfall Gully*) which marks the right-hand extremity of the crag as seen from the valley. The *North* and *West Faces* of this lower part of *Pillar* rise up to form a rounded dome, *Low Man*.

Above *Low Man*, the upper cone rises to form the summit of *Pillar Rock* called *High Man*. On the right of this is the clean *West Face of High Man*, which is an upper extension to the *West Face of Low Man*, the two being separated by a leftward-slanting diagonal rake which forms the lower part of *The Old West Route*, a useful descent.

The 'uphill' side of the *West Face* ends abruptly at a deep chimney which forms a pronounced notch behind the *High Man* called the *Jordan Gap*, which separates the summit of *Pillar Rock* from *Pisgah*, the truncated pinnacle which rises out of the main mountainside to the south. The *Jordan Gap* forms the short southern face of *Pillar Rock*. Continuing around the summit of *High Man*, the *East* and *North Faces* form steep, rough ground, mainly unsuitable for continuous climbing, though there are some routes. One early classic route hereabouts, *Slab and Notch Climb*, forms the easiest ascent to, and descent from, *High Man*.

Pillar Rock can be conveniently described in five main sections:

South and East Faces of High Man

This is the area of sunny short climbs (including *Slab and Notch*) reached by following the *Shamrock Traverse* from the left, over the top of the *Shamrock*.

East and North Faces of Pisgah

The smaller summit between the *High Man* of *Pillar Rock* and Pillar Fell can be gained by an easy scramble from the south (mountain) side.

There are two chimneys on the east side of *Pisgah*, **East Pisgah Chimney Left** (1923) and **East Pisgah Chimney Right** (1892). The *Left* is climbed via its right wall on excellent rock and is rather good (M), but the *Right* is a vegetated scramble.

Pisgah from Jordan Gap	6m	HS		1898

Start from the top of a big block, just opposite the *Central Jordan Climb*.

By the aid of a small foothold a long stride is made to a jug and thin crack on the right. A groove is entered with a distinct lack of holds; a good one, however, is found for the finish. Completely unprotected and hard when wet.

From the highest point of the *Jordan Gap*, **Pisgah West Traverse** (10m, M) traverses an obvious foot-ledge to gain the *West Rib of Pisgah* and thence the summit. This is the quickest way to return to the mountain footpath from the *Jordan Gap* but it is quite exposed.

The routes on *Pisgah West Face* are described on page 293.

South Face of High Man (Jordan Gap)

The *Jordan Gap* is the deep cleft in between the *North Face of Pisgah* and the *South Face of High Man*. It is approached from the east via the easy scramble of *East Jordan Gully* and ends abruptly on the west side at the top of *West Jordan Gully*.

The best **descents** are either by reversing *Slab and Notch* (see page 213) or by abseil from a block near the summit cairn.

Far West Jordan Climb	22m	MS	★	1909

Start from a poised block standing almost against the wall, 2 metres from the top of *West Jordan Gully*.

A delicate move to the left across bulging rock leads to a slabby corner from where a short slab on the left leads to a small pinnacle near the left arête. Follow the short crack just to the right to a fine ridge finish

West Jordan Crack	22m	VD+		1909

Start from a poised block standing almost against the wall, 2 metres from the top of *West Jordan Gully*.

A delicate move to the left across bulging rock leads to a slabby corner. Climb a short slab on the right to a steep crack; up this, then easy scrambling to the top of *High Man*.

Over the Jordan	20m	E1	★	2005

Start from the highest point of the *Gap*, immediately left of *West Jordan Climb* at a short crack.

(5b). Climb the crack and step left to a slab. Go boldly up this into a steep groove to the right of the groove of *West Jordan Crack*. Climb the groove exiting it rightwards by a right-slanting crack.

West Jordan Climb	20m	D	★	1882

Start from the highest point of the *Gap* immediately to the left of *Jordan Bastion*.

A wall with an awkward start up a crack leads to a ledge at 3 metres. A shallow scoop/groove is succeeded by a widening crack on the right, which ends at the top of a huge flake, by which point it has become a chockstoned chimney. An easy wall leads to the top.

Pillar Rock Jordan Gap

1	New West Climb (top part)	VD ***
2	Sundance (top part)	MVS **
3	South-West Climb (top part)	MVS ***
4	West Jordan Gully (top part)	S
5	Far West Jordan Climb	MS *
6	West Jordan Crack	VD
7	Over the Jordan	E1 *
8	West Jordan Climb	D *
9	Jordan Bastion	VS *
V1	Variation	

Jordan Bastion	20m	VS+	★	1919

The obvious steep thin crack between *West* and *Central Jordan Climbs*. Short, but awkward, sustained and strenuous.

(4c). From the middle of the *Gap*, step across a cleft and approach the crack from the left (or gain the same point more easily from the right). Climb the crack on good holds to a step out left; either climb the continuation crack to the top or chicken out by moving right along the sloping ***Gangway Variation*** to finish in the same place.

Central Jordan Climb	20m	VD+	★	1882

Start immediately to the right of the highest part of the *Gap*.

A block corner with a crack in it leads to a big sloping ledge. The steep wide crack in the corner is followed to a huge flake, from where a short wall leads to *High Man*.

Deep River (S, 2006) is a rather pointless girdle traverse that starts up a broken arête just right of ***Central Jordan***, then follows that route almost to the top whereupon a descent is made down the ramp option of ***Jordan Bastion***. It then descends the crack of ***West Jordan Climb***, before crossing the slabs to finish up ***West Jordan Crack***, or, perhaps better, ***Far West Jordan Climb***.

East Jordan Climb	30m	VS+	★	1884

Start from the top of two large jammed chockstones near the bottom of *East Jordan Gully*, directly in line with an open-angled corner, which marks the line of the climb.

(4c). From the chockstones, climb direct to the foot of the corner. Make awkward moves to get established in the corner and climb it to a move left onto a ledge. Make another awkward move up and right onto the wall to grasp a tiny spike on the right (may be harder for the short – a sling can be flicked over this spike prior to committing to the move). Then climb direct to the top.

East Jordan Wall	30m	MVS	★★	1919

Start at the very bottom of ***East Jordan Gully***, and just left of the start of ***Slab and Notch*** below a short corner. The upper section contains some suspect rock, but this does not spoil a superb route. Take a few slings.

(4b). Climb the corner and then step up left and back right into an open groove which leads to a niche at 10 metres. Move up and rightwards out of the niche and follow a vague slim groove (rather bold), then climb directly up the wall to the top.

East Face of High Man

Whitehead's Corner	35m	VD		1850

Start as for ***Slab and Notch***, but having gained the ***Slab***, traverse right near its top to a short corner and climb this to a large grass ledge (possible belay on the right at a horizontal crack). Climb the dirty corner to its top, finishing up the last part of the *Pendlebury Traverse* – better than it looks, but not much.

J.K.C.	35m	MS	★	2006

The short wall between *Whitehead's Corner* and the *Notch* gives a pleasant pitch on super rock.

Start as for ***Slab and Notch***, but having gained the ***Slab***, traverse right near its top to a short corner and climb this to a large grass ledge (possible belay on the right at a horizontal crack). Climb the wall directly above the horizontal crack to reach stacked blocks on the *Pendlebury Traverse*. Finish up the fine crinkly wall on the left.

Slab and Notch Climb	60m	M+	★★★	1863

One of the easiest routes of ascent and descent on the *Rock*; it is described in both directions. Many variations are possible both in ascent and in descent, but the route described gives the most straight-forward way up to and down from the summit of *High Man*. Numerous belay possibilities exist. Start at the foot of *East Jordan Gully* well below *Jordan Gap*.

Climb up on to the large easy-angled ***Slab*** on the right at its top left-hand corner and descend slightly (or gain the ***Slab*** at its bottom left via a crack). Traverse easily across its base and climb either of two steep grooves to the *Notch* (20 metres). Move right along a narrow ledge for 4 metres and then climb the wall/arête direct to another ledge. Move right and climb slabs on the left of a large gully (*Great Chimney*) until it is possible to step right into the upper section of *Great Chimney*, up which the climb finishes.

The Easy Way M 1863

Actually only easier if clad in tweed and nails. It quits ***Slab and Notch*** a metre or so above the end of the traverse of the ***Slab*** and rounds the *Curtain* on the right via the *Ledge*. A 2 metre descent leads into the upper part of *Great Chimney*. Scramble up the *Steep Grass* to its apex. An awkward undercut move up a chimney/groove leads to a junction with the standard route.

Slab and Notch (in descent) 60m M+ ★★

From the summit of *High Man*, move north for 10 metres to an obvious cleft and chimney (*Great Chimney*) splitting the *East Face of High Man*.

Descend the chimney easily for a few metres, move left (facing in) onto a stepped slab, and descend this to a good ledge which leads to a short steep broken arête. Descend the arête for 5 metres to another ledge. From the ledge move left (facing in) to the *Notch* and descend either of the steep grooves beyond to gain the ***Slab***. Traverse the ***Slab*** leftwards (facing in) and climb up its left edge slightly to descend to the foot of *East Jordan Gully*.

Pillar Rock East Face of High Man

Photo: Stephen Reid

1	Pisgah Chimneys	M
2	Pisgah from Jordan Gap	HS
3	Jordan Bastion	VS *
4	Central Jordan Climb	VD *
5	East Jordan Climb	VS *
6	East Jordan Wall	MVS **
7	Whitehead's Corner	VD
8	J.K.C.	MS *
9	Slab and Notch Climb	M **
10	Pendlebury Traverse	M *
11	The Curtain (top part)	HS *
12	The Arête	MS *
13	The Great Chimney	D
14	North-East Chimney (top part)	VD
15	North-East Arête (top part)	S *

Pendlebury Traverse	20m	M+	★	1872

Start at the *Notch* on *Slab and Notch Climb*.

Follow a ledge on the left to a short chimney. Climb over or round a block at the top of the chimney onto a moderate upward traverse, to a junction with *Whitehead's Corner*, then follow a chimney in the corner.

The next two routes, *The Curtain* and *The Arête* are best taken in combination.

The Curtain and The Arête	78m	HS+	★★	1884

This climb runs up the obvious arête (or curtain of rock) which forms the left side of *Great Chimney*. Start by a wall on a flat grassy ledge (cairn), just above the lowest short wall of the arête.

1 26m. *The Curtain*. The wall with good if dodgy holds is followed by an awkward wide crack which starts from a precariously poised block on the right. There is a possible belay above, but not much in the way of anchors: best to continue by climbing up rightwards on good holds and following the narrowing ridge to a good spike belay just before a large flat ledge (the *Ledge* of *The Easy Way*).

2 7m. Traverse the *Ledge* leftwards and climb up to the *Notch*.

3 45m. *The Arête*. Just right of the *Notch*, climb a slightly overhanging corner (the right-hand of two) on good holds. Follow this to a slight headwall which is overcome via a thin left-slanting crack. The arête leads to the top. This pitch can be climbed from the *Notch* in its own right (MS).

Direct Variations 82m VS 2003

The climb can be extended by starting at the very bottom of the ridge, just above the top of *Walker's Gully*.

1 32m (4c). A short groove on the right, or its left rib, leads to a grass ledge and loose spikes. Climb a short wall above to a large grass ledge and cairn (start of the original route). The original route is then followed to the *Ledge*.

2 50m (4b). Climb the arête of the pinnacle above and so reach the *Notch*. Move up the left-hand groove a little to a wide crack in its right wall and go up this rightwards to gain the broken arête between the two grooves. Follow this directly until it joins the original route.

The Great Chimney	80m	D		1887

Better as a reference point than a climb, this prominent cleft splits the *East Face* and runs from near the top of *Walker's Gully* to the summit of *High Man*. The first pitch is a right old struggle; squirm up it to the *Steep Grass*. Above, a short troublesome chimney-cleft lands one gasping at a junction with *Slab and Notch* which is followed easily to the top.

The Old Wall Route		M		1850

It is possible to scramble fairly easily to the top of ***Low Man*** from the scree above ***Walker's Gully***. The scree of the amphitheatre is descended on the left side (looking down) until the foot of the ***Great Chimney*** is reached. A little ridge, which at one time had a wall on it, leading down to the top of ***Walker's Gully***, is immediately in front; this is crossed and easy ledges at the same level lead into ***Stony Gully*** (upper part of ***Savage Gully***), a scramble up which soon leads to ***Low Man***. ***The Old Wall Route*** itself, one of the earliest variations of the climbing on ***Pillar***, goes via this scramble, except that shortly before reaching ***Stony Gully*** a divergence is made to the wide ***Square Chimney***, about 7 metres high, which is seen in a corner up on the left. This chimney is ascended and from the top a junction is made with the final part of the ***Old West Route*** which is followed to ***High Man***.

North-East Face of High Man

This face can be traversed at a higher level than the ***Old Wall Route***. Well up the recess leading to the foot of ***The Great Chimney***, an easy crack will be seen on the right. This leads to a broad ledge which has some large blocks resting on it. Just beyond this is the large mossy V-corner of ***North-East Chimney***. This and the next climb lie about 15 metres left of the ***Square Chimney*** on the ***Old Wall Route***, and are also easily reached by traversing from the summit of ***Low Man***.

North-East Chimney	26m	VD		

1 **16m.** Climb mossy corner crack with interest, and then slabs, to belay under a shallow chimney with a chockstone.

2 **20m.** Overcome the chockstone and continue more easily to the summit of ***High Man***.

The next route climbs the slanting crack just right of Pitch 1 of ***North-East Chimney*** and makes an excellent alternative route from ***Low Man*** to ***High Man***.

North-East Arête	36m	S	★★	1909

1 **16m.** Climb the jagged crack to a scoop and follow the left edge of this to a large sloping ledge and boulder belay.

2 **20m.** Climb steeply up the right-hand side of the blunt arête above. Alternatively, reduce the standard to D by traversing right 2 metres and joining the ***Old West Route***. Continue more easily to the summit of ***High Man***.

Shamrock

The *Shamrock* presents an *East Face* and a far more interesting *North Face*, the latter being divided into an *Upper Tier* and a *Lower Tier* by the *Great Heather Shelf* which runs diagonally across its centre and is reached by scrambling from the left (serious in wet conditions), starting just right of a huge overhanging wall. It is a large rambling crag with several long and interesting routes, in the main on excellent rock though it can be very lichenous and mossy in places. Unfortunately, there is an excess of grassy ledges and dry conditions are desirable for most of the climbs. Some routes, such as *Photon*, *Eros* and *Thanatos*, do dry quickly however, as this section of the crag catches the morning sun.

Most of the climbs end on the summit of the ***Shamrock*** which is capped by a distinctive flat block (the ***Tea Table***), and is divided from the main mass of ***Pillar Fell*** by ***Shamrock Gully*** to the east, and the scree funnel of ***Walker's Gully*** to the west.

The easiest **descent** from the summit of ***Shamrock*** is to descend slightly to gain the hillside at the top of ***Shamrock Gully***, and above the scree funnel of ***Walker's Gully***. Scramble a short way up the fellside, first rightwards, then leftwards, to reach the start of an exposed sloping diagonal rake lying above the crag, called the ***Shamrock Traverse*** (this is at a similar level to the summit of ***Pisgah***). This is well marked and leads down to the open ground on the left of the crag.
The climbs are described from **left** to **right**.

East Face of Shamrock

Sirloin Climb	120m	S		1939

A poor route, which follows a fairly prominent series of ribs bounding the left edge of the sweep of slabs, which form the left wall of ***Shamrock Gully***. If you must, it starts at the exact corner of the ***Gully***, which is also the lowest point of the ***Rock***. A full description can be found on the FRCC website.

Shamrock Gully	160m	S		1890

This gully, although of considerable length, offers very little real climbing, the greater portion of it being composed of grass, loose earth and shifting scree. A very poor route of little merit – climb it at your peril!

Kipper's Chimney	30m	HS	★	1967

The obvious square-cut chimney on the left wall of ***Shamrock Gully***. Classic, steep, hard, on good holds and a little worrying; worth the effort –

Pillar Rock

Shamrock

1	Harlequin Chimneys	D	
2	Graviton	HVS	**
3	Photon	MVS	**
4	Eros	E2	***
5	The Shamrock Chimneys	VD	
6	Photogenic	E1	**
7	Positron	VS	
8	Electron	HVS	***
9	Tower Postern	HS	
10	Lepton	HVS	
11	Boson	HVS	
12	Pauli Exclusion Principle	E3	**
13	Vishnu	E2	
14	Thanatos	HVS	***
15	Thin It Is	E1	**
16	Shamrock Eliminate	HVS	**
17	Shamrock Tower	MVS	**
18	Odin	HVS	**
19	The Magic Rainbow	E1	**
20	Necromancer	E1	**
21	Walker's Gully	MVS	***

Photo: Stephen Reid

it can easily be tagged on to any of the main *Shamrock* routes. Start about 30 metres down from the top of the gully, just above the first steep step.

Climb the groove to the foot of the chimney proper. The square-cut chimney above is climbed using parallel cracks and anything else which makes upward progress possible. Exit left near the top or with more difficulty on the right.

Shamrock Buttress Route 2	148m	VD		1909

The climb improves with altitude but is never very good. Start immediately to the right of *Shamrock Gully*.

1 **75m.** Easy scrambling (with belays at will) leads to a large bilberry-covered platform.
2 **25m.** From the ledge, climb the small buttress straight ahead and traverse into the gully (a diamond-shaped wall is on the right). Climb a mossy wall on small holds to regain the ridge.
3 **20m.** Follow the ridge to a grassy walk into the gully to arrive opposite *Kipper's Chimney*.
4 **18m.** An entertaining pitch. Enter a small niche which is left awkwardly to the right; a steep wall is then climbed with the aid of a crack to a small cave just below the ridge. Exit right to gain the ridge.
5 **10m.** Follow the ridge to the *Tea Table*.

Variation to Pitch 4

A few metres further up the gully, a narrow chimney is seen 4 metres up on the right wall. This is entered with some difficulty and followed to a ledge, about level with the cave on the original pitch. Climb straight up to another ledge on the left, passing a large detached block to finish on the ridge near the top of the climb.

Variation: Route 1 1902

It is possible to climb the whole route at moderate standard by avoiding all the reasonable rock – not recommended unless botany is your bent.

North Face of Shamrock (Upper Tier)

The following climbs (except the first) lie above the *Great Heather Shelf*, a left-to-right-slanting paddock that splits the *Shamrock*. They can be reached from its left-hand end by steep vegetated scrambling, or, better, by ascending a route on the *Lower Tier*.

Harlequin Chimneys	150m	D		1928

Start right of a huge overhang, a prominent feature at the foot of the *Shamrock*. The chimneys form a continuous fault and route finding and belays are obvious.

Graviton	145m	HVS	★★	2005

A companion route to ***Eros*** – and of similar character, taking the fine arêtes to the left of that route. Start by scrambling 60 metres up the ***Great Heather Shelf*** to the foot of a clean groove on the left (***Photon***). Alternatively, reach the same point by climbing a route on the ***Lower Tier*** and descending down the ***Great Heather Shelf***.

1 20m (4c). Climb diagonally across the left wall of the groove to gain the left arête. Go boldly up this to a slight break and continue up the arête until it eases. Down climb the grassy chimney on the left to a stance at the foot of another arête.

2 30m (4b). Climb the crack just right of the arête to a small ledge. Gain the arête and follow it (hidden wires on right) to a groove which leads to a stance.

3 40m (4a). Climb the broken grassy wall to an easy arête overlooking ***Shamrock Gully***. Follow this and climb a cracked slab round to the left of the smooth diamond-shaped wall to regain the arête which is followed to a stance.

4 25m (5a). Climb up a couple of metres to the left of the steep wall of the final tower, then traverse one metre left along a grass ledge (above ***Shamrock Gully***) and climb boldly up the first shallow groove which is followed to the crest of the ridge.

5 30m. Easier climbing along the ridge to the ***Tea Table***.

Photon	147m	MVS	★★	1967

A long and varied climb of a mountaineering character. The stances are large and the protection good. Start by scrambling 60 metres up the ***Great Heather Shelf*** to the foot of a clean-looking but in fact slightly grassy groove on the left. Alternatively, reach the same point by climbing a route on the ***Lower Tier*** and descending down the ***Great Heather Shelf***.

1 25m (4c). Climb the steepening groove to below a sharp arête (***Eros***) – the next pitch takes the groove to the right of the arête.

2 30m (4c). Move right and go up a slabby corner to the foot of the groove. Ascend the steep corner to a bulge and climb this using the steep crack on the right. Continue up the crack to reach a good ledge on the left.

3 37m. Climb the corner above and continue past a huge chockstone to a good ledge. Climb the mossy slab on the left to finish on a ledge overlooking ***Shamrock Gully***.

4 25m (4b). Climb up a couple of metres to the left of the steep wall of the final tower, then traverse 3 metres left along a grass ledge under a shallow groove to climb up into a broken groove, which is followed to the crest of the ridge. Alternatively climb up into the groove from the right.

5 30m. Easier climbing along the ridge to the ***Tea Table***.

Eros	152m	E2-	★★★	1968

An extremely good climb taking bold ribs to the right and left of *Photon*. Start on the immediate right of the first groove of *Photon*.

1 25m (5a). Climb the rib direct to a mossy slab which leads to a good ledge at the foot of a sharp arête. A bold pitch.

2 30m (5b). Gain the steep rib above which is climbed on its right side for 18 metres. Continue up the slab above to a ledge, then traverse left to a grassy corner – a fine and even bolder pitch.

3 22m (5b). Climb the corner-groove above (the right edge of the diamond-shaped wall) with difficulty, using the rib on the right as necessary.

4 20m (4a). Continue to a ledge on the right. Step left across the groove and climb the left edge of a slab to a ridge, which leads to beneath the final tower.

5 25m (4b). As for *Photon*. Climb up a couple of metres to the left of the steep wall of the final tower, then traverse 3 metres left along a grass ledge, under a shallow groove, to climb up into a broken groove, which is followed to the crest of the ridge.

6 30m. Easier climbing along the ridge to the *Tea Table*.

Above: Jim Fairey demonstrating delicate balance moves on the crux of **Eros** (E2), Pillar Rock. **Photo:** Stephen Reid

The Shamrock Chimneys	150m	VD		1894

It's routes like this that give climbing on *Pillar* a bad name! *"Those who do visit the place will find much chimney-sweeping awaiting them"*, according to George Abraham writing in the *FRCC Journal* of 1908. To the right of *Photon* and *Eros* will be seen two chimneys. Start up the rather vaguer left-hand chimney and follow grass and loose rock in the right-hand one to make the first ascent this century.

Photogenic	124m	E1+	★★	2005

The fine arête on the right of *Photon's* Pitch 2 is the highlight of this climb. Start down and left of *Electron's* big corner and just right of *The Shamrock Chimneys*.

1 26m (5a). Start up a short scoop right of ***The Shamrock Chimneys***, and follow the slab above, slightly rightwards at first, then back leftwards, until a traverse can be made left under a square-cut overhang to reach a belay in ***The Shamrock Chimneys*** at the foot of the arête.
2 28m (5b). Move up leftwards onto the arête and climb it on excellent rock. Diligent searching will reveal more runners than first appearances might suggest.
3 35m (5b). Climb the short rib just right of the grassy gully until a step right leads back onto the other rib. Move up and right, to a grassy recess, a few metres below the big grassy ledge, where a bold traverse can be made across to the left arête to reach a belay just above.
4 35m. Traverse along the ridge to the ***Tea Table***.

Positron	124m	VS		1967

Takes the buttress between ***The Shamrock Chimneys*** and ***Electron*** in its lower half, and a rib and crack-line in its upper half to reach the ridge between ***Shamrock Gully*** and ***The Shamrock Chimneys***. This rather vegetated and worrying route starts as for ***Electron***.
1 40m (4c). Gain the upper grass ledge and, from its left end, climb diagonally left to gain a grassy crack. Climb this for a short distance and step left to a grass ledge. Ascend diagonally left to a good crack and follow the steep parallel cracks above. Near the top, step left to a ridge on the edge of ***The Shamrock Chimneys***.
2 24m (4b). Scramble up to a grassy bay. Traverse left into a slabby scoop and ascend this and move left to a small grass ledge and rock rib.
3 30m (4b). Climb the easy rib and crack above, followed by a grooved rib to a ledge, and then a short groove, moving right and up to a grass ledge at the foot of a good crack. A worrying lead!
4 30m (4a). Take the crack-line behind the belay which widens into a corner at half-height. This leads to the ridge between ***Shamrock Gully*** and ***The Shamrock Chimneys***. Easy scrambling along the ridge leads to the ***Tea Table***.

Electron	100m	HVS+	★★★	1966

One of the best and longest routes on the ***Shamrock*** in its own right, but especially so if combined with ***Thanatos***. The layback crack, although not technically difficult, is bold and intimidating and the first pitch is hard, especially if wet, which it usually is. The route starts 15 metres right of ***The Shamrock Chimneys*** at the foot of a vast vertical right-angled left-facing corner with a short hour-glass shaped chimney on its right. This is reached by the inevitable scrambling up the ***Great Heather Shelf*** or, much better, by climbing ***Thanatos***.

1 26m (5a). Climb the vast right-angled corner to a small chockstone at 6 metres. Overcome an awkward bulge and continue up the corner with another awkward move higher up. Belay on a large grass ledge.
2 24m (4b). Climb up the broken groove for 12 metres to a grass ledge and surmount the wall beyond to a large block. Belay at the foot of the imposing (not to mention intimidating) off-width crack.
3 20m (4c). The crux! Climb the crack with bravado. A fine character-building pitch.
4 30m (4b). Move right and go up the grey arête to a slim ledge 2 metres below the top of a pinnacle. Traverse 6 metres right to the foot of a continuation arête and ascend this to the foot of the *Tea Table*.

Tower Postern	85m	HS		1941

A poor route, grassy and vegetated. Start on the ***Great Heather Shelf*** at a grassy groove just right of the huge corner of ***Electron***.
1 25m. Easy scrambling up the grass corner, then climb the corner-crack ahead, which leads to a grassy stance below an apparently impossible finish. By a long and awkward step round the arête on the left, the upper section of a steep corner (***Electron***) is reached which leads to easy ground. By walking to the right an excellent thread belay is reached below a vertical crack.
2 8m. Climb the crack, which is hard, strenuous and exposed, but on good holds, to an excellent stance.
3 25m. Ascend a steep turfy corner. Continue up the steepening corner; the difficulty increases but, after an awkward movement, the final section of the crack is climbed more easily.
4 15m. Climb some ribs on the right to the foot of the *Tower*.
5 12m. The *Tower*. This is climbed to the main ***Shamrock*** ridge which is followed more easily to the top.

Lepton	100m	HVS+		1968

A good line up the buttress to the right of ***Tower Postern***, but spoilt by dirty and worrying rock on the second pitch. Start just right of ***Tower Postern***, below a short square-cut groove.
1 23m (4c). Climb the square-cut groove and slabby rock above for 10 metres. Climb up to some hanging flakes but avoid them by traversing horizontally left to the edge of the buttress and then climb straight up to a worrying belay on the edge of the buttress below a hanging groove.
2 20m (5a). Mantelshelf into the unpleasant groove and turn the overhang on the left; a long reach gives access to a sloping grass ledge. Scramble up to the left and belay below a large corner.
3 27m (4c). Climb across the slab to its left side and gain a short crack; climb this, then traverse right to below an obvious off-width crack

which splits the left wall of the groove. Climb the crack to a slab (several Friends 3.5 and/or 4 useful).

4 30m (4c). Traverse left to cross *The Shamrock Chimneys* above the chockstone. Climb diagonally left, up the left wall, to a crack, which is followed to the summit ridge.

Boson	92m	HVS+		1968

An unbalanced climb whose justification lies in Pitch 3. The rest of the climb is a vegetated Hard Severe. The route follows the obvious corner to the right of *Tower Postern* and starts to the left of the line of the corner at a square-cut groove.

1 12m (4a). Climb the square-cut groove and move right to belay at the foot of the corner.

2 20m (4a). The corner above is climbed direct, moving out left to a rib near the top. Then climb the wide crack on the left to belay just to the left of a steep rib.

3 30m (5b). Climb the steep rib near the right edge to a thin crack, which is followed to a recess below an undercut groove; fingery and strenuous. Attain the groove above with interest (not obvious) and climb it to a ledge. Climb another groove just left of the arête to belay by a dubious spike.

4 30m. Climb the rib on the left to the top.

Pauli Exclusion Principle	85m	E3	★★	1988

Good climbing but a very serious undertaking. Start under a sharp-edged arête, just right of *Boson* and just left of the short corner of *Vishnu* (there is a huge spike belay in the next corner to the right).

1 25m (5b). Virtually protectionless where it matters. Climb the arête on its right-hand side to a good hold at 10 metres, when moves up and right lead to a small spike runner (it is possible, though not necessarily ethical, to traverse rightwards onto a big ledge and place some gear at this point!). Move up the thin crack above the spike and then trend back left to the arête and follow it to a grass ledge.

2 20m (4c). As for *Vishnu*, climb the large flake crack above and an easier wall to a grass ramp which leads to a belay under a short diagonal chimney.

3 25m (5b). Another very serious pitch. Climb out rightwards, onto the slabby base of the buttress and move up leftwards to reach the edge of a grassy gully above the chimney. Pull straight up the blunt leftmost arête above and climb it on a series of flat holds (no further gear after the first 7 metres).

4 15m. Climb the slab on the left and the corner beyond to the top of the *Shamrock*, or perhaps more in keeping with the scary nature of the route, the block-filled chimney above the belay.

Vishnu	92m	E2+		1968

A serious climb, which is reflected in the overall grade, the main pitch being bold, not well-protected, and lichenous to boot. Start beneath a 6 metre high, right-angled corner just right of ***Pauli Exclusion Principle*** and 6 metres to the right of ***Boson***.

1 25m (5a). Climb the corner and continue up the crack above until it steepens, then make an awkward move left to a mantelshelf. There is a ledge a little higher and, 4 metres above this, another ledge is reached with a belay below a steep crack.

2 20m (4c). Climb the large flake crack above and an easier wall to a grass ramp which leads to a belay under a short diagonal chimney.

3 30m (5b). Pull out right on to the slabby base of the buttress. Move up to the left for a couple of metres, then traverse back to the right to the foot of a blank groove. Climb the rib on the right to a mantelshelf. Make an awkward move back left, across the top of the groove to gain a small ledge in the centre of the buttress. Climb the final wall, trending slightly to the right, on good but widely-spaced holds to a large ledge.

4 17 m. Climb the wall behind the belay on the left, then continue up a pleasant slab, which forms the left wall of the corner above, to the top of the crag.

North Face of Shamrock (Lower Tier)

The next routes start below the ***Great Heather Shelf***, at the lowest part of the ***Shamrock***, in the vicinity of where the mountain rescue box 'used to be'. The best reference point is the large left-facing corner with the left-facing overhang at the top: this is the line of ***Thanatos***.

Thanatos	67m	HVS+	★★★	1968

A good pitch which when combined with ***Electron*** provides one of the best outings at its grade on the crag. Start just right of the lowest part of the crag, directly beneath the large roofed corner.

1 27m (4b). Climb a slab and vegetation to a corner. Go up this for a couple of metres, then move left onto the steep slab, which leads to a bilberry ledge. Continue up to a second bilberry ledge at the base of the main corner.

2 30m (5b). An excellent, well-protected pitch. Climb the corner until just below the first overhang. Traverse left onto a rib and enter a groove below the second overhang. Make difficult moves on the left to reach a good ledge.

3 10m. An easy groove leads to the ***Great Heather Shelf***; scramble a further 15 metres up this to belay. ***Electron*** lies round the corner to the left and is reached by a traverse, first down, then up.

Thin It Is	177m	E1	★★	2004

A good outing, essentially the right arête of *Thanatos* in the lower section followed by the fine buttress left of *Odin*, giving four excellent pitches.

1 27m. Follow Pitch 1 of *Thanatos* to the second bilberry ledge.

2 20m (5a). Starting on the right, follow cracks in the right wall to the left end of a small grass ledge. Climb the groove and arête on the left for 4 metres before traversing rightwards to a somewhat convoluted belay on a higher ledge (mid-pitch 3 of *Shamrock Tower*).

3 35m (5b). Climb the thin crack in the left wall, passing a slot with difficulty to gain a good hold over the bulge above. Pull immediately left using a hidden side pull into the base of a hanging groove above the roof of *Thanatos*. Follow the groove to the *Great Heather Shelf* and scramble up this to belay.

4 20m. Scramble further, diagonally rightwards, up the *Great Heather Shelf* to a massive upstanding flake at the upper right extremity, overlooking *Walker's Gully*.

5 40m (5b). Go straight up for 5 metres and traverse to the right along a flake into a short corner. Climb this and the left-trending groove for about 10 metres (all as for *Odin*) until just below a kink rightwards at the start of a long crack. Finger traverse left to the arête and step round it onto a good foothold. Continue the traverse another move to a crack and follow this with decreasing difficulty up the fine wall to a big grass ledge. On the left is a prominent square arête with a short wall to its right leading to a V-groove and bounded on the right by a left-facing corner. Belay in this corner.

6 35m (5a). Climb the corner, moving right to its rib to avoid the bulge. Continue up a second corner and at its top step right to the foot of a slab. Follow cracks up the slab to a short headwall which is overcome directly on blocky jugs.

Shamrock Eliminate	183m	HVS+	★★	1965

These two sets of variations (to *Shamrock Tower* and *Odin*) combine to give good varied climbing the full length of the *Shamrock*, but each can also be climbed in its own right.

Shamrock Variations VS+

Improves with height. A good pitch up the obvious V-groove in the right arête of *Thanatos*. It can be climbed on its own as a start to any of the routes on the *Upper Tier*.

1 23m. Follow Pitch 1 of *Thanatos* as far as the first bilberry ledge and belay in a small corner on the edge of the right arête.

Right: Chris King making the first ascent of Pitch 5 of **Thin It Is** (E1), Pillar Rock.
Photo: Stephen Reid

2 35m (5a). Climb the stepped corner on the left of the arête for 4 metres. Move up and right, round the arête, and up into the bottom of the V-groove. Climb the groove to its top and follow the obvious corner above to a grass ledge. Take the left-hand of short twin grooves to the stance in another short groove on Pitch 3 of ***Shamrock Tower***.

3 45m (4a). Traverse horizontally left for 3 metres round the arête and gain easier rock which leads to the ***Great Heather Shelf***. Scramble diagonally rightwards up this to a massive upstanding flake at the upper right extremity, overlooking ***Walker's Gully***.

Odin Variations HVS+

4 20m (4b). From the upstanding flake, move left and enter the obvious left-slanting hanging groove, which is awkward to start. Climb the groove to a block belay just over the top on the right under a V-groove.

5 25m (4b). From the bottom of the block belay, avoid the V-groove by stepping out right onto the steep buttress. Move up and right, then go straight up excellent rock to a good belay in a left-facing corner crack.

6 20m (5a). Above just on the left is an obvious V-groove just right of the prominent buttress. Climb the steep wall on small holds to gain a grass ledge at the foot of the groove. The smooth groove is difficult to start. After about 6 metres escape right and climb the rib. All quite "top-end".

7 15m (4c). The V-groove above to the top.

Shamrock Tower	176m	MVS	★★	1940

Enjoyable climbing at the top end of the grade.

1 23m. As for Pitch 1 of ***Thanatos*** to the first bilberry ledge and belay in a small corner on the edge of the arête.

2 18m (4b). From the belay, step onto the arête on the right, climb up a little, and then rightwards into a corner (junction with ***Odin***). Ascend the corner to a small ledge and very large block belay.

3 25m (4b). Traverse left for 3 metres and step round the arête into a V-shaped groove; climb this and the wide groove above (mainly on the right) to a pair of small grass ledges at its top. Move up the right-hand of two short corners to another grass ledge and belay in a short V-corner by a large block to the right (or climb the left-hand corner direct at 5a).

4 45m (4a). Move up right onto the block, step right and climb a cracked slab. Cross the ***Great Heather Shelf*** diagonally up and rightwards to a massive upstanding flake at the upper right extremity, overlooking ***Walker's Gully***.

5 40m (4b). Go straight up for 5 metres and traverse to the right along a flake. Turn the arête and climb straight up and then slightly rightwards to gain the huge left-facing corner. This is followed to a large ledge on the right.

6 25m. Continue up an easy rock ridge to the top of the buttress.

Odin	178m	HVS+	★★	1960

An excellent route following the main *Shamrock Ridge*. Even the pitch of heather-bashing to cross the *Great Heather Shelf* does not detract greatly from its quality. Start about 6 metres to the right of *Thanatos* where 30 metres of grassy scrambling leads to the left side of a bay and a spike belay; this is a few metres up and left of a short corner.

1 18m (4c). Step off the spike and go directly up the steep wall and a short groove to a slim ledge on the right and large block belay, junction with *Shamrock Tower*.

2 25m (5b). Climb off the block and into the niche above with difficulty, then step right to avoid the roof and climb directly up steep rock to reach a long slim groove on the right. Climb this for 2 metres, then move back left across the wall to a grass ledge. A mantelshelf leads to another grass ledge and block belay.

3 45m (4b). Climb over the bulge on the left and cross the *Great Heather Shelf* diagonally up and rightwards to a massive upstanding flake at the upper right extremity, overlooking *Walker's Gully*.

4 50m (4c). Go straight up for 5 metres and traverse to the right along a flake into a short corner. Climb this and the left-trending groove and continue up a long crack to a ledge. A superb pitch.

5 40m. Continue up the easy ridge and scramble to the *Tea Table*.

The Magic Rainbow	70m	E1-	★★	1972

A worthwhile route, giving a slightly harder alternative to *Thanatos* to reach routes on the upper buttress e.g. *Necromancer*. Start some 10 metres right of *Thanatos* at a short left-facing corner reached by scrambling 15 metres up rushes – this is a few metres down and right of the spike belay at the start of *Odin*.

1 20m (5b). Climb the corner for two metres until it is possible to move across the steep left wall to gain a slim left-facing groove. Climb the groove to a grass ledge on the right.

2 30m (5a). Climb a short groove just up and right of the belay, or its left wall moving back right at the top to a ledge. Climb up the steep wall above to gain the left end of a narrow ramp. Follow the prominent crack above, pulling out left at the top, and scramble up 8 metres. Alternatively, from the right end of the ramp, follow a thin crack, exiting leftwards.

3 20m. Climb the short wall to the *Great Heather Shelf*.

The Magic Rainbow Direct E1 1994

2 30m (5b). Traverse right along the gangway for 4 metres. Follow a line of good holds diagonally left across the steep wall to a short hanging crack directly above the belay. Make an awkward move into the groove above. Climb the groove to an obvious V-groove above. Climb the awkward groove to a large ledge.

Between ***The Magic Rainbow*** and ***Walker's Gully*** lies a lot of unpleasant looking vegetated rock: **Green Pastures** (S, 1939) wends its way up here before continuing up the overgrown right-to-left-slanting line in the ***Upper Tier*** that can be clearly seen when approaching from Ennerdale. Even the first ascensionists admitted that the climb was somewhat grassy and its full description has been relegated to the FRCC website.

Necromancer	105m	E1-	★★	1968

Worth doing but only for its upper pitches which give fine bold slab climbing. It is best climbed in conjunction with either ***Thanatos*** or ***Magic Rainbow***. The original start followed the left edge of ***Walker's Gully*** but it consists of 60 metres of grassy rock with a short hard wall. From the right-hand end of the ***Great Heather Shelf*** scramble down into ***Walker's Gully*** to a block belay at the top of Pitch 2 of ***Walker's Gully***. It is also possible to gain the belay at the start of the second pitch by traversing rightwards 10 metres from the huge flake at the upper right end on the ***Great Heather Shelf*** (4b).

1 35m (5a). Climb a grassy groove on the left into a wet cave. Exit right from the cave onto a steep slab and ascend it, keeping to the centre for the best climbing. Move up and right to a small stance and large block belay in a fine position overlooking the gully.

2 30m (5a). Climb the slab below the impressive final wall. Move to the left edge and climb the flake crack until it is possible to traverse right to the centre of the wall. Climb boldly up to a small flake, then move right and continue up the slab to a ledge and block belay.

3 40m. Continue up the easy ridge and scramble to the ***Tea Table***.

Direct Start 12m E2 1986

Start from the block belay at the foot of the route, at an obvious crack just left of ***Walker's Gully***.

1 (5c). Climb the crack with increasing difficulty until it fades out after 10 metres. Then move delicately left to join the original route.

The Eightfold Way	178m	E1-		1968

This girdle traverse of ***Shamrock*** starts as for ***Photon***. By combining this route with ***The Link*** and ***The Girdle Traverse*** it is possible to make ***The Greater Traverse*** of over 500 metres. Unfortunately the climbing is nowhere near as good as befits the notion, being largely mossy and lichenous.

1 **25m (4b).** Climb the steepening groove of ***Photon*** or, better, the first pitch of ***Eros*** (5a).
2 **30m (4c).** Walk along the grass ledge and stride across ***The Shamrock Chimneys*** to a large sloping hold. Step down and round the arête and make an ascending traverse, delicate in places, passing a mossy streak to a junction with ***Electron*** above the bulge of the first pitch; climb up the big corner to a ledge at its top.
3 **10m (4b).** Traverse the short wall on the right to the top of a grassy groove. Follow an obvious poorly protected and exposed traverse line across the steep wall on the right. Just round the arête is a small stance and hollow blocks belay, below the crux pitch of ***Lepton***.
4 **18m (4a).** Hand-traverse horizontally into the corner of ***Boson***. Leave this by an easy grass ledge on the right to a belay round the arête.
5 **12m (5a).** From the right end of the ledge, step down and round the corner. Continue traversing to a crack and descend the undercut wall below on moss covered jugs until it is possible to step up right to a ledge.
6 **25m (5b).** Climb the V-groove to the overhang; step to the right onto the wall and traverse (all very dirty) to a good jug round the corner. Mantelshelf on to this and traverse horizontally into ***Odin*** below the steep section. Traverse horizontally past some wedged blocks into the corner of ***Shamrock Tower*** (poor stance).
7 **18m (5a).** Gain a crack on the rib on the right and follow this for a short distance until it is possible to traverse right to the centre of the wall. Climb boldly up to a small flake, then move right and continue up the slab to a ledge and block belay (second half of Pitch 2 of ***Necromancer***).
8 **40m.** Continue up the easy ridge and scramble to the ***Tea Table***.

The Link	75m	E1		1968

A high-level girdle traverse of the walls of ***Walker's Gully*** with extreme exposure. Unfortunately there is rather more grass and lichen than rock and the climbing is serious due to poor belays. This traverse links the girdle of ***Shamrock*** (***The Eightfold Way***) with the girdle of the main crag, making possible ***The Greater Traverse***. Start at the belay at the end of Pitch 5 of ***The Eightfold Way***.
1 **15m (4b).** Drop down rightwards awkwardly on grass to gain a huge flake just above the upper right end of the ***Great Heather Shelf*** and traverse the top of this to swing round the arête at its end. Keep traversing rightwards on grassy rock to a small spike belay overlooking ***Walker's Gully***.
2 **15m.** Abseil straight down the impending wall into the impressive ***Walker's Gully***.

3 **18m (5a).** Follow a slight foot-traverse across the right wall and make a scary pull out onto the rib on the right (it is possible and probably wise to arrange a high side runner on the opposite wall of the gully before starting this pitch). Climb the short wall above to gain a grassy left-slanting groove/ramp (***Side Slip***) which is ascended a short way on sloping holds to a faint depression where a stance may be taken. Arrange a myriad of mostly useless belay points in the vegetation above.

4 **27m (5a).** An intimidating pitch to second – fortunately the protection is good. Continue up the right branch of groove above and mantelshelf onto the thin grass ledge on the right. Follow this to its end; then descend a narrow mossy gangway until it is possible to step to the right to better holds on a rock pedestal. Continue traversing rightwards more easily to a belay at the start of the final pitch of ***Grooved Wall***.

The Original Way

A rather pointless loop in the ***Greater Girdle***.

Start at the belay at the end of Pitch 5 of ***The Eightfold Way***.

1 **25m (5b).** Pitch 6 of ***The Eightfold Way***.

2 **12m (4b).** Gain a crack in the right-hand rib; descend this, and move down diagonally to a large pinnacle belay overlooking ***Walker's Gully*** (first half of Pitch 2 of ***Necromancer*** in reverse).

Walker's Gully	125m	MVS	★★★	1899

One of the few good gully climbs of the district and a very imposing and atmospheric route; it follows the deep cleft separating ***Shamrock*** from the ***North Face of Low Man***. The pitches may be split if necessary. Helmets are strongly advised as there is much loose scree above the gully. The last pitch may be found harder by short people.

1 **27m.** Climb a short easy chimney followed by scree, to the foot of a high green chimney. Climb the right wall of the chimney and gain a sloping grass terrace.

2 **40m (4a).** An exposed groove with poor holds is climbed until it is possible to step on to the first chockstone in the chimney. Another chockstone just above is easily surmounted, followed by scrambling up the bed of the gully for 30 metres. ***Necromancer*** and the ***Right Wall of Walker's Gully*** routes start here.

3 **18m (4b).** Climb rocks on the left of a chimney to a cave in the gully which is usually wet. Climb up behind, then over, a chockstone; then bridge the gully until a sloping chockstone is reached. Another chockstone is very awkward.

4 **25m.** A short scree slope leads to a cave in the gully formed by a large chockstone. The through route is strenuous but short. It can be

avoided by climbing the left wall outside the cave. A further through route leads to a wet cave.

5 15m (4c). More large chockstones are encountered until the cave below the crux is reached (a thread runner may be found high up in the recess between the capstone and the exit wall, but it is awkward to fix). Move across the right wall on sloping holds to a recess under the final capstone. The tall can then back-up - back on the left wall. Otherwise continue climbing strenuously up the right wall.

Original Start 85m 1898

Not as good as the route described above: start some metres to the left of the foot of the gully.

1 15m. Grassy ledges.
2 20m. Traverse left to a corner. Continue the traverse for 3 metres.
3 15m. The chimney, which has good holds.
4 35m. A walk over a grassy terrace to the right; then upwards to join the gully midway up Pitch 2.

Additional Finish 60m D 1909

The climb runs up the ridge on the left and its start is reached by crossing over the top of the capstone.

6 18m. A crack is climbed to a block on the ridge. A steep wall is now ascended on good holds to a platform on the right.
7 12m. Move onto a ledge on the right in order to get onto a ridge on the left as this provides the best climbing.
8 30m. Easy scrambling finishing near the *Tea Table* at the top of the *Shamrock*.

North Face of Low Man

The *North Face* is a large crag, up to 130 metres high, which offers a good variety of worthwhile climbs and some not so worthwhile. Difficults and Extremes lie side by side, many of which are among the best in the district. Due to an excess of grassy ledges, virtually all the routes become very unpleasant in wet conditions.

All the climbs, with the exception the upper routes of the *Right Wall of Walker's Gully* and *Pedestal Wall*, start from *Green Ledge*, a very prominent grassy traverse, which crosses the cliff rightwards from the bottom of *Walker's Gully*. At the right-hand end of *Green Ledge*, the *Bounding Buttress* marks the start of such routes as *North-West Climb*, and just beyond this point it is possible to scramble round to the *West Face* via the *Waterfall* (see page 262 for details).

Descent:

The easiest descents are:

a) by descending ***Stony Gully*** (the grassy gully on the east side of ***Low Man***) a little way to just above a rock step then climb a short wall on the left (looking in) and traverse leftwards over grass and bilberry ledges to the scree above ***Walker's Gully*** from where the ***Shamrock Traverse*** is easily reached;

b) descend ***The Old West Route***, then scramble down and cross the ***Waterfall*** (great care needed in wet conditions) to gain ***Green Ledge***;

c) if the crossing of the ***Waterfall*** does not appeal, then after descending ***The Old West Route***, a path on the opposite side of the scree leads to open hillside that can be descended more easily;

d) follow ***The Old West Route*** to the summit of ***High Man*** and descend from there (see page 210).

The routes are described from **left** to **right**.

Right Wall of Walker's Gully

The first few routes start from the small amphitheatre at the top of Pitch 2 of ***Walker's Gully*** and climb the vertical open right wall of the ***Gully***. They can also be reached from the ***Great Heather Shelf*** on the ***Shamrock***. While the climbing is steep with fine situations, it is so vegetated that it cannot be recommended, although the flowers are very pretty.

Side Slip	57m	VS		1976

This horrible overgrown route follows a prominent line of grooves on the immediate right (true left) of the top half of ***Walker's Gully***. Start immediately out right from the small amphitheatre.

1 15m (4b). Climb the groove on the right of the gully, moving right on to a large ledge.

2 15m (4c). Follow the groove over a small overhang to a small stance.

3 27m (4a). Continue up the left-hand groove to a large ledge and climb the corner to the top.

Over the Hill	50m	E1		1987

When clean, reportedly a fine route with good situations – but now reverted back to nature. Start as for ***Soliton***, just right of ***Side Slip***. Steep and strenuous climbing with good protection though you'll have to dig for it.

1 25m (5b). Traverse out of the gully, as for ***Soliton***, for a couple of metres, then climb a short rock corner to a grassy rake: this point is level with and just to the left of the hand-traverse into ***Soliton***. Move up left into the leftwards-facing diagonal crack and climb it until a long slanting overlap is reached. Move up and right into the continuation of the crack and climb it steeply to a recess. Climb this and

move right round a boss of rock to good belays and junction with the traverse of *The Link*.

2 25m (5b). Move back left into the recess and climb a short delicate groove in a leftward-slanting gangway (*The Link* in reverse). When at the level of a grass ledge, climb straight up the wall into a large recess (*Soliton* moves right here). Make some bold exhilarating moves straight up out of the recess and climb steeply up the wall on widely spaced holds which appear in all the right places, until forced to move right into a large corner recess. Climb this moving right at the top.

Soliton	60m	HVS		1972

This route follows a very prominent narrow chimney-groove right of *Over the Hill* and, although somewhat marred by the wanderings of its second pitch, it was once described as containing some fine steep climbing. Unfortunately it is also marred by being very overgrown nowadays. Start immediately right of *Side Slip*.

1 30m (5a). Traverse out of the gully and move across mixed ground to the foot of an obvious crack and groove-line on the right wall. The start of the crack is very steep and vegetated and is turned by a short scramble up on the left, followed by a horizontal traverse into the crack. Up this by steep jamming and bridging to a short chimney which leads to a good grass ledge and junction with *Grooved Wall*.

2 30m (5a). Traverse left along a grass ledge and continue round a bulge (junction with *Over the Hill*), and into a recess; climb a short delicate groove in a leftward-slanting gangway. When at the level of a grass ledge (the traverse of *The Link* in reverse), there is a large recess above. From a handhold on the right edge of the recess, make a diagonal traverse rightwards across the wall to a good foothold. Continue up the wall above to a groove which leads to the top of the crag.

North-East Face of Low Man

The next few climbs all start in the area between the bottom of *Walker's Gully* and the step up at the start of *Green Ledge*. Once they were all great climbs here, but moss and lichen have reclaimed some of them, and only *Tapestry*, *Grooved Wall* and *Sheol* are worth considering now.

The Black Widow	100m	E2		1968

Ascends the hanging groove in the black wall high up to the left of *Sheol*. The fierce second pitch is sustained and strenuous. Once a fine route – but now gone to seed. Start in *Walker's Gully* by scrambling 12 metres up to the foot of the steep wall on the right of the gully.

1 25m (5a). Follow a line of expanding flakes rightwards, across the wall, to join *Grooved Wall*. Climb the chimney and belay on top of a pinnacle.

High Man
Low Man
Stony Gully
The Hand Traverse
The Nose
Walker's Gully MVS***
1
2
3
4
5
6
7
8
9
10
11
12
15
16
24
25
26
27
28
29
30

Pillar Rock North-East Face of Low Man

1	Side Slip	VS	
2	Over the Hill	E1	
3	Soliton	HVS	
4	The Black Widow	E2	
5	Tapestry	E4	***
6	Grooved Wall	VS	***
7	Cunning Stunts	E2	
8	Sheol	E2	**
9	North-East Climb	MS	**
10	Savage Gully	MVS	*
11	North Climb	MS	***
12	Aknaton	VS	*
13	Klingsor	E2	
14	Patriarch of the Pillarites	E3	*
15	Proton	E1	*
16	Hadrian's Wall	VS	
17	Scylla (upper part)	HVS	**
18	Puppet (middle part)	E2	**
19	Straits of Messina	E4	*
20	Caucus Race (lower part)	E3	*
21	Nor'-Nor'-West Climb	VS	**
22	Roraima (lower part)	E1	*
23	North-West Climb (l. part)	MVS	***

East Face of High Man

24	Slab & Notch Climb (part)	M	***
25	The Curtain and the Arête	HS	**
26	The Great Chimney	D	
27	The Old Wall Route	M	

North-East Face of High Man

28	North-East Chimney	VD	
29	North-East Arête	S	**
30	The Old West Route (part)	M	***

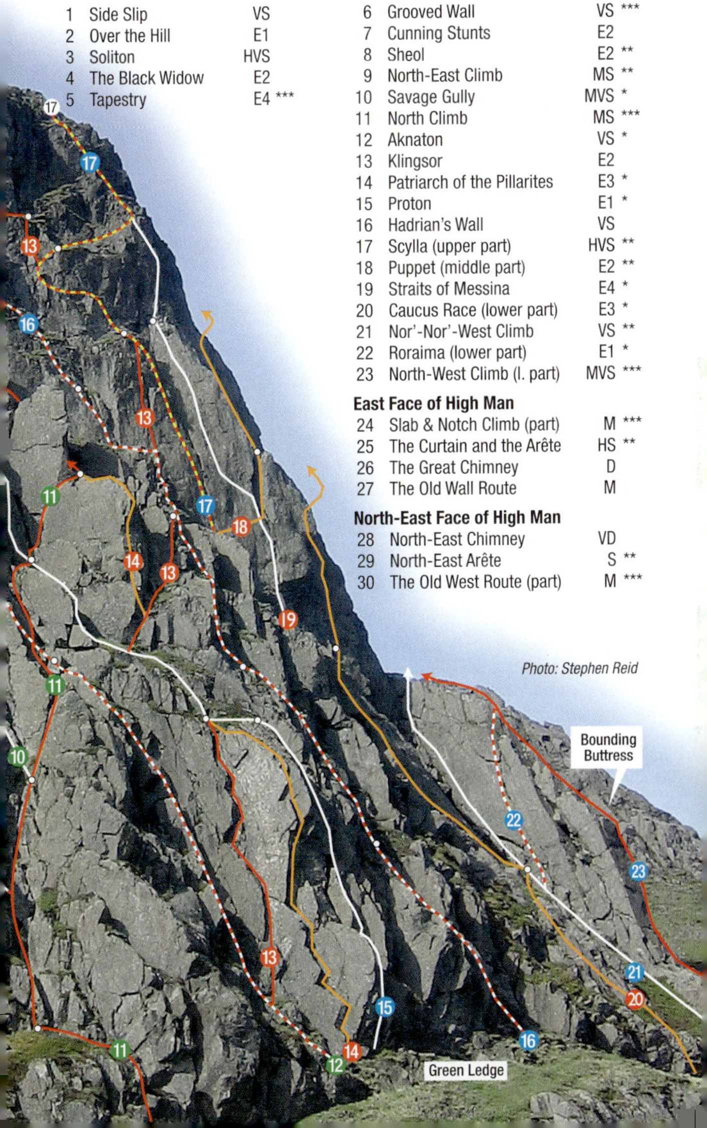

Photo: Stephen Reid

2 25m (5c). Climb up a little and traverse right across a mossy wall to two sloping ledges. Pull round into a groove to reach the overhang. Climb the overhang with some difficulty and up into a niche at the bottom of the groove. Follow the groove on good holds at first and then with difficulty to the final overhang. Traverse right to the arête and pull onto a grass ledge.
3 30m (5a). Traverse right for a couple of metres and climb a crack in the groove to a slab. Climb the slab to a small grass stance (possible belay), then jam up the overhanging twin cracks to a ledge.
4 20m (4c). Climb the crack above and finish up the short groove.

Tapestry	70m	E4	★★★	1980

Fit to hang on any wall – and reasonably clean to boot! Excellent climbing in good situations but with a serious second pitch. Scramble 12 metres up from *Walker's Gully* to start at the foot of its steep right-bounding wall.
1 25m (5b). Climb the centre of the huge pinnacle of ***Black Widow*** Pitch 1 and finish by its left edge (junction with ***Grooved Wall***). Follow ***Grooved Wall*** to belay beneath the overhang on the crux pitch of that climb.
2 20m (6a). Climb the overhang of ***Grooved Wall*** and immediately step right to a shallow corner. Follow this almost to the top (last, tricky to arrange, gear), then gain the wall on its left and climb it, moving right to finish on the belay ledge.
3 25m (5b). From the right-hand end of the ledge, a groove in the arête leads to a soaring leftward hand-traverse. Follow this and then climb a crack back right to finish.

Grooved Wall	124m	VS+	★★★	1928

A good climb, despite the first pitch, taking the prominent series of difficult grooves running up the right wall of *Walker's Gully*. Start on the path just right of the foot of the gully. All difficulties are well-protected.
1 45m (4a). Scramble 15 metres up high grassy ledges which lead up to a wide broken chimney composed of a vast flake for its left-hand side. The chimney is followed to its top.
2 35m (5a). The left-hand groove above is followed and a ledge attained (it is possible to belay on this ledge which will make the next moves safer for the leader as they will have the second to land on should they fall off). Above is an overhanging crack, which is the crux of the climb. Gain the groove above and continue up it to a good spike belay.

Right: Chris King weaves his way up the final pitch of **Tapestry** (E4), Pillar Rock.
Photo: Stephen Reid

3 20m (4b). Continue up the sustained groove to belay by a corner on the side of the groove.

4 24m (4c). The final groove above is not without interest, but ends after 12 metres. Continue up ledges and grass to a rock gateway which opens onto the scree just above ***Walker's Gully***. From the gateway, a Difficult scramble up the ridge above brings you to the foot of the excellent ***North-East Arête*** (S) which makes a fine way to the summit of ***High Man***.

Cunning Stunts	60m	E2		1981

An aptly named climb, with three very different styles of climbing – delicate, tricky and brutal. It takes the prominent corner and arête between ***The Black Widow*** and ***Sheol***. Once worth three stars, but now the first pitch possesses some of the finest looking moss growth on the crag – and that's saying something! Take a large spray can full of Roundup© and start below a short grassy corner just left of the obvious jagged crack of ***Sheol***.

1 25m (5b). The grassy corner leads to a steep jamming crack forming the right side of a huge flake. Climb this and the continuation ramp to a large detached block (thread). Step onto the right wall of the leaning groove (peg runner) and make an awkward move onto the next ramp; up this and the finger-crack to a good ledge.

2 15m (5c). Step left across the overhanging wall to gain a flake-crack on the arête. Levitate strenuously onto the exposed ledge and up twin jamming cracks to belay below the final pitch of ***Tapestry***.

3 20m (5b). Climb the groove in the arête, as for ***Tapestry***, to an overhanging wide crack containing two chockstones. Climb this with grace to the top. Scramble 15 metres rightwards over ledges to the **descent** path which traverses left to the top of ***Walker's Gully***.

Sheol	86m	E2-	★★	1965

The impressive jagged soaring crack in the wall immediately right of ***Grooved Wall***. An excellent first pitch on a route where the difficulties diminish rapidly, although the upper pitches are pleasant enough and on good if dirty rock. Start by scrambling up grass to the foot of the crack.

1 22m (5b). The sustained and awkward crack, which is nearly vertical and tilts slightly to one side, is followed in its entirety to a good stance and chockstone belay.

2 22m (5a). Above are three grooves. Follow ***North-East Climb***, first rightwards then back leftwards, and gain the very steep, and cleaner looking, right-hand groove by traversing in from the left. Sustained bridging gains a ledge and belay.

Left: Martin Armitage searches for holds and runners on the overhanging crux of **Grooved Wall** (VS), Pillar Rock. **Photo:** Stephen Reid

3 15m (4c). Climb the groove on the left exiting it to the right a few metres below the top to a ledge.

4 27m (4a). Climb straight up and finish up the wide square chimney that is the last pitch of ***Savage Gully*** to belay on top of the ***Nose*** of ***North Climb***.

Sheol/Tapestry Connection	67m	E2-	★★★	

It is possible and very rewarding to combine the first pitch of ***Sheol*** with a short section of ***North-East Climb*** and the final pitch of ***Tapestry***, making an impressive way up the crag. For even greater interest the second pitch of ***Cunning Stunts***, which starts from the grass ledge just above the belay at the top of Pitch 1 of ***Sheol***, can also be included (E2).

North Face of Low Man

The next climbs start above the step up at the start of ***Green Ledge***.

North-East Climb	116m	MS	★★	1912

A classic route with atmosphere and good situations in the upper half, despite an abundance of grass. Start as for ***North Climb*** from the very left end of ***Green Ledge*** at a patch of gravel where a short wall leads to a square platform.

1 10m. Pitch 1 of ***North Climb***. An easy mantelshelf and short slab lead to a large ledge at the foot of a broken gully/groove.

2 26m. Climb the gully of Pitch 2 of ***North Climb*** for 10 metres to the second ledge (possible belay) at about half height. Move up a metre, then traverse 3 metres across the rib on the left. A 3 metre chimney leads to a small stance (possible belay). Move round the rib on the left on to a slab. Traverse the slab to grassy ledges.

3 23m. A short chimney leads to a longer one with an awkward finish. Climb the short slab on the left, then walk left to a long V-groove on the wall of ***Walker's Gully***.

4 24m. Climb the groove to a corner with a belay.

5 18m. A mossy wall on the right leads to a good ledge behind a big block (possible belay). A steep chimney is followed by easier climbing to a grassy corner.

6 15m. Another steep chimney is followed by grassy ledges. From here a traverse can be made right to ***Low Man*** or left to the scree above ***Walker's Gully***.

Savage Gully	104m	MVS	★	1901

A climb of some character: the grass should be considered as part of its nature and provides essential handholds. Much harder (and more serious) in anything other than bone dry conditions. Start as for ***North Climb***.

1 35m. Follow Pitches 1 and 2 of *North Climb* to the foot of *Twisting Chimney*.
2 25m (4b). The *Gully* (which is actually more of a V-groove) rises steeply above on the left. Climb the groove on the right for 12 metres and move left, round the rib, and make an awkward pull-up to a grass ledge. Regain the right-hand groove and climb it, passing the chockstone on the right or left, to a good belay.
3 20m (4b). A delicate step left leads to a rock nest. Climb the jamming crack in the corner, then rounded rocks straight ahead lead to a stance in a bay under a wide square undercut chimney on the right.
4 24m (4a). Climb bulging rock awkwardly into the chimney and exit via the right wall to a ledge level with the *Nose* of *North Climb*. Belay 5 metres higher on the right wall of the grassy *Stony Gully* which leads to *Low Man*.

Variation Start 35m 1968

This variation avoids some of the grass and starts 10 metres up Pitch 2 of *North Climb*.

(4c). Move left up slabs to below a steep crack; this is climbed for 10 metres to a ledge, then move right to a groove. Climb the groove direct to a stance in a rock nest, midway up Pitch 3 of *Savage Gully*.

Nose Finish 35m 1931

4 24m (4b). Climb a crack in the wall on the right of the bay to the *Strid Ledge* on *North Climb* and finish via the *Nose* (as for *North Climb*).

North Climb	101m	MS	★★★	1891

A superb classic Difficult with a Severe finish which is considerably harder in wet weather. It has been the scene of many epics and should not be underrated by novice parties. It is possible to avoid the last pitch by taking the *Savage Gully* exit but this is not recommended. Take lots of slings and start from the very left end of *Green Ledge*, at a patch of gravel, where a short wall leads to a square platform.

1 10m. An easy mantelshelf and short slab lead to a large ledge at the foot of a broken gully/groove. This groove is the lower section of *Savage Gully*.
2 25m. Follow the gully/groove until it steepens at a small grassy bay. On the left, the smooth double groove of *Savage Gully* continues in a soaring line. On the right is the deep *Twisting Chimney*.
3 34m. Climb *Twisting Chimney* and then trend leftwards up an open groove. Scramble up to a belay on a small ledge at the meeting of two narrow chimneys.
4 9m. The *Stomach Traverse*. Squeeze up and along the right-hand chimney which curves to the right in its upper half.
5 18m. The be-chockstoned corner is climbed via a capstone, followed by a walk of 6 metres to the *Split Blocks*. Climbed into the *Split*, turn

Pillar Rock North Face of Low Man

1	Necromancer	E1 **
2	Walker's Gully	MVS ***
3	Side Slip	VS
4	Soliton	HVS
5	The Black Widow	E2
6	Tapestry	E4 ***
7	Grooved Wall	VS ***
8	Cunning Stunts	E2
9	Sheol	E2 **
10	North-East Climb	MS **
11	Savage Gully	MVS *
12	North Climb	MS ***

13	Ahknaton	VS *
14	Klingsor	E2
15	Patriarch of the Pillarities	E3 *
16	Proton	E1 *
17	Hadrian's Wall	VS
18	Scylla	HVS **
19	Puppet	E2 **
20	Straits of Messina	E4 *
21	Caucus Race	E3 *
22	Megaton	HVS/E1 ***
23	Goodbye to all That	E1 ***
24	Nor'-Nor'-West Climb	VS **
V	Variation	VS
25	Roraima (lower part only)	E1 *
26	Ximenes	HVS **
27	North-West Climb	MVS ***

North East Face of High Man

28	North-East Chimney	VD
29	North-East Arête	S **
30	Old West Route (part)	M ***

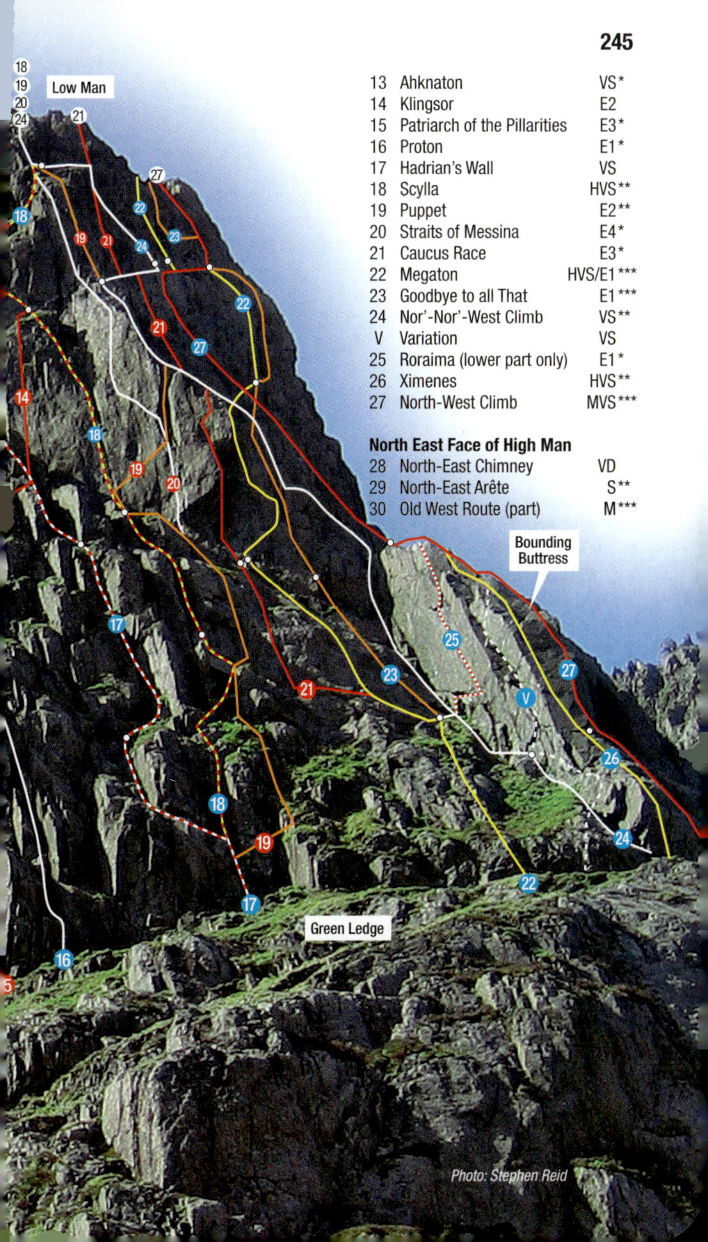

Photo: Stephen Reid

left and wriggle up the chimney to the top of the ***Blocks***. Traverse to the left, making an exposed stride across the fearful void of the ***Strid***, to a big ledge below and right of the *Nose*.

6 5m. *The Nose*. Go left along the ledge to a corner (high runner). From the corner, work out leftwards to stand on the tip of a projecting flake. Will it, won't it moves up and left gain better holds and a ledge just above; belay immediately. The easy grassy ***Stony Gully*** leads to the summit of ***Low Man*** from where ***The Old West Route*** can be joined. Alternatively a rising traverse across bilberry and heather to the left of ***Stony Gully*** crosses a rock ridge after 50 metres and lands you at the foot of ***Great Chimney*** from where a further traverse left and up gains the **descent** of the ***Shamrock Traverse***.

The Hand Traverse 8m HS ★★ 1892

An excellent alternative finish, particularly in the case of a runny *Nose*!

6. From the right end of the ledge below the *Nose*, climb the steep wall for about 3 metres on tremendous holds until the sharp edge of a flake is reached. Traverse boldly left to the top of the *Nose*.

The Nose Direct 5m HVS 2003

6 (5a). As for the *Nose* to the corner. Struggle up this direct, via a huge block.

Descent into Savage Gully VD

Definitely not recommended as a finish to ***North Climb*** and famously dismissed by first ascentionist Haskett Smith as "stooping to conquer", but included for historical completeness. Although technically easy, it involves a long runout with no runners and much rope flicking.

6. Get lowered from below the *Nose* for 12 metres into the amphitheatre near the top of ***Savage Gully***. Traverse left 20 metres around the arête on the left to the foot of a 12 metre chimney/groove. Climb the chimney, followed by an easy upward traverse right for 20 metres into ***Stony Gully*** (the easy upper part of ***Savage Gully***) and so gain the top of the *Nose*. Lower a rope down to bring up your shivering second.

Variation Starts

Two poor alternative starts exist. The first one ***The Intermediate Variation*** (50m, D, 1921) starts 18 metres to the right and climbs mostly grass parallel to the ordinary route, joining that route near the top of ***Twisting Chimney***. The second one starts 55 metres right of the ordinary route and is called ***The Westerly Variation*** (D, 1891). This takes a roughly diagonal line left across the ***North Face*** under the obvious square cut chimney of ***Scylla***, and taking the easiest line to the base of the large clean wall at its right-

Right: Dave Lehane sampling the 19th Century delights of the **Stomach Traverse** on **North Climb** (MS), Pillar Rock and, **inset**, a 19th Century ascent of the same pitch (note the ice axe!) **Photos:** Stephen Reid and FRCC Archive

hand end. Follow grass leftwards to join the ordinary route at the *Split Blocks*.

Akhnaton	88m	VS+	★	1967

A fine direct line up the massive corner some 9 metres along *Green Ledge*; this is the first major feature encountered after *North Climb*. Unfortunately it suffers from being rather dirty and also from having easier options to the left at several points, but is still well worth doing. A highlight is the *Hand Traverse* finish of *North Climb*. Scramble a few metres up a grassy bay to the base of the corner.

1 47m (4c). Climb the groove, surmounting two bulges, to a grass ledge; continue up grass a couple of metres to join the polished corner-crack on *North Climb* Pitch 3 which is follow it to a ledge and block belay on the right.

2 33m (4c). Traverse left into the bottom of the continuation groove which is marked at half-height by a large pinnacle on the right. Carry on up the groove with increasing difficulty and belay just right of the *Nose* on *North Climb*.

4 8m (4b). From the belay, step right and go up the steep wall to hand-traverse left and finish on the top of *North Climb*.

Klingsor	142m	E2-		1974

An eliminate which weaves its way up the face. Pitch 3 is good but hardly justifies the rest of the climb. It starts at the foot of *Akhnaton* and follows the groove system on the steep right wall, before breaking rightwards to the big wall of *Scylla*.

1 30m (5a). Climb the groove and very vegetated crack-line to belay on ledges above.

2 38m. Move up right to a short corner leading to an easy rake. Follow this rightwards (mainly grass) to emerge on a ledge below a very thin crack-line in the steep wall, left of the crack of *Scylla*.

3 27m (5b). Move up to a ledge with a perched block. Step off the block and climb the wall, first right, then left of the crack-line until a short hanging V-groove can be entered. Pull out right to gain a ledge above. Step left onto the steep wall and go straight up to a ledge. A good well-protected pitch.

4 25m (5a). As for Pitch 4 of *Scylla*; from the left end of the ledge, pull up an overhanging wall and traverse left to the foot of a narrow crack, which is climbed to the top of a pinnacle. Climb straight up the short narrow grooves above to a ledge.

5 22m (5b). Step left to the toe of the buttress. Climb up and leftwards, across the steep slab, to a nut runner round the left edge, then traverse right to gain a prominent ledge. Enter a steep shallow groove

on the right edge; go up this and the wall above to belay well back. All rather steep and seriously loose!

Patriarch of the Pillarites	65m	E3	★	1988

An excellent climb which ascends the bold hanging arête immediately right of Pitch 1 of ***Klingsor*** and starts as for that route.

1 35m (5c). Start as for ***Klingsor*** but pull onto the ramp on the right; follow this to a spike runner beneath an impending wall. Bridge up and make a hard pull round the arête on the left onto a steep wall. Climb this (bold) on small spaced holds for 3 metres and step right into the thin corner which leads to the belay.

2 30m (5c). Scramble 10 metres up ***Proton*** and climb the middle of three short corners. Move left to a small niche which is above an obvious crack. Climb the bulge above slightly rightwards to a hollow flake and small pocket. Move delicately up to the overhang and make hard moves right (crux) to a crack which leads to a finishing ledge covered in small debris. Move up to belay at the top of the ***Stomach Traverse*** on ***North Climb***. The route ends here: the continuation up the arête above still awaits the right climber, but a good way to reach the top of the crag would be to climb the chockstone chimney on the right and then traverse right to join ***Klingsor*** at the start of Pitch 3.

Proton	149m	E1-	★	1966

A good but somewhat grubby route. Start 18 metres right of ***North Climb*** at the foot of a long V-groove. The lower block is split by triple cracks. This is just to the right of the huge open groove of ***Akhnaton***.

1 33m (5b). Climb the right-hand crack to a sloping shelf and follow the corner-crack above with a difficult but well-protected start. Belay on a grass ledge.

2 25m. Climb up steep grass to join ***North Climb*** at the foot of the ***Stomach Traverse***.

3 28m (5a). Climb the large and entertaining corner above (just left of the ***Stomach Traverse***), passing three breaks, to rejoin ***North Climb*** at the ***Strid***.

4 18m (5b). A good pitch - much better than it looks. Enter the V-groove on the left by a difficult and quite bold rising traverse from the right. Continue up the groove to a block belay.

5 45m (4a). A worrying lead! Climb leftwards up a disintegrating ramp to its top then back right across a cracked wall via a good finger-crack to a big grass ledge. Bridge up a big groove round on the right then step up the steep wall rightwards and scramble up delicate debris to the summit of ***Low Man***. The original route apparently climbed the initial cracked wall direct but this looks even more lethal.

Hadrian's Wall | 158m | VS- | | 1933

An adventurous climb, with a fair share of grass and lichen it is true, but not worthy of its previous description as a "botanist's dream". Lack of protection on the crux pitch means that the full flavour of climbing as it was in the 1930s can still be enjoyed today (or not as the case may be!). Start as for ***Scylla***, 33 metres right of ***North Climb***, at the last main groove before the green bay.

1 18m (4b). Climb a short broken rib to grass below the main groove and make an awkward traverse left under a small overhang. Follow a grassy corner to belay at a dodgy spike.

2 25m (4b). Trend right for 6 metres and climb up into a large corner which turns into a chockstone chimney. At its top climb a short corner to a belay on the right.

3 15m (4b). Move back left on grass and climb a deep V-chimney to a stance on the right, on a long ledge at the foot of a huge headwall taken by ***Scylla*** whose crack pitch lies 5 metres to the right. Chockstone belay in a short chimney.

4 15m (4c). The short chimney with an overhanging chockstone leads to a higher section of ledge under the headwall. Climb a short crack in the wall to the base of a groove and avoid the groove by a traverse left, then go up to a stance in a corner.

5 35m (4c). The crux! Claw your way up onto a higher grass ledge and scrabble up it to its highest part. Search diligently for any runners you can at this point. On your left is a raised lichenous black slab. Scrub as much of the moss as you can off this and then teeter along it leftwards with a very balancy move to step into a chimney on its left. Thrutch up the chimney to a grass ledge (good spike on left).

6 50m (4c). Climb the V-chimney direct (or escape via its left wall at 6 metres), then follow the arête bounding ***Stony Gully*** to finish on the summit of ***Low Man***.

Liza Groove Start 18m VS 1952

1 18m (4b). Climb a short broken rib to grass below the main groove. Climb the main groove, first by the crack on the right, then moving to the crack on the left. Belay on the left at a dodgy spike.

Guidebook Error Variation 18m VS

Until this guide Pitch 2 had been wrongly recorded since the description was first published, stating "trend left" instead of "trend right", resulting in this inferior variation.

2 20m (4b). Climb a rock rib just right of the spike, then trend left and climb a shallow groove and belay below a short chimney. Climb the chimney and corner above to emerge beneath the chockstone chimney of ***North Climb*** Pitch 5. Climb this and traverse right to the crack and groove in the headwall on Pitch 4 of the proper route.

Scylla	133m	HVS-	★★	1963

A good route of a mountaineering character, which climbs the crack in the centre of the huge wall on the ***North Face of Low Man***. Start at the last major groove on the left side of the grassy bay, just right of a short impending band of rock. When looking up, high on the crag will be seen a blank wall with a crack in it. Below the wall is a square chimney which forms the second pitch of ***Scylla***. If you can see this chimney then you are in the right area. Start up left a few metres at a grassy groove.

1 *35m (4a).* Climb up to the central groove and follow this exiting right. Making the most of the rock above, trend right to a short wide gully and climb it to a stance at a huge chockstone below the very large square chimney.
2 25m (4b). Climb the chimney to belay below a crack in the wall.
3 30m (4c). Climb the crack in the centre of the wall: it becomes a chimney-groove at 12 metres. Avoid a large wedged block by a crack on the left and continue up this crack, and ledges above, to belay on the highest ledge at a hollow block.
4 25m (5a). From the top of the ledge, pull up an overhanging wall. Traverse down and left to the foot of a groove and jamming crack, which is climbed to the top of a pinnacle, from where a swing right leads to easier ground. Take a stance immediately on the grass ledge.
5 18m (4a). Traverse rightwards to the arête on the right and follow it to the summit of ***Low Man***.

Direct Finish 20m E2+ 1966

The overhanging crack above the stance on Pitch 3 of ***Scylla***. An exposed and strenuous pitch.

4 (5c). Traverse across a water-stained groove to start the crack. It is narrow at first, then wider, and is climbed by strenuous jamming. Move out at the top to the ledge and belay at the top of Pitch 4 of ***Scylla***.

Puppet	130m	E2-	★★	1966

This route also ascends the large wall in the centre of the face. A varied climb with difficult and exciting upper pitches but unfortunately rather dirty. Start as for ***Scylla***.

1 26m. Climb up to just below the central groove, but avoid it by traversing right and then scrambling up steep grass and rock to a short wide gully. Climb this to a stance at a huge chockstone below the very large square chimney of ***Scylla***: it is much better to do Pitch 1 of ***Scylla***.
2 24m (4c). Move to the right and climb a short corner for 6 metres, then step back left above the overhang and go up a pleasant crack. Continue over ledges and an overhanging chockstone to below the crack of ***Scylla*** in the centre of the large wall.

Pillar Rock North-West Face of Low Man

1	North Climb (upper part)	MS ***
2	The Hand Traverse	HS **
3	Proton	E1 *
4	Hadrian's Wall	VS
5	Scylla	HVS **
V1	Scylla Direct Finish	E2
6	Puppet	E2 **
7	Straits of Messina	E4 *
8	Caucus Race	E3 *
9	Megaton	HVS/E1 ***
10	Goodbye to All That	E1 ***
11	Nor'-Nor'-West Climb	VS **
12	Ximenes	HVS **
13	North-West Climb	MVS ***
V2	Taylor's Chimney	
14	Charybdis	HVS **
15	Roraima (upper part)	E1 *
16	Gorre	E1
17	Goth	E1 **
18	Gaul	HVS **
19	The Appian Way	HS ***
20	The Hun	VS *
21	The Old West Route	M ***
V3	Slingsby's Crack	D *

B	Split Blocks
C	Le Coin
D	Downlen's Chimney
E	Block Ledge
L	Lamb's Chimney
N	The Nose
O	Oppenheimer's Chimney
T	Taylor's Chimney

Photo: Al Phizacklea

West Wall Traverse
The Terrace
Green Ledge
C
B
N
1
2
3
4
5
6
7
8
9
10
11
12
13
14
15
17
18
19
20

3 18m (5b). Ascend *Scylla* for 6 metres to a thread runner. Traverse across the wall on the right, ascending slightly to gain the deep lichenous pod-like groove. Climb this, or the arête on the right, to a small stance at the top.

4 18m (4b). Continue up the corner and vague arête above, as for Pitch 6 of *Nor'-Nor'-West Climb*, until a few moves to the right lead to a small stance at a rather worrying detached spike.

5 20m (5b). Climb the steep shallow groove above and left; then continue up the steep wall on improving holds to a good ledge: a bold pitch.

6 24m (4a). Move left and follow an easier ridge to the top of *Low Man*.

Straits of Messina	130m	E4	★	1984

A fine eliminate route giving bold delicate climbing up the wall between *Puppet* and *Scylla* and the thin hanging crack above.

1–2 50m (5a). The first 2 pitches of *Megaton* then up left to belay as for *Scylla* below the main wall.

3 33m (6a). Climb the thin crack leading directly to the groove on *Puppet* (starting from the left). Up the groove a little then pull out left onto an obvious square ledge. Move left across the wall for 2 metres, then climb up and continue up a thin crack-line in the slab to the rib; up this to belay below a thin crack in the overhanging wall.

4 23m (6a). Climb the thin crack which is 3 metres right of the crack of *Scylla Direct*. This curves leftwards to pull out onto a ledge above *Scylla Direct*.

5 24m (4a). More easily up the ridge above, as for *Scylla*.

Caucus Race	124m	E3-	★	1993

A strenuous test in chimneying technique up the prominent capped V-groove in the centre of the *North Face* – this is just to the right of *Puppet*, and very obvious when approaching the crag from Ennerdale. Unfortunately the rest of the route does not live up to the main pitch. Start on *Green Ledge*, as for *Megaton*, about 10 metres left of the *Bounding Buttress*, under a steep grassy area.

1 18m (4b). As for *Megaton*, climb a 3 metre wall to heather and then a rock rib to a rightward-slanting grass ledge under slabs; thread chockstone belay on right about halfway along the ledge.

2 *28m (5a)*. From the belay, follow a left-slanting crack under the nose of the slabs to a wide shelf. Traverse this to a thin groove which is climbed with a difficult pull onto the upper slab. Follow this to a grass ledge, climb directly up the wall at the back of the ledge, exiting rightwards, then move back left, to belay as for *Megaton* directly under the menacing V-groove.

3 **22m (6a).** Levitate up the groove to the overhang (good thread runner) and make a wild hand-traverse leftwards to a welcome resting place on the arête. On recovering, climb directly up the wall above to a horizontal break and hand-traverse this rightwards to the arête. Easily up this to a good spike belay. (It is possible to climb the wall direct but this is dirty and not as good).

4 **18m (5a).** Above on the left is a sharply defined V-groove with an arête on its left (***Nor'-Nor'-West Climb***) and on the right a shallower V-groove (***Taylor's Chimney***). Between the two is a very vague groove blocked at half height by a smooth bulge. Climb this groove, overcoming the bulge with difficulty and continue more easily to a small stance and poor belay on the left at a large detached spike (if this belay does not appeal it is just possible, with 50 metre ropes and careful ropework, to continue up the next pitch).

5 **38m (5b).** A complex pitch. From the spike move horizontally right 2 metres to a small quartz ledge with grass on it. Make a bold move directly up the wall into a short shallow groove. Continue up the groove until it peters out and mantelshelf awkwardly into a slim groove on the right. From the top of this, traverse diagonally rightwards on slabs before moving back left to a grass ledge. Climb the corner formed by dubious blocks to a swing into a short groove. Exit rightwards from this and then follow an easy ramp-line back left to the summit of ***Low Man*** taking care with loose rock.

Megaton	120m	E1-	★★★	1972

Mega! Varied, interesting and sustained at a good level. It contains a bold slab on Pitch 2 but this can be avoided at no loss of quality by following the variation described below and reducing the standard to HVS. Start towards the right-hand side of ***Green Ledge***, some 7 metres left of the ***Bounding Buttress***, below the steep grassy bay.

1 **18m (4b).** Climb a 3 metre rib/spike to grass. Make the best of the rock rib above to the lower end of a rightward-rising grass ramp under a steep slab; thread chockstone belay on right about halfway along the ledge.

2 **26m (5a).** From the lower end of the grass ramp, starting some 5 metres from the ***Bounding Buttress*** wall on the right, climb very boldly up the slab above for 9 metres before moving left to gain a vague rightward-curving fault which is followed to easier ground. Follow the general line back leftwards and take a belay well up on the left by a pile of blocks on a ledge under the impressive overhung deep V-groove of ***Caucus Race***.

3 **36m (5a).** Step off the pile of blocks and traverse to the right along two rock ledges to a groove. Climb this for 2 metres then leave it to move leftwards up a gangway to a thin corner-crack which soon

widens and is followed until the angle eases. Climb up rightwards for 12 metres or so to a recess with a dubious spike and a loose pebble thread in a corner.

4 20m (4c). Pull directly over the bulge above into a groove and follow it to a huge shallow niche. Continue in the same line to easier ground under a steep crack. (There is a similar crack some 7 metres to the right which is ***Oppenheimer's Chimney*** on ***North-West Climb***).

5 20m (4c). ***Downlen's Chimney***. Climb the crack (not as bad as it looks!) to the top of ***Low Man***.

HVS Variation 1992

This easier and better-protected variation reduces the standard of the whole climb to HVS with no loss of quality (the pitch itself is actually VS). At the end of Pitch 1, belay at the upper end of the grass ramp, under the wall of the ***Bounding Buttress***.

2 (4c). Start 2 metres to the left of the belay and follow a thin crack directly up the slab (as for ***Goodbye to All That***) until about half-height where it is possible to branch up leftwards to easier ground. Climb diagonally leftwards to the stance.

Goodbye to All That	124m	E1-	★★★	1996

A direct line on excellent rock taking in the prominent ragged crack right of the main pitch of ***Megaton*** and culminating in a sensational top pitch. Start as for ***Megaton***, 7 metres left of the ***Bounding Buttress***.

1 18m (4a). As for ***Megaton***, climb a 3 metre wall to heather and then a vague rock rib to a rightward-slanting grass ledge under slabs. Belay under the bounding wall on the right at the foot of a slab.

2 26m (4c). Two metres left of the ***Bounding Buttress*** wall is a thin crack in the slab. Climb this direct to a narrow bilberry ledge and huge block belay.

3 36m (5b). Climb up into an overhung scoop just left of the belay and pull out awkwardly onto a small ledge on the left. Climb directly up to join ***Megaton*** at the right-hand end of its traverse (***Megaton*** goes left along a narrow ramp into a narrow corner). Continue straight up the crack directly above pulling out rightwards to easier ground. Climb directly up over bulges and slabby rock to belay as for ***Megaton*** and ***North-West Climb*** in a recess with a dubious spike and a loose pebble thread in a corner.

4 20m (5a). Stride out rightwards onto a ledge on the right with a spiky block on it. Climb the arête above on its left side to emerge into a rock bay. Climb the wall on the right to a square pocket and traverse right to a flake on the arête. Go straight up to easy ground below a

Left: Colin Wornham pysching himself up for the bold moves on the final pitch of **Goodbye to All That** (E1), Pillar Rock. **Photo:** Stephen Reid

deep chimney/crack (***Oppenheimer's Chimney***). The best belay is well below the chimney on a small quartz ledge on a superbly exposed rib out on the extreme right.

5 24m (5a/b). A bold pitch. Climb up to the base of ***Oppenheimer's Chimney*** and fix some good runners! Traverse horizontally leftwards on blocks to some tiny footholds on a rib and make a long reach up and left for a jug – much easier if you are tall. (The technical standard now drops to 4c.) Climb directly up the wall above in an exposed position on good holds but with no further protection until a runner can be placed under a chockstone on the left in the final crack of ***Megaton***. Move back right and follow more jugs up a rib to easy ground and the top.

Nor'-Nor'-West Climb	141m	VS+	★★	1932

A helter-skelter of a route that wends its way up the ***North Face*** giving a good scare on every pitch. Start at the right side of a large grassy bay in the corner under the ***Bounding Buttress***.

1 30m (4a). Follow the line of the huge corner formed where the ***Bounding Buttress*** meets the grassy bay – various lines are possible. Belay on a grass ledge under slabs.

2 25m (4b). Continue up the corner to a huge chockstone, pass this on the left and carry on directly to a bilberry ledge. Exit steeply up a wide crack on the right to the ***Terrace***. Junction with ***North-West Climb***.

3 25m (4c). Climb a short V-groove just left of the rock glacis to a break (***North-West Climb*** reaches this point from the right). Make an exposed traverse down leftwards and round with difficulty into a niche. Climb boldly out of the niche by its right edge and continue diagonally leftwards to gain the final couple of metres of the crack of ***Megaton*** which leads to a belay on a large sloping ledge with a good spike just below it.

4 30m (4c). A serious pitch. Go up the groove above for 9 metres until just before it steepens up and becomes ***Taylor's Chimney*** (***North-West Climb original way***). Step onto the arête on the left and climb it until a few delicate moves to the right (possible at two levels) lead to sloping ledges and a large detached spike. The latter part of the pitch is just to the left of ***Taylor's Chimney*** (***North-West Climb***). Make an exposed traverse to the right across the top of ***Lamb's Chimney*** and belay on small ledges under the obvious off-width crack of ***Downlen's Chimney*** (the left-hand of two such cracks, and Pitch 4 of ***Megaton***).

5 16m (4c). A puzzling short crack in the left wall (2 metres left of ***Downlen's Chimney***) leads to a ledge. Move up and left, up grass and fractured rock to a large grass ledge.

6 15m (4a). The arête on the left of the grass ledge leads to the top.

Variation Start 56m VS 1936

This route takes in the obvious chimney in the left wall of the ***Bounding Buttress*** to join *Nor'-Nor'-West Climb* on the *Terrace*. Start just left of *Nor'-Nor'-West Climb*.

1 16m (4a). Climb the wall at the left corner of the slab. Ascend the slab using a thin crack then step right across the top of the initial crack of *Nor'-Nor'-West Climb*. Climb the short wall on the right then ascend a slab to the left of the buttress. Make a rising traverse leftwards just above the vegetation, passing a crack, to a large block lying against the buttress. Just beyond, a large pinnacle provides a belay.

2 40m (4c). Climb the awkward left-hand crack to gain the chimney. Move up the left rib and heave yourself over the chockstone (if you dare!). Avoid the continuation crack by traversing rightwards onto the front of the buttress and climb directly to the *Terrace*.

Direct Finish: Downlen's Chimney 20m VS 1954

5 20m (4c). The overhanging black chimney crack (since incorporated into *Megaton*) to the left of the parallel ***Oppenheimer's Chimney*** looks formidable but its bark is worse than its bite. Scrambling leads to the top of *Low Man*.

Roraima | 122m | E1- | ★ | 1981

An eliminate on good rock if occasionally spooky rock but whose main justification lies in Pitch 2. The lower part of the route takes the obvious crack in the left wall of the ***Bounding Buttress***, to the left of the chimney of the *Variation Start to Nor'-Nor'-West Climb*, and the upper part lies between *North-West Climb* and *Charybdis*.

1 24m. As for *Nor'-Nor'-West Climb*. Or better, the *Variation Start to Nor'-Nor'-West Climb*, and continue to a grass ledge and unsound blocks just left of the prominent hand-jam crack in the steep wall.

2 30m (5b). Climb the sustained crack and then more easily to a spike belay on the lower left edge of the *Terrace*.

3 24m (4c). As for *Strider*. Up the short pink groove behind the stance and then up the cracked stepped arête above. Step left to belay below a cracked groove, just right of *North-West Climb*.

4 22m (4b). Up the cracked groove to a ledge below another groove capped by an overhang. Avoid this by swinging onto the right arête overlooking *Goth* (as for *Charybdis*). Follow the arête direct on good holds and belay as for *Charybdis*.

5 22m (4c). As for *Charybdis*. Climb the shallow groove above, just to the right of ***Oppenheimer's Chimney***. Move to the right over the bulge; then follow a slanting crack back left up the wall to the top.

Ximenes	51m	HVS+	★★	1968

A good approach to several routes on the ***West Face*** (such as ***Goth***), which takes the front of the buttress leaning against ***Low Man***. Start 2 metres right of the left edge of the ***Bounding Buttress*** at an overhung recess below a crack. This is just left of the initial gangway of ***North-West Climb*** and is the left-hand of two cracks.

1 18m (5a). Gain the crack from the recess and follow it strenuously to an easing. Move left and climb the slab to the foot of the crack in the prow of the buttress, just left of the wide chimney on ***North-West Climb***.

2 33m (5b). Climb the crack, which is awkward and strenuous but well-protected, to a ledge (possible belay), and continue up easy slabs to the ***Terrace***, at the left-hand end of the ***West Wall Traverse***.

North-West Climb	130m	MVS	★★★	1906

A fine route giving varied climbing and good situations. Start at the right-hand end of ***Green Ledge***, underneath the ***Bounding Buttress***, at an obvious rightwards-slanting short gangway.

1 20m. Climb the gangway to a ledge and follow a chimney for 10 metres to a slab. Avoid the continuation chimney by traversing left across the slab to belay at the foot of a much wider chimney.

2 36m (4a). The wide chimney is taken direct to finish on a grassy slab in a corner (possible belay). Avoid the chimney-crack ahead by climbing up a short crack onto the crest of the buttress on the left and follow another crack up this until the angle eases at the ***Terrace***. Cross the large platform rightwards for 9 metres to belay at the base of a smooth glacis.

3 25m (4b). Ascend the slab and a short grassy corner to a grassy ledge under a prominent steep V-groove. Avoid this by traversing the ledge leftwards around a rib and climb up into the first of a series of three recesses (***Le Coin***). Carry on up into a second recess which contains a dubious pointed spike, a solid blunt spike, and a loose but threadable pebble in a short corner.

4 25m (4a). The undercut groove directly above the belay is part of ***Megaton***. To the left of this groove are three other vague grooves, the first of which is known as ***Lamb's Chimney***. To gain this, traverse left to a nose and ascend it to ***Block Ledge***. Climb the groove above (***Lamb's Chimney***), mainly on the left, and pull out left at its top. Stride immediately back right and go up to a belay below the impending crack of ***Downlen's Chimney*** above, which is the final pitch of ***Megaton***.

5 24m (4b). Traverse rightwards under bulges and go up to the foot of another impending crack (***Oppenheimer's Chimney***). After an awkward

start it becomes more reasonable and easy scrambling then leads to the top of *Low Man*.

Kirkstile Variation 60m S 1937

A rather pointless variation on an otherwise fine route. Start about 10 metres right of the ordinary start.

1–2. Climb a gangway leftwards and traverse left below the first chimney of ***North-West Climb*** to a scoop which is climbed. Continue up a buttress, make for a chimney up on the right and ascend this. On the right is a steep wall which is followed to a pyramid of rock, which is climbed by a crack.

Taylor's Chimney (Original Way) 1906

4. Climb downwards from the belay until a short traverse left can be made to an open chimney (***Taylor's Chimney*** – the left-hand of the three vague grooves) which is climbed for about 10 metres. At its top, a traverse is made back right over the top of ***Lamb's Chimney*** to rejoin the more direct climb at the belay under ***Downlen's Chimney***.

Variation Finish 30m 1913

5 (4a). ***Oppenheimer's Chimney*** can be avoided by traversing rightwards lower down and then ascending a crack and going to the right round the corner. Climb an exposed steep wall on the right, which leads to an easier wall which can be climbed on the right or left. Finally make a resolution with yourself to go and finish the climb properly.

Charybdis	129m	HVS	★★	1964

A climb of many parts which follows slabs then a series of grooves in the arête between the ***North*** and ***West Faces of Low Man***. Start from ***Green Ledge*** as for ***North-West Climb***.

1 15m. Follow Pitch 1 of ***North-West Climb*** to a stance and belay at the top of the 10 metre chimney.

2 30m (4c). Continue up the same chimney then ascend a wall split by cracks to the ***Terrace***.

3 20m (4c). Move to the right to a glacis. Ascend this and go up the corner. Belay below the obvious deep overhanging groove.

4 15m (5a). Climb into the groove (chockstone runner). Descend a little and climb the left wall by laybacking a big flake. Return along an awkward gangway to the top of the groove and go over a loose block to a sloping stance and thread belay on the right. (The main groove can be climbed direct).

5 12m (5a). Climb the green groove above (the left-hand of two grooves) moving left at the top to a ledge.

6 15m (4b). Climb the groove on the right, or much better, the fine bold arête on the right of the groove, to a large block belay and junction with ***Goth***.

7 22m (4c). Climb the shallow groove above, just to the right of ***Oppenheimer's Chimney***. Move to the right over the bulge, then follow a slanting crack back left up the wall to the top.

Below Green Ledge

The large rambling tiered area below ***Green Ledge*** looks interesting on first sight, but close acquaintanceship renders it less so. There is good rock, but it is mainly vegetated and the protection is poor. **Pedestal Wall** (S, 1937) is the only climb to have been described, though no doubt many variations have been made by those attempting to follow its rather vague description. Only the first pitch could be located with certainty and it has been consigned to the FRCC website.

West Face of Low Man

This is one of the best faces of *Pillar Rock* with excellent rock that dries quickly after rain and catches the afternoon sun. This face is reached from below the *North Face* by following *Green Ledge* rightwards to where it drops away into a wide wet gully which cuts deeply into the hillside below the *West Face of Low Man*, and is known as the *Waterfall* (or *West Waterfall Gully*). An awkward scramble leads almost horizontally, starting with a one metre rock step round into the gully before dropping down the last few metres. It then crosses the gully and goes up a short slimy wall onto the scree on the other side of the *Waterfall* where a scramble leads up to the *West Face of Pillar*. This is all very nasty if wet and has serious prang potential if you muff it. Another option is to leave *Green Ledge* before the one metre rocky step where the normal traverse into the *Waterfall* goes and scramble down a steep grass trench to cross the gully at a lower point by a dripping black wall. Go under this wall via a fault-line and continue in this line, well beyond the steeper rocks, until you gain open hillside to the west of the *Rock*, whereupon a scrambly ascent can be made to join the normal path to the *West Face*.

Alternatively it is possible to avoid crossing the ***Waterfall*** by climbing **Waterfall Climb** (50m, D 1913), up a groove system in the rocks which bound it on the left side to the same point.

When approaching this face from Buttermere or Ennerdale, the ***Waterfall*** crossing is avoided by ascending the unremitting scree-ridden fellside well to the right of the ***Waterfall*** until a horizontal path is gained which leads round to the ***West Face***.

From the *Western Scree*, under the *West Face*, the climbs are reached by following the *West Wall Traverse*, a slightly worn scramble that starts some 10 metres up the scree from the head of the *Waterfall*. This point is also about 40 metres down the scree from the start of *The Old West Route* and slightly below the level of the lower approach path that ends on the other side of the scree. An exposed scramble traverses slightly downwards, passing under a long low smooth wall, then rising a little to a huge block on a grass ledge at the foot of *The Appian Way*. A slight descent from here leads round the edge of the crag to the *Terrace*, half way up the *North Face* at the top of the *Bounding Buttress* and at the start of *Goth*.

Descent:

All the routes end on the summit of *Low Man* from whence the lower section of *The Old West Route* makes a good descent: from just below the summit of *Low Man*, scramble rightwards down a well marked way to an exit onto scree near the foot of *Rib and Slab Climb*. Alternatively follow the upper section of *The Old West Route* to the summit of *High Man*, or better still traverse round to the left and climb *North-East Arête* instead.

The climbs are described from **left** to **right**.

Gorre	75m	E1+		1992

An eliminate line following the fine series of arêtes between *Goth* and the upper pitches of *Charybdis*. Unfortunately the climb looks rather better than it is and, though the second pitch is good, most of that is either *Goth* or *Charybdis*. Start as for *Goth*.

1 25m (5b) Follow *Goth* for about 5 metres, then step down left and traverse horizontally left on small holds to pull awkwardly into a hidden groove in the arête. Follow the groove to a rightwards-sloping ramp. Climb the short dark groove above (between the black mossy groove of *Goth* Pitch 2 on the right and the *Green Groove* of *Charybdis* Pitch 4 on the left) to a hanging belay below the steep wall.

2 30m (5b) Climb the steep wall, as for *Goth*, and make a strenuous pull up to gain a standing position on the hand-traverse holds of that route. Move leftwards on to the fine arête and follow it (mainly on the right) to a ledge. Climb up rightwards for 2 metres to a stance.

3 20m (4c) Climb the wide crack and step right to a short arête. Up this to a flake ledge. Climb the centre of the short wall above.

Variation to Pitch 1: Charysma 1999

Gain the groove in the arête by a long step right from a few metres up the groove of *Charybdis* Pitch 3 – all rather dirty and unpleasant and with poor protection – yum!

Pillar Rock West Face of Low Man

1	Charybdis (upper part)	HVS **	15	Thor	VS **
2	Gorre	E1	16	Err	VS **
3	Goth	E1 ***	17	Ledge and Groove Climb	S **
4	Gaul	HVS **	18	Devil's Exit	HVS *
5	The Appian Way	HS ***	19	West Wall Climb	VD ***
6	The Hun	VS *	20	Mallory's Route	HVS **
7	The Terrorist	E2	21	The Old West Route	M ***
8	Appian Wall	VS **	V	Slingsby's Crack	D *
9	Attilla	HVS	22	The Pulpit Route	VD *
10	Triton Direct	VS **	23	The Crumb	HS
11	Mirror, Mirror	E2 **			
12	Nook and Wall Climb	MS **			
13	The Devil's Eliminate	HVS **			
14	The Devil's Entrance	VS **			

P	The Pedestal
FN	First Nook
SN	Second Nook
L	The Pulpit

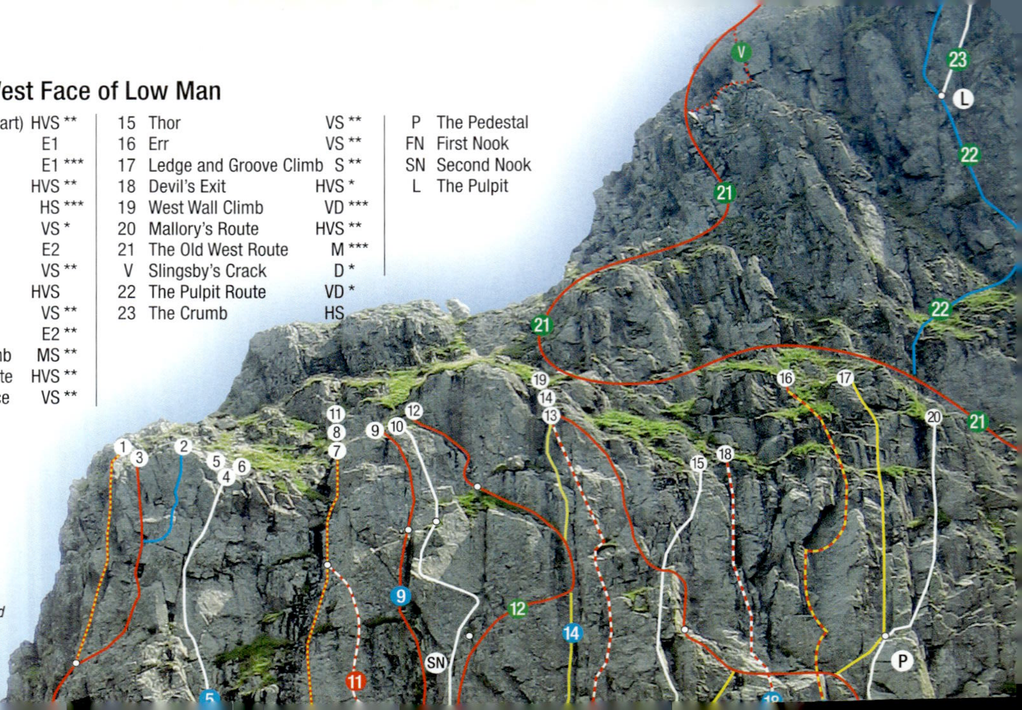

Photo: Stephen Reid

The Terrace
West Wall Traverse
Block
The Waterfall
FN
1
2
3
4
5
6
7
8
9
10
11
12
13
14
15
16
17
18
19
20

Goth	75m	E1+	★★★	1959

This route follows the huge open curving groove at the junction of the *North* and *West Faces of Low Man*. A fine climb with a well positioned but intimidating crux that requires very small wires for protection and probably warrants E2 if you are short. Follow the ***West Wall Traverse*** leftwards to a huge block on a grass ledge at the start of ***The Appian Way***. Scramble down and left, passing a smaller block, to another grass ledge at the foot of an open-book corner with an undercut arête on its left (left again is the deep overhanging groove of ***Charybdis*** with a large flake on its left wall). A blunt spike belay will be found at this point. A good alternative approach is to climb ***Ximenes*** from ***Green Ledge*** to the ***Terrace***.

1 20m (4c). Climb the vague open groove to a hanging stance in the grassy V-groove, 4 metres below the huge overhang.
2 35m (5b). Traverse left for 2 metres to the foot of a mossy groove leading up to the left end of the roof of the overhang. This is climbed until a dubious block in the roof of a small overhang is reached; then break out left across a small slab to an arête and runners. The overhanging wall above is inadequately protected by tiny wires. Climb it to a narrow sloping ledge and either hand-traverse strenuously to the corner on the right, or move up (to gear!) and foot-traverse instead. Continue up this corner until a small overhang bars the way. Traverse left across the wall to a stance on a quartz ledge.
3 20m (4a). Climb up to a short curving crack on the right. Ascend this and finish up rough slabs taking a line almost on the left arête.

Gaul	73m	HVS+	★★	1974

An excellent main pitch at the upper limit of the grade makes this a route not to be missed. Start as for ***Goth*** at the blunt spike belay.

1 20m (4b). Cross grass rightwards to a short greasy chimney-groove. Climb this and the left-slanting slab above to a grass ledge in a V-groove below the big roof on ***Goth***.
2 35m (5a). Climb onto the slab on the right and cross it to a groove. Follow this and the wall above with sustained difficulty to an easier groove (***The Appian Way***) which leads to a grass terrace and block belay. A good pitch.
3 18m (4a). Ascend the crack on the left as for ***The Appian Way***.

The Appian Way	65m	HS	★★★	1923

A very pleasant and exposed route with delicate wall climbing and good situations. Follow the ***West Wall Traverse*** leftwards, first downwards slightly under a long low wall, then diagonally upwards over grassy ledges for some 70 metres, to a huge block on a grass ledge.

1 20m. Avoid the mossy groove by climbing up grassy rock on the left for 3 metres and then traversing to the right across the top of the

groove to gain a grassy corner-ramp which is followed to its top; flake and crack belay.

2 **15m.** Climb the thin corner-crack and, from its top, traverse delicately left across the imposing wall to a worrying spike on the skyline. (It is best to belay on wires just left of the base of the spike and back this up with gear in a crack on the left).

3 **12m.** Move left and ascend a series of steep ledges straight ahead (all rather bold) to a grassy terrace and a large block leaning against the wall; thread belay.

4 **18m.** The slightly overhanging 8 metre crack (right-hand branch) on the left of the block is followed by slabs. The overhanging crack may be avoided by climbing up grassy ledges to the right, but you'd only feel guilty!

The Hun	60m	VS	★	1966

The route ascends the bottomless chimney just right of the overhang of ***Goth***. The climbing is exhilarating and exposed although on rather doubtful rock to start. Start as for ***The Appian Way*** at a large block reached via the ***West Wall Traverse***.

1 **30m** (4c). Ascend the shallow groove just left of the mossy corner for 2 metres, stepping left and up, then layback the worrying detached flake above for 6 metres – this flake can be avoided via the groove of ***Appian Wall*** to the right. Move left to a large block below the bottomless chimney. Climb into this then go up the right wall to a stance by a spike at the top of Pitch 2 of ***The Appian Way***. (It is best to to belay on wires just left of the base of the spike and back this up with gear in a crack on the left).

2 **30m** (4b). Continue up Pitches 3 and 4 of ***The Appian Way***.

The Terrorist	55m	E2		1988

Steep and fingery climbing but in the end a rather unbalanced route. Start as for ***The Appian Way*** at a large block reached via the ***West Wall Traverse***.

1 **48m** (5c). Follow ***The Hun*** as far as the pinnacle above the layback flake. Climb the steep crack-line up the wall above to an overlap, pull out rightwards to the arête and climb the cracked wall to reach good holds on the traverse of ***The Appian Way***. Climb the wall above directly via a V-shaped slot to grass ledges.

2 **7m.** Climb the wall behind to the top. A good spike belay can be found by scrambling some 20 metres further up.

Appian Wall	57m	VS+	★★	2004

A direct line through ***The Appian Way*** – superb but scary! Start as for ***The Appian Way*** at a large block reached via the ***West Wall Traverse***.

1 **25m (4c).** Bridge the mossy groove direct and continue up the clean rock groove above until just below the right end of an overlap. Step right onto the arête and follow cracks up the wall to the traverse on ***The Appian Way*** which is followed leftwards to a dodgy spike. (It is best to to belay on wires just left of the base of the spike and back this up with gear in a crack on the left).

2 **25m (4b).** Move carefully up off the spike and traverse boldly rightwards towards the middle of the wall before climbing straight up to grass ledges. Go rightwards up these to a crevasse stance. A virtually runnerless pitch.

3 **7m.** Climb the blunt arête above the stance. A good spike belay can be found by scrambling some 20 metres further up.

Direct Variation HVS 2004

(5a). Combine Pitches 1 and 2 by climbing straight up the upper wall via a V-shaped slot from the traverse of ***The Appian Way*** (as for ***The Terrorist***).

Attila	65m	HVS		1967

The curving line of stepped overhangs and grooves bounding the right-hand side of the wall crossed by ***The Appian Way***; unfortunately the climbing is not as good as the line it follows, being very green in the upper half. Start 4 metres to the right of ***The Appian Way*** at the top of a short grassy chimney under a convex wall.

1 **20m.** Ascend a fault in the wall to a spike at 4 metres. Move to the right, then trend back left to the belay at the top of Pitch 1 of ***The Appian Way***.

2 **18m (4c).** The corner-crack of ***The Appian Way*** leads to an overhang, which is climbed on the left (awkward) to a belay on the arête, directly below the second overhang.

3 **20m (5a).** Step left and climb leftwards, under the overhang, to a V-groove, which leads to an enormous block belay.

4 **7m.** Step left from the block and ascend the wall via little niches and then slabs above; spike belay some 20 metres higher.

The next routes all start from the lowest rock on the face, immediately above the ***Waterfall***, where a smooth vertical 5 metre wall slants down slightly leftwards. The ***West Wall Traverse*** runs down easy slabs under this wall. The wall is broken on the right by a steep dark crack (***Thor***) and on the left by a chimney that doesn't quite reach the ground (***Nook and Wall Climb***).

Triton Direct	75m	VS	★★	1974

An enjoyable eliminate line up the rib between the two nooks of ***Nook and Wall Climb***. Start 3 metres left of the chimney of ***Nook and Wall Climb*** at an easy-angled groove.

1 **38m (4c).** Climb a metre up the groove then, before it gets dirty, pull blindly out rightwards into a good crack. Climb this and the rough slab above to a terrace. Follow the rightward-slanting grassy ramp of ***Nook and Wall Climb*** above to its top, then pull awkwardly leftwards into a broken groove on the left wall and go up this to easy slabs. Climb up to a shallow open groove on the right-hand side of a sharp arête. Climb this on the right, almost moving into the grassy *First Nook*, before pulling back left. From the top of the groove, move up, then stride out left to a stance on top of the sharp arête, under a flake hand-jam crack.

2 **28m (4c).** Climb the hand-jam crack to a junction with the flake traverse on ***Nook and Wall Climb*** and take a shallow groove above to easier ground. Overhead is the *Bad Corner* – a steep grass-filled corner-crack: climb up to get established in the base of this, then either continue up the grassy crack or, much better, make an exposed traverse leftwards to the arête which is climbed to a huge block belay.

3 **9m (4c).** Stand on the block and make a long reach up the smooth wall to a high jug (just right of the small niches/crack of ***Attila***). Pull up and climb a slab to the top; spike belay some 20 metres higher.

Mirror, Mirror…	70m	E2	★★	2005

An out there, "on the wall" experience, with such pesky distractions as runners kept well below the absolute minimum on Pitch 2. Take several thin slings and a cool head and start as for ***Nook and Wall Climb***.

1 **33m (5b).** Step left onto the wall and move left into the chimney which is climbed to a terrace. A narrow rightward-slanting grassy ramp is followed until moves can be made straight up the wall to gain a standing position on a blocky projection. Sidle round the arête and up to easy slabs, then trend left to belay in a leftward-facing corner at the top of ***The Appian Way*** Pitch 1.

2 **30m (5a/b).** Step one metre left from the corner and climb straight up the wall on incuts to the traverse-break of ***The Appian Way*** (spike runner on left, and gear in crack above). Step right to the left-hand end of a slim overhang and move up through the bulge (wire beside hollow hold). Climb boldly up the wall above, firstly rightwards, then leftwards, on good holds (but with no gear) until finally a barely adequate spike runner allows breathing to resume just below the steeper headwall. Climb directly through the headwall to a crevasse stance.

3 **7m.** Climb the blunt arête above the stance; a good spike belay can be found by scrambling some 20 metres further up.

Nook and Wall Climb | 81m | MS+ | ★★ | 1920

A meandering but interesting and historic route featuring some very exposed climbing. Start from a flat rock platform on the ***West Wall Traverse***, just right of the bottomless chimney towards the left-hand end of the smooth vertical 5 metre wall. The best belay will be found 3 metres to the right at the crack of ***Thor***.

1 33m. Step left onto the wall and move left into the chimney which is climbed to a terrace. A narrow rightward-slanting grassy ramp is followed until it steepens. Climb up for a couple of metres, then traverse right to a grassy corner. Follow the rib ahead on the right to a flake belay.

2 15m. Traverse the flake leftwards into the ***First Nook*** (a big grass ledge at the foot of a right-angled corner). Climb the corner to a rock ledge about halfway up, then traverse left along a huge flake and left around the arête into the ***Second Nook***. There is a very mossy wall on the left.

3 24m. Easy rock on the right leads to below the ***Bad Corner***. (This is the grass-filled hanging groove above which can be climbed at a Very Severe (4c).) Avoid this by moving one step down to the right and boldly cross the wall with the aid of a flake to regain the main corner. Climb the corner moving out left below a bulge at its top to gain a large sloping ledge and huge block belay.

4 9m. A short chimney, just to the right of the belay, finishes on a grassy terrace; spike belay some 20 metres higher.

Variation MVS 2004

1 (4a). From the terrace a short clean white blocky rib, a metre or so left of a perched block, and 2 metres right of the grassy ramp, can be climbed to join the top of the ramp – a better way, especially in the case of a damp ramp.

The Devil's Eliminate | 66m | HVS | ★★ | 2004

An exciting final pitch up the arête to the right of ***The Devil's Entrance*** is the making of this climb. Start as for ***Nook and Wall Climb***.

1 26m (4b). Pull out left towards the chimney but immediately step back right and climb a thin crack up the wall to a terrace. Step off a perched block and climb directly up the wall to a grassy niche. Climb rock to the left of a grassy crack to gain the left edge of a large flake. Belay on the right of the flake under an impressive slab.

2 40m (5a). Step off the flake and climb boldly up the left edge of the slab (just right of the groove of ***The Devil's Entrance***) to a small quartz ledge at its apex. Above is the corner of ***The Devil's Entrance***. Make an exposed stride of 1.5 metres horizontally rightwards to a steep crack and climb this to a small ledge. A short groove leads to a bigger ledge. Climb the short mossy wall above, moving out left to semi-mantelshelf up a clean rib to another ledge. The groove above the pinna-

cle on the right is part of ***West Wall Climb*** and the groove around the arête to the left is the ***The Devil's Entrance***. In between them is a shallow open groove. Climb boldly up this and the rough slabby rib above. Belay slightly higher on a chockstone on ***The Old West Route***.

The next three routes all start at the steep dark right-hand crack in the smooth vertical 5 metre wall which slants down slightly leftwards just above the ***West Wall Traverse***. This crack is 3 metres right of the chimney start to ***Nook and Wall Climb***.

The Devil's Entrance	65m	VS-	★★	1972

A direct version of ***Nook and Wall Climb***.

1 25m (4c). Climb the jamming crack of ***Thor*** and move up right onto the slab then back left immediately onto a rib. Climb the rib to grass and step right into a slim rightward-facing groove/crack; follow this to a flake belay.

2 40m (4b). Step off the flake and climb the left edge of the slab for a metre, before traversing left into the left-facing corner of ***Nook and Wall Climb***, just above the ***First Nook***. Climb the corner to a small quartz ledge at the apex of the slab on its right. Continue up the steeper corner above, moving right at a bulge near its top, to belay on a chockstone on ***The Old West Route***.

Thor	65m	VS-	★★	1967

An enjoyable climb with good situations and excellent rock.

1 30m (4c). Climb the jamming crack and move up and right to ascend an easy-angled rightward-slanting slab using a flake-crack. Climb directly up a steeper slab above (just right of a corner-groove), to just below a slim open groove on its right-hand side. Traverse right 2 metres, past a large flake, and climb up to a small rock ledge and flake belay. Alternatively, climb a short way up the slim groove that forms the right-hand side of the main slab and traverse right 3 metres higher to gain a stance on top of the flake.

2 35m (4c). Climb a steep crack/groove above to a small overhang. Turn this on the left and continue up to the top of a pinnacle (and a junction with ***West Wall Climb*** which follows the groove on the left). Move up and then make an airy rising traverse across the wall on the right to a grass ledge; scramble up to a belay.

Overleaf: Chris King and Stephen Reid making the first ascent of the stunning **Mirror, Mirror…** (E2), Pillar Rock. The leader is placing vital runners prior to making the crux moves through the bulge just left of the small roof to his right.
Photo: Jonathan Preston

Err	75m	VS+	★★	1970

A rising girdle start, initially indecisive and linking together bits of several other climbs, culminates in a fine top pitch.

1 **35m (4c).** Climb the jamming crack of ***Thor***; then follow ***Thor*** up right onto a slab. Traverse to the right across the broken slabs to a perched block (all part of ***Ledge and Groove Climb***) and then follow ***West Wall Climb*** up rightwards to a rock glacis.

2 **40m (4c).** Climb the corner-crack behind the belay then step left onto easy-angled rock; ahead is a lichenous groove. Make a bold move onto the clean rib to the right of this and pull rightwards into the base of a hanging capped groove. Climb the groove to the overhang which is avoided by some timely holds appearing on the slab on the right. Continue up grassy ledges to a belay on ***The Old West Route***. A fine pitch.

Ledge and Groove Climb	80m	S	★★	1933

A meandering but enjoyable climb on excellent rock: however, an exposed downward traverse on Pitch 2 makes this an unsuitable route for nervous seconds. Start at a one metre high groove, below a smooth wall, at the top of clean slabby steps on the ***West Wall Traverse***, and more or less directly above the ***Waterfall***. This is 6 metres down and left from ***West Wall Climb*** and just right of the hand-jam crack start of ***Thor***.

1 **22m.** Climb the groove and then diagonally rightwards up a narrow ramp to below a V-groove (***West Wall Climb***). Traverse delicately left along the exposed ***Ledge*** to its end and ascend slabby rocks rightwards to a grass ledge 5 metres below a large flake.

2 **34m.** Climb up to just below the flake and then step down and cross a little wall on the left. Climb up to a detached flake crack system and follow this until it is possible to move out right. Climb the slab to a tiny ledge at its top. There is a short groove leading up to a scoop with cracked blocks up on the left (the original belay) and a steep mossy groove up high on the right. Instead of going up to the original belay, keep traversing awkwardly rightwards, well below the mossy groove, to make an exposed downward step across the top of a groove and gain a good stance on the ***Pedestal*** on the right: the ***Pedestal*** has a wide crack up its left-hand side. This traverse is part of ***West Wall Climb*** in reverse.

3 **24m.** The steep shallow groove directly above (the left-hand of two shallow grooves above the ***Pedestal***) is hard to attain, but once entered the holds improve, though it is still quite bold. Exit on the right, cross grass to the right, and go up a short easy crack behind a block, beyond which easy steps lead to ***The Old West Route***.

The Devil's Exit	62m	HVS+	★	1975

A direct line up an obvious feature, but often wet, and always mossy – though not a bad route despite this. Start as for ***West Wall Climb***.

1 **25m** (4a). Follow Pitch 1 and part of Pitch 2 of ***West Wall Climb***, to a square glacis.

2 **37m** (5b). Climb the mossy crack to the left of the corner-crack up the wall above to an awkward landing, then climb straight up a scoop into the mossy groove above and struggle to the top. Belay to the right of a flake on the right or scramble up 8 metres to ***The Old West Route***.

West Wall Climb	65m	VD	★★★	1919

An excellent route of continuous interest. Follow the ***West Wall Traverse*** a few metres to a platform below a 3 metre wall.

1 **15m.** A short crack leads to a grass rake. Cross this and make a hard start up a V-groove until it is possible to pull out left to a sloping ledge and flake belay.

2 **15m.** Step right; steep rocks then lead to a rock glacis. A superb crack in the wall on the right, to the right of the corner-crack, leads to a small sloping ledge some 3 metres below the end of the crack. Belay on the ***Pedestal*** just above.

3 **15m.** Descend leftwards slightly from the ***Pedestal*** and make an awkward traverse leftwards, well under a mossy groove to a short groove on the left. Climb this to a large scoop and belay on blocks at the base of a cracked pinnacle.

4 **20m.** Climb the pinnacle via its left arête and from its top climb a short awkward groove, and/or the wall on its left. Easier rock leads to the top of ***Low Man***.

Mallory's Route (North-West-by-West)	65m	HVS-	★★	1913

Long overlooked – an outstanding lead for its day. The first 15 metres are in common with ***West Wall Climb***. Follow the ***West Wall Traverse*** for a few metres to a platform below a 3 metre wall.

1 **40m** (4b). A short crack leads to a grass rake. Cross this and make a hard start up a V-groove until it is possible to pull out right onto a sloping ledge. Traverse right and climb up behind a large block. Gain a V-groove above and then follow the prominent crack in the right wall to a fine belay on the ***Pedestal***.

2 **25m** (5a). Just worth the grade. Step right off the ***Pedestal*** and climb awkwardly up into a shallow groove (the right-hand of two shallow grooves above the ***Pedestal***). Climb this (still awkward) to grass, then a corner on the right and so to the top.

Auld Lang Syne | 52m | HS | ★ | 2006

This climb makes the most of the delightful clean white rock under ***The Old West Route***, well to the right of the other climbs on the ***West Face of Low Man***. The climbing is fairly straight-forward but protection is scant. Begin at the start of the ***West Wall Traverse***, at a rightward-slanting rib.

1 **35m.** Climb the rib then a wide crack to a ledge on the right of a slab. Step up left onto the slab and puzzle your way up it to easier rock which leads to a grass terrace and block belay at the foot of another slab.

2 **18m.** Step off the block and climb the slab by its right edge. Continue up the easier slab above to belay on ***The Old West Route***.

Strider | 200m | VS+ | ★★ | 1974

A girdle of the ***West Face of Low Man*** which takes in many of the best pitches. Start under the ***North Face*** towards the right end of ***Green Ledge***, as for ***North-West Climb***.

1–2 **56m.** Climb the first 2 pitches of ***North-West Climb***. Belay at a good spike on the lower left edge of the Terrace.

3 **26m (4c).** Climb the short pink groove, then continue up the cracked rib on the right until level with the top of the huge groove of ***Charybdis*** on the right. Stride across the groove to a sloping ledge and thread belay.

4 **12m.** Traverse to the right along easy ledges to the belay on ***Goth*** at the top of Pitch 1.

5 **26m (4c).** Gain the slab on the right and cross it to the groove of ***Gaul***. Move right around a steep rib, then swing across to the chimney of ***The Hun***. Continue up ***The Hun*** to the large spike on ***The Appian Way***. It is best to belay just left of the base of this and avoid using the spike.

6 **20m (4b).** Reverse the traverse of Pitch 2 of ***The Appian Way*** to a ledge below the overhang of ***Attila***. Climb the crack of ***Triton*** on the right and traverse the flake of ***Nook and Wall Climb*** to a slim ledge and belay halfway up the initial groove of Pitch 2 of the ***The Devil's Entrance***.

7 **20m (4a).** Climb the groove of the ***The Devil's Entrance*** for 6 metres to a small quartz ledge under where it steepens, reach rightwards to a crack and ascend this for two metres then traverse down and rightwards, crossing the groove of ***Thor*** below a small overhang; stance and belay round the corner at the cracked pinnacle of ***West Wall Climb***.

8 **40m (4c).** Descend a few metres and traverse rightwards until under a lichenous groove. Make a bold move onto the clean rib to the right of this and pull rightwards into the base of a hanging capped groove. Climb the groove to the overhang which is avoided by taking to the

slab on the right. Continue up grassy ledges to a belay on *The Old West Route*. A fine pitch - the last pitch of *Err*.

The Old West Route	150m	M	★★★	1826

Pillar's Low and *High Men* are separated by this obvious and well polished scramble: the original route of ascent. From the *Western Scree*, follow the left-slanting rake-line that divides the *West Faces of Low* and *High Men* to the summit of *Low Man*. From there, move towards *High Man* and up to slightly higher grassy ledges until a more rocky right-to-left stepped diagonal line leads to a short steep corner and small pinnacle. A determined heave-ho will gain you easier terrain that leads to to the summit of *High Man*.

Variation: Slingsby's Crack 5m D- ★ ca.1890

From *Low Man*, follow the standard route to the highest grass ledge on the right. The crack lies up the right-hand side of a large pinnacle flake, some 12 metres to the right of the usual finish.

West Face of High Man

The most impressive face of *Pillar Rock* and also the quickest to dry. The notes on the *West Face of Low Man* (on page 262) provide the approach details for this area. The climbs are reached from the *Western Scree* or by scrambling up the *Old West Route*.

Descents:

The best descents are either by reversing *Slab and Notch Climb* (see page 213) or by abseil from near the summit cairn, followed by *Western Gully*. Care is needed not to dislodge scree in *Western Gully* which starts where the separate pinnacle of *Pisgah* merges in with the main mountainside. An alternative descent is provided by *The Old West Route* which follows the rounded ridge down from the summit of *High Man* to the top of *Low Man*, where the descent from *Low Man* can be followed. Don't try to descend *West Jordan Gully* from the *Jordan Gap*.

The climbs are described from **left** to **right**.

The Pulpit Route	61m	VD	★	1934

Varied and interesting climbing to the left of the great nose of rock upon which *Gondor* lies. Start high on *The Old West Route* where the latter crosses the top of a gully (dodgy spike belay - find something better!).

1 **30m.** Climb a mossy wall to the right of a large ill-defined pinnacle and gully/chimney to a sloping grassy terrace. Traverse rightwards

Pillar Rock West Face of High Man

1	The Old West Route	M	***
V1	Slingsby's Crack	D	
2	The Pulpit Route	VD	*
3	The Crumb	HS	
4	Gondor	E2	***
5	Gomorrah	VS	***
V2	Direct Start	VS	
V3	The Ridge Variation	VS	***
V4	Original Finish	VS	
6	Vandal	HVS	***
7	Pillar of Salt	E1	**
8	Hawkeye	HVS	**
9	Sodom	VS	*
10	Cheekwoolly	S	**
11	Rib and Slab Climb	HS	***
12	Rib and Rib Climb	E1	**
13	New West Climb	VD	***
V5	Western Trod	MS	*
14	The South-West-by-West Climb	VS	**
15	Sundance	MVS	**
16	South-West Climb	MVS	***
17	West Jordan Gully	S	*
18	Sentinel	E1	*
19	Pisgah West Ridge	MS	*
V6	Variation	S	*
L	The Pulpit		

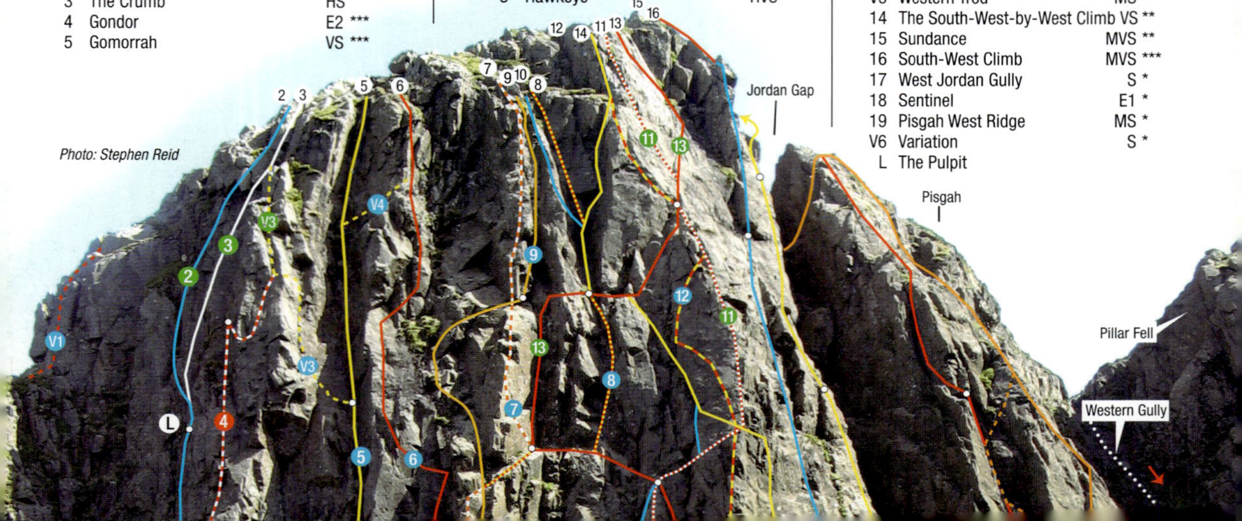

Photo: Stephen Reid

1
2
3
5
6
7
7
8
8
9
9
V2
10
11
V5
12
13
14
15
16
17
18
19

across a grassy gully and climb a short wall to a ledge with blocks. Climb a groove system running up left which leads up onto the *Pulpit*.

2 31m. Step up left and traverse a wall leftwards for 2 metres before traversing back right and ascending the rib on the right to an alcove and a large rock ledge just above. Go up the chimney above (or the open groove round to the right) and then traverse right on grass ledges to a dubious block on the right arête. A final short rib ends the climb near the top of *High Man*.

The Crumb	57m	HS		1974

Really *Pulpit Route Direct*. A steep line up the left flank of the tower of *Gondor*. The climbing is better than it looks, but that isn't saying much. Start at a deeply cut chimney, half-way up *The Old West Route*.

1 27m. Climb the chimney and groove above. Cross the grassy gully and climb straight up to a grass ledge below a groove.

2 30m. Climb the crack above to the *Pulpit* (a large flake – possible belay) and move right into a groove. Follow this to the summit of *High Man*.

Gondor	70m	E2	★★★	1967

An impressive and exposed climb which is both strenuous and delicate. The route follows the bulging arête on the left of the prominent groove of *Gomorrah*. Start at the base of the ridge left of *Gomorrah*.

1 25m (4a). Pitch 1 of *Gomorrah*.

2 18m (5b). Climb the groove in the arête to the bulge. Above on the left is a large triangular hold. Pull up and move boldly up right until the angle eases. Belay in a small corner below a grass ledge.

3 27m (5c). Climb down from the stance for 2 metres and traverse delicately right round the nose onto the wall. Climb up and left to easier climbing, following a groove to a large ledge and block belay. An alternative way to start this pitch (the original way) is to climb the overhanging arête on the right wall for 2 metres (very bold), then move onto the wall and continue up as above.

Gomorrah	80m	VS	★★★	1919

A superb climb which ascends the big groove on the left side of the *West Face of High Man*. Start on a small grass ledge, well below and left of the huge triangular roof, reached by scrambling up *The Old West Route* some 40 metres to a belay on a spike just left of a rough rib.

1 25m (4a). Follow the rib to a green ledge on the left. A wall and slab lead to huge block belays.

2 20m (4b). Step up right and traverse round the rib and across the corner to ledges. Step down and climb an awkward right-slanting crack/groove on the right to gain a ledge below the big groove. Climb

the groove, taking care with poised blocks, to a stance under a roof.

3 35m (4b). Overcome the bulge and continue up the groove to the top.

Direct Start 30m VS 1967

1 (4b). Worth doing if you've already done the ordinary start. As for ***Vandal***, follow the grassy corner to a stance beneath the roof (possible belay) or better, follow the ordinary start but trend right to the same point. Move left up a slab and ascend the groove over a slight bulge. Continue up left to join Pitch 2 and follow this to the stance in the main groove.

Above: Martin Armitage employing traditional techniques in the chimney of **Gomorrah** (VS), Pillar Rock. **Photo:** Stephen Reid

The Ridge Variation VS ★★★ 1932

A very good alternative. Quite wild!

3 30m (4c). From the belay, traverse left with difficulty to gain the foot of a steep crack. Climb this over a slight overlap and pull onto a slab that forms the left side of a slight groove. Exit left into another groove which leads to a ledge and blocks from where easy climbing attains the top of ***High Man***.

Original Finish 35m VS

3 (4b). Originally the route quit the upper groove at an obvious break on the right, traversed along this for 4 metres to a hollow block belay and then finished up a hollow rib.

Vandal	80m	HVS+	★★★	1959

A fine route, steep and well-protected in its lower half but becoming rather worrying with height. It takes the groove-line arising from the large triangular overhang of the ***West Face***. Start directly below the triangular roof.

1 25m (4c). Climb the grassy corner to about 5 metres below the triangular roof where a line up the wall on the right leads with a difficult move to a small ledge. The short curving crack on the right is followed to a good stance.

2 35m (5a). A fine pitch. Climb the main crack passing another large overhang on its right to a small overhang at 12 metres. Move left round this and either traverse left to the left arête or move up and

traverse left a few metres higher. Climb boldly up the slab above until it is possible to traverse right into an easier slabby amphitheatre and eventually find a runner. Climb up leftwards to a poor flake belay on a ledge at the foot of a flaky rib (possibly better to continue and stretch the rope out).

3 20m (4b). Climb the hollow rib to the top. Alternatively, go back down into the amphitheatre and traverse diagonally rightwards through a gap in the jagged arête to climb up the final few metres of the chimney of ***Sodom*** – this was the original finish.

Pillar of Salt	85m	E1	★★	1997

An eliminate line between ***Sodom*** and ***Gomorrah***. The rock is clean and very rough, particularly on the final pitch which follows the arête left of the chimney shared by ***New West Climb*** and ***Sodom***. Start as for ***Vandal***.

1 25m (5a). Follow the first pitch of ***Vandal*** as far as the small ledge. Climb the thin crack on the left to the stance on ***Vandal***.

2 30m (5a). Move up one metre and then make a rising traverse rightwards along an obvious series of holds across the wall on the right to the arête. Climb the arête direct until it eases under a bulge (junction with ***Sodom***) and traverse right along a slim ramp to belay on the chockstone at the foot of the chimney on the ***New West Climb***.

3 30m (5c). Pull up the short wall on the left to a ledge. Make a hard series of moves up the wall above (Wallnut 0.5 in thin crack above finger pocket) to get established on a sloping ledge on the arête. Follow the arête more easily to a slab on the left of the continuation arête (***Sodom*** crosses from left to right at this point). Reach a huge jug on the edge of the continuation arête and mantleshelf on to it. Follow the arête above on fine holds to another break (The original finish of ***Vandal*** crosses from left to right at this point). Finish directly up the jagged edge above, resisting the temptation to bridge across the chimney on the right.

Hawkeye	84m	HVS	★★	1995

A line up the rib between ***Vandal*** and ***Sodom*** but finishing right of the latter. Start 3 metres right of ***Vandal*** beneath a crack.

1 17m (5a). Climb the crack onto a pedestal below a blunt arête. Climb the arête directly (quite bold) moving right at the top to a flake belay and stance on the right (junction with ***Sodom***).

2 30m (5a). Climb the prominent groove directly above the stance and, when it eases, step left onto a rock ledge on the front of the rib beneath a shallow groove. Go up this to a large flake runner (junction with Pitch 3 of ***Sodom*** which goes up, then left). Continue a

Left: Stephen Reid in a fine position on **Gomorrah's Ridge Variation** (VS).
Photo: Martin Armitage

short distance until a short ramp leads rightwards to the foot of the chimney on *New West Climb*.

3 12m (5a). Immediately on the right of the chimney is an overhung V-groove. Climb this over a bulge and step right to a grass stance in a prominent groove (junction with *The South-West-by-West Climb*).

4 25m (4b). Climb to the overhang. Go up the groove on the left a short distance and pull out right to finish up another groove and short wall above.

Sodom	88m	VS	★	1919

Enjoyable but scary friction climbing based around the arête to the right of *Vandal*. Be warned it is a bold climb – Pitch 3 offers little more in protection now than it did in Kelly's day. Start 12 metres up *The Old West Route*, on a ledge 3 metres above it.

1 20m. An easy slab is climbed for 12 metres then a groove followed by steep rock which leads to a grassy niche (belay above on the left).

2 20m (4a). Move 3 metres to the right to a clean corner (shared with *Cheekwoolly*). Climb the corner to a resting place below a steep slab then traverse horizontally left on sloping rock steps to the left-hand side of a grassy corner (spike belay high up on the rib on the left).

3 28m (4b). A serious lead. Ascend the rib on good holds stepping left into an exposed groove. Follow this and where it eases move up the left-hand side of the rib, overcoming a bulge and thin slab to gain a shallow corner. Step up left to blocks and climb the wall just left of these to gain a slab. Traverse rightwards and down slightly, passing through a gap in the rib, to gain the chimney on *New West Climb* at the point that that route quits it to traverse right (chockstone belay).

4 20m (4b). The chimney.

Cheekwoolly	85m	S	★★	1974

An excellent line on superb rock. Protection is spaced but adequate. Start just right of *Sodom* in the back of a huge groove, reached by scrambling 5 metres leftwards up grass from the pale dike at the start of *Rib and Slab Climb*.

1 45m. Climb the open groove-line which trends slightly to the right, to belay on the traverse on Pitch 3 of *New West Climb* under the right-hand of two grooves to the right of the chimney on *New West Climb*.

2 40m. Climb the right-hand groove to where it opens out (part of *South-West by West Climb*). Traverse left into the left-hand groove and climb its left rib to the top, just right of the top pitch of *Sodom*.

Above: Ennerdale drumlins bathed in evening sunlight. **Photo:** Phil Rigby

Rib and Slab Climb	90m	HS	★★★	1919

One of the best climbs of its grade in the Lakes and an extremely enjoyable way to the summit of ***Pillar Rock***. Start just above the start of a right-slanting intrusion of pale rock, 2 metres below the large embedded block which is at the foot of ***New West Climb***.

1 26m. Traverse left along a footledge and continue leftwards to a steep rib with a groove. Climb this to break out left at a small ledge. Climb the slab right of the groove, or the rib on its right, to a ledge. A bold pitch.

2 20m. The groove above is hard to start (crux) but the difficulties soon ease. Climb the steep rib on the left of the groove of ***New West Climb*** to a stance at the top.

3 20m. Traverse right and upwards, crossing a groove, onto a superb rough slab; climb it, rising rightwards to a rib which is followed to the "pile of blocks" belay on ***New West Climb***.

4 24m. Follow the crack of ***New West Climb*** for about 3 metres then traverse leftwards via a block. Climb the blistered slab and rib above directly to the top.

Rib and Rib Climb	90m	E1-	★★	2005

An eliminate style series of variations on ***Rib and Slab Climb*** giving great climbing on fantastic rock. Unfortunately the protection on Pitch 1 is poor and this pushes it up a grade. Start as for ***Western Trod***, at the foot of a great right-slanting pale rock intrusion, just a couple of metres below the start of ***Rib and Slab Climb***.

1 30m (5a). Follow the intrusion for 5 metres to a short shallow wide chimney. Step leftwards onto a rib that is just right of the groove of ***Rib and Slab Climb*** and climb the rib to a jagged overhang. Step left onto ***Rib and Slab Climb*** and go up a few moves to place an inadequate selection of paltry protection. Traverse horizontally rightwards onto the overhang, pull over it, and follow the rib to the stance at the top of Pitch 1 of ***Rib and Slab Climb*** below a short V-groove. Climb the wall to the right of the groove and go up a few metres to a stance on the ***New West Climb*** just below a small square roof. A bold pitch but never desperate.

2 36m (5a). Climb a slim groove to the left of the roof (just right of the groove of ***New West Climb***), until good jugs on the right wall allow a traverse rightwards above the roof to the arête. Follow the arête to gain the traverse on ***Rib and Slab Climb***, then climb diagonally leftwards up the fine slab to its left edge before bold moves up rightwards allow the arête to be regained. Follow it to the "pile of blocks belay" on ***New West Climb***. A great pitch.

3 24m (5a). Step out leftwards off the top block and make a fingery hand-traverse onto a nose on the left. Continue the traverse leftwards round into a slim groove and climb this to join the last moves of ***Rib and Slab Climb***.

New West Climb	87m	VD+	★★★	1901

A very fine climb which finds its way through areas of rock usually reserved for harder things. The situations are superb making it one of the best routes of this standard in the Lake District. Start just above a big embedded block in the scree, 25 metres or so down from ***West Jordan Gully***.

1 20m. Follow easy rock in a shallow chimney trending slightly to the left to a rib which leads to a small corner. Follow a steep staircase on the right to belay on a good ledge.

2 10m. Climb a wide shallow chimney which leads to a small platform and traverse horizontally left for 4 metres to step down to a good belay. (It is possible to reach this belay direct from Pitch 1, but this is harder, grassy and not as good).

Left: Sally Baxendale and Richard Tolley tackle the magnificent slab pitch on **Rib and Slab Climb** (HS), Pillar Rock. **Photo:** Stephen Reid

3 17m. Climb the obvious groove to ledges and make an awkward traverse left to the foot of a chimney (chockstone belay).

4 20m. The imposing chimney above is climbed or thrutched, depending on ability and girth, to a chockstone at 9 metres (possible belay). Avoid the chimney above (***Sodom***) by traversing horizontally right and around a rib with difficulty. Continue rightwards, then up, to surmount a pile of blocks which form a magnificent belay.

5 20m. Climb the crack up the slab above to a small ledge and finish via the slab on the left.

Western Trod MS ★ 1995

A pleasant variation start up the obvious right-slanting intrusion of pale rock. Start 3 metres below the large embedded block which is at the foot of *New West Climb*.

1 25m. Follow the light coloured rock dike rightwards to join Pitch 1 of *New West Climb* just before the belay.

Direct Finish S 1911

4 29m. From the chockstone belay, climb the chimney direct to the top. A lot more awkward and not as good (later incorporated into ***Sodom***).

Original Finish

5 25m. From the pile of blocks belay, traverse into a block-filled grassy groove on the right and climb it to the summit.

The South-West-by-West Climb | 80m | VS+ | ★★ | 1938

A contrived but worthwhile and increasingly good climb. Start a few metres to the right of *New West Climb*, by the big boulder under *West Jordan Gully*.

1 18m. Traverse left on loose rock to the rib which bounds *New West Climb* on the right and follow it to belay on that climb.

2 25m (4c). The left edge of a smooth rectangular slab on the right leads to a horizontal ledge below another larger slab. Climb this until the rock steepens, then move left across a crack to a good foothold before making a few hard moves up to a stance half-way up Pitch 3 of *Rib and Slab Climb*.

3 15m. Traverse left into an easy groove and climb this to the traverse of *New West Climb*. A more difficult alternative can be made by traversing right, climbing between ***Rib and Slab Climb*** and *South-West Climb* and reversing the upper traverse of *New West Climb*.

4 22m (4c). Traverse left and climb the groove above to the overhang; turn this on the right (crux, and quite bold) and pull out right onto the arête which is followed to the top.

Right: Martin Armitage on the exposed moves out of the chimney on **New West Climb** (VD), Pillar Rock. **Photo:** Stephen Reid

Sundance | 75m | MVS | ★★ | 1995

A rather unbalanced but pleasant climb directly up the face between ***The South-West-by-West Climb*** and ***South-West Climb***. Start 6 metres below and left of ***South-West Climb***.

1 16m (4b). Climb the wall and corner above to a large grass ledge and traverse 3 metres right to a flake belay.

2 35m (4c) Move one metre left and ascend a thin crack up the slab to a bulge. Pull over this via a crack and ascend the slab on the left to a rock ledge. Go directly up via a second ledge to a corner. Climb the corner or the wall on its left to a ledge. Continue up the slab to a stance beneath the prominent arête.

3 24m (4b). Bridge up into the corner above and pull out right onto the arête as soon as possible. Follow the left-hand side of the rib above to join ***South-West Climb*** for the last few moves.

South-West Climb | 75m | MVS | ★★★ | 1911/1919

Delectable climbing on small but positive holds. A justly popular route. The start is one metre left of the entrance to ***West Jordan Gully***.

1 35m (4b). A short groove leads to a small ledge under a slab containing a deep-cut hold. Gain the hold from the left, move awkwardly right and continue up the slab to where it steepens. Pull up boldly on good holds which lead to a small ledge. Continue up the rib on the edge of the gully for another 10 metres to a good square ledge.

Above: Getting some gear in for the delicate moves on **South-West Climb**, MVS, Pillar. **Photo:** Mark Gear

2 22m (4b). Traverse diagonally left for 3 metres, then step up, move back right onto the slab and climb it, keeping to the right until a slight steepening is reached. Climb boldly up the slab above until a short traverse right under a large block can be made, towards ***Jordan Gap***, to a small stance. Quite a serious pitch.

3 18m (4b). Return under the block and climb up a steep rib and short crack to the summit of ***High Man***.

Original Way 19m 1911

2. From the belay on Pitch 1, traverse left and ascend a grassy slab to a wide V-chimney (usually wet) which is followed to the top (as for the original final pitch of *New West Climb*).

Boot Strap | 104m | VS | ★ | 1967

A mini-girdle taking in only the *West Face of High Man*. A sustained route which contains some good if not original climbing. Start as for *South-West Climb*.

1 22m (4b). Follow *South-West Climb* for about 20 metres to a sitting belay about 3 metres above the overlap.

2 24m (4a). Traverse left onto *South-West-by-West Climb*, cross this and traverse round the corner to gain the belay at the top of Pitch 3 of *New West Climb*.

3 16m (4b). Follow the traverse of *New West Climb* and continue past the chimney to attain the small sloping ledge on the rib of Pitch 3 of *Sodom*. Climb this to a small ledge.

4 12m (4a). Step down and left and traverse to the rib overlooking *Gomorrah*. Make a long step onto this climb and go up to a belay beneath an overhang.

5 30m (4c). A wild pitch! From the belay, traverse left with difficulty to gain the foot of a steep crack. Climb this over a slight overlap and pull onto a slab that forms the left side of a square groove. Exit left into another groove which leads to a ledge and blocks. Easy climbing attains the top of *High Man*.

The Girdle Traverse | 446m | VS | | 1931

An expedition combining a few fine pitches with a lot of rather vegetated scrambling. Originally climbed in reverse with even more descending. As is common with other long mountain crag traverses some prior knowledge of the crag will be an advantage.

1–3 100m (5a). Pitches 1 to 3 of *Grooved Wall*.

4 35m. A mossy wall on the right leads to a good ledge behind a big block, as per *North-East Climb* Pitch 5. Follow horizontal grass ledges rightwards to the open amphitheatre near the top of *Savage Gully*; dodgy block belay in the centre of the gully.

5 15m (4a). Step further across the gully and ascend a crack in the right wall leading to the ledge beneath the *Nose* on *North Climb*.

6 25m. Cross the *Strid* and descend the *Split Blocks*. Go down the grass ledge on the right to a crevasse stance beneath a short crack/groove the left edge of the main headwall (taken by *Scylla*).

7 20m (4b). As for *Hadrian's Wall*, ascend the crack until it turns into a dirty groove, at which point take to the wall on the left which is climbed to grass ledges. Climb up and right to a ledge on the right

and the hollow block belay on *Scylla*.

8 25m (4c). Cross the water-stained groove at a level with the belay, and go awkwardly round the arête on the right to the large detached block stance on *Nor'-Nor'-West Climb*. Continue the traverse rightwards to small ledges under *Downlen's Chimney* (top pitch of *Megaton*).

9 24m. Traverse easily rightwards under the foot of *Oppenheimer's Chimney* and climb a short crack to a ledge. Traverse right to a large flake leaning against the wall at the stance below the final pitch of *The Appian Way*.

10 20m. Traverse right on grass and then follow a slightly rising rock crevasse to a vast block belay on *Nook and Wall Climb*.

11 30m (4a). Descend the slab below the block slightly, and pull up a short wall on the right to gain the top of *Ledge and Groove Climb*. Scramble up right to belay on *The Old West Route*.

"They are enthusiastic fellows, these climbers. They ascend their favourite mountains time after time (one honoured pioneer of Lake District climbing has made ninety-nine ascents to the summit of Great Gable); they are unwearied in finding new ways up everywhere, and their talk, when they get together, is of nicks and notches, ladders and ledges, gullies, ghylls, and chimneys, and even of cols, arêtes and couloirs. All Cumberland and Westmorland is familiar to them; they are at home on the Blencathra Edges, looking down to the waters of the dark tarn which is said to reflect the stars at noon-day, on the precipices of Scafell, and Striding Edge on Helvellyn. They have clambered among the waterfalls of Piers Ghyll, climbed the precipice of Pavey Ark and the crags of Lingmell, crossed the sloping stones wedged in the caverns at Dungeon Ghyll, scaled the front of Great End; yet ever do they return with greater fondness to the most enticing peak of all – the redoubtable Pillar Rock of Ennerdale."
CN Williamson, ***The Climbs of the English Lake District, All Year Round*** *(1884).*

12 24m. Scrambling down *The Old West Route* to the start of *Gomorrah*.

13 25m. Climb Pitch 1 of *Gomorrah* or the *Direct Start*.

14 40m (4b). Continue up Pitch 2 and part of Pitch 3 of *Gomorrah* until not far below the top when it is possible to traverse to the right to a stance at a hollow block on the arête (as for *Vandal*).

15 12m. Descend the sloping grass ledges below and traverse to the right to belay at the chockstone at the top of the chimney of *New West Climb*.

16 11m. As for *New West Climb*; traverse right around the rib and keep traversing until a short ascent leads to the pile of blocks belay.

17 40m (4b). Traverse right to the arête and finish up *South-West Climb*.

Original Finish

A fairly pointless exercise.

15 17m. Descend the sloping grass ledges directly below the stance and keep climbing straight down the sloping and poorly protected rocks of *Sodom* until a lower gap in the arête enables a traverse to the right to belay at the chockstone at the bottom of the chimney of *New West Climb*.

16 30m. Traverse right and climb the slab of Pitch 3 of *Rib and Slab Climb* for 12 metres. From here a horizontal traverse to the right across a V-groove leads to the top of Pitch 1 of *South-West Climb*.

17 40m (4b). Continue up Pitches 2 and 3 of *South-West Climb*.

The Greater Traverse	516m	E1		1969

Joining *The Eightfold Way*, *The Link* and *The Girdle Traverse* creates a route of alpine proportions – the longest climb in the Lake District. Sadly, length isn't everything.

West Jordan Gully	30m	S	★	1898

This is the prominent cleft separating *Pisgah* from *High Man*. An interesting and atmospheric climb deep inside the mountain.

The way is obvious and the capstone can be surmounted either on the left or on the right. It is also possible to climb a crack on the left wall at the start of the climb which leads to a niche on the left-hand capstone route.

West Face of Pisgah

This is the small buttress to the south (right) of *West Jordan Gully*. The routes on its *East* and *North Faces* are described on page 209.

Sentinel	55m	E1	★	1967

This route contains a hard first pitch and then is much easier. It takes a direct line up the steep crack above the start of *Pisgah West Ridge*. Start immediately right of *West Jordan Gully* at a blunt arête below the crack.

1 20m (5b). Climb the arête to runners below the crack. Surmount the overhang with difficulty and follow the crack more easily to a stance.

2 35m. Continue up the easier crack above for 6 metres then move out left and make a short traverse to a V-groove which is climbed to the easy-angled slabs of *Pisgah West Ridge*. Continue up these to the top.

Pisgah West Ridge	55m	MS	★	1909

A pleasant climb which starts by a corner just to the right of *West Jordan Gully*.

1 43m. Ascend the wall immediately right of the corner to a small pedestal ledge or gain it more easily from the right. Climb the broken

arête above to a large crack and follow this trending right to a grassy groove. Traverse left onto a slabby buttress and follow the crest to a ledge.

2 12m. A short wall and easier slabs lead to the top of the *Pisgah*.

Variation 25m S ★ 1909

At the top of the large crack, level with the base of the grassy groove, an exposed traverse left is made to a corner with a grassy stance. A crack on the left is awkward to enter. As soon as it widens, trend up rightwards to join the upper part of the original route.

West Cove

GR **NY 170 124** Alt **750m** F **North**

There are still possibilities for exploration on the crags at the head of the cove on the west side of *Pillar Rock*. So far the only route of worth is *West Cove Eliminate*.

West Cove Chimney (grade unknown, 1908) lies left of **Wide Gully** (S, 1913) which splits the crags from top to bottom, its start being 90 metres from *West Jordan Gully* at a slightly higher level than the foot of the latter. **Branch Gully** is an easy scramble that leads off right out of *Wide Gully* after about 10 metres.

West Cove Eliminate | 55m | E1+ | ★★ | 1964

A technically interesting route which follows the line of the corner-groove rising from the junction of *Wide* and *Branch Gullies* and is well seen from the *West Face of the Rock*.

1 5m (4c). Climb a short groove and wall to a large grass ledge at the foot of the main groove.

2 20m (5b). The groove is difficult to start, not that easy in the middle and difficult to finish. It is fortunate that there is a lie down ledge at the top as it may well be needed.

3 30m (4b). Move out to the right to a huge block and stand on it. Climb the wall above, keeping near the right edge, on good holds but with no runners for far too long a distance. Continue up easier slabs to the top.

Above: Martin Armitage makes a rare ascent of **West Cove Eliminate** (E1), West Cove. **Photo:** Stephen Reid.

Long Chimney (VD, 1908) starts 15 metres to the right of *Wide Gully*. The chimney is followed, with some loose rock in its upper part, to a ridge which leads past the top of *Branch Gully*. Straight ahead is another chimney (VD) but an easier alternative chimney lies some distance to the right and round the corner.

Mirk (or Wind Gap) Cove

Mirk Cove (NY 160 123) is the cove to the west of Pillar Cove. It is actually two subsidiary coves, Wind Gap Cove and Mirk Cove, divided by vague ridge, near the top of which is situated *Black Crag*. It is one of the most beautiful and most remote coves in the Lake District, but it should be noted that this area was subject to some route preparation ("gardening") that provoked heated discussion in 2005 concerning the ethics of vegetation removal – see the section on **Caring for the Natural Environment while you Climb** (page 14) for a summary of current best practice.

Wind Gap & Mirk Coves
Ennerdale

1 Black Crag Evening Buttress
2 Black Crag Lower Slabs
3 Black Crag Upper Buttress
4 Cove Crag
5 Spire Crag
6 Scoat Fell Crag
7 Steeple East Buttress

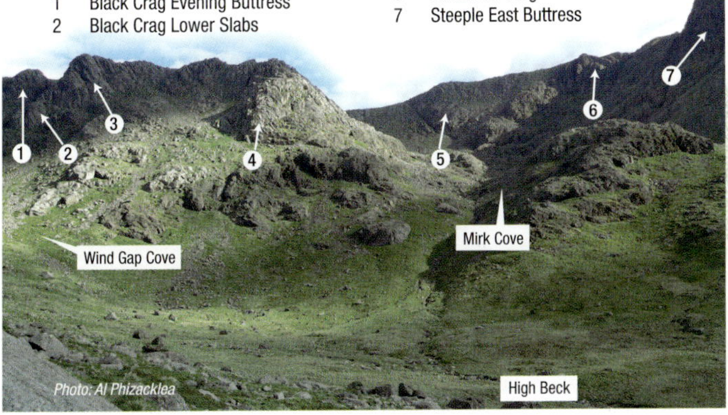

Approaches:

There are two main approaches:

From **Ennerdale**, the most direct way is to ascend alongside High Beck (a tributary of the Liza). The upper woodland part of this path is not marked on the OS map but is actually pretty good if a bit boggy in places. Those using bikes should follow the approach as for ***Pillar Rock***, then keep cycling westwards along the upper forest track until, just after crossing High Beck, a path will be seen leading up through the trees (2hrs 30mins – 3hrs).

From **Wasdale**, the path up Mosedale (as for Pillar Fell), and tedious slog up to Wind Gap is followed. Once Wind Gap is reached, follow the ridge westwards (left) to a cairn (828m); the summit of ***Black Crag*** is only 50 metres or so away. Alternatively, it is more interesting and involves less scree crawling, to follow Mosedale Beck to source, then reach the col between Red Pike and Scoat Fell whereupon a path traverses rightwards to join the Scoat Fell – Pillar Fell ridge and passes near the top of ***Black Crag*** (2hrs 30mins).

All the above approaches are very long for a single day's climbing but there is good flat ground in the base of the cove which would make an excellent campsite less than half an hour from the crags.

Black Crag

Grid reference:	**NY 164 117**	Altitude:	**750m**
Faces:	**North-North-West**	Approach:	**2hrs 30 mins – 3 hrs**

Black (or *High*) *Crag* is situated high up the north slope of Scoat Fell which goes down to Wind Gap. The routes vary in length from one to four pitches, and the rock in the main is superb, though it can be very blank in places so it is advisable to pick climbs well within your grade to start with, and to carry a good range of gear including micro-cams and micro-nuts, as well as larger stuff and thin slings. There are good climbs at all but the hardest grades and the crag would well repay a visit especially in the afternoon and evening when the sun is upon it.

On entering the lower cove take the left fork of the stream towards Wind Gap. The cliff lies a little to the right of this and should not be confused with the more broken crags still further to the right, or those encircling the combe (*Mirk Cove*) of the right fork of the stream. When approaching from Wasdale, if a line is struck leftwards, at the same level as the Wind Gap, across the rather steep and rough fellside, the foot of the crag is reached in less than 10 minutes from Wind Gap.

Descent:

Black Crag conveniently splits into five separate climbing buttresses and the first marked feature encountered towards the left side of the crag (looking up) is the wide scree-filled *Descent Gully*, which gives an easy but unpleasant descent from all routes. A much more pleasant descent is via the gully to the right of the crags.

Black Crag
Evening Buttress

1	Blonde on Blonde	VS *
2	Evening Chimney	VD
3	Wounded Knee	E1 *
4	The Flying Fin	HVS *
5	Flying Fin Direct	E2

Evening Buttress

The first buttress is high on the left-hand side of the *Descent Gully*. The routes end almost on the summit of the ridge between Scoat Fell and Pillar.

Blonde on Blonde	50m	VS	★	2006

Not as good as it looks though the finish is great. Start just right of the main arête of the buttress and 10 metres left of *Evening Chimney* at a wide crack.

1 30m (4c). Climb up to a pinnacle flake then up the crack and left onto the arête. Move up until forced back right into a grungy chimney. Make a hard move up this and pull out left. Cross back rightwards, across the crack, and climb the wall on the right. Scramble up loose ledges to a block belay on the highest just left of the upper arête.

2 20m (4c). Climb the arête on hollow blocks to the top of a huge flake. Move awkwardly left to a short groove, go up this to a slab and finish up the arête on the left.

Evening Chimney	60m	VD+		1940

Start in the gully at the foot of a dark undercut chimney 6 metres right of the main arête.

1 35m. Struggle up into the undercut chimney, follow it to grass ledges and trend to the right over easy rocks to the highest grass ledge under a right-slanting corner system.

2 25m. Follow a broken rib to a block. Either climb the strenuous mossy corner on the left (S) or better, step right to a notch and climb the crack and V-chimney straight above.

10 metres right of *Evening Chimney* is massive hanging fin of rock with a large slab forming its left face. The remaining climbs are on this slab.

Wounded Knee	30m	E1+	★	2006

The wavy crack up the left side of the slab gives a sustained pitch at the top end of the grade. Start from a grass ledge below a short sharp arête.

(5b). Climb the arête to a grass ledge containing two blocks. Climb the crack on the left side of the slab above; hard to start, and even harder to finish.

Right: Stephen Reid and Sally Baxendale making the first ascent of **Blonde on Blonde** (VS), Black Crag. **Photo:** Sarah Bailey

The Flying Fin	30m	HVS+	★	2006

A great pitch. Start from a grass ledge below the arête of the massive hanging fin of rock, just right of the short sharp arête start of ***Wounded Knee***.

(5a). Climb easily up leftwards to two blocks on a grass ledge. Step off the blocks and make a thin traverse rightwards to the arête. Climb up to a jug and then traverse back left to pull up onto a thin foot-ledge with the crack of ***Wounded Knee*** on its left. Move up the crack a metre, then traverse back right and follow a thin crack to better holds on the right. Traverse these rightwards to the arête which soon leads to the top.

Flying Fin Direct E2 2006

(5b). As for the original route but from the jug, make an airy step out and up rightwards until under a small roof. Avoid this on the left then climb up rightwards to rejoin the original route at the arête.

The next route starts immediately right of the ***Descent Gully*** and just left of the ***Lower Slabs***.

The Main Ridge Climb	111m	D	★	1929

A fine long outing though artificial in that it is possible to turn difficulties on the left and escape into the ***Descent Gully***. Start at the foot of a short steep buttress with a huge block on top, some 4 metres left of a gully that bounds the left side of the ***Lower Slabs***.

1 18m. Climb the obvious line on the crest of the buttress on good holds moving slightly right onto a grass ledge. Climb the short wall to emerge just to the left of a huge block.

2 15m. Scramble right for 6 metres and cross the upper part of a gully to another steep buttress. Move slightly down and right and traverse onto the ridge then climb directly to the top of the buttress.

3 30m. Ridge scrambling followed by an awkward wall leads to a huge rock glacis (which descends into the ***Descent Gully***). Belay at some large boulders.

4 18m. Walk leftwards up grass just to the right of a large freestanding pinnacle to below a short chimney-crack in the steep wall on the left of the glacis

5 15m. The short chimney-crack or rocks on the left, leads to a wide sloping rock ledge. This is followed by a right-facing corner and ends on another large rock glacis (which also descends into the ***Descent Gully***).

6 15m. Ascend the right edge of the glacis to a fine summit.

Right: Stephen Reid on the first ascent of **The Flying Fin** (HVS), Black Crag.
Photo: Sally Baxendale

Lower Slabs

Thirty metres right of the *Descent Gully* and just right of *The Main Ridge Climb* is a superb face of rock about 35 metres high. It can be recognized by a mossy recessed step towards the right in the ground under the crag and a leftward-trending grassy area on the left. It stands above the *First Terrace*.

Lower Slabs Ordinary Route	42m	VD	★★	1929

A good little route which also gives an interesting variation start to ***The Main Ridge Climb***. Start 20 metres right of ***The Main Ridge Climb*** and 4 metres left of the mossy recess.

Follow grassy rocks up left for 6 metres to an obvious foot-ledge which leads rightwards to a step up to a grassy ledge and block. Step back left and climb a shallow groove with a crack to a rock ledge on the right. Move left onto the arête and follow the left side of the crest pleasantly to a rock platform.

Lower Slabs Super Direct	35m	E1	★	1987

A bold direct start and worrying finish to ***Lower Slabs Direct***. Start 2 metres left of the large mossy recess.

(5a). Climb the wall direct via a small V-groove, with an awkward move right to a grass ledge (Friends 3.5 and 2 just above). From the right side of the ledge, easier but unprotected climbing up a slightly left-slanting ramp leads to a rock ledge. An upward traverse right is made past a reasonably solid flake to a worryingly poised one. Climb delicately upwards past the poised flake and directly up the wall to the top.

Lower Slabs Climb Direct	38m	HVS	★★	1929

A very pleasant though quite serious climb which weaves its way up the face covering some interesting ground. Start 2 metres left of the large mossy recess as for ***Lower Slabs Super Direct***.

(4c). Climb a rightward-trending (almost horizontal) dog-leg crack to reach a shallow left-slanting groove, immediately above the top of the mossy recess. Follow this to a grass ledge (Friends 3.5 and 2 just above). From the right side of the ledge, easy but unprotected climbing up a slightly left-slanting ramp leads to a rock ledge. An upward traverse right is made past a reasonably solid flake to a worryingly poised one. From the poised flake, make a long stride rightwards and then climb up and rightwards to a small triangular niche, then rightwards from the top of this to a good ledge.

Black Crag
Lower Slabs & Middle Buttress

1	Lower Slabs Ordinary Route	VD	**
2	Lower Slabs Super Direct	E1	*
3	Lower Slabs Climb Direct	HVS	**
4	Debutante's Slab	MVS	**
5	Ellison's Eliminate	HVS	*
6	Left Central Slab Climb	S	*
7	Overhanging Central Slab Climb	HS	**
8	Poet Laureate	E1	*
9	Central Corner	HS	
10	Central Slab Climb	S	
11	Perfect Day	E1	**
12	Solo Slabs	D	
13	Limerick	HVS	*
14	Poetry in Motion	E1	
15	Ode to Boby	VS	***
16	West Gully	D	

Photo: Al Phizacklea

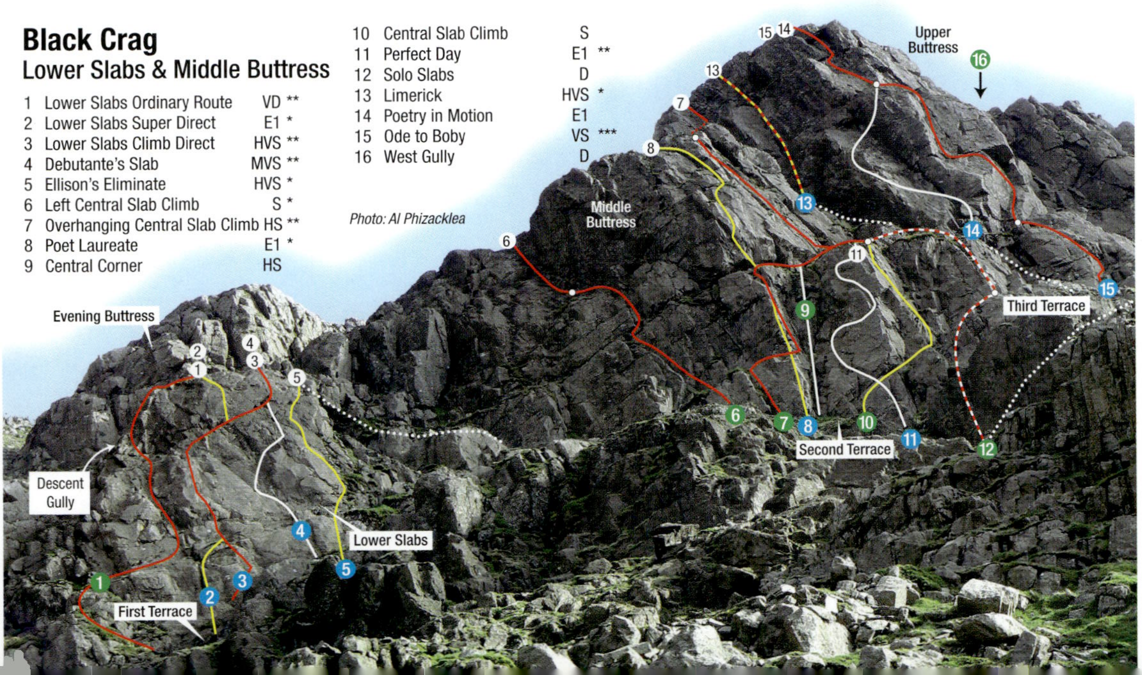

Debutante's Slab	30m	MVS	★★	1990

A good slab climb on fantastic rock with a wild finish. It is very bold in the lower two-thirds but the climbing is fairly straightforward. Start from a higher grass ledge above the mossy recess under the slabs, beneath a very thin left-facing corner at some wonderfully bubbly rock. Alternatively, use the start of ***Lower Slabs Climb Direct*** to reach the same place.

(4b). Climb the bubbly rock and thin corner direct to easy ledges (it is possible to traverse left at this point and place the Friends mentioned in the descriptions above). Continue up and slightly leftwards until it is possible to move back and up to the right to gain a ledge and large blunt spike (first runner - protection is adequate from here). Ascend the intimidating headwall above the spike, first leftwards to a small triangular niche, then rightwards from the top of this to a good ledge (the last few moves are in common with ***Lower Slabs Climb Direct***).

Ellison's Eliminate	30m	HVS-	★	2006

Pleasant climbing on fine rock up the edge of the slab. Start at the right-hand side of the buttress at some mossy streaks just right of ***Debutante's Slab***.

(5a). Climb the wall on big holds to a ledge. Move up rightwards to gain the start of a leftward-slanting diagonal crack (and some gear!). Follow the crack, then step right and up and make an awkward mantelshelf onto a tiny ledge under the headwall. Stride left to join ***Debutante's Slab*** and move up to the base of the triangular niche on that route, but then traverse right a metre or so and climb diagonally rightwards up the steep headwall on excellent holds.

Middle Buttress

The next climbs to the right start from the *Second Terrace*, about 30 metres higher than the *First Terrace*, which can be reached via an opening a few metres round from the large mossy recess, or from the top of the *Lower Slabs* by a short descent to the right. The cliff rises steeply to attain its greatest height. On the left side, the crag is cut away in its upper reaches by a large leftward-leaning impending diedre or fault. Right of this a small band of overhangs run horizontally across the crag to peter out on the right side. Running down from the overhangs is a series of ribs and corners.

Left: Stephen Reid catches the last of the evening sun on **Lower Slabs Climb Direct** (HVS), Black Crag. **Photo:** Sarah Bailey

Left Central Slab Climb	46m	S+	★	1929

An interesting and atmospheric if somewhat mossy climb. Start left of centre of the main face at a slabby wall, right of a fault running up the left side of the crag and in a grassy corner just right of a rib with a small overhang at 5 metres. This is just left of a large slabby boulder at the base of the crag.

1 32m. Climb the slabby wall, right of the rib and a grassy groove, to a grass ledge. Climb the narrow left-slanting slab above by its left edge to a possible stance by perched blocks. Move right past the blocks into a short corner and trend left into a large grassy recess under the impending head wall.

2 14m. A better pitch than it looks. The leftward-trending slabby corner is climbed to the top, ending on a large grassy rake.

Overhanging Central Slab Climb	86m	HS	★★	1929

A continually interesting series of pitches with varied climbing giving a good if escapable route to the top of the buttress. Start 5 metres right of *Left Central Slab Climb* below the left-hand of two leftward-slanting ribs and just right of a large slabby boulder at the base of the crag.

1 27m. Climb the first rib to just below a grassy ledge and traverse out to the right round the arête and into the rather vegetated right-facing *Central Corner*. Climb the *Corner* for a few moves until it is possible to make a hard pull out to the left edge, then swarm over the final bulge by liberal use of a large hollow flake. Belay immediately (thread under the overhang).

2 7m. It is best to traverse right on grass and rushes and re-belay at a large block.

3 22m. Make a low traverse leftwards across the cracked upper slab and go up its left side to a large block. Continue directly up the slab above, just left of a grassy chimney, to belay at the top of a wide easy-angled grassy rake. A fine pitch.

4 30m. The final tier gives another fine pitch. Follow a slab with a crack in its left side to gain a large grassy corner on the right. A final slab and corner on the left ends on a large rock glacis.

Poet Laureate	46m	E1	★	1987

A direct route up the highest section of *Middle Buttress*. There is a short hard bold section at the start of the second pitch, otherwise the climbing is straight-forward. Start 6 metres left of the toe of the buttress at a clean arête which bounds a right-facing corner and 2 metres right of *Overhanging Central Slab Climb*.

1 24m (4b). Climb the arête direct (bold at mid-height) to a block belay on a grass ledge below a short V-corner/groove

2 **22m** (5b). Make gymnastic moves off the block leftwards to the foot of the groove (small nut runner in the groove and in a small crack around the rib on the right). Climb the groove for a few moves before making difficult moves into a small crack in the rib on the right. Ascend the short delicate slab above to easier ground. Follow the slabs pleasantly via a short left-facing corner.

Central Corner	24m	HS		1987

The dirty corner is a reasonable line but unpleasantly vegetated. It gives a direct start to ***Overhanging Central Slab Climb***. Start at the foot of the corner immediately right of ***Poet Laureate***.

Climb the corner direct with a move out right at the top to below Pitch 3 of ***Overhanging Central Slab Climb***. Block belay on the right.

Central Slab Climb	27m	S		1929

Really a variation start to ***Overhanging Central Slab Climb*** and not as good as the main route described but easier and more escapable. Start below a short shallow groove, 3 metres right of ***Central Corner*** and 5 metres left of a grassy rock rake.

1 **12m.** Climb the groove for 4 metres to a slight overhang and traverse right along a narrow ledge to a grassy corner immediately followed by another higher grassy corner.

2 **15m.** Climb a slabby corner by its left edge to a big grassy ledge and block belay. Either continue as for Pitch 3 of ***Overhanging Central Slab Climb*** or **descend** an easy gully to the right.

Perfect Day	25m	E1–	★★	2006

An excellent pitch on superb rock up the wall to the right of ***Central Corner***. Protection is good on the crux but there is a long bold section above this to reach the top. It can be climbed in its own right or makes a good start to either ***Limerick*** or ***Poetry in Motion***. Start at clean rib at the lowest point of the wall; this is just right of the groove of ***Central Slab Climb*** and just left of a wide grassy ramp.

(5b). Make a hard move to start the rib and climb it first leftwards then via a step right to a small grass ledge and up to a small roof. Traverse leftwards down a ramp (crossing ***Central Slab Climb***) to a short corner and go up this, pulling out left at its top. Climb the shallow blocky left-facing groove above until it peters out then traverse rightwards and gain a slim groove in the arête (good hidden wire placements just below the base of the groove). Climb the groove (last gear) to gain a good ledge above. Exit the ledge on the left, move up 2 metres and traverse horizontally rightwards to another slim groove in the arête. A couple more moves up this will allow your heart rate to return to normal. Block belay on right. From the belay, the starts of ***Limerick*** and ***Poetry in Motion*** lie above and right, or a gully on the right can be **descended**, or Pitch 3 of ***Overhanging Central Slab Climb*** takes the slabs on the left.

Solo Slabs	39m	D		1937

An escapable route that follows a parallel line to ***Central Slab Climb***. Start 5 metres up the grassy rock rake at a short grassy corner.

1 **24m.** Climb the corner to its top, move up to a higher ledge and traverse right over the top of the small buttress to belay at slabs bounded on the right by a grassy gully.

2 **15m.** Follow the slabs ahead slightly leftwards and move left to the block belay below Pitch 3 of ***Overhanging Central Slab Climb***. Either continue as for Pitch 3 of ***Overhanging Central Slab Climb*** or **descend** an easy gully to the right.

Upper Buttress

From the right-hand end of the *Second Terrace*, a rock and grass rake slants up rightwards to the *Third Terrace* and a short upward scramble leads to the foot of the impressive *Upper Buttress*, with a hanging corner left of centre and a huge overhang on its right, and which is bounded on its far right by *West Gully*. On the left side of the crag lies a leftward-slanting grassy gully which affords a means of ascent or descent from the top of *Middle Buttress*.

Several small buttresses below ***Upper Buttress*** have been climbed (1929) but the exact lines are not known.

The routes on the main crag are described from **left** to **right**.

Limerick	35m	HVS	★	1988

A good climb which follows an obvious stepped leftward-slanting corner on the extreme left side of ***Upper Buttress***. The route has excellent protection throughout, but is rather slower to dry than the other routes on the crag. Start about 30 metres up and left from ***Ode to Boby*** near the top of a grassy gully which separates ***Middle Buttress*** from ***Upper Buttress***.

(5b). Follow the slabby corner to a small overhang. Step up and right into another small corner then climb this for a couple of metres until another overhang forces moves right into the final corner. Climb this with pleasant layback moves to an obvious grass terrace (possible belay). Immediately above is an overhanging slanting crack which is both hard and strenuous. Climb the crack direct; long reaches are

Black Crag Upper Buttress

1	Overhanging Central Slab Climb (part)	HS **
2	Poet Laureate (part)	E1 *
3	Central Corner (part)	HS
4	Perfect Day (part)	E1 **
5	Central Slab Climb (part)	S
6	Solo Slabs (part)	D
7	Limerick	HVS *
8	Poetry In Motion	E1
9	Ode to Boby	VS ***
10	Tower Buttress	VD ***
V	Variation	MS
11	West Gully	D

required to overcome its difficult upper section. It is also possible to climb the wall on the left. The rest is followed more easily to the top.

Poetry in Motion	73m	E1		1987

Some good but serious climbing up the hanging slab on the left side of the buttress. Start as for *Ode to Boby*.

1 15m (4a). Follow *Ode to Boby* to the grassy ledge below the corner gangway. Move left a couple of metres to belay under a large triangular block.

2 35m (5a). Climb up past the large block and onto the left-slanting corner/slab. Climb the corner for a couple of metres (it is allegedly possible to climb the dirty corner direct at a slightly harder standard, though why anyone should want to…). Traverse delicately left (crux) onto a resting point on the edge of the slab. Move up steeply to a small ledge and rejoin the corner. Continue to a small overhang and finally get some runners though none of them are that good. Climb steeply up right to a grass terrace.

3 23m (4c). As for the last pitch of *Ode to Boby*.

Ode to Boby	71m	VS+	★★★	1971

An entertaining climb that weaves its way up the buttress. Start 7 metres left of *Tower Buttress* at a stepped recess which is in the middle of a small slabby buttress leaning against the main crag.

1 15m (4a). Easy rightward-trending steps lead to an awkward wall on the left and are followed by a rightwards-leaning corner/gangway.

2 18m (4c). A fine pitch. Make awkward moves onto the mossy gangway and follow it to the right-hand end of the prominent rectangular overhang (good thread). Traverse left under the overhang, step round the edge, and continue a delicate traverse left to a triangular niche.

3 15m (4b). Another good pitch. Climb the imposing corner above to a large grass ledge.

4 23m. (4c). Follow the grass ledge leftwards until it ends. Above is an obvious greenish concave slab; climb the steep slab boldly on small holds to a groove on the right followed by easier rock to the top.

Direct Finish 15m VS+ ★ 1987

4 (4c). Rather artificial and serious in its lower half but the top section is great. Climb the rib to the left of a choked crack and follow it to the top of the crag.

Left: Sally Baxendale approaching the crux moves on the superb rock of **Tower Buttress** (VD), Black Crag. **Photo:** Stephen Reid

Tower Buttress	57m	VD+	★★★	1929

A superb climb on excellent clean rock and with considerable exposure. Start at the lowest point of the slabby buttress, just right of *Ode to Boby*, and some 20 metres down and left from *West Gully*.

1 18m. The pleasant slab to a large grass terrace.

2 27m. Climb the right edge of the buttress for a few metres, then traverse left to the base of a wide crack level with a rectangular overhang. Traverse left above the overhang for a metre and then go straight up to ledges below the final slabs. The wide crack can also be climbed at a similar grade.

3 12m. Either climb the slab 2 metres left of the thin crack in a shallow groove ahead or the thin crack itself or start up the thin crack but, once above a ledge, quit it just below the top for a hand-traverse right – this last is most spectacular.

Variation MS

3 12m. Struggle up the undercut wide crack right of the original finish.

West Gully (D, 1929) bounds *Upper Buttress* on the right. It offers about 40 metres of vegetated easy climbing.

Western Buttress

Right again is *Western Buttress*, a very broken easy-angled and grassy area of rock. *Crack, Chimney and Slab* follows the left edge of this buttress.

Crack, Chimney and Slab	35m	VD		1929

This climb forms the right-hand ridge of *West Gully* and is a traditional subterranean chimney climb. Start up and right from the first chockstone in *West Gully*.

1 15m. A narrow slab leads to the foot of a prominent black cleft.

2 20m. The black cleft and through-route, which are often wet, lead to a continuation of the chimney or a much more pleasant slab on the left.

Two other routes, **Left-Hand Route** (D, 1929) and **Right-Hand Route** (D, 1929), have proved impossible to trace.

Cove Crag

Grid reference: **NY 162 118** Altitude: **675m**
Faces: **North** Approach: **2 hrs 30 mins – 3 hrs**

Not named on the maps. In the centre of Windgap Cove, 250 metres west of and slightly lower than *Black Crag*, lies a low rocky spur which curves up to join the main Scoat Fell ridge (pleasant in winter conditions). The base of the spur terminates at a set of water-streaked slabs of immaculate rock. The routes are easily combined with a visit to *Black Crag*. Most of the rock is quick-drying but a few wet streaks can linger for several days after rain.

Fifteen metres left of the lowest point of the buttress are a pair of short left-leaning and right-leaning ramps that almost form a V. To the right of the right-hand of these two is a left-leaning ramp that leads to the same point. The effect is of a W without the right-hand stroke.

Deja Ewe	65m	VS+	★★	2006

Superb rock and the quickest drying line on the crag. Start at the left-hand left-leaning ramp.

1 25m (5a). Climb the ramp then traverse left to a short corner. Make a hard move up this and step right onto the slab above. Immediately move up left and climb easily up to a large platform. Move left then climb back right follow a grassy right-slanting groove to a large mossy ledge.

2 20m (4b). From the right-hand side of the ledge, climb the wall diagonally leftwards until it is possible to pull up rightwards onto a ledge in an open left-slanting groove. Climb a crack on the far wall of the groove to a ledge and zigzag up ledges to a huge block belay on the right.

3 20m. Left of the belay block is a large slightly protruding block. Start left of this and climb up just right of a smaller poised block. Continue in the same line to a grass ledge and then climb the groove on the right behind the tower.

Prophylactics	65m	E1-	★★	1988

This route hardly lives up to its name being very poorly protected at the start. Start at the left-hand left-leaning ramp.

1 25m (5a). Follow the short ramp to the foot of a short impending crack and scoop directly above. Climb this with difficulty and worry, then move slightly right and follow a rib to a large mossy ledge on the left.

Cove Crag

1	Deja Ewe	VS	**
2	Prophylactics	E1	*
3	No Ewe Turns	MVS	**
4	Baxi's Bomber Beetles	HVS	**

Photo: Al Phizacklea

2 20m (4c). From the left-hand side of the ledge, climb up to the edge of a slab and cross it leftwards until overlooking a black groove. The delicate rib above ends with a superb flake hold; finish at a higher ledge – an exciting pitch.

3 20m. Climb the easy groove to the top or just walk off leftwards.

No Ewe Turns	67m	MVS	★★	1988

A great climb – don't be put off by the mossy start. Start right of the previous route at the central right-leaning ramp.

1 25m (4a). Up the ramp to a ledge, follow the crack on the right of a smooth wall until it trends left, then climb straight up to a ledge, 2 metres down and right of the large mossy ledge.

2 20m (4b). Move up rightwards until 2 metres right of a blocky lump in the left-leaning central corner. Climb the slabby wall above to a diagonal crack, follow this leftwards to its high point, then continue up the wall above, via a short groove, to a huge block belay.

Right: Sally Baxendale on **Baxi's Bomber Beetles** (HVS), Cove Crag, during the first ascent. **Photo:** Stephen Reid

3 14m (4a). Stand on the block then trend left and then right up the rib, to belay beneath a cracked tower.

4 8m (4b). The left-hand crack provides a strenuous finish.

Baxi's Bomber Beetles	67m	HVS	★★	2006

Another interesting route on great rock. Start at the rightmost left-leaning ramp.

1 25m (5a). Climb the ramp to a junction with *No Ewe Turns* and follow it to the foot of the crack on the right of the smooth wall. Swing out left and hand-traverse up a slim ramp to a short groove. Climb this to a ledge, then a smooth corner on the left to a stance 2 metres down and left of a large mossy ledge.

2 20m (4c). Climb up rightwards crossing *No Ewe Turns* and up block holds just left of the right arête until just below a grass ledge on the right. Climb the obvious clean left-leaning groove on the left and continue in the same line up a short corner to a big ledge and huge block belay. A great pitch.

3 22m (5a). Stand on the block then climb the arête direct until some gear can be placed under a block. Step back down onto a tiny foothold on the arête and traverse right into a corner. Climb this to a grass ledge then go up a short corner to a cracked tower. Climb diagonally rightwards to the right arête of the tower and then follow this to the top.

Spire Crag

Grid reference:	**NY 160 114**	Altitude:	**770m**
Faces:	**North**	Approach:	**2hrs 30 mins**

Not named on the maps, this small slab of immaculate clean rock is set amongst danker outcrops on the steep headwall of Mirk Cove, 120 metres north-east of the summit of Little Scoat Fell and 200 metres left of *Scoat Fell Crag*. (On the 1:25000 OS map, it is just above the "8" of spot height 841 of Little Scoat Fell). It provides phenomenal friction and dries very quickly. On the minus side it is rather a long way from anywhere and spends much of the day in the shade.

Approach:

From **Wasdale**, either follow Nether Beck all the way past Scoat Tarn to the top of Scoat Fell, (6.5km) or take the Mosedale path directly to the same point (5km): both of these approaches are arduous (2hrs 30mins). From the summit of Scoat Fell, walk 150 metres east towards Pillar Fell until the dry stone wall ends abruptly at a crag. Below here a cairn can

Spire Crag

1	Ring a Ring o' Ouzels	VS *
2	Spire Route	MVS *
V1	Variation	VS
3	Where the Ousel Wasn't	HS *
4	Inspired Slab	E2 **
V2	Original Finish	E3
5	Fred Dibnah, Steeplejack	E2 *
6	Impatience Slab	S *
7	Perspire Crack	E3 *
8	Ouzely Does It	D *

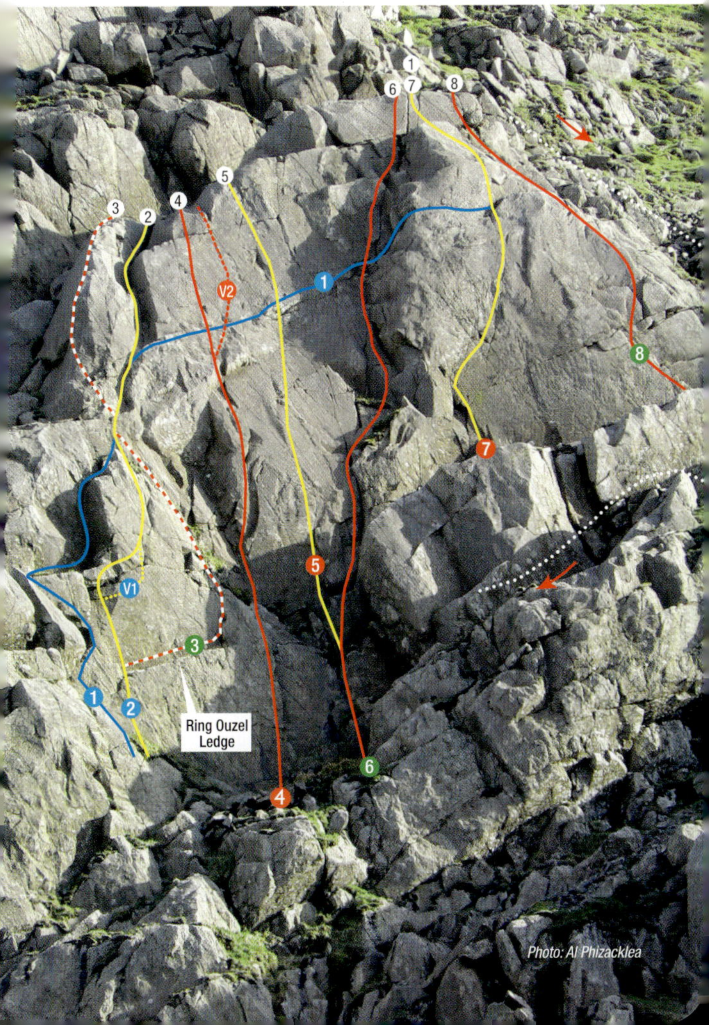

be seen on a boulder; scramble down to this cairn and drop down left for another 50 metres to the top of the crag.

From **Ennerdale**, follow the Mirk Cove approach branching right once above the treeline (at least 2hrs 30mins).

The routes start from a grass ledge below the main slab - this is a few metres above the scree. The best **descent** is to the right.

Ring a Ring o' Ouzels	30m	VS+	★	2006

An enjoyable left-to-right girdle. Start at the upper left end of the grass ledge as for *Spire Route*.

(4c). Climb the right-hand side of a large block and follow the crack leftwards to stand on the block. Pull up onto the ledge above, and climb a short corner on the right to an awkward exit and a junction with *Spire Route*. Climb up to just below the final groove of *Spire Route*, and swing right onto the face, and follow an obvious finger-traverse rightwards into the big corner of *Impatience Slab*. Go up this one metre and then traverse right around the arête and follow another finger-traverse rightwards into the top section of *Perspire Crack*; finish up this.

Spire Route	23m	MVS	★	2005

Start at the upper left end of the grass ledge.

(4a). From the right-hand side of a large block climb up into a shallow corner. Follow this to a ledge and short corner. Step back down and foot-traverse right to reach a crack in the centre of the wall above. Climb this past a spike and finish up a groove.

Variation VS 2005

(4c). The foot-traverse can be hand-traversed.

Where the Ouzel Wasn't	23m	HS+	★	2006

Pleasant wall climbing with a bold finish. Start at the upper left end of the grass ledge as for *Spire Route*.

On the right, just above the belay, is the long narrow *Ring Ouzel Ledge*. Gain the ledge and traverse it to its right end, then climb up leftwards to a spike (junction with *Spire Route*). Climb straight up until under the arête to the left of the final groove of *Spire Route* and climb it on its left-hand side (easier than it looks).

Inspired Slab	24m	E2-	★★	2005

Immaculate rock and a good line. Start in the centre of the ledge just left of the big corner of *Impatience Slab*.

(5b). Climb a short right-facing groove to a ledge. Move up to the base of a recess and pull right to a crack and pod which leads past a scarred nut placement and up leftwards to an overlap. Pull boldly over this to a thin break, then go straight up the thin crack in the wall above (technically harder if you are short).

Original Finish E3 2005

(6a). From the thin break, climb diagonally rightwards with difficulty to finish up a short crack.

Fred Dibnah, Steeplejack	24m	E2	★	2005

More good rock on the slabs left of the big corner of *Impatience Slab* but rather spoilt by being too close to that climb for most of its length. Start as for *Impatience Slab*.

(5c). Pull onto a grass ledge and follow a thin short crack to a nut out right. Climb the crozzly wall above the crack (spike on right) and move into a slight depression where a step right enables a variety of dubious wires to be fixed (or stretch right and place a stonker on *Impatience Slab*). Follow the thin crack up leftwards to the top.

Impatience Slab	22m	S	★	2003

The pleasant corner starting at the foot of a large block.

Climb the lower flake to grass ledges and follow the groove to the top.

Perspire Crack	15m	E3	★	2005

Bold thin climbing up the left-slanting crack in the upper right-hand wall. Start from a higher ledge, above and right of the other routes.

(6a). Pull up using a small flake to climb the thin crack-line – it's thin and sustained all the way; a skyhook protects the initial moves, thereafter the gear is good.

Ouzely Does It	12m	D	★	2006

Pleasant pottering up the right-hand side of the crag. Start a metre from the right edge and 4 metres right of *Perspire Crack*.

Climb the wall on jugs then move right onto the arête. Follow this avoiding grass to the right to finish up the headwall via the left side of a protruding block.

Scoat Fell Crag

Grid reference:	**NY 158 115**	Altitude:	**765m**
Faces:	**North-East**	Approach:	**2hr 30 mins**

Scoat Fell Crag faces north-east just below the summit of Scoat Fell and can be identified by the obvious but unpleasant *East Gully* which splits the crag to form the tower-like *East* and *West Buttresses*. Further right, the cliff develops ledge systems. Only a few routes have been

Scoat Fell Crag

1 Travesty Cracks HS
2 The Dream Merchants MVS
3 The Faux Pas VS
4 Twin Ribs Climb MVS *
5 Octopus HVS
6 Serendipity Ridge D *

Photo: Al Phizacklea

recorded here and, whilst the underlying rock is good and there is scope for more, the greasy grassy nature of the place, combined with the long walk in, will hopefully put most people off the idea. Best left to nature or winter climbers!

East Buttress

This is the steep buttress to the left of *East Gully*. At its base are two short chimneys divided by a vertical rib. The left-hand one is clean, but the right-hand is green and wet.

Travesty Cracks	57m	HS		1971

The prominent line of cracks towards the left side of the *East Buttress*. The top quarter is good but unfortunately the rest is very overgrown. Start at the left-hand of the twin chimneys.

1 **37m.** Climb the chimney past a capstone to steep grass. Pull to the right to a ledge on the rib then climb a little slab on the right to a large spike. Continue up the short wide crack moving left to a ledge (possible belay). Climb the layaway crack immediately to the left of the vertical crack on *The Dream Merchants*. Ledges are reached giving access to an obvious system of short grassy grooves and cracks trending left. Follow this line to a corner with a chock belay.

2 **20m.** The imposing chimney-crack ahead has an overhanging top. Follow it past doubtful chockstones to a small ledge. Avoid the

unpleasant looking direct finish and traverse left for 2 metres to a rough clean slab. Climb this boldly to the top.

The Dream Merchants	60m	MVS		1971

The prow of the ***East Buttress*** makes a reasonable route. Start at the left-hand of the twin chimneys.

1 33m (4b). Climb the chimney a few metres to step right onto a ledge. Make a hard move up the groove ahead and then climb more easily to a ledge under a thin crack; this proves awkward to gain and strenuous to quit. Continue up the arête to a grassy ledge.

2 27m (4b). Climb a short crack on the ridge to small ledges then bridge up the overhanging scoop immediately above. Move slightly left onto a wall which is ascended direct to a gangway sloping right. Return to the arête on the right and climb past a huge block to the top of the crag.

The Faux Pas	55m	VS		1971

A varied climb (!) up the right side of the ***East Buttress***. Start at the right-hand mossy chimney.

1 15m. Squeeze up the lurid dripping green chimney until it eases and then pull out onto the rib on the right, followed by steep grass to belay under a leftward-slanting fault-line on the wall above. A character-building pitch.

2 20m (4c). The hold encrusted wall is ascended, first via the fault-line, then straight up using two thin cracks to a large grass ledge. Climb the fine steep corner/chimney/crack at the right end of the ledge. Grassy niche and chock belay. A good pitch.

3 20m (4b). Climb a short slab on the left to the arête then move up rightwards to a narrow grass ledge and finish up the wall. A reasonable pitch.

To the right lies ***East Gully***, the great central vegetated gully that divides the buttresses. Not surprisingly, it is only known to have been climbed in winter.

West Buttress

Two slightly better climbs are to be found on the *West Buttress*, the buttress to the immediate right of *East Gully*. Two prominent steep parallel ribs run up to a large overhang. Start by scrambling 6 metres up grass to the right of the foot of the ribs and belay in a grassy corner.

Twin Ribs Climb	67m	MVS	★	1945

The best route on the crag though that isn't a tremendous claim to fame – quite bold.

1 27m. Climb the wall for 3 metres then traverse left to the edge of the right rib which is followed for a few metres. Cross the groove to the left rib via a small foot-ledge and climb it to a good ledge below the overhang. Swing out to the left under the overhang and pull up on good holds then climb a wall to a grass ledge.

2 40m. Easier climbing up the broken rib leads to a large grassy ledge from where rough scrambling leads to the top of the buttress.

Octopus	65m	HVS		1946

Not a bad pitch, and would probably merit a star if it was a tad cleaner, plus a bit more gear might be revealed. Start as for *Twin Ribs Climb*.

1 25m (4c). Climb the wall for about 3 metres and step to the right to the slim groove above (2 metres left of the wide chimney). Climb the groove until it peters out then continue boldly up the wall to a small ledge on the left under the overhang. Swing up right (steep but on good holds) until a foothold is reached. Climb the vertical wall by means of a small crack until a short traverse left can be made to join *Twin Ribs Climb*.

2 40m. As for *Twin Ribs Climb*.

Serendipity Ridge (115m, D ★, 2003) takes the very right-hand edge of the crag by a variable line and provides a pleasant scramble.

Steeple – East Face

Grid reference:	**NY 158 116**	Altitude:	**700m**
Faces:	**East**	Approach:	**2hrs 30 mins – 3 hrs**

There is a lot of broken rock on the *East Face of Steeple* overlooking Mirk Cove. The following climb makes the best of it.

Steeple Buttress	160m	VD	★★	1957

A long and worthwhile mountaineering route that has the benefit of ending right on the summit of the mountain. Many variations are possible. Start towards the back of the cove where a clean grey rib descends from its right-hand side almost to the floor.

1 30m. Scramble easily leftwards up the first section of the ridge to a grass ledge at the foot of a slightly undercut wall.

2 25m. Ascend the wall to a square ledge; then take a crack on the right (or the rib to its left) and follow it to a recess and block. Traverse left to a spike belay.

3 20m. Step back right and climb the steep wall on good holds to a grassy knoll.
4 30m. Easy scrambling up the edge of the buttress, or the grassy rake. Belay to the right of the base of the hanging rib leading to the summit.
5 25m. Move up and traverse left onto the steep rib. Climb this to a large block belay.
6 30m. Move up to the base of the obvious groove with two greasy chimneys; avoid this by stepping left into a slim V-groove in the hanging rib; climb this and easier rock to finish at the summit cairn.

Mirklin Cove

Mirklin Cove (NY 152 117) lies west of Mirk Cove, divided from it by the long north ridge of Steeple. From some distance away the cirque of crags of Mirklin Cove look quite impressive but on closer acquaintance it is only *Haskett Buttress* along with the *West Face of Steeple* to its left that provide continuous rock for climbing.

Approaches:

From **Ennerdale** the best approach is to cross the concrete bridge on the River Liza before Gillerthwaite and take the path up onto Lingmell. Continue eastward to Low Beck which is followed pleasantly up to the crags. From Bowness Knott car park, it's a 7 km walk with a 600 metre ascent to reach the crags in about 2-2½ hours (a bicycle would reduce the time taken).

From **Wasdale** the crags can be reached in about 2 hours from Nether Beck Bridge. Follow Nether Beck for about 4 km and where Nether Beck veers north-east, continue north to the broad col between Haycock and Scoat Fell. From here follow the 700 metre contour across the Ennerdale side of the hill, first in a north-east direction, then easterly to the foot of the crags.

All the above approaches are very long for a single day's climbing, but there is good flat ground in the base of the cove which would make an excellent campsite less than half an hour from the crags.

Steeple – West Face

Grid reference:	**NY 156 117**	Altitude:	**700m**
Faces:	**West**	Approach:	**2hrs 30 mins – 3 hrs**

Steeple presents a *West Face* looking out towards Ennerdale Water and a *South-West Face* angled towards *Haskett Buttress*. It gives long mountain routes on clean rock in a pleasant setting but slightly spoilt by some loose holds and a niggling lack of good runners.

Steeple West Face

1 Contravallation Ridge S *
2 Moving Finger Grooves VS *

Photo: Stephen Reid

Descent:

The easiest descent is down a grassy scramble and gully on the right.

Contravallation Ridge	90m	S	★	1969

This route takes a line of continuous rock running up the centre of the crag on the right edge of the *West Face*. A pleasant climb on superb rock, but quite bold. Start just left the arête at the junction of the two faces and 18 metres up and right from the lowest point of the crag.

1 **12m.** Climb the rough slabs. After 6 metres move to the right to an awkward scoop with an exit on the left. Move left to a ledge with high belays.
2 **18m.** Climb straight up, just left of two juniper patches, and step rightwards onto the second. Climb up a little and then step round left under a steep clean arête to a grass ledge (spike belay high on left).
3 **45m.** Follow a groove up the the left side of clean arête ahead and traverse to the right to a perch on the ridge. The same point can be gained via a gangway and groove on the right side of the arête. Slabs lead to a narrow ledge below a steep sharp ridge. The slabby rock just left of the crest is climbed on small holds to a grassy corner.
4 **15m.** A short wall is followed by scrambling to a block belay.

Moving Finger Grooves | 75m | VS | ★ | 1969

A discontinuous line of grooves and ribs up the centre of the crag. Start some 15 metres up and right from *Contravallation Ridge* in a grassy bay below an unpleasant-looking vertical mossy groove which is usually wet.

1 **35m (4c).** Avoid the wet groove by traversing horizontally left and climbing up cleaner rock to the left end of a long juniper ledge. Traverse the ledge rightwards, under an inviting corner-crack, and step delicately rightwards under overhanging rock to a poor landing in the groove on the edge of the crag. Follow this steeply to a ledge.

Above: Mike and Pippa Cocker on **Moving Finger Grooves** (VS), Steeple West Face. **Photo:** Stephen Reid.

2 **15m (4a).** Traverse horizontally left to gain a fine position on the front of the exposed nose then ascend directly to a wide ledge. Traverse rightwards up stepped bilberry ledges to the foot of a vertical rib on the right edge.
3 **25m (4b).** Climb the awkward green scoop just left of the rib, exiting leftwards. Move back diagonally rightwards to the crest, step up, then climb the steep final wall to a block belay. Quite a bold lead.

Moving right (south) for about 200 metres, across scree and grass, brings one to ***Haskett Buttress***, the finest crag in the cove.

Haskett Buttress

Grid reference: **NY 155 114** Altitude: **750m**
Faces: **North-West** Approach: **2hrs – 2 hrs 30 mins**

Haskett Buttress is the most impressive buttress among the crags at the head of Mirklin Cove. It is divided into three by two gullies, *Haskett Gully* on the left and *Western Gully* on the right. The right wall of *Haskett Gully* is split by an impressive crack (*The Dolorous Stroke*), while the front of the buttress has several steep corner-lines and on the right-hand side at about one third height is a long horizontal overhang.

Descent:

The descent from ***Haskett Buttress*** is either down the easy scree gully on the immediate right of ***West Buttress*** (the scrappy buttress to the right of ***Haskett Buttress*** when facing the crag) or better the grassy rib to the right again.

East Buttress	92m	S		1942

The buttress to the left of ***Haskett Gully***. The route starts at the base of the buttress, at the foot of a short rib.

1 20m. Climb the rib and step left at the top. Ascend an awkward corner on the right to a narrow ledge. From the left end of the ledge, work upwards to a block, and continue straight up to a rib above and left to a ledge.
2 25m. Easy climbing up rough rock to a sweep of slabs. Climb the slabs for a short distance, then make an awkward traverse right to climb a mixture of grass and rock to some blocks at the foot of a large steep wall.
3 22m. Climb the wall above the blocks to a flake in the wall. Climb onto the tip of this and step right to a small ledge. Continue up the wall on good holds and, where the rock impends, work right and up a groove to a short wall (avoidable) which is climbed to blocks.
4 25m. Scramble up the easy ridge to the top of the buttress.

Haskett Gully (1908) is about 90 metres long and consists of appallingly steep vegetation interspersed with bits of rock at a Severe standard. Best left until frozen.

The Dolorous Stroke	90m	E1	★	1969

The right (westerly) wall of ***Haskett Gully*** is cut along its entire length by a superb crack-line. Except for the first pitch, it is a very fine if at present somewhat lichenous climb and, although it has a serious feel about it, it

Haskett Buttress

1	The Dire Straits	E3 *
2	The Devious Slash	VS
3	The Detrital Slide	VS *
4	The Seriously Dyslexic	VS *
5	The Determined Sally	HVS *
6	The Dextrous Shuffle	E3
7	The Dipso Sonambulist	E2 *
8	The Deleterious Sting	E2 *

Photo: Stephen Reid

is well-protected by large friends. Well worth the effort. Start immediately right of ***Haskett Gully*** at the lowest point of the buttress.

1 30m (4a). Climb an indefinite rib to ledges below a corner. Rock steps lead to a wall. Climb a vertical groove on the right, stepping right at the top to a bilberry terrace.

2 24m (5b). The sharp rib on the left, overlooking the gully, has a slabby right face. Climb this to a niche below the crack proper. Surmount the first overhang (hard) and climb with difficulty to a poor resting place below the final bulge. Continue, still not easy, to a comfortable bilberry ledge.

3 18m (4a). The continuation crack is followed more easily to another ledge.

4 18m (4c). Traverse 3 metres left and gain a higher small grass ledge. The fine open and impending corner/groove above provides a delicate and fitting finish to the climb.

The Dire Straits	96m	E3	★	2006

A fine though rather lichenous battle up the obvious hanging corner in the left arête of the main crag. Start 3 metres right of left arête of the crag.

1 30m (4a). Climb diagonally left and follow the arête keeping to the cleanest rock and finishing up a slim groove.

2 26m (5c). Gain the corner above and climb it, with increasing difficulty and rather less protection than one would like, to a desperate move before exiting rightwards.

3 40m (4c). Climb the arête on the left via a thin crack, then go up grass leftwards to blocks. Step up right onto the continuation arête and then scramble to the top.

The Devious Slash	84m	VS		1969

The most obvious feature of lowest band of ***Haskett Buttress*** is a vertical corner situated in the centre. The climb starts some 9 metres below this, and about 20 metres up and right from the start of ***The Dolorous Stroke***.

1 27m (4c). An indefinite rib and grass is followed by the imposing vertical corner. Scramble diagonally left for 6 metres to a terrace.

2 15m (4b). Surmount two grass ledges to where the rock steepens. An awkward pull up to the left leads to steep slabs, which lead to a wall containing a steep crack. Avoid the crack by moving right to the corner-crack and exit on the right; then move to the right, up slabs, to a grassy ledge with a large block.

3 42m (4b). From the left end of the ledge, climb a wall to another ledge. A steep wall with a crack and good holds is followed by a slab and step right onto a pleasant ridge which leads to the top.

The Detrital Slide	84m	VS+	★	1969

Start just right of ***The Devious Slash***.

1 27m (4a). Broken rocks lead to a sloping grass terrace. Ignore the corner-groove (Pitch 1 of ***The Devious Slash***) and go up 5 metres rightwards to step off a rock and climb straight up an enjoyable wall to a ledge. Immediately above is a smooth-looking V-groove with an undercut start. Good crack belay one metre to the left.

2 15m (4c). A fine, sustained and quite bold pitch – take some micro-wires. Pull directly over the bulge just left of the belay (and a metre or so left of the groove), and climb diagonally up leftwards and through a bulge to gain a smooth-walled sentry-box. Leave it via the rib on the left to reach a good runner. The steep slabs above lead to a grassy ledge and block belay at the top of Pitch 2 of ***The Devious Slash***.

3 42m (4a). Climb the wall behind the block for 3 metres then traverse to the right along a ledge for 6 metres to a small clean buttress/arête. Ascend this on fine rock then continue easily, just left of a grassy chimney, to a short slab split by a thin crack. Step off a pillar to gain this. Scrambling leads to the top.

Original Way

2 15m (4c). Make an awkward entry into the overhanging groove to the right of the belay and climb for 2 metres until a traverse left leads across and then up into the sentry-box.

The Seriously Dyslexic	84m	VS+	★	2005

Start 2 metres right of ***The Devious Slash*** just left of a short grassy chimney.

1 27m (4a). Broken rocks lead to a sloping grass terrace. Climb the obvious diagonal crack-line in the right arête of the initial corner of ***The Devious Slash***. Immediately above is a smooth-looking V-groove with an undercut start. Good crack belay one metre to the left.

2 15m (4c). Make an awkward entry into the overhanging groove and climb the corner above directly to a belay in a short corner at the right end of a grass ledge (the block belay at the top of Pitch 2 of ***The Devious Slash*** is at the left end of this ledge).

3 42m (4b). Above is a short square recess. Climb this and then diagonally leftwards up the wall above. Follow the clean rib above to surmount a detached pinnacle. Climb the wall behind and scramble to the top.

The crag now swings right into a deep scree-filled cleft (***Western Gully***) which has a left wall of good clean rock. At its lower edge is an obvious roof above a great slab.

The Determined Sally	77m	HVS	★	2006

The curving groove above the left end of the roof is the main pitch of this climb. Start 10 metres or so down and left of ***Western Gully***.

1 25m (4c). An easy slab leads to a shallow chimney which is climbed to a belay on a large ledge.

2 25m (5a). As for ***The Dextrous Shuffle***, climb the wall to a slab under the roof and a decaying peg. Move boldly up the wall just left of the roof (reassuring rusty peg!), exiting leftwards into a right-slanting groove. Follow this easily until it steepens when more thought-provoking climbing leads to a belay on a grass ledge.

3 27m (4a). As for ***The Detrital Slide***, climb the clean, small buttress/arête behind the belay on fine rock; then continue easily, just left of a grassy chimney, to a short slab split by a thin crack. Step off a pillar to gain this. Scrambling leads to the top.

The Dexterous Shuffle	65m	E3		1988

A serious intimidating route with very poor protection. Start by scrambling left from the foot of the gully to belay below the left-hand end of the roof.

1 35m (5c). Climb up the slab to the remains of a peg runner at the first belay on ***The Delectation Sinistrose***, then up the bulging wall to another aging peg. Traverse right on undercuts, across the very lip of the roof to reach a good hold, and continue delicately rightwards to reach a vertical crack. Follow this to a ledge and block belay.

2 30m (4b). Pitch 2 of ***The Dipso Somnambulist***.

The Dipso Somnambulist	63m	E2	★	1988

A superb steep climb on excellent rock. Start at the foot of the slab below the right-hand end of the roof.

1 33m (5b). Climb up to the roof then swing right and follow the thin crack-line direct to a ledge and block belay.

2 30m (4b). Either climb the easy rocks behind to finish up the cleanest slab or abseil from the block to the base of the crag (sling required).

The Deleterious Sting	60m	E2	★	1988

Good but nerve-wracking wall climbing taking a parallel line 2.5 metres to the right of ***Dipso***. Ennerdale's version of ***Bloodhound*** but with poorer protection. Start just right of ***The Dipso Somnambulist***.

1 30m (5b). A short steep juggy wall leads to the slab of ***Dipso***, then move right across and up the wall to gain a good narrow ledge in its centre (crux). Follow a thin crack to a bulge, then step left (good crack further left provides the first solid gear!) and back right round some hollow blocks to where a shallow scoop leads to a ledge. A crack above is followed (-ish) to a ledge and block belay.

2 30m (4b). Pitch 2 of *The Dipso Somnambulist*.

The Dactylic Springald	60m	E1		1988

Although only really a variation start to ***The Deleterious Sting***, it gives some good climbing. Start higher up the gully at a grassy patch below an obvious clean groove.

1 30m (5b). Climb out left to gain a small pinnacle on the steep wall. Step up to a crack then traverse delicately left across the fine ramp to reach *The Deleterious Sting* at the scoop. Finish up this.

2 30m (4b). Pitch 2 of *The Dipso Somnambulist*.

The Ductile Slant	50m	MS		1969

Start 6 metres above the previous route and some 6 metres below a steep rib that divides the gully.

1 20m. The left wall of the gully is climbed diagonally leftwards, crossing the foot of a break in the wall and continuing left to doubtful flakes and blocks. Three metres after a small rock finger is past, step right and ascend the blunt nose on good holds to a block belay on the ridge. The break crossed previously is now immediately on the right.

2 30m. Step up and left on to a pedestal of rock then swing onto the wall and gain the crest of the rib on the left. Climb this to a small ledge and traverse left across a rib to a good ledge. Climb the wall behind the ledge and follow the excellent open slab on the right to the summit.

The Delectation Sinistrose	103m	VS		1970

A left-to-right girdle traverse of ***Haskett Buttress*** giving sustained delicate climbing. Start as for *The Dipso Somnambulist*.

1 25m (4a). Steep rock steps lead onto the slab proper. Climb directly up the right edge to the overhang then, keeping as high as possible, traverse the entire length of the slab under the overhang to a poor stance at its top left corner.

2 12m (4b). Move across and down the small smooth slab on the left to moderate holds in the groove of Pitch 2 of *The Detrital Slide*. A short delicate traverse left then leads to a smooth-walled sentry box; exit via the rib on the left. A block belay lies on the cramped overhung rock ledge above.

3 16m (4b). Move left awkwardly to gain an overhung groove then step left again to the steep slabs of Pitch 2 *The Devious Slash*. Ascend these for 2 metres then traverse 2 metres to the right into the corner-crack. Pull out of it and follow slabs up right to a grassy ledge with a large block.

4 26m (4c). Traverse left along a diminishing ledge, and cross the top of the bottomless groove of ***The Dire Straits*** to the left edge of the buttress. Climb up over slabby rock to a rounded blistered nose and ascend an exposed crack on its left side to a grassy bay containing a pile of large unstable blocks.

5 6m (4a). Cross the blocks, swing left across the gully wall, and descend slightly to the rock crevasse below the last pitch of ***The Dolorous Stroke***.

6 18m (4c). Traverse 3 metres left and gain a higher small grass ledge; then climb the fine open impending corner above. (Pitch 4 of ***The Dolorous Stroke***).

Almost opposite the start of ***The Dactylic Springald*** in ***Western Gully***, on the right wall of the ***West Buttress***, is a prominent crack-line, easily seen from the summit of the main buttress.

Steeple Crack	36m	VS		1975

This short but interesting route climbs the prominent crack-line.

(4c). Climb the wide crack past the initial steepening in the chimney. The crack and groove above are followed to the top.

Crag Fell

Crag Fell (NY 097 143), the mountain falling into the south-west corner of Ennerdale Lake, has four areas of cliff. The most obvious is the impressive ridge of *Crag Fell Pinnacles* at half-height, well seen from Ennerdale Bridge. These can mainly be ascended by easy scrambling and only offer short pitches.

The band of cliffs below the summit ridge of the mountain and a similar band above the dam appear to offer nothing more than a few short vegetated pitches.

The spur of the fell protruding into the lake however has rock of a marginally better calibre. This cliff, ***Anglers' Crag*** is often dry when ***Pillar Rock*** is wet and has some of the lowest lying climbs in the valley. Unfortunately the rock is lichenous and not above suspicion and the climbs are short.

Anglers' Crag

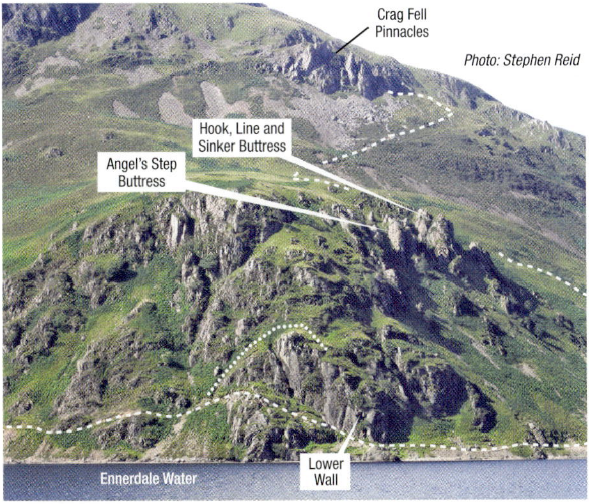

Anglers' Crag

Grid reference: **NY 100 150** Altitude: **130m**
Faces: **North** Approach: **20 mins**

This collection of buttresses is situated just above the lakeshore path. The most westerly, *Hook, Line and Sinker Buttress,* has a huge overhang. More central is *Angel's Step Buttress,* an impressive square tower. Both these buttresses are situated above some unpleasantly steep vegetated ground and are best reached from the top, via a traverse in from the diagonal path over the summit of *Anglers' Crag*. They do however contain the best climbing on the crag.

Approach:

From **Ennerdale Bridge**, take the first road to the Ennerdale Water and follow it to a car park near the pumphouse (NY 085 154). A track leads past the dam and round the south shore to a small headland under the crag (20mins).

Lower Wall

The lakeside path continues under the lowest point of the crag to a rather mossy wall approximately 40 metres high and only just above the water. Though some of these routes are good, many of the others, which were once clean, are now very dirty and do not merit full descriptions. The routes are described from **left** to **right**.

Dan's Groove (18m, D, 1980) climbs the groove 5 metres to the left of **Dan's Mine** (18m, D, 1980), the grassy chimney/gully at the far left (east) end of the wall: a Severe finish (**Cow Pie**, 30m, 1980) can be made up the right wall – follow *Dan's Mine* to a grassy ledge, then transfer to the right wall, climb up, swing into a groove and follow a crack. The buttress to the right contains the following routes all of which are very dirty. **Desperate Dan** (30m, VS 4b, 1980), a poorly protected direct variation on *Forgotten Wall*; go up the arête right of *Dan's Mine* for 3 metres to a break in the overhang, then the centre of the wall crossing *Forgotten Wall*. **Dan the Man** (30m, VS, 1995), as for *Desperate Dan* to the break in the overhang, move left, and follow a small corner, groove and crack. **Forgotten Wall** (30m, HS, 1958) starts 2 metres right of *Dan's Mine*, at a shallow crack and follows it for 4 metres, before moving diagonally left up a shallow groove-line and then straight up, passing a huge detached block on the left – best forgotten!

The next section is even more vegetated (it has a large oak at 8 metres) but to the right again and just left of the lowest point of the crag is the *Main Wall* which presents a smooth slab-like aspect some 35 metres high. Just right of centre of this wall is an obvious deep 15 metre high V-groove, ending at the left side of a horizontal heather ledge. This is *Phantom Groove*. The routes on this wall may have been clean once but they certainly aren't now!

The first two routes finish at a small block with an old bolt belay of Brunellian proportions. There is also a cemented in peg 3 metres up and left. To **descend**, scramble diagonally leftwards up steep grass to gain a scree gully on the left of the crag.

A Face Remembered	35m	VS		1985

A direct version of *Shadow Wall* with just adequate protection – if you can dig it out. Start 4 metres left of *Phantom Groove*.

(4a). Make a hard start diagonally left up whitish rock to the edge of the face and follow this directly to the top, passing an in situ peg and finishing up the left arête. All very mossy.

Shadow Wall	35m	S		1958

Serious and dirty but often top-roped by outdoor ed groups – for once this should be encouraged! Start up a vague weakness just left of a mossy streak 3 metres left of *Phantom Groove*. Protection is very sparse.

Climb the wall direct on good but moss-covered holds to an in situ peg at 15 metres, then straight up, keeping just left of a shallow vegetated hollow. Trend left up the buttress above.

For the next few routes, **descent** can either be as above or abseil from a stout holly on the lip of the crag on the far right (looking up).

Phantom Groove	45m	MS		1938

A once pleasant but now very dirty climb and badly protected to boot.

1 15m. Climb the groove to the ledge then move right to belay on a tree.

2 30m. Move back left and climb the shallow continuation of the groove, then a wall, to the top. Scramble 7 metres up grass to a tree belay on the right.

The short slab right of *Phantom Groove* has recorded on it **Andrea's Revenge** (HVS 5a, 1983) and **Temptation** (S, 1958). Both are very overgrown. It is possible to climb anywhere on the faces between *Dan's Mine* and *Temptation* at 4c/5a, if you have the nerve and a good trowel.

A couple of metres right of *Temptation* is a dirty roofed chimney/gully containing hollies (M). Just right of this is a pleasant blocky ridge.

Like It or Lump It	50m	D	★	

A fine little climb. Start just left of the lowest point of the buttress.

Climb the blocky ridge/slab moving right at its top. The broken heathery rib above is followed by 20 metres of steep grass to a tree belay.

Mortuary Slab	33m	HVS		1983

(5a). Climb the vague groove between *Like it or Lump it* and *Midge Arête*, then go straight over the black overhanging wall and directly up the slab and steep wall to a difficult finish at the base of a large holly.

Midge Arête	50m	MS	★	

Another good little route; nicely exposed. Start at the rib at the lowest point of the buttress.

Gain the rib from the right and follow it with a hard step up a bulging thin groove to easier ground. Move up left, and follow a broken heathery rib and then steep grass to a tree belay.

The remainder of *Lower Crag* offers many vegetated problems. The only climb worth recording lies 100 metres to the right, up a shallow groove in a smooth face of rock.

Shep	25m	VS		1959

A good pitch but with poor protection above very steep grass and a very deep lake. Start just down and left of a fern-filled chimney, formed where a block ridge meets the crag

(4c). Climb short overlapping slabs to a small overhang. Step right and up a wall to a ledge. Move right round a bulge and climb a groove on good holds to a huge boulder belay. The huge boulder is a landmark and helps locate the route.

Angel's Step Buttress

This is the largest and most impressive buttress on the crag and is easily recognisable by the overhang in its centre. It lies to the right of, and above, *Lower Wall*, and can be reached by a scramble up the grassy fell rightwards. However it is much better gained by taking the diagonal path which goes over the top of *Anglers' Crag* and dropping down to the routes. From the summit, look for a narrow rock ridge with a small holly on top. **Descend** the gully to its left (looking out). The routes are described from **left** to **right**.

Comfortably Numb	30m	E1		1996

A good exposed line but snappy rock and barely adequate protection make this route an adrenalin pumping experience.

(5a). Follow *Angel's Step* to the first ledge, then climb the wall directly to the roof and move onto the left arête via a horizontal crack. Climb the arête, first on the left, then on the right and so to the top.

Angel's Step	30m	HVS	★	1961

A fine little climb on good rock. Start at the foot of the buttress.

(5a). Climb a bulging rock pillar to a ledge. Continue up a groove to the overhang. Move to the right and make a precarious mantelshelf onto a small ledge (crux). Move up to a bigger ledge and go straight up the wall above to the summit.

Gog	30m	E1		1959

A worrying pitch up the obvious flake crack on the right of the buttress that is likely to have you goggle-eyed: although the climbing is good, the 5 metre flake, which provides most of the handholds, footholds and protection, seems barely attached to the crag and has an ominous hollow ring to it. Start at a brittle spike below a groove just right of *Angel's Step*.

(5a). Climb the groove and then the flake until it ends. On the left is the mantelshelf of *Angel's Step* (and a decent runner). Move up delicately then climb the wall above on small holds to the top.

Between *Angel's Step Buttress* and *Hook, Line and Sinker Buttress* (100 metres across to the right), a number of short problems on various unattractive bits of rock have been recorded. The only one worth a mention is **Aneurysm** (10m, VS 4b, 1982) which ascends the middle of a short red buttress of rock just right of *Angel's Step Buttress*.

Hook, Line and Sinker Buttress

This is the clean-looking buttress on the far right of the crag: best gained by taking the diagonal path which goes over the top of *Anglers' Crag*. From above it can be recognised as the most westerly (left-hand, looking out) buttress: also it has several boulders on its top. Scramble down a wide grass gully on its left (looking out) to a large holly on the right side of the base of the crag. The routes are described from **left** to **right**.

Catalepsy Corner	40m	HVS		1982

Start 10 metres down and left of the large holly below a vegetated red groove leading to a small holly at 5 metres. Not very good.

1 25m (5a). Climb the groove until under the holly then ascend the slab on the right. Move left above the holly to below a reddish overhang. Traverse left under the overhang and up on loose undercuts to a grass ledge.

2 15m (4a). Climb the dirty V-groove to the top.

Live Bait	25m	E2		1997

A bold and exposed route on worrying rock up the fine pillar to the left of the groove of *Hook, Line and Sinker*. Start as for *Catalepsy Corner*.

(5b). Follow *Catalepsy Corner* to the slab, but continue directly up the slab to gain the top of an undercut block at the base of the central groove. Make a blind pull out left to stand on a nose on the face of the pillar above the red roof and climb rapidly up the bulging wall above before your arms expire.

Variation

The pillar can also be gained from the left more easily.

Hook, Line and Sinker

30m | E1 | ★ | 1959

The best of the harder routes on *Angler's Crag*. Start as for *Catalepsy Corner*.

(5b). Follow *Catalepsy Corner* to the slab but continue directly up the slab to gain the top of an undercut block at the base of the central groove. Climb the groove to the overhang and move up diagonally leftwards under this with difficulty to gain a ledge on the left. Finish direct.

Original Start

The route originally started up the reddish left-slanting break 4 metres right of the start described above and 6 metres down and left of the big holly. This was once graded E1 (5b) but most of its holds have since fallen off and it is not known to have been ascended in its current state.

Above: Walter Phipps on the variation start to **Live Bait** (E2), Anglers' Crag.
Photo: Stephen Reid

Crystal Groove

30m | HS | ★ | 1959

An excellent little climb up the main groove. Due to the awkward line of the climb, care is required with rope management and the placing of protection. Start at the large holly on the right side of the buttress.

Squeeze past the holly and climb out left along a sloping gangway until it peters out. Gain the groove running up to the overhang; then traverse to the right, under the overhang, and follow a slab and easy rib to the summit.

Hey, Fat Lip

24m | S | ★ | 1996

Another pleasant route though slightly artificial. Start as for *Crystal Groove*.

(4b). Follow *Crystal Groove* for 3 metres onto the ramp, then traverse rightwards across the wall under a small holly to gain the arête and climb up to a slab, above and right of the main overhang. Traverse left along the top of the main overhang, below a second, smaller overhang, and pull directly over the centre of this using a flake or move even further left before climbing up.

Crag Fell Pinnacles GR **NY 096 148** Alt **280m** F **North**

The *Pinnacles* rise impressively at approximately half-height on the mountain and are best reached via the diagonal path to the top of *Anglers' Crag*, then by a zig-zag path above. They are worth visiting for the novelty factor alone, and the fine outlook. One hundred metres to the east of the *Eastern Pinnacle* is a stout pinnacle which gives a pleasant route up its long side (**Far Eastern Pinnacle Face**, 15m, D, 2000). The larger detached *Eastern Pinnacle* is best climbed via **Magog** (27m, VS 4b ★, 1948) – this takes an obvious right-slanting crack in the *East Face* to a ledge, then up the right arête and a rightwards traverse to the top. **Crag Fell Chimney** (MS, 2000) is the obvious chimney between the *Eastern* and other pinnacles. The isolated rock near the west end is *Robinson's Pinnacle*: **Eastern Crack** (12m, 1948) is Severe, **The Short Side** (6m, 2000) is a strenuous E1 (5b), and **Robinson's Route** (ca 1890) climbs the *West Face* via a mossy groove (MS).

Grike GR **NY 081 148** Alt **200m** F **North**

Grike is a collection of small buttresses in and above the forest plantation: they are heavily vegetated and slow to dry, and although visited in the past they are better left in the obscurity they deserve.

Above: Evening at Black Crag – Stephen Reid wonders if he is going to make last orders!
Photo: Sarah Bailey

Area Crag Name	Aspect	Alt (m)	Approach Time (mins)	Drying Time
Great Gable				
Kern Knotts	SW	520	75	F
The Napes	SW	700	105	F
Westmorland Crags	S	800	120	F
Gable Crag	N	800	90–120	S
Green Gable				
Green Gable Crags	W	750	75–120	F
Kirk Fell				
Boat How Crags	N & W	700	120–135	M
Black Sail Buttress	N	620	120	S
Ennerdale				
Bowness Knott	SW	130	5	F/M
Raven Crag	N	350	120	M/S
Hind Cove	NE	600	150	S
Great Doup	N	750	150	M/S
Pillar Rock	N,S,E,W	600	150	F/M/S
West Cove	N	750	150	M/S
Black Crag	NNW	659	150–180	M/S
Cove Crag	N	660	150–180	S
Spire Crag	N	770	150	F
Scoat Fell Crag	NE	765	150	S
Steeple – East Face	E (!)	700	150–180	M
Steeple – West Face	W (!)	700	150–180	M
Haskett Buttress	NW	750	120–150	M
Anglers' Crag	N	120	20	M/S

Crags Suitable for Groups

The only crag that has been regularly used for group instruction in the area covered by this guide is the *Lower Wall* of *Anglers' Crag*, Ennerdale

Route Lengths (m)	Total Routes 487	M D VD	MS S HS	MVS VS	HVS E1	E2 E3	E4+
8–50	48	6	2	11	10	13	6
10–123	85	17	14	24	11	11	8
9–150	32	4	8	13	5	2	
12–150	55	5	9	17	13	10	1
13–80	21	8	8	4	1		
27–170	34	6	6	2	9	9	2
75	2			2			
40–80	7	3	1	2		1	
80–100	2	1	1				
40–80+	5	5					
30–40+	3	1	2				
6–185	119	16	20	29	37	15	2
55+	3	1	1		1		
24–111	22	6	4	3	9		
65–75	4			2	2		
12–30	8	1	2	2		3	
57–70	5		1	3	1		
160	1	1					
65–70	2		1	1			
36–103	14		2	5	3	4	
24–50	15	1	5	2	6	1	

(NY 100 150). However, it is not really suitable, being very mossy with poor belays and with a steep scramble on grass to descend. It is described on page 333.

Climbing Walls

There is a good range of climbing walls available to those living in or visiting the Lake District. They are described here for use on those occasional rainy days and dank evenings:

Ambleside: St Martin's College (ex-Charlotte Mason's College)

Low cost revamped wall at the college, with good bouldering but no leading. Open 13:30 to 21:30 Monday to Friday; 12:00 to 17:00 on Saturdays, but only during the term time. It may be open for reduced hours in the holidays. Not open on Sundays. Tickets available at the wall.

Access check – tel: 015394 30300, www.ucsn.ac.uk

Barrow in Furness: Park Leisure Centre

Good access and low cost, but very limited lead climbing and a cramped bouldering area. Excellent other facilities. Open all day until 21:45 weekdays; 10:00 to 18:00 weekends.

Access check – tel: 01229 871146, www.barrowbc.gov.uk

Carlisle: The Sands Centre

Reasonable, low cost, climbing facility in a large sports centre. Good bouldering and leading. Very good access and excellent general facilities. Open 09:30 to 22:30 seven days a week.

Access check – tel: 01228 625222, www.thesandscentre.co.uk

Carlisle: St Aidan's County High School

Good freeform featured leading wall open to the public. Bouldering may be possible but you might need your own mat. Open 17:00 to 21:00 Monday to Friday (last admission 20:00), 10:00 to 17:00 Saturday and Sunday (last admission 16:00).

Access check – tel: 01228 607469, www.st-aidans.cumbria.sch.uk

Cockermouth: Leisure Centre

Varied bouldering with natural stonework and Bendcrete. Low cost and good access. Other sports facilities available. Open 08:00 to 22:00 Monday to Thursday; 08:00 to 21:30 Friday; 09:00 to 17:00 weekends.

Access check – tel: 01900 823596, www.allerdale.gov.uk

Egremont: Wyndham Sports Centre

A good facility located in the centre of Egremont on the west coast, only half an hour from Wasdale Head. There are practice areas, bouldering, leading walls and a huge roof. Unfortunately no longer open to the public except on a club booking basis.

Access check – tel: 01946 820356

Ingleton: Inglesport Climbing Barn

Best of the small walls. Very good use of space with leading and bouldering. Regular innovations. Relaxed friendly atmosphere. Cafe and shop nearby. Open 09:00 to 22:00 Monday to Thursday; 09:00 to 17:30 Friday; 08:30 to 18:00 weekends.

Access check – tel: 015242 41146, www.inglesport.co.uk/wall.html

Kendal: The Lakeland Climbing Centre

A magnificent indoor climbing facility with excellent bouldering and leading. Includes a very impressive 18 metre main wall (with fixed gear) and a huge roof. Located on the Lake District Business Park, across the A6 from Morrison's supermarket. Changing and shower facilities. Open Winter (September to April): 16:00 to 22:00 Monday; 10:00 to 22:00 Tuesday to Friday; 10:00 to 19:00 weekends and Bank Holidays. Summer (May to August): 10:00 to 22:00 Tuesday to Friday; 10:00 to 17:00 weekends and Bank Holidays.

Access check – tel: 01539 721766, www.kendalwall.co.uk

Keswick: Keswick Climbing Wall and Activity Centre

Located on Southey Hill Industrial Estate, at the western end of the town. There is quite extensive bouldering, some leading and top-roping walls. Open 10:00 to 21:00 every day, with an extra hour (ie to 22:00), Tuesday to Thursday, from October to March.

Access check – tel: 017687 72000, www.keswickclimbingwall.co.uk

Penrith: Penrith Leisure Centre – Eden Climbing Wall

An excellent wall adjoining the town's swimming pool. Good bouldering and leading walls. Open 10:00 to 21:30 weekdays; 10:00 to 21:00 weekends.

Access check – tel: 01768 863450, www.leisure-centre.com

Useful Contacts

Climbing

British Mountaineering Council
0870 0104878 www.thebmc.co.uk
Fell & Rock Climbing Club www.frcc.co.uk
National Mountaineering Exhibition, Rheged, Penrith
01768 868000 www.rheged.com

Lake District Weather

Fell Top Weather Forecast 0870 0550575
http://www.lake-district.gov.uk/weatherline/home/index.php

Lake District National Park Authority www.lake-district.gov.uk

Bird Restrictions
017687 79633 http://www.frcc.co.uk/rock/birds.htm
Brockhole National Park Centre
015394 46601
Head Office
01539 724555

Tourist Information

Cumbria Tourism
015394 44444 www.golakes.co.uk
Egremont
01946 820693
Keswick
017687 72645
Camping Barns
01946 758198

Journey Planners

Cumbria County Council www.cumbria.gov.uk
Traveline
0870 6082608 www.traveline.org.uk

Where to Stay

Black Sail Youth Hostel nestles in magnificent surroundings in Ennerdale. The mountain in the centre is Great Gable with Green Gable to the left. The Prow of Boat How Crag can be seen up on the far right. **Photo:** Phil Rigby

This list of Youth Hostels, Campsites and Camping Barns in the north-west of the Lake District is fairly comprehensive, but there are no doubt more, and fuller details will be available from Tourist Information Offices. This information is current in 2007 but will almost certainly alter and it is probably best to make telephone contact before going to a particular hostel, site or barn.

Youth Hostels

www.yha.org.uk	Grid Ref	Telephone
Eskdale	NY 195 010	0870 770 5824
Wastwater	NY 145 045	0870 770 6083
Ennerdale	NY 142 141	0870 770 5820
Black Sail	NY 194 124	07711 108450
Cockermouth	NY 118 298	0870 770 5768
Buttermere	NY 178 168	0870 770 5736

Honister Hause	NY 226 135	0870 770 5870
Keswick	NY 267 235	0870 770 5894
Borrowdale – Longthwaite	NY 254 142	0870 770 5706
Derwentwater – Barrow House	NY 268 200	0870 770 5792

Camping Barns

www.lakelandcampingbarns.co.uk	**Grid Ref**	**Telephone**
Wasdale, Murt Barn	NY 131 040	01946 758198
Gosforth, Mill House Barn	NY 100 044	01946 758198
St Bees, Tarn Flatts Hall Farm	NX 947 146	01946 692162
Ennerdale, High Gillerthwaite	NY 142 141	01946 758198
Buttermere, Crag Barn	NY 174 172	01946 758198
Loweswater		
Waterend Farm, Swallow Barn	NY 116 226	01946 758198
Holme Wood Bothy	NY 123 216	01946 816940
www.holmewoodbothy.org.uk		
Newlands, Catbells Barn	NY 243 208	01946 758198
Rosthwaite, Dinah Hoggas Barn	NY 259 151	01946 758198
Caldbeck, Hudscales	NY 331 375	017687 72645
St Johns in the Vale,		
Low Bridge End	NY 316 205	01946 758198
www.campingbarn.com		
Thirlmere, Causeway Foot	NY 294 218	017687 72290

Campsites

	Grid Ref	**Telephone**
Eskdale		
Fisherground	NY 152 001	019467 23319
Hollins Farm	NY 178 010	019467 23253
Holmrook, Seven Acres	NY 073 018	01946 822227
Wasdale, Santon Bridge	NY 111 017	019467 26286
Nether Wasdale, Church Stile	NY 126 042	01946 758198
www.churchstile.com		
Wasdale Head	NY 185 088	019467 26384
www.ntlakescampsites.org.uk		
Wasdale Head, National Trust	NY 185 073	019467 26220
St Bees, Seacote Park	NX 962 120	01946 822777
www.seacote.co.uk		
Buttermere		
Sykes Farm	NY 173 171	017687 70222
Dalegarth	NY 186 159	017687 70233
Gatesgarth	NY 191 148	017687 70256

Lorton		
Wheatsheaf Inn	NY 155 259	01900 85199
Whinfell Hall	NY 150 254	01900 85260
Braithwaite, Scotgate	NY 235 236	017687 78343
www.scotgateholidaypark.co.uk		
Keswick, Castlerigg Hall	NY 280 225	017687 74499
www.castlerigg.co.uk		
Castlerigg	NY 283 223	017687 72479
www.castleriggfarm.co.uk		
Derwentwater	NY 260 232	017687 72392
www.campingandcaravaningclub.co.uk		
Threlkeld		
Burns Farm	NY 305 242	017687 79225
Setmabanning	NY 322 247	017687 79229
Thirlmere		
Dale Bottom	NY 295 220	017687 72176
Bridge End Farm	NY 315 192	017687 72166
Borrowdale		
Ashness	NY 192 271	017687 77361
Grange, Hollows Farm	NY 250 167	017687 77298
Stonethwaite, Langstrath	NY 268 133	017687 77234
Stonethwaite, Chapel Farm	NY 257 140	017687 77602
Seatoller	NY 245 139	017687 77232
Seathwaite Farm	NY 232 122	017687 77394

Mountain Accidents

by Dr John Ellerton (LDSAMRA)

Procedure for climbers in the Lake District

Mountain rescue in the Lake District is well served by 13 voluntary teams backed up by special search and cave/mine rescue units. They are equipped to a high standard and work closely with the RAF helicopters and Air Ambulance services. Consequently, only minor casualties should come within the scope of treatment and evacuation by the climber's companions. The rule for all other cases is; to make the casualty safe, to start first aid, and to send for a Mountain Rescue Team.

Sending for Help

A reliable member of the party, with full information about the nature of the injuries and the position of the incident (including, if possible, the map reference) should be sent to find the nearest telephone. He should dial 999, and ask for the Police, who will notify the appropriate team/agency. The sender of the message should stay by the telephone until he receives instructions from the Team Leader. Mobile phones can save a considerable amount of time – please use them to call the Police. Have the mobile phone number handy and keep within reception range. Reception is often better on the tops or ridges of the mountains. Do not switch the phone off – the team leader will call back.

Lack of help

You have a difficult decision to make when the casualty is severely injured, possibly unconscious, and you are alone. You should try to summon help from nearby climbers or walkers by shouting, giving the distress call on a whistle (6 blasts repeated regularly), flashing a torch (6 flashes repeated regularly), or sending up a red flare. If there is no response then assess the relative dangers of leaving the casualty, or of failing to get help, and then act decisively in the interest of the casualty.

Emergency precautions and first aid

While waiting for the rescue team, you should check for further danger, and then carry out basic first-aid treatment.

Safety first

Are you and the casualty safe from further danger?
If not try and make yourselves safe: either by moving, or anchoring yourselves, or both. Is the casualty responsive?

Is the casualty's Airway open?

If necessary, open it by a simple jaw thrust or lift. If possible, avoid moving the neck after trauma. An open airway is essential if the casualty is unconscious or semi-conscious as reduced consciousness can cause death from asphyxia as the tongue falls back blocking the airway. The position of the casualty, in particular his head and tongue, should be adjusted to open the airway and continually reassessed.

Is the casualty's Breathing?

Look, feel and listen for breathing. Basic Life Support should be started, if you are trained, when the casualty is unconscious and shows no signs of breathing, and it can be continued until help arrives and where there is a chance of recovery (lightning, drowning, heart attack). It is usually futile in casualties with internal injuries and is probably best to defer in cases of severe exposure/hypothermia until expert help is available. An unconscious and breathing casualty should be put in the Recovery Position if possible. Check the airway is still open.

Is the casualty's Circulation adequate?

Stop any bleeding from wounds by elevation and direct pressure with dressings or clothing. The pressure needs to be applied continuously for at least 10 minutes. Raising the legs and/or lowering the head may be appropriate. Internal haemorrhage should be suspected if the casualty has sustained blows to the chest or abdomen or broken the femur (thigh bone). The condition often deteriorates and all steps should be taken to facilitate the rapid arrival of the Mountain Rescue Team and, if possible, a helicopter. A record of the pulse rate and consciousness level is very helpful.

Is the casualty Disabled due to damage to head or spine?

Record the casualty's consciousness level – alert, responsive to voice, responsive to pain or unresponsive? Has the spine been damaged? If so, do not move the casualty unless essential for safety reasons. Maintain the head in the normal straight position using your hands.

Check the limbs for fractures

If present, immobilise the limb by the simplest method available. In the case of the arm, pad it and bandage it to the chest, and in the case of the leg, pad it and bandage it to the other leg.

Prevent hypothermia (exposure)

Shelter the casualty from wind and rain. Wrap them in as many layers of clothing as possible and encase them in a 'poly bag' or other impermeable barrier. Do not forget to insulate the head and underneath the casualty.

A **helicopter** may arrive before the mountain rescue team. Extinguish all flames and secure all equipment. The downdraught can knock you over, so get in a safe position. Do not approach the helicopter until clearly signalled to do so by the pilot.

Further points to consider

Large **organised groups** should bear in mind that Mountain Rescue Teams are a finite resource and it is wrong to assume their availability.

The majority of climbers killed in the Lake District as a result of a climbing accident die from a head injury. A **helmet**, whilst not being 100% effective, can make the difference between living and dying.

Whilst **mobile phones** can be very useful in emergencies, any temptation to use them in the hills to call the emergency services in non-emergency circumstances should be resisted. If you are not sure whether it is an emergency or not, please investigate a little yourself first before reaching for your phone.

GPS systems, whilst also useful, are no substitute for carrying a **map** and **compass** and knowing how to use them.

The routine carrying of a suitable **head-torch** would save many needless call-outs.

Lake District Mountain Rescue Teams are made up of unpaid volunteers and rely on charitable contributions. Your consideration and a "Thank you" go a long way to ensure the service continues.

The **Lake District Search and Mountain Rescue Association** (LDSAMRA) acts as an umbrella body for the Lakeland Mountain Rescue Teams. It has a website at:
http://homepages.enterprise.net/ldsamra
which gives contact details for the individual teams.

Right: An RAF Search and Rescue Sea King helicopter picks up a casualty on Great Gable. **Photo:** Phil Rigby

First Ascents

Alternate and varied leads are indicated by (alt) and (**var**)

Gable, Green Gable & Kirkfell

1884 Sept 1 **Needle Ridge** – WP Haskett Smith, JW Robinson
Most of the difficulties were avoided by a traverse into Needle Gully. The first true ascent of the Ridge was made by G Hastings, E Haskett Smith C Hopkinson, JW Robinson and WC Slingsby on 6th March 1887, though WP Haskett Smith had descended it in 1886 on the day he climbed the Needle. It was climbed from the lowest point by AG Woodhead, SF Jeffcoat, J Laycock, 2nd January 1911.

1886 June 27 or 30 **The Wasdale Crack, Napes Needle** – WP Haskett Smith
A solo tour de force, and widely reckoned to mark the birth of rock climbing as a sport separate from mountaineering.

Above: Walter Parry Haskett Smith around the time he made the first ascent of **Napes Needle**.
Photo: FRCC Archive

"From the top of the crack there is no trouble to reach the shoulder, whence the final stage may be studied at ease. The summit is near, being as they say in Trans-Atlantic cities 'only two blocks away,' but those same blocks are set one upon the other and the stability of the top one looks very doubtful. My first care was to get two or three stones and test the flatness of the summit by seeing whether anything thrown-up could be induced to lodge. If it did, that would be an indication of a moderately flat top, and would hold out hopes of the edge being found not too much rounded to afford a good grip for the fingers. Of the three missiles one consented to stay, and thereby encouraged me to start, feeling as small as a mouse climbing a milestone."
WP Haskett Smith 'The First Ascent of Napes Needle' (*FRCC Journal* 1914).

11 July 1910. By the left end of the Mantelshelf – LB Smith, WB Brunskill, J Mallinson, TC Pattinson. This may have been done previously by GB Gibbs. On this date TC Pattinson passed through the crack from west to east.

1889 Mar **The Sphinx** or **Cat Rock** – WP Haskett Smith and "five or six of the strongest climbers in England"

1890 **Easy Sheep Walk** – JW Robinson
A sketch and descriptions by Robinson of routes on Gable Crag points out a scramble: *"E. is an easy ascent, the upper part being grass, up which it has been suggested you may drive a sheep!"* The sketch points to the large steep area of grass to the left of Sledgate Ridge and continuing up the side of Engineer's Chimney. The upper part has now been incorporated into the descent scramble from the Engineer's Slabs area.

1891 Apr 23 **The Lingmell Crack, Napes Needle**
OG Jones, CGM, WE Sumpner.
This predates the previously recorded first ascent on 23rd April 1892 by OG Jones, Mrs Commeline and JN Collie.

1892 Apr 15 **Eagle's Nest Ridge Direct** – GA Solly, WC Slingsby, GP Baker, WA Brigg
A route years ahead of its time. Requiring combined tactics in an incredible situation with no protection. A photo by GP Baker taken at the time shows patches of snow around the base of the crag. *"I went first and found it difficult enough to get to the little platform. When there I sat down to get my breath with my back to the ridge and a leg dangling over each side. The party below made some uncomplimentary remark as to what I looked like perched up there, and I suggested that I looked more like an eagle on its nest. That is, I fear, the very unromantic but truthful origin of the name. Those who have visited the spot know that no bird would ever build a nest on so windswept a ridge. Standing up, I found that the first steps of the next pitch were very difficult, and that the rock rather pushed one out. The others got*

Above: Godfrey Solly who made the outstanding first ascent of **Eagle's Nest Ridge Direct** (MVS) in 1892. **Photo:** FRCC Archive

out the rope, and Slingsby, climbing up as far as possible, stood on a little step just below, with his hands on the platform. I put one foot on his shoulder and, as I climbed up, making room for him, he raised himself and finally stood on the platform, helping me as far as possible. I went on and climbed the second step. Then when I came to the third I did not like it. Retreat was even less inviting, and consultation with the others impracticable. After looking round, something of a hold for each hand and foot was discovered, and I went on, with the knowledge that if even one hand or foot slipped, all would be over."

Godfrey Solly, 'Some Early Recollections', ***FRCC Journal*** (1909).

Pope's Variation, HR Pope, ETW Addyman, 11th September 1910.

1892 Apr 17 **Eagle's Nest Ordinary Route** or **West Chimney**
GA Solly, M Schintz

1892 Apr 17 **Arrowhead Ridge**
to the recess behind the Arrow: WC Slingsby, H Walker, RW Brant, GP Baker, WA Brigg;
finishing along the ridge: GA Solly, M Schintz, RW Brant, HC Bowen, 31st March 1893.

1892 Dec 31 **Oblique Chimney** – J Collier, B Goodfellow, E Talbot, HJ Woolley, SB Winser

1893 Aug 28 **The Crowley Route, Napes Needle** – EA Crowley

1893 Dec 26 **The Crack** OG Jones, WH Fowler, JW Robinson

1893 Dec 26 **Kern Knotts Chimney** OG Jones, WH Fowler, JW Robinson
Variation on left of slab, FO Wethered, C Schuster, H Kempson, 28th April 1894.

Prior to 1894 **Pinnacle Ridge**
Certainly climbed prior to 1897 as its ascent is described by Owen Glynne Jones in ***Rock Climbing in the English Lake District***.

WP Haskett Smith mentions that Westmorland's Crag is *"full of neat 'problems,' and it is customary to pay it a visit on the way to Gable Top after a climb on the Napes,"* ***Climbing in the British Isles*** (1894).

1894 May 8 **Crowley's Chimney Route** – EA Crowley (solo)
The first and rather circuitous ascent of Rainbow Ridge originally referred to as Ridge to West of Arrowhead Ridge.

1894 Sept 17 **The Arête, Napes Needle** – WH Fowler
Slingsby's Variation was climbed by WC Slingsby on 21st January 1904.

1895 Dec 31 **Square-Cut Gully** – EA Crowley, M Travers

1896 Mar 14 **Arrowhead Ridge Direct** – AG Topham, H Walker, WC Slingsby
Direct over the top of the Arrowhead. However GA Solly, M Schintz, RW Brant, HC Bowen may have made the first direct ascent on 31st March 1893. Their description follows:

"They kept rather more on the ridge itself than the former party (17th Apr 1892) *had done, on the way to the Arrowhead."*
South-East Variation, F GRAHAM, 8th October 1925.

1896 Apr 7 **The Central Gully, Direct Finish, Gable Crag** – F LEACH, V BLAKE, TS BOOTH
Chimney between Direct and Easy exit, HV READE, G ARBUTHNOT, 28th September 1903.

1896 Apr 26 **Doctor's Chimney** – DR. SIMPSON, CW PATCHELL

1897 Apr 27 **Kern Knotts West Chimney** – OG JONES, CW PATCHELL

1897 Apr 28 **Kern Knotts Crack** – OG JONES, HC BOWEN
"Robinson held strong views about the unwisdom of making the ascent of Kern Knotts Crack. It was then unclimbed, and he urged that its conquest would lead to unjustifiable attempts by other less skilful climbers, and disaster would result. Again Jones disagreed. I remember Robinson's last 'Parthian shot,' as he turned towards Borrowdale. 'Well, Jones,' he said, smiling, 'if you climb that crack, I'll never speak to you again!' Two months later Kern Knotts Crack was added to the list of Cumbrian courses."
George D Abraham, ***Mountain Adventures at Home and Abroad*** (Methuen 1910).

Above: Ogwen Glynne Jones, or the *Only Genuine Jones* as he styled himself. **Photo:** Abraham brothers

Lower Part of the Crack Direct, WR READE, WP McCULLOCK, July 1898.

1899 July 30 **Engineer's Chimney** – GT GLOVER, WN LING
Variation – HS GROSS, MH HEWSON, 20 June 1924.

1899 Oct 15 **Ling Chimney** – WN LING, GT GLOVER

1908 Sept **Mallory's Left-Hand Route** – GHL MALLORY, GL KEYNES

1908 Sept **Mallory's Right-Hand Route** – GHL MALLORY, GL KEYNES
Variation Start – PL FEARNEHOUGH, G OLIVER, July 1968.

1909 Apr 7 **Abbey Buttress** – FW BOTTERILL, J DE V HAZARD
Originally named ***Abbey Ridge***. On the first ascent Fred Botterill wrote about the 80ft. main pitch: *"I was enabled to rest my arms by placing my hands behind my back, my cheek resting affectionately against the rock... The holds are all good and only ice or high winds need be feared!"*

1909 Apr 9 **Smuggler's Chimney**
JS SLOANE, M GIMSON, A GIMSON, JG HENDERSON

1912 Apr 12 **Kern Knotts West Buttress** – GS Sansom, SW Herford

1912 Aug 26 **The Obverse Route, Napes Needle** – SW Herford, WB Brunskill.

1913 Sept 7 **Abbey Buttress Variations** – GHL Mallory, A Goodfellow
Upper part only, called ***Mallory's Variation***. Remainder on 17th June 1924 by HS Gross, MH Hewson. These variations were combined to make an independent route, but recently the first pitch has disappeared in a large rockfall.

1913 Sep 7 **Chockstone Chimney** – JL Prescott, Miss E Seatree
Long overlooked, the description of this climb only came to light in 2005. "*…closely resembles Kern Knotts Chimney. It is not so stiff as the latter but is intermediary between it and the easy way up Eagle's Nest Arête. The rock is of the finest and the fact of finishing directly up to Westmorland's Cairn renders this climb much more worthy of consideration than appears to be the custom.*" JL Prescott, ***Wasdale Climbing Book*** (1913).
Possibly climbed before by WP Haskett Smith ca.1884

1913 **The Back Staircase** – GF Woodhouse, AB Cowburn
Part of the route is now used as a descent scramble from the top of Tophet Wall into Great Hell Gate.

1919 June 13 **Tophet Bastion** – HM Kelly, EH Pryor, AR Thomson, Mrs Kelly, CG Crawford.
Kelly noted that the climb may have been done before, and it seems likely that it is the same, or nearly the same as **South-East Arête** which was climbed by G Hastings, E Greenwood, J Firth and WC Slingsby, 7th July 1894, but of which no description survives.

1919 July **Scimitar Ridge** – CF Holland

1919 Aug 5 **Kern Knotts Buttress** – HM Kelly, REW Pritchard
"*Utterly severe. The first two pitches are extraordinarily strenuous and tiring; while the swing round the corner which starts the upper section seemed to me quite desperate*". CF Holland in a note to HM Kelly, *Harry Kelly Diaries*.

1919 Aug 7 **Central Climb South Face** – HM Kelly, REW Pritchard, AP Wilson
Variation Start, JH Jameson, September 1933.
Central Climb Variation, JA Austin, RB Evans, 31st March 1956 (not named at the time); the start of this variation has since been incorporated into the Kraken (1974).

1919 Aug 7 **Flake Climb** – HM Kelly, REW Pritchard, AP Wilson, GH Jackson

1920 May 30 **The Slab Climb** – HM Kelly, GS Bower

1920 Aug 30 **Sabre Ridge** – HM Kelly, REW Pritchard

1921 Apr 9 **Innominate Crack** – GS Bower, B Beetham, JB Wilton

1921 Nov 10 **The Buttress** – F Graham

1921 Nov 11 **Chantry Buttress** – F Graham

1921 **The Higher Needle Girdle, Napes Needle**
Unknown, but ascended this year or before as there is a photo of an ascent in the *FRCC Journal* of 1921.

1922 June 5 **Buzzard Wall** – F Graham, M Wood

1922 July 27 **Cutlass Ridge, The Napes** – F Graham

1922 July 27 **Rainbow Ridge** – F Graham
Variation, FG Balcombe, CJA Cooper, June 1934.

1923 July 14 **Tophet Wall** – HM Kelly, REW Pritchard

Above: Harry Mills Kelly pioneer of many new Lakeland climbs. **Photo:** FRCC Archive

"As before, we looked around for a belay, hoping that since our last visit a rocky piton might have crept up in the night, but there was nothing except that ridiculous stump of a juniper bush which our minds scorned as aid, but to which our hearts clove to with a sickly feeling. The second man wound his rope round it two or three times and assured the leader that it "wasn't necessary really, but he might as well." The leader now started at the left hand end of the ledge and working slightly to the right up the wall on small holds, found himself, much to his surprise, at the top of it and crawling gingerly back to the left along a rocky ledge some fifteen feet long." HM Kelly 'Tophet Wall' (*FRCC Journal* 1924).
"G (Blanche Eden-Smith) got up to Great Hell Gate to see the finish of the climb and had thoughtfully carried a basket of strawberries up. A new climb, followed by strawberries at the foot of it – what more could one wish for!", Harry Kelly Diaries.
The party then tried, but failed on, the **Direct Start**. This was eventually soloed by M de Selincourt on the 15th August 1925, in front of a startled FRCC group who were just then discussing its feasibility.

1924 Apr 20 **The West Route** – HM Kelly, REW Pritchard

1924 June 16 **The East Buttress, Kern Knotts** – HS Gross

1924 June 19 **Eagle's Corner** – CD Frankland, B Beetham
Variations – HS Gross, MH Hewson, June 1925.
Variations – M Schatz, GG Macphee, 12 October 1946.

1924 Sept 25 **Zeta Climb** – F Graham

1925 Apr 19 **Sea Wall Arête, East Buttress** – G Basterfield, T Graham Brown

1925 Apr 19 **Starboard Chimney** – G Basterfield, T Graham Brown

1925 May 30 **Hatchway and Rigging** – LC Letts, T Graham Brown

1925 May 31 **Breakwater Slabs and Lighthouse** – G Basterfield, G Lee, T Graham Brown

1925 June 7 **Larboard Arête** – G Basterfield, KB Milne

1925 Aug 19 **Tricouni Rib** – CD Frankland, MM Barker

1925 Sept 8 **Belfry Crack** – F Graham, GM Wellburn

1925 Oct 9 **Aaron** – F Graham

1925 Oct 9 **North Face** – F Graham

1925 Oct 16 **Lucifer Crack** – F Graham

1925 Dec 30 **Esplanade Climb** – T Graham Brown, EH Pollitt

1925 Publication of first FRCC guidebook to Gable, ***IV. Great Gable and Borrowdale,*** Gable author HS Gross, editor RST Chorley.

1926 Apr 3 **Longshoreman's Arête** – J De V Hazard, T Graham Brown

1926 Apr 3 **Coastguard Climb** – J De V Hazard, T Graham Brown

1926 Apr 3 **Starboard Arête** – J de V Hazard, T Graham Brown
Originally called **Starboard Arête by Clinker** but the Clinker (a flake) has now disappeared.

1926 Apr 4 **Stern Girdle Traverse** – J de V Hazard, T Graham Brown

1926 Apr 4 **Horizon Climb** – J de V Hazard, T Graham Brown

1926 May 24 **Prayer Mat Buttress** – G Wood-Johnson, E Wood-Johnson, TR Burnett, K Ward, WG Hennessy, A Wood-Johnson

1927 Oct 23 **Alpha** – GC Macphee, HS Gross, CM Barnard

1927 Oct 23 **Eta** – GG Macphee, HS Gross, CM Barnard

1927 Oct 29 **Gamma** – GG Macphee, CM Barnard

1927 Oct 29 **Theta** – CM Barnard, GG Macphee

1927 Oct 29 **Beta** – CM Barnard, GG Macphee
Top Pitch Direct, GG Macphee, Kate Ward, 12th May 1928.

1927 Nov 27 **Epsilon** – GG Macphee, GS Bower, HS Gross

1928 Apr 11 **Long John** – HG Knight, HM Kelly
"I remember standing on nothing to make a series of stretches, all of them several inches longer than my reach, to ledges of the 'one-sixteenth of an inch' order, which we are said to use as holds; of Kelly saying: 'Splendid, carry on. Can't you reach that roughness two feet higher?'; of Mrs Eden-Smith watching apparently thousands of feet below; of a fairly large ledge which allowed me to traverse to the piton in Ling and sob…
'Long John' is Kelly's name for the climb, not mine, and he seemed to think I ought to be rechristened to suit."
HG Kight 'Addenda Montana' (***FRCC Journal*** 1928).
Top Pitch added by CJA Cooper, E Wood-Johnson, EDG Lewers, June 1932.

1928 Apr 27 **Kern Knotts Chain** – HG Knight, WG Standring, HM Kelly
Left to Right. The same team reversed the route two days later.

1928 Apr 29 **Direct Obverse from the Gap, Napes Needle**
HG Knight, HM Kelly, WG Standring
Also the ***Direct Variation***. *"Kelly suggested going round by the Napes and seeing if a long reach was of any use in trying to get up the Needle Direct from the gap. After careful inspection from the foot with a magnifying glass, and two or three failures, the lower difficulties were overcome and a long arm grabbed the flake fifteen feet up and all was over bar the cheering. In this ascent, Kelly was brought up to the shoulder before I finished the top of the Obverse, but despising myself for such cowardice I managed it again in one run-out."* HG Knight 'Addenda Montana' (*FRCC Journal* 1928).

1928 May 12 **Delta** – GG Macphee, K Ward

1928 May 12 **Epsilon Chimney** – GG Macphee, K Ward
Though probably climbed by numerous members on an FRCC meet, May 1910.

1928 May 28 **Breakwater Slabs, Grooved Arête** – HS Gross, G Basterfield, B Tyson

1930 June 22 **Sepulchre** – JA Musgrove, N Richards, ES Wilson, M Beaty, J Brady, AJ Buck
Sadly destroyed by an earthquake in 1981.

1932 June **Tophet Ridge** – S Watson, R Holmes, B Porter, C Cowen
The original ascent used combined tactics in a very exposed position.

1932 June **Westmorland Ridge** – S Watson, R Holmes, B Porter, C Cowen

1932 June **Kern Knotts Corner** (by easy exit) – S Watson, R Holmes, B Porter, C Cowen
Direct Finish, S Watson, A Watkins, P Brown, 1934.

1933 Sept **Fie** – CJA Cooper

1934 June 7 **The Buttonhook Route** – FG Balcombe, CJA Cooper

1934 June 8 **Engineer's Slabs** – FG Balcombe, JA Shepherd, CJA Cooper
A magnificent lead which was not repeated for over 11 years.

1934 June **Lucifer Ridge** – FG Balcome, JA Shepherd

1934 June **Engineer's Slab – Unfinished Arête**
FG Balcombe, JA Shepherd

1934 June **Hell Gate Pillar** – FG Balcome, CJA Cooper, MM Barker

1935 Apr 28 **Starboard Fender** – TH Savage, RH Fidler, RM Lupton, D Usher

1937 Publication of the second FRCC guidebook to Gable, ***3. Great Gable, Borrowdale, Buttermere***, Gable author CJ Astley-Cooper, editor HM Kelly.

1938 Aug 28 **Brimstone Buttress** – AT Hargreaves, SH Cross, RE Hargreaves, JJ Heap, AM Nelson

1939 June 17 **Moss Slab** – A Gregory, F Grundy

1939 **Barney Buttress** – B Beetham

1940 June 2 **The Prow of the Boat** – SH Cross, AT Hargreaves, RE Hargreaves, AM Cross
1940 June 16 **Eagle's Crack** – RJ Birkett, R Holmes, G Rawlings
1940 June 21 **Starboard Arête Direct** – DMK Home
1940 Oct 13 **Tophet Grooves** – RJ Birkett, V Veevers
1941 June 16 **The Needle Perimeter, Napes Needle** – RL Plackett, A Burnstead
1942 June 25 **Back of the Napes** – TAH Medlycott, Miss Medlycott
1944 Apr 10 **Kirk Fell Ghyll** – L Kellett, JE Blackshaw, CEF Dee
1944 Sept 7 **Windy Ridge** – AR Dolphin, C Smith, J Skinner
1945 Apr 10 **Demon Wall** – AR Dolphin, AB Gilchrist
The Upper Traverse – J Lamb, C Downer, 12th October 1974.
1945 Apr 11 **Tophet Girdle** – AR Dolphin, B Black
1945 Sept 6 **Eagle's Chain** – J Wilkinson, J Umpleby
1946 July 14 **Gremlin's Crack** – D Haworth
1947 Apr 18 **Heinz Route** – B Beetham
1947 Sept 27 **Little John** – JG Ball, JW Cook
1948 Publication of the third FRCC guidebook to Gable, ***Great Gable, Green Gable, Kirkfell, Yewbarrow, Buckbarrow***, authors CJ Astley-Cooper, W Peascod, AP Rossiter, editor HM Kelly. Reprinted, 1958, 1961.
1951 Sept 16 **Jaga** – GB Fisher, F Bantock, P Taylor
1954 **Skorkian Crack** – P Ross, D Fielding
1954 Oct 10 **Salome, The Napes** – G Fisher, D Oliver
Variation Pitch 1 – P Ross, D Fielding, the same day.
1955 Apr 20 **The Cenotaph** – P Ross, R Scott, D Wildridge
1958 June 15 **Corkscrew Slabs** – AH Greenbank, J Wilkinson, AE Wormell
1958 June 15 **Sledgate Ridge** – AH Greenbank, J Wilkinson, AE Wormell
1958 July 5 **Moonshiner** – J Wilkinson, J Umpleby
1958 July 5 **Sundowner** – J Wilkinson, RS Knight, J Umpleby
1959 May 17 **Girdle Traverse, Green Gable** – JD Oliver, KC Ogilvie
1959 Aug 11 **Aaron's Slab** – J Wilkinson, AE Wormell, PB Wormell
1960 Apr 23 **Crocodile Crack** – G Oliver, G Arkless, P Ross, N Brown
1960 May 22 **Alligator Crawl** – G Oliver, G Arkless
1962 Oct **Pyfo** – DN Greenop, E Ivison (alt)
1965 Aug **Scrimshanker** – L Brown, J S Bradshaw
1966 Sept 30 **The Tomb** – AG Cram, W 'Bill' Young
1 point of aid used on Pitch 2 at the overlap. Now climbed free.
Variation climbed by P Nunn on second ascent.
1967 June 1 **Interceptor** – PL Fearnehough, NJ Soper

Left: Combined tactics by S Watson, R Holmes, B Porter and C Cowan on the first ascent of **Tophet Ridge** (VS), The Napes, in 1932. **Photo:** Abraham Brothers

1967 June 27 **The Troll** – AG Cram, L Rodgers
1 point of aid used on Pitch 1 at the block overhang. Now climbed free.

1968 July **Belfry Buttress** – JE Howard, PL Fearnehough

1968 July **The Pod** – PL Fearnehough, G Oliver

1968 Aug **The Slant** – M Burbage, LJ Griffin, PL Fearnehough, G Oliver
The top pitch had previously been led by P Nunn in 1955.

1968 Sept **The Merry Monk** – PL Fearnehough, G Oliver

1969 May 24 **Three Blind Mice** – NAJ Rogers, CH Taylor, I Roper (alt)

1969 May 27 **The Cat Run** – CH Taylor, J Taylor, A Kelly

1969 June 1 **Numenor** – I Roper, NAJ Rodgers
Three points of aid used on first ascent. Climbed free by WS 'Bill' Lounds, K Bliss, 30th August 1973.

1969 June 14 **Landlubber** – I Roper, NAJ Rogers

1969 June 14 **Fanghorn** – I Roper, NAJ Rogers
Thee points of aid used on first ascent. Pitch 1 climbed with 1 point of aid, WS 'Bill' Lounds, K Bliss, 30th August 1973. Climbed free and with Pitch 2 *Alternative Finish* by D Birkett, Sue Wood, P Ross 25th June 1995.
Paul Ross took a 10 metre fall direct onto Dave.
"I was on minute holds, one minute I was there the next I was not!"

1969 June 15 **The Vikings** – AR McHardy, P 'Tut' Braithwaite
A gem stolen from under the noses of the locals by a marauding Lancashire team, who established the first E3 on Great Gable. An on-form Richard McHardy placed a single Moac on the crux second pitch! A very bold lead – an attempt by another team had resulted in a broken arm the week before.

1969 Publication of the fourth FRCC guidebook to Gable, ***Great Gable***, author PL Fearnehough, editor J Wilkinson.

1970 June 4 **The Jabberwock** – R Valentine, J Wilkinson
Pitch 3 originally the **Direct Finish to Engineer's Slab – Unfinished Arête**, first climbed by P Ross, DP Lockey, 15 June 1958.

1970 June 4 **Trundle Ridge** – R Valentine, J Wilkinson

1970 June 13 **Potheen** – D Miller, J Wilkinson

1970 June 13 **The Bandersnatch** – D Miller, J Wilkinson

1970 June 20 **The Serpent** – C Read, W L Robinson (alt)

1971 Sept 11 **Spirit Level** – AG Cram, W 'Bill' Young (var)
One point of aid used on Pitch 1. Now climbed free.

1973 May 19 **Crinkler's Crack** – R Valentine, J Wilkinson

1974 Apr 6 **El Vino** – A 'Tony' Stephenson, S Miller

Left: Geoff Cram and Bill Young on the first ascent **The Tomb**, Gable Crag, in 1966.
Photo: Chris Eilbeck

1974 Apr 6 **The Kraken** – S Miller, A 'Tony' Stephenson
The initial corner had previously been climbed as a ***Variation to Central Climb South Face*** by JA Austin and RB Evans, 31st March 1956.

1974 May **Vindolanda** – P Long, J Adams
One point of aid used on first ascent. Climbed free by P Botterill, J Adams on 10th July 1977.
Variation Start now incorporated into the climb, K Phizacklea, A Phizacklea, 6th June 2006.

1976 Oct 24 **The Crysalid** – S Clegg, J Lamb (alt)

1977 July **Supernatural** – P Whillance, DW Armstrong (var)
Originally graded E4, and later upgraded to E5. All the pitches were climbed on separate evenings after a mad dash from the end of the working day in Carlisle.
Direct Finish added by P Whillance, DW Armstrong, 22nd July 1984.

1977 July 10 **Sarcophagus** – P Whillance, DW Armstrong (alt)

1977 Aug 9 **The Cayman** – P Whillance, DW Armstrong

1977 Publication of the fifth FRCC guidebook to Gable, ***Great Gable***, author PL Fearnehough, editor J Wilkinson.

1978 Apr 23 **Triffid** – P Botterill, J Lamb

1978 May 21 **Golden Calf** – P Botterill, J Lamb (var)

1978 June 18 **Sacrificial Crack** – J Lamb, P Botterill, J Taylor
The challenge laid down by PL Fearnehough in October 1976 is successfully taken on. Not repeated for 9 years. The last of the 'big three routes' on Tophet Wall which left their mark on the 1970s.

1979 June 3 **The Angel of Mercy**
J Lamb, P Botterill
Variation – A Phizacklea, K Phizacklea, 6th June 2006

1979 **Feline Crack** – J Lamb, M Hetherington, J Fotheringham

1981 June 28 **Triffid Right-Hand Finish**
J Lamb, P Botterill (var)

1981 June 28 **Sylvester** – T Furness, PC Rigby (var)

Above: Pete Botterill, who with Jeff Lamb (see page 34) bagged **Sacrificial Crack** (E4) and **Golden Calf** (E5), on Tophet Wall. **Photo:** Trevor Jones

1981 June 28 **Sepulchre Direct** – J Lamb, P Botterill
A solution to the problem created by the loss of the original first pitch of Sepulchre in a rockfall.
A ***Direct Finish*** which the present route uses was climbed as a variation in 1975 by J Lamb.

1981 June 28 **Cenotaph Left-Hand** P Botterill, J Lamb
Four extremes in one day from a strong Carlisle team brings Kern Knotts up to date.

1981 Aug 9 **Misfit** – A 'Tony' Stephenson, W 'Bill' Young
Aid point used for cleaning on first ascent. Now Free.

1982 Apr 29 **Time and Place** M Leoroyd, H Griffith

1984 Aug 15 **Incantations** – P Whillance, DW Armstrong (var)
Pitch 3 added by P Whillance, DW Armstrong, 22nd August, 1984. The direct finish of Supernatural was originally to be the third pitch of Incantations. However to give a true first ascent for the Lakeland Rock TV series, another pitch had to be cleaned and climbed live for the programme.

1985 Publication of the FRCC guidebook supplement to Gable, ***New West***, author W 'Bill' Young, editor D Miller.

1986 July 15 **Snicker Snack** – C Downer, A Hall
Colin Downer noticed the fine unclimbed crack-line of Snicker Snack in a picture of Engineer's Slabs whilst browsing through a copy of *Hard Rock*. It had been overlooked by many teams. Hampered by poor weather, Downer made over a dozen visits to the crag to clean and climb three superb routes – Snicker Snack, Powder Finger and Dream Twister.

1987 Apr 25 **Hell Bent** – A Phizacklea, D Kirby

1987 Apr 25 **The Tartarus Trip** – A Phizacklea, D Kirby

1987 May 16 **Powder Finger** – C Downer, A Redfearn

1987 June 20 **Amos Moses** – P Long, T Parker

1987 July 13 **Dream Twister** – C Downer, A Hall

1987 Aug 8 **The Tormentor** – A Phizacklea, AH Greenbank
'There he is! My tormentor!', shouted Tony Greenbank, glancing up and seeing Al Phizacklea peering through the mist on the stance above, while being totally bereft of any idea as to what his next move should be.

1987 Sept 27 **Hell Raiser** – A Phizacklea, AH Greenbank, JC Lockley

1988 Apr 24 **Calculus** – S Brailey, S Hubball
The upper section was originally ***Alpha Variation*** by A Wood-Johnson, Mabel M Barker, 21 April 1935.

1988 Apr 24 **Omega** – S Hubball, S Brailey

1988 Apr 24 **Abacus** – S Hubball, S Brailey

1988 Apr 24 **Caleb** – S Hubball, S Brailey
Four new routes in one day, the first for 55 years.

1988 May 7 **Timshel** – S Hubball, S Brailey

1988 May 15 **Smaug** – A Phizacklea, RE 'Bob' Wightman (alt)

1988 May 15 **The Gable End** – RE 'Bob' Wightman, A Phizacklea

1988 May 16 **Arjuna** – S Hubball (solo)

1988 May 21 **Murin Buchstansangur**
A Phizacklea, RE 'Bob' Wightman

1988 May 22 **American Dream** – S Brailey, S Hubball, S Day

1988 May 30 **East of Eden** – S Hubball, S Brailey

1988 May 30 **Greenpeace** – S Brailey, S Hubball

1988 June 5 **Close to the Wind** – R Kenyon (unseconded)
Incorporating ***Awe***, a variation on The Buttonhook Route, GWB Tough, JE Harding, 29 August 1965

1988 June 12 **Nothing to Declare** – A Phizacklea, D Kirby

1988 June 12 **Strike While It's Hot** – A Phizacklea, D Kirby
The result of industrial action during a long hot summer.

1988 June 15 **The Tombstone** – A Phizacklea, S Carruthers
Pitch 2 top roped on first ascent, then led.

1988 June 15 **The Short Crack** – A Phizacklea, S Carruthers

1988 June 27 **The Slay Ride** – A Phizacklea, C Gregg

1989 May 29 **The Satanic Traverses**
A Phizacklea, RE 'Bob' Wightman, D Lampard

1989 June 17 **Mome Rath** A Phizacklea, D Kirby

1989 Apr 25 **Eastern Bloc** A Phizacklea

1989 Apr 25 **Pussy**
A Phizacklea, PW Cox

1990 May 28 **Moggy Traveller**
A Phizacklea, A Rowell

1990 May 28 **Fat Freddie's Cat**
A Phizacklea, A Rowell, D Kells

1991 July 18 **Tophet Grooves Direct** – SJH Reid, J Grinbergs (alt)
Only the cleft pitch was new, and even this showed signs of previous ascents.

Above: Al Phizacklea on the first ascent of **Pussy** (E4), Kern Knotts. **Photo:** Dave Kells
Left: Pete Whillance (left) and Dave Armstrong, looking at the top pitch of **Incantations** (E6), The Napes, before the first ascent for the *Lakeland Rock* TV series in 1984. **Photo:** Chris Bonington

The ***Direct Start*** was climbed by PL Fearnehough and JE Howard in June 1968, and ***Pitch 2 Direct*** was added by J Grinbergs and A Davis in June 1989.

1991 Aug 14 **Aquiline Slab** – A Phizacklea, JL Holden

1991 Aug 14 **Tosspot** A Phizacklea, JL Holden

1991 Aug 14 **The Young Shavers** A Phizacklea, JL Holden

1991 Aug 14 **West Buttress Eliminate** – A Phizacklea JL Holden
Superdirect Start added by DW Armstrong, N Barraclough 14th May 2000.

1991 Aug 31 **Pharos** – S Clegg, K Clegg, I Carr, R Valentine

1991 Publication of the sixth FRCC guidebook to Gable, ***Gable and Pillar***, Gable author D Kirby, editor DW Armstrong.

1992 May 16 **Caterwaul** – SJH Reid, S Frame

1992 May 20 **Centennial Climb** – T Marr, M Tooke

1992 June 6 **Conversation Killer** – F Wardropper, B Swale, J Wilkinson

1993 June 8 **Golgotha** – I Turnbull, C Downer
Pre-top roped and pre-placed Rock1 and RP4.

1995 June 25 **Flagship** – D Birkett, Sue Wood, P Ross

1995 July 2 **End Zone** – M Lynch, B McKinley

1996 Aug 2 **Scenic Cruise** – P Ross, P Greenwood

1996 Sept 20 **Dehydroepiandrosterone** – A Ross, P Ross

1997 Apr 16 **Final Voyage** – P Ross, P Armstrong
Pitch 1 Direct – RO Graham, E 'Ted' Rogers 29th July 1999.

1997 July 22 **Trim and Incline** – A Phizacklea, K Phizacklea

1998 May 17 **Grimalkin** – K Telfer, J Gilhespie, P Morgan
The same line was also claimed by D Booth, I Turnbull as **Brown Badger** around the same time but they were not entirely certain of the date.

1999 July 11 **Cannon Stone** – M Armitage, T Kennedy

1999 July 12 **Sick Heart River** – SJH Reid, RJ Kenyon
The first new route on the Needle for over 50 years – climbed after work on a fine summer's evening.

"Reaching down, I dabbed tiny crucial footholds with chalk so that I wouldn't miss them in the gloaming, and then stepped up. The poor high layaway for my left hand, a wide reach for a hidden side-pull with the right, and then I delicately moved my feet up, an inch at a time, until my cramped left made the ledge. Next, not even daring to think about it, my right hand arced up for a tiny nick in the rock above, pinched it between thumb and forefinger, and I stepped onto the ledge. On my left a blunt chisel-shaped spike took a miserable excuse of a sling, but I didn't care; one move round the arête and I was on The Shoulder and talking nineteen to the dozen as I set up a belay." Stephen Reid 'Sick Heart River' (*FRCC Journal* 2000).

The ***Direct Variation*** from the Platform was climbed by K Telfer on the second ascent, 7th May 2000, and the super direct line of ***The Thirty Nine Steps*** was added by PC Rigby, K Avery, 12th May 2002.

Above: Stephen Reid on **Sick Heart River** (E2), Napes Needle. **Photo:** Colwyn Jones

1999 July 29 **Numenor with Direct Finish** RO Graham, E 'Ted' Rogers

1999 July 29 **Voyager** E 'Ted' Rogers, RO Graham

1999 July 29 **Jolly Roger** E 'Ted' Rogers, RO Graham
First pitch only, the route finished up the second pitch of Fanghorn.

1999 Aug 22 **Keel Haul** – E 'Ted' Rogers, RO Graham

1999 Aug 28 **Poseidon Adventure** – RO Graham, A Jones
Pitch 2, E 'Ted' Rogers, RO Graham, 22nd August 1999.

2000 May 29 **Nine Lives** – PC Rigby, J Williams

2000 June 26 **Breathless** – J Dunne, A Jack
Originally graded E10 (7a) and a contender at the time for the hardest route in the Lakes, if not the UK. It had been inspected by many extremely talented climbers over the previous decade and only finally succumbed after some 14 attempts.

"John continued to push himself for three years after Hard Grit was filmed, until he found

Above: John Dunne first ascentionist of **Breathless** (E9), Tophet Wall. **Photo:** Adrian Berry

*himself fighting for life on the first ascent of Breathless – a crimpy, dangerously run-out E10 in the Lake District. 'I nearly ****** it.' Crimpy climbing has always been John's least favourite style. 'It wasn't a John Dunne route – it was a Dave Birkett route,' John says, referring to the second ascentionist, and his superior crimping abilities. John's experience on Breathless made him question the pressure of having to climb hard, necky routes for little money. 'I was tired of having to keep pushing things.'"*
Extract from an interview with John Dunne by Adrian Berry, *Hard Grit – Where are they now?* (www.planetfear.com 2005).
Has had two repeats to date.

2000 July 9 **The Cat's Whiskers** – DW Armstrong, PC Rigby

2000 July 14 **Mausoleum** – PC Rigby, R Fone
Pre-top-roped.

2000 July 22 **Cat Napping** – PC Rigby, R Fone

2000 July 23 **The Loch Ness Monster** – PC Rigby, J Pattison

2002 Sept 15 **The Wasdale Roof, Napes Needle** – PC Rigby, T Foster
The first alternative way to climb the top block on Napes Needle for over 90 years!

2003 Mar16 **Rusty's Rib** – SJH Reid, JE Reid

2003 Apr 10 **Tubular Balls** – SJH Reid, C King

2003 Apr 10 **Not a Cairn in the World** – SJH Reid, C King (alt)
Variations – TJ Suddaby, SJH Reid (alt), 6th July 2003
The lower variation now incorporated into the main description.

2003 Apr 10 **Cairn Nuts Crack** – C King, SJH Reid (alt)

2003 Apr 10 **Pinncairnle Rib** – C King, SJH Reid (alt)

2003 May 25 **Tormentil** – A Phizacklea, JL Holden
Tormentil is a yellow flower found on Gable.

2003 May 25 **Turdus torquatus** – A Phizacklea, JL Holden
Named after a Ring Ouzel (*T.* ***torquatus***) which was singing at the crag.
Pitch 3 (***Eagle's Nest Super Direct***) was climbed by J Morgan and P Johnson, 13th October, 1985.

2003 May 30 **Hamshanker** – A Phizacklea, JL Holden

2003 May 30 **Chantry Buttress Direct** – A Phizacklea, JL Holden

2003 May 30 **Gharial** – A Phizacklea, JL Holden

2003 June 15 **Cairn Direct** – SJH Reid, IJW 'Jack' Reid

2003 June 15 **Crackerjack** – SJH Reid, IJW 'Jack' Reid

2003 June 15 **Dad's Day Slab** – SJH Reid, IJW 'Jack' Reid

2003 June 22 **R & R Special** – SJH Reid, C Read (alt), A Gladstone

2003 June 22 **The Cairnbrian** SJH Reid, C Read (alt), A Gladstone

2003 June 29 **Sparrowfart Rib** – SJH Reid, IJW 'Jack' Reid

2003 June 29 **Hell Gate Chimney** – SJH Reid, IJW 'Jack' Reid

2003 June 29 **School's Out** – SJH Reid, IJW 'Jack' Reid

2003 June 29 **Wha's the Crack** – SJH Reid, IJW 'Jack' Reid

2003 June 29 **Chocks Away** – SJH Reid, IJW 'Jack' Reid
2003 June 29 **Cairnshung Face** – SJH Reid, IJW 'Jack' Reid
2003 June 29 **Cairn Climb** – SJH Reid, IJW 'Jack' Reid
Seven new routes in one day by a father and son team!
2003 Aug 15 **Westmorland Crack** – TJ Suddaby, SJH Reid
2003 Aug 15 **Hellfire and Brimstone** – SJH Reid, TJ Suddaby
2003 Aug 15 **Adam's Groove** – TJ Suddaby, SJH Reid
2003 Aug 15 **Caitlin's Climb** – TJ Suddaby, SJH Reid
2004 Feb 29 **Leap Year** – A Phizacklea, JL Holden
2004 May 23 **Red Arrow** – A Phizacklea, JL Holden
2004 May 23 **Burning Sphinxter** – A Phizacklea, JL Holden
2004 July 17 **Rob and Angie's Wedding** – C Richards, P Cooper
2005 June 27 **Calaboose** – BJ Clarke (solo)
2005 June 28 **Coronet** – BJ Clarke (solo)
2005 June 28 **Solenelle** – BJ Clarke (solo)
2005 June 28 **Transpire** – BJ Clarke (solo)
2005 June 28 **Inca Grooves** – BJ Clarke (solo)
2005 July 7 **Notre Dame** – BJ Clarke, J Holden
2005 Aug 17 **Mayan Slab** – BJ Clarke (solo)
2006 May 25 **Isis Crack** – BJ Clarke (solo)
2006 May 25 **Tango Magenta** – BJ Clarke (solo)
2006 May 25 **Thee Groove** – BJ Clarke (solo)
2006 May 25 **Ringing Flakes** – BJ Clarke (solo)
2006 May 30 **Chequered Cracks** – BJ Clarke (solo)
2006 May 30 **Blazonry** – BJ Clarke (solo)
2006 May 30 **Borrowed Time** – BJ Clarke (solo)
2006 May 30 **Of Beauty** – BJ Clarke (solo)
2006 May 30 **Chestnut Edge** – BJ Clarke (solo)
2006 May 30 **Lost Ridge** – BJ Clarke (solo)
2006 June 3 **Marie Celeste** – BJ Clarke (solo)
2006 June 3 **Troubadour** – BJ Clarke (solo)
2006 June 3 **Cerca Trova** – BJ Clarke (solo)
2006 June 3 **Groyne Strain** – A Phizacklea, JL Holden
2006 June 3 **Sea Shanty** – A Phizacklea, JL Holden
2006 June 3 **The Golden Rivet** – A Phizacklea, JL Holden
2006 June 3 **Bilge and Ballast** – A Phizacklea
2006 June 3 **Bowspit** – JL Holden, A Phizacklea (alt)
2006 June 15 **Topsail** – E 'Ted' Rogers, K Forsythe
2006 June 15 **Spinnaker** – K Forsythe, E 'Ted' Rogers
2006 July 2 **Lost Arrow Spire** – A Phizacklea, JL Holden
2006 July 13 **Bonjour Matelot** – BJ Clarke (solo)
2006 July 16 **Guest Appearance** – A Phizacklea, JL Holden, N Wharton
2006 July 23 **Jongleur Wall** – BJ Clarke, J Holden

Above: Peter Rhodes slacklining Napes Needle. **Photo:** Barnaby Whiteside

2006 July 28 **Napes Needle on a slackline!**
On this day P Rhodes and J Ritson walked a line rigged between Needle Ridge and the summit block of Napes Needle!

2006 Aug 24 **Hotel du Lac** – BJ Clarke, J Ford

2007 Apr 6 **Abbot** – A Phizacklea, JL Holden

2007 Apr 6 **Costello** – A Phizacklea, JL Holden

2007 Apr 6 **A Laudable Ox** – A Phizacklea, JL Holden

2007 Apr 6 **Crumbs from a Rich Man's Table** – A Phizacklea, JL Holden
Variation Finish added the same day by the same team.

Ennerdale

1826 July 9 **The Old West Route**
J Atkinson
See **Historical** on page 39.
Slingsby's Crack is thought to have been climbed by WC Slingsby ca.1890–1900.

Above: Slingsby's Crack (D), Pillar Rock. A variation to the Old West Route first climbed by WC Slingsby 1887.
Photo: Abraham Brothers

1850 **Old Wall Route**
CAM Baumgartner
"Sheep occasionally manage to get across, and the Old Wall was built many years ago to prevent their passage, but it is now ruined. Sometimes, ignoring Badminton, they still venture across without a rope..." Owen Glynne Jones, ***Rock-Climbing in the English Lake District*** (Longmans 1897).

"(From the Jordan Gap, Auld Will Ritson) pointed out to me a narrow track on a level ledge of rock winding round the side of the Pillar Stone. This I followed till it brought me to the north side of the Rock, losing site of Ritson. When I reached the back of the Rock, or rather the front of it, looking towards Ennerdale and Buttermere, it was simply a matter of climbing up by the hands more than the feet." CAM Baumgartner quoted by RST Chorley, Some Notes on Pillar History (***FRCC Journal*** 1926). However it is hinted in this article that this route is likely to have been climbed earlier, though George Seatree (Reminiscences of Early Lakeland Mountaineering ***FRCC Journal*** 1910) maintains that Baumgartner ascended the Old West Route and that the Old Wall Route was not climbed until 1866.

1850 **Whitehead's Corner** – JG Whitehead
It is with some hesitation that this ascent is recorded, as it has not been described in previous guides nor mentioned in earlier first ascent lists. However HM Kelly refers to it in his historical, stating *"... and Mr Whitehead's, who claims, according to Mr JW Robinson, to have done the Corner above the Slab, ie, the one into which the Pendlebury Traverse leads"*. Whitehead, a doctor from Whitehaven, is recorded as having climbed Pillar again in 1853 and 1881 so was likely a keen and competent mountaineer. However it is strange that Kelly did not record the route in his guide, nor make any attempt to repeat it (at least none that is recorded in his diaries). Perhaps he doubted

the claim. It was definitely soloed by JW Robinson in 1885, albeit with a rope hanging nearby just in case. *"Over the 'notch' we went for our first climb and entered our names as usual, then ran down and tried Pendlebury's Crack which leads you into the upper part of the 'corner' and thought it rather easy. We hung the rope down at the corner as a precaution, but it was not used. I then descended and attacked the 'Corner'. HS and I had been a little way up on a former visit, and Whitehead claims to have gone that way in 1850, the only known ascent. It is two chimneys and they miss each other, and this makes the only real difficulty at that point. I drew myself up by the hands entirely."* John Wilson Robinson (Camping amongst the Crags in 1885, ***FRCC Journal*** 1917).

1863 Aug 14 **Slab and Notch Climb** – JWE Conybeare, AJ Butler, E Leeke, JC Leeke, TRC Campbell, JD Poyer, JW Pratt

It seems likely that both the Notch Route and the ***Easy Way*** were climbed. *"The Notch Route was the first we tried, but when, from the top of the Curtain, I saw the steep grass, I called to the rest to try whether there was no lower way of reaching it. Thus was found the Easy Way, by which most of us went up that day, and by which we all came down"* Letter of 1864 to WP Haskett Smith, ***CC Journal*** 1905.

However, the route is also recorded as having been ascended by the *"keeper of the St Bees' Lighthouse and four friends in 1861,"* George Seatree, Reminiscences of Early Lakeland Mountaineering (***FRCC Journal*** 1910).

1872 Sept **Pendlebury Traverse** – F Gardiner, WM Pendlebury, R Pendlebury, J Hasking, HJ Priest

GD Abraham, in 'The Climbs of the English Lake District' (***FRCC Journal*** 1908), and in other publications, repeats a story related to him by Richard Pendlebury that he walked from Keswick in his smoking room slippers and the team actually climbed Whitehead's Corner. This was denounced as *"bosh"* by William Pendlebury when he was interviewed shortly before his death by Godfrey Solly in 1921 (***FRCC Journal*** 1922), and it seems likely that his brother was confusing the details of more than one event. Fred Gardiner was a noted alpinist and made the first ascent of Mt Elbruz.

1882 Aug–Sept **West Jordan Climb** – WP Haskett Smith

"Dear Kelly, You ask about the naming of the climbs. You must blame me for Pisgah and Jordan. In those days people mainly reached the rock via the fell top and were apt to march on up the former in the belief that it led to the top, but found, like Moses, that Jordan cut them off from the Promised Land." WP Haskett Smith, 19th November 1936 (letter to Harry Kelly, FRCC Archives)

1882 Aug–Sept **Central Jordan Climb** – WP Haskett Smith

Right: West Jordan Climb (D), Pillar Rock, circa 1900. **Photo:** Abraham Brothers

Prior to 1884 **The Arête** (and maybe **The Curtain**) – WP Haskett Smith
It is uncertain when these climbs were first done, but the date of the third ascent of The Curtain is given as 18 April 1899 and Williamson mentions the Arête (by which he seems likely to mean the Curtain as well) as having been climbed in his article 'The Climbs of the English Lake District' of 1884. In the same article he mentions that Haskett Smith had ascended Pillar Rock by more than twelve distinct routes. There is some evidence to suggest that the original route up the Curtain avoided the off-width crack by a traverse to the left (George D Abraham, ***British Mountain Climbs*** 1909), and it is mentioned that *"it was climbed direct, without divergence, in August, 1909, by FW Botterill and E Roberts,"* rather implying that previous ascents had not been so.
Direct Variations – SJH Reid, C King (alt), 25th September 2003.

1884 Aug-Sept **East Jordan Climb** – WP Haskett Smith
On 27th July 1919 the East Jordan Climb was made independent of the Central Jordan Climb by giving it a new start and a slightly different finish, HM Kelly, CG Crawford, CF Holland, NE Odell.

1887 Mar 5 **The Great Chimney** – WP Haskett Smith
Although OG Jones records it (***Rock Climbing in the English Lake District*** 1897) as having been climbed by Haskett Smith in 1884, and George Seatree ('Reminiscences of Early Lakeland Mountaineering' ***FRCC Journal*** 1910) maintains it was first climbed in 1866.

1889 Jun 5 **Great Doup Buttress** – WP Haskett Smith and party
Originally named Smoking Rock. *"For fear of the name being adduced as a proof of recent volcanic action it is well to say that it is so called not as itself smoking but because a well-known climber of the old school loved to smoke an evening pipe on it."* WP Haskett Smith, ***Climbing in the British Isles*** (Longmans 1894).

1890 Dec 29 **Shamrock Gully** (by Right-Hand Route of the Great Pitch)
G Hastings, C Hopkinson, JW Robinson
A previous ascent had been made by the help of a snowdrift. On 29th December 1896 the Left-Hand Route of the Great Pitch was first climbed by OG Jones, WJ Williams, GD Abraham, AP Abraham though this was very much a winter ascent.

1890 **Robinson's Route** – JW Robinson
Climbed around this time.

1891 July 27 **North Climb (Savage Gully Exit)** – WP Haskett Smith, G Hastings, WC Slingsby
This was by the ***Westerly Variation***, but the Stomach Traverse Route as far as the Split Blocks had been climbed by Haskett Smith and his brother Edmund previously when exploring the North Face. ***The Hand Traverse*** was first done (also by the Westerly Variation) by GA Solly, G Hastings, HA Gwynne, E Greenwood and

Above: At the split blocks on **North Climb** (MS), Pillar Rock. The central figure is the photographer Ashley Abraham. **Photo:** Abraham Brothers

WC Slingsby, 13th February 1892. "*It is a weirdly sensational feeling to be performing a kind of aerial flight along that great cliff; the grip of the fingers seems strangely inadequate, and there is always the unnerving thought that it may give out before the exhausting final part of the traverse is reached.*" George D Abraham, *Mountain Adventures at Home and Abroad* (Methuen 1910).

The Nose was first climbed about 1893 by J Collier, SB Winser, and probably others.

Intermediate Variation, HM Kelly, REW Pritchard, JH Doughty, H Coates, 26th August 1921.

The Nose Direct C King, SJH Reid, 25th September 2003.

1892 Apr 21 **East Pisgah Chimney Right** – OG Jones

1892 **Jordan Gap crossed on a rope!** – FW Newmarch

114 years before the Needle Gap was slacklined – though it is doubtful that he walked a hemp rope in nailed boots!

1894 Sept 23 **The Shamrock Chimneys**

RS Robinson, JW Robinson, LR Wilberforce, WH Price

1897 Jan 1 **Hind Cove Gully** – RC Gilson

First ascent was evidently made on this date, and the only name mentioned in connection therewith is that of RC Gilson, though there were probably others. It may well have been in winter conditions as it was a particularly hard winter.

1898 Mar 31 **Pisgah from Jordan Gap** – JS Sloane, T Brushfield, S Mason

1898 July 21 **West Jordan Gully** – WP McCulloch, WR Reade

Alternative Start by HB Gibson, GS Sansom, 9th September 1912.

Alternative Finishes by HM Kelly, Morley Wood, H Coates, 3rd September 1921.

1899 Jan 7 **Walker's Gully** – OG Jones, GD Abraham, AE Field

Named after an unfortunate young man who fell to his death down it in 1883.

The first ascent was via the ***Alternative Start*** route. A famous epic as the gully was in very bad condition, being covered in melting ice.

"Next the right wall was tried, and I blessed the previous three months' monotonous training with heavy dumb-bells. The strain on the arms was excessive. Fortunately, there was no running water there, or the cold would have been unendurable. At the worst corner, by hanging on with the right hand, and with the left looping part of my rope through a recess at the side of the boulder, a good grip was improvised. Of natural holds there were none on that smooth icy wall, and the loop was a perfect boon. Even a perfect boon is hard to utilise when hands and feet are benumbed and all one's muscles are racked with prolonged tension. But the loop served its purpose, and after a few more struggles in the crack a ledge was reached from which it was evidently an easy scramble to the head of the gully. 'Réussi – parfaitement – messieurs – send up my coat and boots.' The gasping message was finished in English to save delay, but I shiveringly waited many minutes in soft snow before the rope could be untied and the articles in question slung up on it. A cherished pair of socks fell out of the coat-pocket as it was hauled over the edge of the top boulder, and took a preliminary drop of two or three hundred feet. It gave us quite a shock at the time, for we thought it was a packet of sandwiches." Owen Glynne Jones quoted by George D Abraham, ***Mountain Adventures at Home and Abroad*** (Methuen 1910).

Direct Start – JF, RW and H Broadrick, 5th September 1898.

Additional Finish – FW Botterill and others. June 1909.

1901 May 26 **New West Climb** – GD Abraham, AP Abraham, CW Barton, JH Wigner

A breakthrough – the first route on the West Face since The Old West Route.

"An awkward sensational corner was the beginning of the traverse, and a little clumsiness was excusable, for the holds were rather spaced and difficult to find. One of our party found here that even the weight of the whisky flask upset his delicate balance, and had to return to the chimney to remedy the nuisance, and when, later on, we huddled together in the mist, under the

summit cairn, there was no temptation left for the teetotallers of the party." George D Abraham, 'A New Climb on Pillar Rock' (***CC Journal*** 1901).
It is not certain who first climbed the normal final pitch.
The ***Direct Finish*** was climbed by O Tindale and party on 12th September 1911.
Western Trod was recorded by D Johnson and M Johnson, 9th July1995, but had been climbed before by many parties confused by the old description of New West Climb which instructed them to start from below the embedded block. Examination of old photographs reveals that this block shifted its position some time after the first ascent of New West Climb.

1901 Aug 27 **Savage Gully** – CW Barton, GD Barton, LF Meryon
The **Top Pitch** had previously been led as a finish to North Climb, GA Solly, Easter 1892 or '93.
PA Thompson previously led the main pitch of the gully on 3rd June 1901, but his second could not follow, and he then accepted the moral support of a rope from the platform on North Climb for the last two pitches.
Nose Finish – A Bridge, HM Kelly, M Linnell, 3rd April 1931.
Variation Start – W 'Bill' Young, JC Eilbeck, WS 'Bill' Lounds, 18th June 1968.

1906 June 8 **North-West Climb** – FW Botterill, LJ Oppenheimer, A Botterill, JH Taylor
Originally climbed via Taylor's Chimney.
"The day was fine, the rocks warm and all went well. Fred Botterill led us throughout and as he had been over most of the ground three times there was not much hesitation. After passing the top of the buttress the climb seemed to me to be the steepest of the height that I had been on, but it was satisfactory to find so many good belay pins and little resting places. Twice the leader has to run out 80 feet, the second time over the piece where Dr Taylor found the way, which is very stiff indeed… This was my day of days on Pillar – the fullest of delights that the climber alone can enjoy in their fulness…" Lehmann J Oppenheimer, ***The Heart of Lakeland*** (Sherrat & Hughes 1908).
"… the start is well marked by boot-nail scratches, most of which have doubtless been made by returning parties… A slip on the part of the leader on the upper section would almost certainly mean that none of the party would take any further interest in old age pensions." George D Abraham, 'The Climbs of the English Lake District' (***FRCC Journal*** 1908).
Lamb's Chimney – R Lamb, WL Collinson, R Horton, EW Steeple, 23rd August 1906.
Variation Finish – DG Murray, EB Beauman, 1913?
Kirkstile Variation – F Graham, RST Chorley, 1st August 1937.

1907 Aug 20 Death of John Wilson Robinson (at the early age of 53), who was one of the two great pioneers of Lakeland climbing, the other being WP Haskett Smith. Among his many achievements he made over 100 ascents of Pillar Rock and discovered the High Level Route. The memorial cairn and bronze plaque overlooking Pillar Rock were erected by his friends the following year.

1908 Apr 18 **West Cove Chimney**
JD Hazard, EE Roberts

1908 Apr 22 **Long Chimney, West Cove**
JD Hazard, B Hoessly, F Boyd, EE Roberts

1908 Apr 22 **Haskett Gully** – WP Haskett Smith, LJ Oppenheimer, H Scott-Tucker
"The floor of the cave was very sloping and bad to stand on, so Tucker anchored himself firmly high

Top: The inscribed bronze plaque at Robinson's Cairn in memory of John Wilson Robinson 1853–1907.
Above: The building of **Robinson's Memorial Cairn** on a knoll by the side of the **High Level Route** in sight of Pillar Rock. The figure in the hat standing on the cairn is WP Haskett Smith.
Photo: LJ Oppenheimer (*FRCC Journal* 1907).

up in it and held both of us in, while I gave Haskett Smith a shoulder. He did not find anything much to pull up by, and called for the ice-axe to try what sort of ledges there might be above. 'Give me the escarbadientes, or I suppose I ought to say patio,' for at breakfast-time Craig had been speaking about the coarseness of the English word toothpick and its Spanish equivalent, and enlarging on the superior politeness of the Portuguese language. 'Palatio – piolet – or piolito would perhaps be a more suggestive portmanteau word,' said Haskett Smith, but his philological ingenuity did not help him to find the holds, and we had to resort to ingenuity of another kind. We passed a loop of rope over a chockstone near the mouth of the cave, and by dint of a pretty free use of one another's shoulders, and of the loop, first as a handhold and later on as a stirrup, Haskett Smith and I got over the pitch." Lehmann J Oppenheimer, ***The Heart of Lakeland*** (Sherrat & Hughes 1908).

1909 May 6 **West Jordan Crack** – HB Gibson, WB Brunskill

1909 May 6 **Far West Jordan Climb** – HB Gibson, WB Brunskill

1909 May 24 **Shamrock Buttress Route 2** – HB Gibson, FW Botterill, JH Davidson
Originally a variation but proves to be the best climbing.
The original route (***Route 1***) – GD Abraham, AP Abraham, WG Clay, HG Beeching, Easter 1902.

1909 June 4 **Pisgah West Ridge** – FW Botterill, HB Gibson
Both the ordinary route and ***Variation***.

1909 June **North-East Arête** – FW Botterill, H Williamson, E.S.
Pitch 2 – WF Hurford, SJH Reid, 18th September 2003.
North-East Chimney is thought to have been climbed about the same time.

1911 Sept 29 **South-West Climb** – HR Pope, WB Brunskill
The party finished via the original finish of New West Climb.
Direct Finish to Jordan Gap – CF Holland RF Stobart, Dorothy E Pilley, 24th July 1919.
Direct Finish to High Man – HM Kelly, CF Holland, CG Crawford, NE Odell, 27th July 1919.

1912 Apr 21 & 22 **North-East Climb** – GD Abraham, AP Abraham
The last pitch-and-a-half were avoided by a traverse right along the good ledge on Pitch 5 to join the easy scrambling of the Savage Gully Exit to North Climb. The finish as described was climbed by CF Stocks, Miss Capper, CS Worthington, J Gaspard, 30th May 1912.

1913 Sept 11 **Branch Gully** – EE Roberts

1913 Easter **Waterfall Climb** – DG Murray, EB Beauman, JC Muir

1913 Easter **Wide Gully** – DG Murray, EB Beauman

Above: North-East Climb (MS), Pillar Rock, first climbed in 1912. The two climbers are on the 'vertical 20ft wall' above the 'remarkable 100ft groove' – Pitch 5 in the guidebook. **Photo:** Abraham Brothers

1913 Sept 8 **Mallory's Route (North-West-by-West)**
GHL Mallory, A Goodfellow
Long overlooked, this was the first route on the West Face of Low Man. Kelly failed to locate it, but the line is fairly certain. The original description was written up in the ***Wasdale Head Book*** and a somewhat different account appeared in the ***CC Journal*** 1914. The line of the climb was researched and what was in all likelihood the second ascent made by SJH Reid and C King in 2005. When GD Abraham wrote *"Considering its nearness to such a*

famous course as the North West Climb the new discovery is scarcely likely to become popular", (***Alpine Heights & British Crags*** 1919), he could hardly have realised how accurate his statement was to prove!

1919 July 29 **Rib and Slab Climb** – CF Holland, HM Kelly, CG Crawford
"Parallel to the groove and on the right of it is a narrow corner or crack and I made my way up this until it was possible to break onto the slab, an operation, to me, of considerable difficulty, though the others seemed to find it easy. Once on the face of the slab direct progress upwards was simplified by the excellence of the holds, though I was gradually forced away to the extreme right where there is a good belay about fifty feet up… From the belay we kept to the New West for a few feet and then stepped across to the left onto slabs of the most marvellous rock, sound as a bell, and almost incredibly rough. Gabbro itself is scarcely more destructive to finger tips and rubber soles." CF Holland, 'New Climbs in the Wasdale District', (***FRCC Journal*** 1919).

1919 July 29 **West Wall Climb** – HM Kelly, CF Holland, CG Crawford
Originally named West Face of Low Man. A good day out by anyone's standards – as well as two major new routes, the party also climbed Savage Gully and made the first descent of Walker's Gully.

1919 Aug 3 **East Jordan Wall** – CG Crawford, CF Holland

1919 Aug 3 **Jordan Bastion** – CG Crawford, CF Holland

1919 Aug 9 **Sodom** – HM Kelly, CF Holland
Known as **Route 1** in early editions of the guide.
O Tindale and others did the last two pitches of this route as a ***Direct Finish to New West Climb***, 12th September 1911.

Above: Charles Holland who named **Sodom** and **Gomorrah**. **Photo:** C Douglas Milner. FRCC Archive

1919 Aug 9 **Gomorrah** – HM Kelly, CF Holland
Known as **Route 2** in early editions of the guide.
The initial intention was to climb the line of what is now Gondor, *"A further steep slab brings one to an impasse – an impossible (?) steep arête. A big steep wall on the left of this was not tried, but instead a short traverse was made away to the right to a big triangular recess. Efforts to break out on to the arête (nose to left) were unavailing. A long V-chimney (reaching to the top of High Man), grassy in places, was entered. After ascending this for about 60' a further unavailing attempt was made*

to get on the arête on the left. Chimney still ascended for about 50', but owing to unpleasant grass ahead, a traverse was done to rib on right. (Holland joined me here by a variation, missing out the 50' just mentioned)". HM Kelly, ***The Climbing Diaries***. Holland's variation was in fact to fall off and take a big swing. Kelly held him though he had no belay! *"The line we intended following soon brought us up against obstacles of a most uncompromising character and Kelly was forced into a chimney, or rather a right-angled corner of extreme severity. I found this too hard at one point and had the unpleasant experience of falling off backwards and dangling, as Kelly was seated on a projection. Hardly had I re-established myself when the rope most unkindly removed my pipe from my mouth and not long afterwards completed my discomfiture by dislodging a stone which hit me on the head."* CF Holland, 'New Climbs in the Wasdale District', (***FRCC Journal*** 1919). This was the penultimate day of an amazing holiday for Kelly when in sixteen days he was only prevented from climbing on two by rain. On the remainder, from his base in Wasdale, he alternated visits to Scafell, Gable and Pillar, climbing an inordinate number of routes, many of them new. On the 9th August, in addition to making the first ascents of Sodom and Gomorrah, he and Holland also ascended Savage Gully, and made the first descent of Rib and Slab Climb.

The names of Routes 1 and 2 have been changed, to Sodom and Gomorrah respectively. These were, in fact, the original names as is best explained by a quote from a letter received from HM Kelly: *"It was Holland, under the stress of a slight contretemps on Route 2, which might have ended in disaster, who suggested Sodom and Gomorrah as titles, on the way home on that memorable day. But the suggestion was for a time kept to ourselves and the more prosaic titles entered in the Hotel Log Book, I think the same day".*

The Ridge Variation – M Linnell, AS Piggott, 15th May 1932.

Direct Start – W 'Bill' Young, R Schipper, 19th June 1967.

1920 Sept 11 **Nook and Wall Climb** – HM Kelly, CF Holland, REW Pritchard

"We afterwards attempted another route to the left (of West Wall Climb), and after some good climbing, especially up a wall and along a ledge, following which was an exhilarating traverse along a flake reminiscent of the Great Flake but on a smaller scale, we reached an impasse – a ferocious groove with impossible walls on either side. We retraced our steps and decided to explore from above another day. The expedition was very interesting as we all agreed" HM Kelly Diaries, 31st Aug 1920.

Variation Start – BJ Clarke, SJH Reid, 7th September 2004

1923 May 24 **Hind Cove Buttress** – HM Kelly, B Eden-Smith

1923 May 24 **Routes 1 and 2, Hind Cove** – HM Kelly, B Eden-Smith

1923 May 26 **East Pisgah Chimney (Left)** – HM Kelly

Probably done before.

1923 July 16 **The Appian Way** – REW Pritchard, HM Kelly (var)
Rumour has it that the route was named as a pun on 'a pee on the way', however, 'Appie' was Pritchard's nickname, so this is a more likely source of the name.

"Pritchard led the first two pitches. All went well to here. After digging some time we unearthed a moderate flake belay. Pritchard attempted wall as well as crack but did not succeed in making any progress. Self had a go at the crack (slimy and wet) and got nearly to the top of it; a loose block at the finish sent me down. It was then arranged between us that should I be successful with the crack and not like the look of the succeeding traverse across the wall, Pritchard should go up the flake pitch of Nook and Wall (some 30 feet away on the right – same level) and give the moral support of a belay from there. This he did, after I had managed to get up the crack and tested the wall in question. Self then decided to descend from the steep grassy corner, where situated, to top of crack, kick block down, and try wall from that level. All this was successful, and after getting across the wall, Pritchard came down from the flake to the foot of the crack and soon climbed it, and wall, to me." (HM Kelly Diaries).

1923 Publication of the first FRCC guidebook to Ennerdale, ***Pillar Rock***, author HM Kelly, editor HM Kelly.

1925 June 21 **Rib and Gully Climb** – HM Kelly, B Eden-Smith

1926 July 9 Centenary of Pillar Rock ascent by *"...public orators, children, dogs, maidens, grey-haired ladies, as well as strong bearded men with boots, led by a cheerful person in a top hat, all chattering and clattering upwards, roped or unroped as the fancy took them..."* Sir WH Beveridge, 'The Pillar Rock Centenary', (*FRCC Journal* 1926).

1927 Aug 6 **Great Doup Pinnacle** – G Wood-Johnson, E Wood-Johnson, MM Barker

1928 Apr 28 **Grooved Wall** – HM Kelly, HG Knight, WG Standring
Standring led the last pitch.

"The party spent 8 hours in cleaning up the climb. There was enough earth sent down into Ennerdale to provide soil for the whole of the reafforestation scheme. All climbers should be grateful for the work put in by Standring and Knight, for without the abnormal terrier like qualities they displayed on this occasion the Grooved Wall as a climb would not exist." (HM Kelly Diaries).

"After lunch we got under way, whilst everyone else spread themselves comfortably in the sun. Good time was made to the overhang, and with Standring well anchored on the Pinnacle, Kelly and his understudy got busy. I was tied firmly to the flake in such a way that if it came off under Kelly's weight he wouldn't be alone in his fall, and one of the lengths of rope was made into a loop and hung from its tip. I must say at this point that, though the flake looks preposterously unsound, no amount of pulling or twisting had made it even vibrate. Kelly now made a determined attack

on the overhang and, with loud applause from everyone except himself, his back-view disappeared into the groove. Rope ran out pretty steadily till, safeguarded by a thread in the crack, he was able to rest for a few minutes. In the following section, before the big belay was reached, one of his rubbers was half pulled off in the crack. One of those helpful little touches which make the leader feel so secure."
HG Knight, 'Addenda Montana', (***FRCC Journal*** 1928).

1928 May 28 **Harlequin Chimneys** – HG Knight, WG Standring, W Eden-Smith

1929 June 26 **Main Ridge Climb** – E Wood-Johnson, A Wood-Johnson, EW Milne, WG Hennessy
However: *"an interesting climb was had on Black Crag on the Ennerdale side of the Steeple"* by JW Robinson, G Hastings and W Dickham King, ***Wasdale Hotel Climbing Book*** 27th December 1891 – but this may well have been in winter conditions.

1929 June 26 **Lower Slabs Ordinary Route** – E Wood-Johnson, EW Milne

1929 June 26 **Tower Buttress** – E Wood-Johnson, CJ Astley Cooper, A Wood-Johnson, WG Hennessy
"After a meal the captain led off up Tower Buttress. At one point, christened the Nose, he had to stand on a very thin hold for the left foot, reach round a corner for a left hand hold, change feet on the small stance, get his left foot on to a little knob right on the edge, and about twelve inches above the overhang – which was cut away horizontally underneath for at least six feet – then stand firmly on the left foot and look for more holds above".
WG Hennessy, 'Eleven Days in Wind Gap', (***FRCC Journal*** 1929).

1929 June 26 **Left-Hand Route, West Buttress** – A Wood-Johnson, E Wood-Johnson, CJ Astley Cooper, WG Hennessy

1929 June 26 **Right-Hand Route, West Buttress** – A Wood-Johnson, E Wood-Johnson, CJ Astley Cooper, WG Hennessy

1929 June 27 **Lower Slabs Climb Direct** – E Wood-Johnson, CJ Astley Cooper, A Wood-Johnson, WG Hennessy
Originally climbed in several pitches. **Pitch 3** and ***Direct Finish***, E Wood-Johnson, WG Hennessy, 28th June 1929.

1929 June 28 **Left Central Slab Climb** – E Wood-Johnson, WG Hennessy, A Wood-Johnson

1929 June 28 **Overhanging Central Slab Climb** – E Wood-Johnson, WG Hennessy, A Wood-Johnson
Variation: Central Slab Climb, E Wood-Johnson, A Wood-Johnson, EW Milne, WG Hennessy, 25th June 1929.

1929 June 28 **West Gully, Black Crag** – A Wood-Johnson, WG Hennessy

1929 June 28 **Crack, Chimney and Slab** – A Wood-Johnson, WG Hennessy
The last route of a remarkable few days of exploration from the team who had set up a camp at Wind Gap in order to test tents destined for the Himalaya.

1931 **Girdle Traverse, Pillar Rock** – M Linnell, AB Hargreaves, AW Bridge

The party started up South-West Climb and finished up Grooved Wall.

CJ Crowther and TW Gallon had the idea of a Girdle in the opposite direction but missed out many of the best pitches, 24th April 1957.

1932 June 25 **Nor'-Nor'-West Climb** – AT Hargreaves, GG Macphee

Variation Start by WG Standring, WC Light, 3rd August 1936.

Direct Finish (Downlen's Chimney) – WF Downlen, R Greenwood, 18th March 1954, now incorporated into Megaton.

1933 Apr 14 **Hadrian's Wall** – AT Hargreaves, W Clegg, W Eden-Smith, RE Heap, WG Milligan

Liza Groove Start added by D Hopkin and JN Mather on 26th May 1952 under the impression they had climbed a new route.

Guidebook Error Variation was recorded by SJH Reid and C King, 10th May 2006, though it had no doubt been climbed numerous times before by bewildered parties.

1933 Oct 22 **Ledge and Groove Climb** – AT Hargreaves, G Barker, RE Heap

1934 Apr 1 **The Pulpit Route** – AS Piggott, GR Speaker, HM Kelly

1935 Publication of the second FRCC guidebook to Ennerdale, ***1. Pillar Rock and Neighbourhood***, author HM Kelly, editor HM Kelly.

1937 Aug 1 **Pedestal Wall** – RST Chorley, F Graham

Alternative Start by F Graham, MW Guinness, 10th October 1938. This originally stepped left onto the Original Route. Continued directly by R Kenyon, C King, SJH Reid, 24th July 2005.

1937 **Centipede** – DJ Cameron, W Heaton Cooper

1937 **Scarab** – DJ Cameron, W Heaton Cooper

1937 **Solo Slabs** – JB Chadwick

1938 Whit **The South-West-by-West Climb** – A Birtwistle, WK Pearson

1938 June 20 **Phantom Groove** – J Williams

1939 Apr 7 **Green Pastures** – SH Cross, AT Hargreaves, RE Hargreaves, AM Nelson, CJA Cooper

1939 May 28 **Sirloin Climb** – AT Hargreaves, SH Gross, RE Hargreaves, AM Nelson, CJA Cooper

1940 May 12 **Shamrock Tower** – SH Cross, AT Hargreaves, AB Hargreaves, RE Hargreaves, AM Cross

"The party was suitably impressed by the grunts, which later became groans, of the leader who was climbing in stockinged feet," AT Hargreaves, 'Land of Plenty' (*FRCC Journal* 1936).

1940 May 18 **Evening Chimney** – JB Chadwick, HR Carter

1941 June **Tower Postern** – SH Cross, AT Hargreaves

1942 Aug 9 **East Buttress, Steeple** – W Peascod, A Barton, FL Jenkins

1943 July 23 **Western Buttress, Great Doup** – FL Jenkins
1945 July 19 **Twin Ribs Climb** – J Wilkinson, DW Jackson
1946 Apr 15 **Octopus** – J Wilkinson, CA Bunton, H Ironfield
1948 July 21 **Magog, Eastern Crack** – J Williams, D Williams
1950 Feb 19 **Black Crack Route** – W Peascod, WJ Allen
1950 Apr 10 **Hailstorm** – W Peascod, G Rushworth (alt)
1952 Publication of the third FRCC guidebook to Ennerdale, ***Pillar Rock and Neighbourhood***, authors HM Kelly and W Peascod, editor HM Kelly.
1957 Apr **Steeple Buttress** – DA Elliott
It should be noted that E Banner Mendus climbed two 'benign' routes in this cove, **Rook's Flight** and **Knight's Route,** the descriptions of which were lost with his early death at 35 in 1952.
1957 **Snowstorm** – F Crosby, A Watson
1959 June 3 **Labyrinth** – AG Thorburn, R Macleod
1959 July 6 **Green Gash** – AG Thorburn
1959 June 13 **Vandal** – G Oliver, JM Cheesmond, L Willis
1959 June 13 **Goth** – M de St Jorre, N Hannaby
Two hard routes done in one day. It was 18 years since the last new route had been done on the Rock.
1960 Apr 18 **Odin** – B Ingle, P Crew (alt)
Pitches 1–3 only. **Upper Pitches** added by AG Cram, K Robson, 30th April 1967.
1961 May 14 **Angel's Step** – D Byrne, J Young, W 'Bill' Young
1963 June 9 **Scylla** – AG Cram, W 'Bill' Young
Direct Finish climbed using aid by AG Cram, 1966, climbed free, J Lamb, P Botterill, May 1974.
1964 Sept 12 **West Cove Eliminate** – AG Cram, T Martin
A piton was used as the overhang was wet.
1964 Sept 30 **Charybdis** – AG Cram, W 'Bill' Young
1964 **Skyhook** – AG Cram, W 'Bill' Young (alt)
1965 Apr 2 **Sheol** – AG Cram, T Martin
1965 Oct 23 **Shamrock Eliminate** – P Ross, CJS Bonington (alt)
The party started via Pitches 1–3 of Odin.
The lower two pitches were climbed as a ***Variation to Shamrock Tower*** in 1986 but it is not recorded by whom.
Pitch 3 added by C King, SJH Reid, 13th June 2004.
1966 Apr 30 **Puppet** – AG Cram, B Whybrow
Pitches 1–4. **Pitch 5** was climbed by D Yates and party as a finish to Scylla, July 1963.
Climbed complete, AG Cram, L Rodgers, 19th June 1967.
1966 Sept 20 **The Hun** – L Brown, S Bradshaw
The layback crack was avoided.

Above : Pillar Rock explorers of the 1960s (from left to right): Chris Eilbeck, Roelof Schipper, Bill Young (with his back to the camera) and Geoff Cram. **Photo:** Jim Young

1966 Sept 29 **Electron** – AG Cram, JC Eilbeck

"Like all the best discoveries, this one was accidental. We were engaged in an abortive attempt at a high level girdle. Geoff got off to a good start with a greasy mantelshelf and a hairy tension traverse, but soon the line petered out into grassy ledges. The Girdle was quickly forgotten when Geoff saw a large layback diedre looming above us. (You see, he gets withdrawal symptoms if he doesn't do at least one layback a week). It was only by pointing out some dangerous chocks that I persuaded him that a top-rope might be best. This was soon done and several stones were dechocked, leaving one or two sounder ones. On the way down – surprise, surprise, a big 100ft. corner below the layback pitch looking inviting but greasy. Next day saw me lowering Cram and his MacInnes ice axe down the big corner – a sort of suspended Gardening Club – leaving a thin film of dust on all the holds and a 10ft. pile of sods at the bottom. Day three saw us climbing upwards at last. The big corner was still dirty, but Geoff had brought his brother's hairbrush to provide the master's touch. After the big corner the layback seemed easy and several pitches later we arrived at Ennerdale Bridge in time for a celebration pint." Chris Eilbeck quoted in ***Rocksport*** (ca.1966).

1966 Sept 29 **Proton** – R Schipper, W 'Bill' Young (alt)

Two slings were used for aid on Pitch 1.

Climbed free by T Martin on the second ascent, 1966.

1967 Apr 15 **Attila** – R Schipper, W 'Bill' Young

A ***Variation*** by E Spofforth, J Ratcliff, 22nd June 1975, was later incorporated into Triton.

1967 Apr 16 **Sentinel** – R Schipper, T Martin
Three slings were used for aid.
Climbed free by AG Cram, W 'Bill' Young on the second ascent, 1967.

1967 Apr 29 **Gondor** – AG Cram, K Robson
One peg for aid.
Climbed free by G Tinnings taking a slightly different line, 1978.

1967 Apr 29 **Akhnaton** – W 'Bill' Young, R Schipper (alt)

1967 June 13 **Thor** – R Schipper, CJS Bonington

1967 July 22 **Boot Strap** – JC Eilbeck, PW Lucas

1967 July 22 **Positron** – JC 'Chris' Eilbeck, PW Lucas

1967 Sept 16 **Photon** – WA Barnes, A Jackman, JC Eilbeck, DA Elliott (var)
The party finish up Shamrock Gully.
Pitches 4 and 5, WS 'Bill' Lounds, JC Eilbeck, 18th May 1968.

1967 Sept 23 **Kipper's Chimney** – WA Barnes, A Jackman, DA Elliott
Kipper was Chris Eilbeck's nickname – his friends reputedly stole the line off him and named it in his honour.

1968 Apr 12 **Ximenes** – AG Cram, W 'Bill' Young

1968 Apr 12 **Necromancer** – AG Cram, W 'Bill' Young (var)
Variation Start – R Kenyon, AG Cram, 29th June 1986.

1968 May 18 **Eros** – WS 'Bill' Lounds, JC Eilbeck

1968 May 18 **Thanatos** – WS 'Bill' Lounds, JC 'Chris' Eilbeck (alt)

1968 May 19 **Lepton** – WS 'Bill' Lounds, JC 'Chris' Eilbeck (alt)

1968 May 29 **Tyrozet** – DN Greenop, A McGregor, D Bonney

1968 June 1 **Boson** – WS 'Bill' Lounds, JC 'Chris' Eilbeck (alt)
"The name is in line with the other Shamrock Route names – a boson is a particle with integer spin (as opposed to fermions which have half-integer spin)." Chris Eilbeck (a particle physicist).

1968 June 21 **Eightfold Way**
WS 'Bill' Lounds, JC 'Chris' Eilbeck (alt)
Pitch 2 – W 'Bill' Young, T Martin, June 1968. The original Pitch 2 took a higher and dirtier line.

1968 July 6 **Vishnu** – WS 'Bill' Lounds, JC 'Chris' Eilbeck (alt)

Above: Bill Lounds, first ascentionist of such Pillar Rock classics as **Eros** (E2) and **Thanatos** (HVS) in late 1960s. **Photo:** Chris Eilbeck

1968 July 13 **The Black Widow** – T Martin, J Wilson, G Cowan
Four pitons for aid.
First free ascent, WS 'Bill' Lounds, A Charlton, 8th August 1969.

1968 July 29 **The Link** – W 'Bill' Young, JC 'Chris' Eilbeck (alt)

1968 Publication of the fourth FRCC guidebook to Ennerdale, ***Pillar Group***, author AG Cram, editor J Wilkinson.

1969 Apr 5 **Contravallation Ridge** – DN Greenop

1969 Apr **The Greater Traverse** – W 'Bill' Young, R Schipper (alt)
The first complete crossing in 5½ hours(!) of The Eightfold Way, The Link and The Girdle Traverse of Pillar.

1969 May 3 **Moving Finger Grooves** – DN Greenop, G Jennings (var)

1969 May 28 **The Marriage** – DN Greenop, G Jennings

1969 June 12 **The Dolorous Stroke** – G Jennings, DN Greenop, R Briggs
A hammered in chair-leg was famously used for protection on the crux.

1969 July 15 **The Ductile Slant** – DN Greenop

1969 Aug 29 **The Detrital Slide** – DN Greenop, G Jennings (var)
Variation to Pitch 2 – C King, SJH Reid, 17th July 2005.

1969 Sept 6 **The Devious Slash** – DN Greenop, A McGregor (var)

1970 May 29 **The Delectation Sinistrose** – DN Greenop, G Jennings (alt)

1970 Aug 29 **Err** – WL Robinson, KS Perry (alt)

1971 May 2 **Travesty Cracks** – DN Greenop, AD Baldwin (alt)

1971 May 2 **The Dream Merchants** – DN Greenop, AD Baldwin (alt)

1971 May 2 **The Faux Pas** – DN Greenop, AD Baldwin (alt)

1971 Sept 11 **Ode to Boby** – DN Greenop, H Thomas (var)
Named after a rather attractive Czech mountain guide! However the same line may have been climbed by CJS Bonington in the early 1960s.
Direct Finish, J Loxham, 26th May 1987.

1972 May 20 **Megaton** – W 'Bill' Young, WA Barnes
Pitch 4 (*Downlen's Chimney*) was first done as a direct finish to Nor' Nor' West Climb – WF Downlen, R Greenwood, 18th March 1954.
HVS Variation – SJH Reid, J Campbell, 12th June 1992.

1972 Aug 15 **The Devil's Entrance** R 'Bob' Bennett, Miss R Lavender

Above: Bill Young, pioneer of many Pillar Rock routes around the 1970s including the classic **Megaton** (E1). **Photo:** Ian Roper

1972 Aug 26 **Soliton** – WS 'Bill' Lounds, JC Eilbeck, KA Willis

1972 Oct 14 **The Magic Rainbow** – DW Hodgson, J Workman
Pitch 1, W 'Bill' Young, I Singleton, 1966.
Direct Variation to Pitch 2 added by PC Rigby, P Kane, May 1994.

1974 May 4 **Klingsor** – C Read, WL Robinson

1974 May 15 **Triton Direct** – A 'Tony' Stephenson, RG Willison
The climb (named Triton) originally started via Pitch 1 of The Appian Way, and finished via the Direct Finish of Nook and Wall Climb. Part of it had been climbed before as a variation to Attila. The extended start and alternative finish were added by SJH Reid and BJ Clarke (alt), 9th September 2004.

1974 June 15 **Strider** – JD Wilson, P Semphill, B Smith

1974 June 25 **Gaul** – JD Wilson, T Martin

1974 June 30 **The Crumb** – R 'Bob' Bennett, Miss R Lavender

1974 July 14 **Cheekwoolly** – R 'Bob' Bennett, Miss R Lavender
Cheek, so called because it had the cheek to cross so many famous routes, originally finished up New West Climb.
It was given an independent finish on May 14th 1988, by A Phizacklea and RE 'Bob' Wightman who thought they had climbed a new line which they called Woolly West.

1975 July 6 **The Devil's Exit** – R 'Bob' Bennett, Miss R Lavender

1975 July 22 **Steeple Crack** – RG Hutchinson, JW Earl (alt)

1976 Aug 28 **Side Slip** – W 'Bill' Young, AG Cram (alt)

1977 Publication of the fifth FRCC guidebook to Ennerdale, ***Pillar Group***, author AG Cram, editor J Wilkinson.

1980 Mar 16 **Dan's Groove** – K Ball

1980 Mar 16 **Cow Pie** – K Ball

1980 Mar 16 **Desperate Dan** – K Ball, D Martin

1980 Mar 16 **Dan's Mine** – K Ball, D Martin

1980 Apr 20 **Tapestry** – A 'Tony' Stephenson, C Sice (alt), W 'Bill' Young, RG Wilson
Pitches 2 and 3 only. **Pitch 1** added by A 'Tony' Stephenson, W 'Bill' Young, April 1982.

After a decade of E4 and above grades elsewhere, Pillar had its first modern route of the so called new wave, cleaned and inspected prior to first ascent. A fine effort by a strong local team.

"We'd last seen the pitch during the previous autumn, when Chris and myself scrubbed away, memorising every fold and crease. A tremendous looking route, and we wanted it badly. It would give a climb of character, that's for sure; emerging from the confines of Walker's Gully by a tenuous layback line, which petered out in the middle of nowhere. What a position! Brushing from the abseil rope, it looked badly protected, but there were holds. Anyway, it only looked 5b, and that wouldn't be a problem, would it? April 1980. Bitterly cold. The hubris which brought me here gives me

wings – laybacking on smears, passing tiny RPs, and I'm soon lunging leftwards onto the only decent hold, to be confronted by the 6a moves which guard the final wall, and by now totally committed. It's irreversible, and falling off this pitch is not an option. Seduced by the Siren rock ledges below. Fingers uncurling. 'Oh Jesus! NO!' Panic, like a rising tide, engulfs. 'I'm coming off!' This terrible scene shifts; replaced by total stillness, and I now see it all, from another place. Removed. He's still attached to the pitch; alive. Absolute stillness. Beautiful. The adrenalin surge is immense, and it's me! I'm on the belay ledge, gasping for air. No longer drowning. I look down the pitch, at the ropes snaking through space, and the ashen faces, far below. We join on the ledge – four friends, all aware of just how close this one has been, and summed up by Chris in typical fashion – 'That should send the price of diarrhoea crashing!' Tony Stephenson (2007)

1981 Apr 8 **Cunning Stunts** – A 'Tony' Stephenson, W 'Bill' Young
Cunning punning – Dr Spooner would have approved!

1981 Apr 13 **Wall Street** – W 'Bill' Young, A 'Tony' Stephenson
Variation Pitch 2 – A 'Tony' Stephenson, 8th April 1981.

1981 Aug 9 **Roraima** – J Grindley, B Thompson

1982 Mar 13 **Catalepsy Corner** – K Ball, D Martin

1982 Mar 13 **Aneurysm** – K Ball, D Martin

1983 Nov 19 **Andrea's Revenge** – W Chapman, K Ball
Named after an indiscretion by the leader.

1983 Nov 19 **Mortuary Slab** – K Ball, W Chapman

1984 June 10 **Straits of Messina** – P Whillance, DW Armstrong (alt)

1985 **A Face Remembered** – S Maskrey, G Greenhow

1985 Publication of the FRCC guidebook supplement to Ennerdale, ***New West***, author W 'Bill' Young, editor D Miller.

1987 Apr 28 **Lower Slabs Super Direct** – J Loxham
Solo with a back rope.

1987 Apr 28 **Poet Laureate** – J Loxham
Cleaned and soloed with a back rope.

1987 May 26 **Poetry in Motion** – J Loxham
Cleaned and soloed with a back rope.

1987 July 14 **Over The Hill** – J Loxham, P Botterill (alt)
Named to reflect the age of the first ascentionists.

1988 Apr 23 **Prophylactics** – A Phizacklea (solo)

1988 Apr 23 **No Ewe Turns** – A Phizacklea (solo)

1988 May 7 **The Dexterous Shuffle** – A Phizacklea, RE 'Bob' Wightman

1988 May 7 **The Deleterious Sting** – A Phizacklea, RE 'Bob' Wightman

1988 May 7 **The Dactylic Springald** – RE 'Bob' Wightman, A Phizacklea

1988 May 7 **The Dipso Somnambulist** – RE 'Bob' Wightman, A Phizacklea
Nice routes, a shame about the names.

1988 May 14 **Pauli Exclusion Principle** – RE 'Bob' Wightman, A Phizacklea
A bold onsight lead, rare these days!

1988 May 14 **The Terrorist** – A Phizacklea, RE 'Bob' Wightman
Even rarer on Pillar these days. Three new routes climbed in one day – the team also added **Woolly**, now incorporated into Cheekwoolly.

1988 June 6 **Patriarch of the Pillarites** – S Miller, J Loxham
The result of an earlier visit by S Miller. The combination of ***Klingsor Variation Start*** (May 1981), and a new hard pitch gave another hard addition to the rock.

1988 June 20 **Limerick** – J Loxham (solo)
Cleaned and top-roped before being climbed with a back rope. The last section of the route (the overhanging crack) had been climbed before as a ***Variation to Poetry in Motion*** by RE 'Bob' Wightman and A Phizacklea, 7th May 1988.

1990 July 14 **Debutante's Slab** – J Loxham, A Loxham

1991 Publication of the sixth FRCC guidebook to Gable and Pillar, ***Gable and Pillar***, author J Loxham, editor DW Armstrong.

1992 June 12 **Gorre** – SJH Reid, J Campbell
An attempt was made to gain the groove in the arête on Pitch 1 direct from below but was abandoned due to poor rock under the roof. Charybdis and Roraima both utilise the upper section of the arête on Pitch 2. The variation ***Charysma*** was climbed by R 'Bob' Bennett and M White, 22nd August 1999, as part of a new route nearly all of which was Gorre. The short groove at the top of Pitch 1 was also first climbed by them and has been incorporated into the main description.

1993 May 24 **Caucus Race** – SJH Reid, C Fanshawe, J Campbell

1995 July 27 **Dan the Man** – D Johnson (solo)
After top-rope practice.

1995 Aug 5 **Hawkeye** – C Read, GL Swainbank
Pitch 3 had been climbed before and recorded as a ***Variation to Cheekwoolly*** – A Phizacklea and RE 'Bob' Wightman, 14th May 1988.

1995 Aug 6 **Sundance** – GL Swainbank, C Read (alt)
Incorporated part of the ***Original Finish to South-West Climb***.

Above: Stephen Reid udges his way up the crux groove of **Caucus Race** (E3), Pillar Rock during the first ascent. **Photo:** John Campbell

1996 Aug 28 **Comfortably Numb** – D Johnson, R de Kelsey, D Shirley

1996 Sept 4 **Hey, Fat Lip** – D Johnson (solo)

1996 Sept 8 **Goodbye to All That** – SJH Reid, SR Stout
Pitch 3 originally followed Megaton for 4 metres before moving out onto the arête. As described, M Armitage, SJH Reid, 3rd May 2007.

1997 July 10 **Live Bait** – S Miller, D Johnson
Left-hand Variation – W Phipps, SJH Reid, 1998

1997 Sept 10 **Pillar of Salt** – SJH Reid, J Preston

2000 June 18 **Crag Fell Chimney** – SJH Reid, J Fairey

2000 June 18 **The Short Side** – SJH Reid, J Fairey

2000 June 18 **Far Eastern Pinnacle Face** SJH Reid (solo)

2003 June 14 **Serendipity Ridge** – C Wells, M Cocker, P Cocker
Despite perfect weather, the team actually thought they were on Tower Buttress, Black Crag!

2003 June 14 **Impatience Slab** – M Cocker, P Cocker, C Wells

2004 June 13 **Thin it is** – SJH Reid, C King (alt)
Lower Tier only. **Upper Tier Pitches** added by C King, SJH Reid (alt) and R Kenyon, 24th July 2005.

2004 Sept 7 **Devil's Eliminate** – BJ Clarke, SJH Reid (alt)

2004 Sept 9 **Appian Wall** – C King, SJH Reid (alt)
The top section of Pitch 1 and much of Pitch 2 had been climbed before – the latter being the upper part of the Terrorist.
Direct Variation climbed by the same team on the same day.

2005 May 5 **Graviton** – SJH Reid, C King (alt)
Pitches 1 and 2 had been climbed before as a ***Variation to Harlequin Chimneys***.

2005 June 10 **Mirror, Mirror...** – C King, SJH Reid, J Preston, Karen Wigglesworth
Pitch 1 added by C King and SJH Reid, 10th May 2006

2005 June 11 **Spire Route** – A Phizacklea, JL Holden

2005 June 11 **Inspired Slab** – A Phizacklea, JL Holden
Straight up finish, C King, SJH Reid, 13th July 2006

2005 June 11 **Fred Dibnah, Steeplejack** – A Phizacklea, JL Holden

2005 June 11 **Perspire Crack** – A Phizacklea, JL Holden

2005 July 10 **Photogenic** – A Phizacklea, JL Holden
Pitches 1 and 3 only.
Pitch 2 had been climbed as a ***Variation to Photon*** only two days earlier by C King and SJH Reid. Phizacklea and Holden thought they were doing a completely new ascent when Al shouted down *"There's only one thing wrong with this new route John, it's got chalk on it!"*

2005 July 8 **Over the Jordan** – C King, SJH Reid

2005 July 8 **Rib and Rib Climb** – C King, SJH Reid (alt)

2005 July 17 **The Seriously Dyslexic** – C King, SJH Reid (alt)

2006 June 6 **Deep River, J.K.C** – BJ Clarke (solo)

2006 June 7 **Auld Lang Syne** – SJH Reid, Sally Baxendale, R Tolley

2006 June 8 **Blonde on Blonde** – SJH Reid, Sally Baxendale, Sarah Bailey

2006 June 14 **The Flying Fin** – SJH Reid, Sally Baxendale

Direct Variation – C King, SJH Reid 16th July 2006.

2006 July 5 **Baxi's Bomber Beetles** – SJH Reid, Sally Baxendale

2006 July 6 **The Determined Sally** – C King, SJH Reid (alt)

2006 July 6 **The Dire Straights** – SJH Reid, C King (alt)

2006 July 13 **Ring a Ring o' Ouzels** – SJH Reid, C King

2006 July 13 **Ouzely Does It** – SJH Reid (solo)

2006 July 13 **Where the Ouzel Wasn't** – SJH Reid, C King

2006 July 16 **Deja Ewe** – C King, SJH Reid, Sally Baxendale (alt)

2006 July 16 **Wounded Knee** – C King, SJH Reid

Just after this ascent the leader tore a cartilage in his knee and had to crawl/walk backwards nearly all the way back to the forest road.

2006 Sept 23 **Perfect Day** – SJH Reid, Sally Baxendale

2006 Sept 23 **Ellison's Eliminate** – SJH Reid, Sally Baxendale

Named in memory of Peter Ellison, the best tractor driver in the world.

Details of the first ascents of the following routes are not known; any information or claims would be appreciated. Please note them on the FRCC website (www.frcc.co.uk).

Kern Knotts: *The Kraken Variation.*

Lower Kern Knotts West: *The Slab and Chimney Route.*

Boat How Crags: *Sea Wall Arête, East Buttress Variation, Starboard Fender Variation.*

The Napes: *Sphinx Ridge.*

Bowness Knott: *The Bowness Girdle, Left Wall.*

Raven Crag: *Central Corner.*

Pillar Rock: *North-East Chimney, Shamrock Tower Variation.*

Black Crag: *Central Corner.*

Anglers' Crag: *Crystal Groove, Gog, Hook Line and Sinker, Forgotten Wall, Like or Lump It, Midge Arête, Shadow Wall, Shep, Temptation.*

Index

Key to Major Crags
1 Kern Knotts
2 The Napes
3 Gable Crag
4 Green Gable Crags
5 Boat How
6 Bowness Knott
7 Pillar Rock
8 Black Crag
9 Haskett Buttress
10 Anglers' Crag
to Maryport
A66
Workington
A595
Whitehaven
Rowrah
A5086
Ennerdale Bridge
Sandwith
A595
Cleator Moor
Cleator
St Bees
Egremont
Calder Bridge
Holmrook
Legend
Butter-mere
Lake
River
Mountain Ridge
Cultivated Land
Rough Pastureland and Mountains